MASTERING THE
OLD TESTAMENT

THE COMMUNICATOR'S COMMENTARY SERIES
OLD TESTAMENT

MASTERING THE OLD TESTAMENT

EXODUS

MAXIE DUNNAM

LLOYD J. OGILVIE, GENERAL EDITOR

WORD PUBLISHING
Dallas•London•Vancouver•Melbourne

[Formerly, *The Communicator's Commentary Series, Old Testament*]

Library of Congress Cataloging in Publication Data
Main entry under title:

Mastering the Old Testament
[The Communicator's commentary.]
   Bibliography: p.
   Contents: OT2. Exodus/by Maxie D. Dunnam.
   1. Bible. O.T.—Commentaries. I. Ogilvie, Lloyd
John. II. Dunnam, Maxie D., 1934–
BS1151.2.C66   1993   221.7´7   93-39330
ISBN 0–8499–3541–5 (v. OT2) [pbk]
ISBN 0–8499–0407–2 (v. OT2) [hd]

Printed in the United States of America

349 AGF   987654321

This book is dedicated to
the memory of my dear friend
Buford A. Dickinson
about whose death I have written
briefly at the close of chapter 8.
The memory of our relationship is
still fresh every morning and
continues to be a source of inspiration.

Contents

Editor's Preface

God has called all of His people to be communicators. Everyone who is in Christ is called into ministry. As ministers of "the manifold grace of God," all of us—clergy and laity—are commissioned with the challenge to communicate our faith to individuals and groups, classes and congregations.

The Bible, God's word, is the objective basis of the truth of His love and power that we seek to communicate. In response to the urgent, expressed needs of pastors, teachers, Bible study leaders, church school teachers, small group enablers, and individual Christians, the Communicator's Commentary is offered as a penetrating search of the Scriptures of the Old and New Testament to enable vital personal and practical communication of the abundant life.

Many current commentaries and Bible study guides provide only some aspects of a communicator's needs. Some offer in-depth scholarship but no application to daily life. Others are so popular in approach that biblical roots are left unexplained. Few offer impelling illustrations that open windows for the reader to see the exciting application for today's struggles. And most of all, seldom have the expositors given the valuable outlines of passages so needed to help the preacher or teacher in his or her busy life to prepare for communicating God's word to congregations or classes.

This Communicator's Commentary series brings all of these elements together. The authors are scholar-preachers and teachers outstanding in their ability to make the Scriptures come alive for individuals and groups. They are noted for bringing together excellence in biblical scholarship, knowledge of the original Hebrew and Greek, sensitivity to people's needs, vivid illustrative material from biblical, classical, and contemporary sources, and lucid communication by the use of clear outlines of thought. Each has been selected to contribute to this series because of his Spirit-empowered ability to help people live in the skins of biblical characters and provide a "you-are-there" intensity to the drama of events of the Bible which have so much to say about our relationships and responsibilities today.

The design for the Communicator's Commentary gives the reader an overall outline of each book of the Bible. Following the introduction, which reveals the author's approach and salient background on the book, each chapter of the commentary provides the Scripture to be exposited. The New King James Bible has been chosen for the Communicator's Commentary because it combines with integrity the beauty of language, underlying Hebrew and Greek textual basis, and thought-flow of the 1611 King James Version, while replacing obsolete verb forms and other archaisms with their everyday contemporary counterparts for greater readability. Reverence for God is preserved in the capitalization of all pronouns referring to the Father, Son, or Holy Spirit. Readers who are more comfortable with another translation can readily find the parallel passage by means of the chapter and verse reference at the end of each passage being exposited. The paragraphs of exposition combine fresh insights to the Scripture, application, rich illustrative material, and innovative ways of utilizing the vibrant truth for his or her own life and for the challenge of communicating it with vigor and vitality.

It has been gratifying to me as Editor of this series to receive enthusiastic progress reports from each contributor. As they worked, all were gripped with new truths from the Scripture—God-given insights into passages, previously not written in the literature of biblical explanation. A prime objective of this series is for each user to find the same awareness: that God speaks with newness through the Scriptures when we approach them with a ready mind and a willingness to communicate what He has given; that God delights to give communicators of His word "I-never-saw-that-in-that-verse-before" intellectual insights so that our listeners and readers can have "I-never-realized-all-that-was-in-that-verse" spiritual experiences.

The thrust of the commentary series unequivocally affirms that God speaks through the Scriptures today to engender faith, enable adventuresome living of the abundant life, and establish the basis of obedient discipleship. The Bible, the unique word of God, is unlimited as a resource for Christians in communicating our hope to others. It is our weapon in the battle for truth, the guide for ministry, and the irresistible force for introducing others to God.

A biblically rooted communication of the Gospel holds in unity and oneness what divergent movements have wrought asunder. This commentary series courageously presents personal faith, caring for individuals, and social responsibility as essential, inseparable dimensions of biblical Christianity. It seeks to present the quadrilateral Gospel in its fullness which calls us to unreserved commitment to Christ, unrestricted self-esteem in His grace, unqualified love for others in personal evangelism, and undying efforts to work for justice and righteousness in a sick and suffering world.

A growing renaissance in the church today is being led by clergy and laity who are biblically rooted, Christ-centered, and Holy Spirit-empowered. They have dared to listen to people's most urgent questions and deepest needs and then to God as He speaks through the Bible. Biblical preaching is the secret of growing churches. Bible study classes and small groups are equipping the laity for ministry in the world. Dynamic Christians are finding that daily study of God's word allows the Spirit to do in them what He wishes to communicate through them to others. These days are the most exciting time since Pentecost. The Communicator's Commentary is offered to be a primary resource of new life for this renaissance.

It has been very encouraging to receive the enthusiastic responses of pastors and teachers to the twelve New Testament volumes of the Communicator's Commentary series. The letters from communicators on the firing line in pulpits, classes, study groups, and Bible fellowship clusters across the nation, as well as the reviews of scholars and publication analysts, have indicated that we have been on target in meeting a need for a distinctly different kind of commentary on the Scriptures, a commentary that is primarily aimed at helping interpreters of the Bible to equip the laity for ministry.

This positive response has led the publisher to press on with an additional twenty-one volumes covering the books of the Old Testament. These new volumes rest upon the same goals and guidelines that undergird the New Testament volumes. Scholar-preachers with facility in Hebrew as well as vivid contemporary exposition have been selected as authors. The purpose throughout is to aid the preacher and teacher in the challenge and adventure of Old Testament exposition in communication. In each volume you will meet Yahweh, the "I AM" Lord who is Creator, Sustainer, and Redeemer in the unfolding drama of His call and care of Israel. He is the Lord who acts, intervenes, judges, and presses His people into the immense challenges and privileges of being a chosen people, a holy nation. And in the descriptive exposition of each passage, the implications of the ultimate revelation of Yahweh in Jesus Christ, His Son, our Lord, are carefully spelled out to maintain unity and oneness in the preaching and teaching of the Gospel.

This volume on Exodus was written by an outstanding pastor, author, and leader of spiritual renaissance. Dr. Maxie Dunnam is pastor of the Christ United Methodist Church in Memphis, Tennessee. I have visited this pivotal church and have seen firsthand the impact of his biblical teaching and leadership. His church is a laboratory of church renewal and contemporary discipleship. Dr. Dunnam's faithful exposition of the word, coupled with dynamic programs, is bringing new life to church members and new members into the new life.

Prior to becoming pastor of his Memphis church, Dr. Dunnam was executive director of *The Upper Room*, a daily Bible study and devotional guide. During that period of his ministry, his calling as a world Christian statesman was firmly established. Now as a pastor of a local church, he has continued his commitment to providing materials and programs for individual and church renewal. In addition to his prolific pen, Maxie Dunnam is in constant demand as a speaker, conference and retreat leader, and resource person for clergy leadership seminars. He speaks and writes out of his authentic ministry on the firing line in a local church involved in personal spiritual renewal and active social responsibilities. He leads a vital parish on the move with Book of Acts intensity and involvement in human needs.

Many readers of this volume on Exodus will have enjoyed and been enriched by Maxie Dunnam's contribution to the New Testament series of the Communicator's Commentary in Volume 8, *Galatians, Ephesians, Philippians, Colossians, Philemon*. This volume is receiving broad acclaim and extensive use by preachers and teachers around the world. This exposition of some of the most crucial of Paul's epistles reveals the author's in-depth approach and reverence for the Scriptures. The volume is rich in the use of metaphors, parables from daily life, and personal and classical illustrations which distinguish Dr. Dunnam's preaching and teaching.

The same quality of vivid communication is the mark of excellence in this volume on Exodus. In his introduction to this volume, Maxie

12

Dunnam refers to Exodus as "a book for everyone." The same could be said of this commentary! Although directing his insights primarily to communicators of Scripture, Dr. Dunnam speaks to everyone who wishes to grapple with the contemporary relevance of Exodus and experience its implication for individual and church life today.

By careful interpretation of the text, Maxie Dunnam makes the distant history of the Israelites clearly understandable to the modern reader. This commentary reflects prolonged, careful scholarship. With help from his commentary, we can understand what God was doing in ancient Egypt and the exodus—and what He is doing today.

Maxie Dunnam's use of contemporary literature is particularly enlightening. Bits from plays, poems, and prose pieces dot the landscape of this commentary. They portray vividly the timeless message of Exodus in a way which speaks in our cultural setting. And they provide the biblical communicators with rich sources of information for teaching and rich sources of illustration for teaching and preaching.

I am especially moved by Dr. Dunnam's frequent personal illustrations. He speaks as a man steeped in the ministry of Christ to broken people. Many of his stories are filled with emotion as well as practical wisdom. I appreciate his honest vulnerability as he shares his pastoral heart with us. Here is a man who can help us to communicate the moving story of Exodus with profound depth and contemporary bite.

Life is exodus. The Lord is constantly calling us as individuals and as churches to trust Him to release us from bondage and press us to claim our destiny as chosen, called, and cherished people. The Book of Exodus is sublimely our own story and our adventuresome pilgrimage to freedom. Maxie Dunnam has shown us how to preach and teach from Exodus in a way which will meet the aching needs and restless hopes of people today. It's a joy to commend this crucial volume to you.

LLOYD OGILVIE

Acknowledgments

There are many people to be thanked for the contribution they made to this writing project:

The congregation of Christ United Methodist Church (Memphis, Tennessee), who heard and responded to almost a year of sermons from Exodus as I researched and preached my way through this exciting book. A pastor/preacher could hardly have the luxury of writing a book such as this if it did not become the "stuff" of weekly preaching and teaching.

Mary Gissendanner Marino (Mrs. Michael A. Marino), my secretary, who patiently worked with the manuscript preparation, and Robbie McQuiston (Mrs. Paul G. McQuiston) who assisted with typing;

Dr. Jim Eoff, lay Bible teacher, who assisted with bibliography at the outset of the writing project;

The Reverend Harold R. Chandler who did bibliographical research;

Dr. Bobbie E. Oliver, Phyllis Gregory, and Melissa Miller of the Memphis Theological Seminary Library;

And, of course, Jerry, my wife, who helps protect my study time, who understands and supports my work style, and by so doing frees me to be productive, and by her love and affirmation enhances my creativity.

Introduction

Exodus, the second book of the Bible, is one of the most exciting in all of Scripture. This book is to the Old Testament what the Gospels are to the New Testament. The redemptive activity of God is clearly proclaimed in Exodus, even as it is in the Gospels. As the Gospels firmly root God's activity in history ("The Word became flesh" [John 1:14]; "When the fullness of time had come, God sent forth His Son, Jesus, born of a woman" [Gal. 4:4]), so God hears the groans of His people in bondage and moves to redeem them.

It is also to be noted that there is a close connection between Moses, the primary actor in Exodus, and Jesus. We will see this in our specific commentary, but note again in this introduction, as above, that Moses is to Exodus what Jesus is to the Gospels. Both fulfill the calling of God in the selfless giving of themselves. Both also portray the living covenant of those who have chosen to follow a redeeming God.

There is a sense in which the New Testament is the most authentic commentary on the Old Testament and especially on Exodus. For that reason, this commentary will seek to make that connection throughout. We will be seeing this word of God as it comes to us in Exodus in light of "the Word became flesh," the Word incarnate in Jesus Christ, and other Scriptures in the New Testament concerning His birth, life, teaching, passion, death, and resurrection.

A Book for Everyone

Exodus is a book for everyone. Though it is the exciting story of God's delivering Israel out of Egyptian bondage, protecting and sustaining them through their wilderness wandering and eventually bringing them to Canaan, the Promised Land, it is far more than that. It is the picture of our spiritual journey out of the world of bondage to sin and into the freedom of forgiveness and the full inheritance we have in Jesus Christ. So, here in Exodus, God calls us from the anguish of our bondage and the humdrum purposelessness of our settled life in Egypt. He bids us to set our feet on a new way. Though that way may be accompanied, as it were, by plague and the hardship of the wilderness, we too will be led by a cloud by day and shining light by night; we will know His overshadowing presence.

Because of its significant place in the Bible, and because of the many sources of its message, Exodus has demanded the attention of professional scholars who have spent hours analyzing the sources. But Exodus is not only for the scholar, it is for the sincere believer who wishes to receive a fresh word from the Lord. It is for the minister who wants to feed his flock on the bread of life. It is for the lay teacher who has been called to that ministry of teaching within the body of Christ. To each the word may come with a different sound, a different accent, but the message will be discerned, the presence of God will be felt, His call will come to us, and His promise of deliverance will lift our weary souls.

Name

The title "Exodus" is quite appropriate, though that was not the original name in the Hebrew text. That text followed the custom of describing a book by its opening words, in this case, "These are the names" (Wĕ'ēlleh shĕmôth), or more simply, "names" (shĕmôth). The title "Exodus" came through the Latin Vulgate which refers to the book as Liber Esodus. The Vulgate, however, is dependent upon the title that appears in the Septuagint, a Greek translation of the Old Testament made in the third century B.C. The Septuagint referred to the book by the simple title Exodus, which means "exit" or "departure." The occurrence of that word comes from the Greek text of Exodus 19:1, "On the third new moon after the people of Israel had gone forth [tēs exodou] out of the land of Egypt."

The name itself conveys the pivotal event of the Old Testament that brought Israel into being as a people of God, a covenant people. It is to be noted, however, that the book deals with more than that specific Exodus event. It deals with the wilderness wandering, the building of the tabernacle, the giving of the Law, the ritual life for the people, and the daily ordinances by which they were to live.

18

The Place of Exodus in the Bible

The Exodus event was determinative for much of biblical thought, and puts this book at the very center of Scripture. In the books of the Old Testament, God is championed as the One who led His people out of Egypt, and the Exodus was the big sign of His redemptive action. The psalmist never tired of extolling this action of the Lord, and the Exodus motif is reflected in nearly twenty psalms (cf. 18; 44; 60; 68; 74; 75; 78; 80; 81; 83; 89; 95; 100; 105; 106; 114; 135; 136).

Likewise the prophets recall the deliverance of Israel out of bondage to make that action the basis upon which they appealed to their own generation (cf. Amos 2:10; 3:1; 9:7; Mic. 6:4; 7:15; Hos. 2:15; 11:1; 12:9, 13; 13:4; Isa. 11:16; Jer. 2:6; 7:22–25; 11:4, 7; 16:14; 23:7; 32:21; 34:13).

This is true not only in the Old Testament but also in the New. In fact, the Exodus theme finds even fuller expression in the New Testament. Exodus, wilderness, and conquest are as important for the New Testament as for the Old. Look at the words that are used to express the saving work of Jesus Christ: "Redeem" and "redemption," "deliver," "ransom," "purchase," "bondage," "freedom." This is the vocabulary of the Exodus event.

Look at the parallels between Jesus and Moses. Pharaoh put out a decree to have all the Hebrew children killed; Moses escaped. Herod put out a similar decree in the first century, and Jesus escaped. (It is interesting that Jesus escaped to Egypt and came out of Egypt back into Israel to begin His public ministry.) Moses crossed the Red Sea and spent forty years wandering in the wilderness; Jesus crossed the River Jordan and spent forty days and forty nights in the wilderness enduring His temptation experience. On Mount Sinai, God gave Moses the commandments—the Law by which Israel would live. Jesus gave the law of the new kingdom in His Sermon on the Mount.

This book clearly has a crucial place in the Bible.

Unifying Theme

Roy L. Honeycutt, Jr., has perceptively suggested that the manifold themes within the Book of Exodus have as their focus of unity the revelation of the Lord's power. "The Exodus is superbly characterized by a triumphant shout of victory much akin to that of the

New Testament resurrection: The Lord has triumphed, to Him belongs the victory! This is well expressed in what may be the oldest written couplet in the Book of Exodus: 'Sing to the Lord, For He has triumphed gloriously! / The horse and its rider He has thrown into the sea' (15:21). The entire song of Moses is a grand exaltation of the Lord's victory and power; Yahweh is triumphant Lord, Lord of all. He is 'glorious in power' and 'in the greatness of His majesty He overthrew His adversaries' (15:6–7). With climactic joy and victory, the triumph song concludes, 'the Lord shall reign forever and ever' (15:18)."[1]

Dr. Honeycutt enumerates those moments in Israel's life that underscore the Lord's sovereign power: the descent of a people into Egypt, their providential sustenance and their eventual redemption under the leadership of Moses (not only the confrontation with and triumph over Pharaoh but also over the gods of Egypt and their representatives), the plague narratives, the crossing of the Red Sea, and the miraculous acts in the wilderness. These demonstrate Yahweh's lordship, His triumph over hostile powers, and His demonstrated power over demonic forces.

The covenant is also a revelation of Yahweh's lordship, bearing witness to His sovereign power.

So, Dr. Honeycutt shapes his study of the Book of Exodus around the unifying theme of "the lordship of Yahweh." Though we will use a different outline in this commentary, Dr. Honeycutt does provide a very helpful outline that focuses on this theme: Yahweh as Lord of history (1:1–7:7), Yahweh as Lord of creation (7:8–18:27), Yahweh as Lord of man (19:1–24:14), and Yahweh as Lord of worship (25:1–40:38).

Authorship

A lengthy tradition identifies Moses not only as the author of Exodus, but of the entire Pentateuch, although the burden of Bible scholarship would deny that. In a technical sense, Exodus is anonymous. This does not mean at all that at least portions of this book are not to be accredited to Moses. Within the book itself, there are occasions when it is clearly stated: "Then the Lord said to Moses, 'Write this for a memorial in the book and recount it in the hearing of Joshua, that I will utterly blot out the remembrance of Amalek from under heaven'" (17:14); "And Moses wrote all the words of the Lord. . . . Then he took the Book of the Covenant and read in the hearing of the people" (24:4, 7); "Then the Lord said to Moses, 'Write these words, for according to the tenor of these words I have made a covenant with you and with Israel'" (34:27).

Some of the most important references for the authority of the authorship of Moses come from the New Testament: "And Jesus answered and said to them, 'Because of the hardness of your heart he [Moses] wrote you this precept'" (Mark 10:5); "For if you believed Moses, you would believe Me, for he wrote about Me" (John 5:46). (Cf. also Matt. 19:8; Mark 12:26; Luke 24:27, 44; John 7:19, 23; Acts 13:39; 15:5; 28:23; 1 Cor. 9:9; 2 Cor. 3:15; Heb. 9:19; 10:28.) That the hand of Moses is clearly in this book cannot be denied. Even so, a majority of Old Testament scholars tend to hold that the authorship of Exodus is much too complex to ascribe to a single person. The problem of authorship is so complex that if all the evidence were to be considered, forging one's own opinion would be a time-consuming, arduous, complicated task. Therefore, we will not pursue authorship in that fashion because that is not our present purpose. Let us simply conclude that both oral and written materials that went into the making of this book may be ascribed to Moses. It does not detract from the book, however, to see the hand of God working through the traditions of the people of Israel, their worship, their priestly traditions, the development of their laws, and the literature that came out of each of the kingdoms when Israel was divided into South and North. Biblical authority does not depend upon who the author is but upon the One who inspires the author.

Authority of the Bible

That leads me to say a specific word about the authority of Scripture. The authority grows out of Scripture's being the inspired revelation of God. In its wholeness and its unity, the Bible is the word of God, so it has the authority of God behind it. For us who would be God's people, the Bible is our divine mandate, our moral duty, our pattern for life, and our hope for eternal life.

For Christians, the ultimate authority is Jesus Christ; therefore, the authority of the Bible is related to Him. He claimed, "All authority has been given to Me in heaven and on earth" (Matt. 28:18)—and we accept His claim. The Bible must always be seen in the light of the lordship of Christ. Our acceptance of the Bible's authority is not dependent upon inerrancy of word and phrase, perfect consistency of all events, or perfect and consistent understanding of God by His chosen servants. Rather, Jesus Christ is the authentic witness to its authority as the word of God.

It must be noted that this is not a subjective judgment. Our understanding of who Christ is as the Son of God and the Word made flesh, of His saving work through His death and resurrection, of His eternal lordship is to be tested by Scripture, not by our own subjective experience and judgment. Therefore, the Bible is to be accepted by Christians as the authoritative guide for all matters of faith and practice; and the written word is found in the authority of the living Word that comes to us through the guidance of the Holy Spirit.

So, the lordship of Christ and the voice of His Holy Spirit, not the compulsion of literalism or the obligation of proof, are what guide us.

Conclusion

What follows is an effort to interpret Scripture in that fashion—in the light of the lordship of Jesus Christ; His ultimate authority in our lives as Savior, Redeemer, and Lord; and the guidance that is ours as this living Christ indwells us by the power of the Holy Spirit.

NOTES

1. Roy L. Honeycutt, Jr., *The Broadman Bible Commentary* (Nashville: Broadman Press, 1969), 1:298.

An Outline of Exodus

I. A People Who Refused to Die: 1:1–22
   A. Covenant: 1:1–7
   B. Change: 1:8
   C. Conflict: 1:9–14
   D. Commitment: 1:15–22
   E. Death and Life
   F. Life and Choice
   G. Confirmation and Certainty
II. The Providence of God in Moses' Formative Years: 2:1–25
   A. A Miracle Child: 2:1–10
   B. Moses Grows Up: 2:11–15a
   C. Moses' Exile in Midian: 2:15b–22
   D. When Are We Most Like God: 2:23–25
III. The Call of Moses: 3:1–4:17
   A. Lessons from the Burning Bush: 3:1–6
   B. A Redeeming God and a Redemption That Is Complete: 3:7–10
   C. A Reluctant Prophet: 3:11–4:12
   D. Moses' Refusal and God's Anger: 4:13–17
IV. The Testing of Faith: 4:18–5:21
   A. Faith Tested on the Journey Back to Egypt: 4:18–31
   B. Faith Tested in Confrontation with Pharaoh: 5:1–5
   C. Faith Tested in the Renunciation of Moses by His People: 5:6–21
V. The Triumph of Faith: 5:22–7:13
   A. Live the Questions: 5:22–6:13
   B. The Family Tree: 6:14–27
   C. Aaron's Miraculous Rod: 6:28–7:13
VI. The Plagues: Revelations of God's Power: 7:14–10:29
   A. The First Plague: The Nile Turned to Blood: 7:14–25

XV. Covenant Law at Sinai: Civil, Criminal, and Covenant: 21:1–24:18
    A. The Law Concerning Servants: 21:1–11
    B. The Law Concerning Violence: 21:12–27
    C. Animal Control Laws: 21:28–36
    D. Responsibility for Property: 22:1–15
    E. Moral and Ceremonial Principles: 22:16–23:19
    F. Ministering Angel: 23:20–33
    G. Israel Affirms the Covenant: 24:1–18

XVI. Camping with God: The Tabernacle and the Priest: 25:1–31:18
    A. Materials for the Sanctuary: 25:1–9
    B. The Tabernacle: 26:1–37
    C. The Ark of the Covenant and the Mercy Seat: 25:10–22
    D. The Table of Showbread: 25:23–30
    E. The Gold Lampstand: 25:31–40
    F. The Altar of Burnt Offering: 27:1–8
    G. The Altar of Incense: 30:1–10
    H. The Bronze Laver: 30:17–21
    I. The Ransom Money: 30:11–16
    J. The Holy Anointing Oil and the Incense for the Altar: 30:22–38
    K. The Court of the Tabernacle: 27:9–19
    L. The Care of the Lampstand: 27:20–21
    M. The Garments of the Priesthood: 28:1–43
    N. The Consecration of the Priests: 29:1–46
    O. The Appointment of Craftsmen: 31:1–11
    P. Keeping the Sabbath: 31:12–17
    Q. With the Finger of God: 31:18

XVII. Rebellion: 32:1–33:6
    A. The People's Faithlessness: 32:1–6
    B. It's Tough to Be God: 32:7–14
    C. Taught by a Golden Calf: 32:15–29
    D. Powerful Intercession: 32:30–35
    E. The Command to Leave Sinai: 33:1–6

XVIII. Renewal of the Covenant: 33:7–40:38
    A. Moses' Third Intercession: 33:7–17
    B. Show Me Your Glory: 33:18–34:9
    C. Renewal of the Covenant: 34:10–35
    D. Construction of the Tabernacle: 35:1–40:38

CHAPTER ONE

A People Who Refused to Die

Exodus 1:1–22

The doctor and his nurse had responded to the anguished plea of a farmer. The farmer's wife was desperately ill. The doctor, with his familiar black bag, and the nurse were ushered upstairs to where the farmer's wife lay. The farmer and his family waited anxiously downstairs in the parlor. After a few minutes the doctor came down with a worried look on his face and asked for a screwdriver. After another few minutes the nurse came down and nervously asked for a can opener. Soon after that, the doctor reappeared, tense and visibly upset, and asked for a hammer and chisel. By this time the distraught farmer couldn't contain himself any longer.

"Tell me, Doc, whatever in the world is wrong with my Bessie?" "Don't know yet," the doctor answered. "Can't get my black bag opened."

That is one of the reasons the Bible is not alive for many of us. We haven't opened the bag yet. We don't have the key, or a key that will get us into the bag. As we begin this study of Exodus, I suggest a key for "getting into the bag." One key is to put ourselves into the picture. When we read Scripture, we are to read it not as spectators, but as participants. Objective information is important, but unless we get involved, unless we put ourselves into the picture, we will not receive the word as God's word for us. For instance, as indicated in the Introduction, Exodus means "the way out," or "exit." Speaking in objective terms, it records Israel's journey from Egypt to Canaan, the promised land of God; but it is also the picture of our own spiritual journey out of the world of bondage to sin into the freedom of forgiveness and the full inheritance we have in Jesus Christ.

We need to keep in mind Paul's admonition: "Now all these things happened to them [the Israelites] as examples, and they were written for our admonition" (1 Cor. 10:11). Four words will help us put ourselves into this story of a people who refused to die. These words are a kind of outline for this first chapter: covenant, change, conflict, and commitment.

COVENANT

> 1:1 Now these *are* the names of the children of Israel who came to Egypt; each man and his household came with Jacob:
> 2 Reuben, Simeon, Levi, and Judah;
> 3 Issachar, Zebulun, and Benjamin;
> 4 Dan, Naphtali, Gad, and Asher.
> 5 All those who were descendants of Jacob were seventy persons (for Joseph was in Egypt *already*).
> 6 And Joseph died, all his brothers, and all that generation.
> 7 But the children of Israel were fruitful and increased abundantly, multiplied and grew exceedingly mighty; and the land was filled with them.
> *Exod. 1:1–7*

No one can understand what the Bible *means* until he or she knows what it *says*. So, throughout our study, it is important to be thoroughly familiar with what the passage says. You may find it helpful to read the entire first chapter at this point, before we consider it in shorter segments.

Exodus is a sequel to Genesis, and the first seven verses of Exodus connect with the account of Genesis. While Genesis closes with the death of Joseph, Exodus 1:6 tells us that *"Joseph . . . , all his brothers, and all that generation"* have died—three hundred and fifty years have passed. Here is another expression of the fulfillment of the covenant God has made with Israel.

You can't understand the Bible, especially the Old Testament, unless you understand the covenant. The covenant was God's ongoing agreement with Israel: "And I will have mercy on her who had not obtained mercy; / Then I will say to those who were not My people, 'You are My people!' / And they shall say, 'You are my God!'" This word of Hosea (2:23) is repeated as an expression of the new covenant which Peter saw fulfilled in the New Testament church, "who once were not a people but are now the people of God, who had not obtained mercy but now have obtained mercy" (1 Pet. 2:10). So *covenant* is the key word describing God's relationship to the people He has chosen.

It began with Abraham. "Now the Lord had said to Abram: 'Get out of your country, / From your family / And from your father's house, / To a land that I will show you. / I will make you a great nation; / I will bless you / And make your name great; / And you shall be a blessing'" (Gen. 12:1–2). Then came that magnificent response of faith: "So Abram departed as the Lord had spoken to him" (Gen. 12:4).

That was the beginning of a great journey of faith as Abraham responded to God's call. When he was ninety-nine years old, the Lord appeared to him again and said, "I am Almighty God; walk before Me and be blameless. And I will make My covenant between Me and you, and will multiply you exceedingly" (Gen. 17:1–2). Abraham fell on his face and God said to him, "Behold, My covenant is with you, and you shall be a father of many nations. No longer shall your name be called Abram, but your name shall be Abraham; for I have made you a father of many nations" (Gen. 17:4–5).

This story of a covenant God who keeps faith with His people is thrilling. One pivotal part of the story is God's giving to Abraham and Sarah a son. Abraham was ninety-nine and Sarah was ninety, yet this miracle-working God moved into the life of this old couple to give them a son. Absurd? Yes, Abraham thought so. When the angel told Abraham this, he fell down on the ground laughing. The angel came to announce it a second time, and Sarah laughed. Responding to her laughter, the angel says, "Is anything too hard for the Lord? At the appointed time I will return . . . and Sarah shall have a son" (Gen. 18:14). And He did, and she did. Scripture puts it cryptically, "The Lord did to Sarah as He had promised" (Gen. 21:1, RSV). A son through whom He would continue to fulfill His covenant was born. His name was Isaac. Isaac had a son named Jacob, and Jacob had a son named Joseph. It was this favored son of Jacob—Joseph—who was sold into slavery in Egypt by his jealous brothers. God continued to move in a mysterious way. By the time famine arose in the land of Jacob and all his family was starving, Joseph had gained favor in Egypt. In fact, he had become a kind of prime minister of the nation. Pharaoh, through Joseph, invited Jacob and his people to come to Egypt and enjoy the "best of all the land" (Gen. 45:20).

Joseph saw the hand of the Lord vividly at work. "And Joseph said to his brothers, 'Please come near to me.' So they came near. Then he said, 'I am Joseph your brother, whom you sold into Egypt. But now, do not therefore be grieved or angry with yourselves because you sold me here; for God sent me before you to preserve life. . . . to preserve a posterity for you in the earth, and to save your lives by a great deliverance'" (Gen. 45:4–7).

In the forty-sixth chapter of Genesis, Jacob had come to Beer-sheba and was making a sacrifice to God, and God gave him a vision. In that vision God said, "I am God, the God of your father; do not fear to go down to Egypt, for I will make of you a great nation there" (v. 3). This is the transitional link with Exodus, where that promise of God to Jacob is verified. *"But the children of Israel were fruitful and increased abundantly, multiplied and grew exceedingly mighty"* (1:7).

The lesson in that history is: Our God is faithful. We can depend upon Him. He keeps His promises. When He makes a covenant, we can count on it. I believe the key verse in the entire Book of Exodus is verse 2 of chapter 20: "I am the Lord your God, who brought you out of the land of Egypt, out of the house of bondage."

Put yourself into the picture. If you are a Christian, you are in covenant with God. That covenant has been sealed by the blood of the Cross, as the covenant in the Old Testament was sealed with the blood of the Passover lamb. God Himself, in Jesus Christ, has made the ultimate sacrifice. He has said to us, "As far as the east is from the west / So far has He removed our transgressions from us" (Ps. 103:12). We can trust that. We are forgiven. He has promised that having "begun a good work" in us, He will bring it to completion (Phil. 1:6). His word is clear: "I will never leave you nor forsake you" (Heb. 13:5; cf. Deut. 31:6, 8).

Whatever is going on in our lives today, whatever adversity we may be experiencing, whatever sorrow and pain we may know, we don't give up. We don't lose faith. The God whom we serve is a faithful God. He is the God who brought Israel out of the land of Egypt, out of the house of bondage, and He will do the same for us.

He is the God of the covenant who promises, "Lo, I am with you always, even to the end of the age" (Matt. 28:20).

CHANGE

1:8 Now there arose a new king over Egypt, who
did not know Joseph.

Exod. 1:8

The next word to get us into the picture is *change. "Now there arose a new king over Egypt, who did not know Joseph."* Who this king of Egypt was is not of great importance, except as he represents a dramatic shift in attitude toward the Hebrews. It seems probable that he was Ramses I, or his son Seti, the great conqueror known for having carried his victorious army as far as Mesopotamia. The flight of Moses to Midian (Exod. 2:15b ff.) would have taken place under Ramses II, under whose reign Egyptian civilization reached its highest point.

This pharaoh *"who did not know Joseph"* brought tumultuous change for the Hebrews. The fact is that change is inevitable.

The essence of the Christian faith is not certainty, but trust. Kings that don't "know Joseph" are always rising up in the land. A wise old rabbi knew. He was breathing his last breaths of life. All the younger rabbis gathered around his deathbed to hear his final words of wisdom.

"Speak to us one last truth, Great Teacher," one of them whispered in his ear. In a barely audible voice, the wise old man said, "Life is like a river." Everybody was anxious to hear what the answer was. So it passed from one rabbi to another—all the way down the stairs to a seminarian standing on the front porch. "Life is like a river . . . life is like a river . . . life is like a river." But the seminarian failed to understand and asked the man in front of him, "What does it mean?"

So up the stairs the inquiry went, "What does it mean . . . what does it mean . . . what does it mean?" until it got back to the old wise rabbi who was dying. The last person gently asked the question up close to the old man's ear, "What does it mean?" And the old rabbi responded, "So, life is *not* like a river."

31

Paradoxical? Yes. That's the way life is. Life is like a river—and what does that mean? Life is not like a river. This is the enigma and paradox of life. Change is certain, and what does that call us to? It calls us to trust, to trust the Lord of the covenant who is constant in His love and in His self-giving in the midst of change.

How often are we in situations where "a king who did not know Joseph" comes into power? A new president takes over our company, and we are not certain of our position. Modern technology is so phenomenally fluid and dynamic that our skills become archaic, and we get nervous about how to keep up.

Or, the change may be at other levels of life. Death comes to our family, as it did to Israel with the death of Joseph. Our family has been left without a father, or a mother, and that means a whole new way of doing things.

Perhaps you've gone through a divorce, and you feel devastated and defeated. Your self-esteem is shattered. Or, you may have just received a diagnosis from your doctor that verifies his suspicion— there's a malignancy, and now your whole life seems different. The future is foreboding. You don't know how to talk about it or how to express your fears, so you are silent. You feel all alone and helpless.

Change—it can bring despair, defeat, devastation. But there is another alternative: trust. Trust the God of the covenant who is constant in His love and in His self-giving.

CONFLICT

1:9 And he said to his people, "Look, the people of the children of Israel *are* more and mightier than we;

10 "come, let us deal shrewdly with them, lest they multiply, and it happen, in the event of war, that they also join our enemies and fight against us, and *so* go up out of the land.'

11 Therefore they set taskmasters over them to afflict them with their burdens. And they built for Pharaoh supply cities, Pithom and Raamses.

12 But the more they afflicted them, the more they multiplied and grew. And they were in dread of the children of Israel.

13 So the Egyptians made the children of Israel serve with rigor.

14 And they made their lives bitter with hard bondage—in mortar, in brick, and in all manner of service in the field. All their service in which they made them serve *was* with rigor.

Exod. 1:9–14

The third word to help us put ourselves into the picture is *conflict*. The new king who arose over Egypt said to his people, *"Look, the people of the children of Israel are more and mightier than we; come, let us deal shrewdly with them, lest they multiply, and it happen, in the event of war, that they also join our enemies and fight against us, and so go up out of the land"* (vv. 9–10).

How true to life. Not only change but conflict is inevitable. Look closely at the text; see the foolishness of Pharaoh. *"Let us deal shrewdly with them."* Never mind justice. Don't worry about kindness. Human life isn't the issue. We can only think of survival.

That shrewdness proved folly. (It always does.) Pharaoh was afraid that the Israelites, if allowed to grow, might discover their strength and seek to emigrate, or if they were invaded by another land, these Israelites might join the invader and overthrow the ruling powers of Egypt. So he set out to weaken them with hard bondage.

He made the same mistake that the ruling powers of South Africa have made with their policy of apartheid. He did not see that he was driving the Israelites to wish for what he was trying to prevent. Alexander Maclaren said it well: "The only way to make men glad to remain in community is to make them at home there. The sense of injustice is the strongest disintegrating force. If there is a 'dangerous class,' the surest way to make them more dangerous is to treat them harshly. It was a blunder to make 'life bitter,' for hearts also were embittered. So the people were ripened for revolt, and Goshen became less attractive."[1]

The long years of ease had multiplied the nation. Now the period of conflict and oppression stirred them out of their comfortable nests and made them willing to risk the bold Exodus for freedom. Isn't it true that conflict, especially life's sorrows and burdens, gives us perspective that nothing else will? It's easy to be at home in Egypt, easy to settle down in the comfort and security of our way of life, easy to cling tightly to the earth. Perhaps we need to be detached from all that in which we trust, all that upon which we depend for security, in order that we might depend wholly upon God. As long as we are happy in Goshen, we will not yearn for Canaan.

COMMITMENT

1:15 Then the king of Egypt spoke to the Hebrew midwives, of whom the name of one *was* Shiphrah and the name of the other Puah;

16 And he said, "When you do the duties of a midwife for the Hebrew women, and see *them* on the birthstools, if it *is* a son, then you shall kill him; but if it *is* a daughter, then she shall live."

17 But the midwives feared God, and did not do as the king of Egypt commanded them, but saved the male children alive.

18 So the king of Egypt called for the midwives and said to them, "Why have you done this thing, and saved the male children alive?"

19 And the midwives said to Pharaoh, "Because the Hebrew women *are* not like the Egyptian women; for they *are* lively and give birth before the midwives come to them."

20 Therefore God dealt well with the midwives, and the people multiplied and grew very mighty.

21 And so it was, because the midwives feared God, that He provided households for them.

22 So Pharaoh commanded all his people, saying, "Every son who is born you shall cast into the river, and every daughter you shall save alive."

Exod. 1:15–22

That leads to the final word: *commitment.*

In Pharaoh's wisdom, which turned out to be folly, it wasn't enough to make the lives of the people of Israel "bitter with hard bondage"; he felt he had to stamp them out altogether. So he instructed the Hebrew midwives to kill all the sons that were born to the women of Israel. And here comes a glorious chapter in that early preparation for the Exodus: *"But the midwives feared God, and did not do as the king of Egypt commanded them, but saved the male children alive"* (v. 17).

When we make a commitment like that, desperate though we may be and though we may have all the odds of the world against us, we will be sustained in that commitment. God will move in to bless. This is the answer to the potential devastation and defeat of change and conflict. This is putting feet on our trust. God honors our commitment, and at the point of our obedience He takes over to work His mighty work. *"God dealt well with the midwives, and the people multiplied and grew very mighty. And . . . because the midwives feared God . . . He provided households for them"* (vv. 20–21).

A human interest story from the 1984 New York Marathon illustrates God's reward for commitment. Fourteen hundred people ran that marathon. The course took them twenty-six miles through the boroughs of New York City. Not everyone completed the course; in fact, far more always drop out than finish. The winning time is almost always somewhere between two and three hours.

Linda Down was the last person to complete the race. It took her eleven hours. She has cerebral palsy, and she runs with the help of crutches. When asked by an interviewer why she even tried, Linda replied, "We are living in negative times. Things feel impossible today. I thought that if I could try to do it, it might be an inspiration to others, and maybe they would try some big things, too." Then she added, "But the last eleven miles were an act of God."

"What do you mean, 'an act of God'?"

"With eleven miles to go, I ran out of my own strength. I didn't have any more. I finished the race on borrowed power!"

As the midwives learned, all who trust God, and take that ultimate step in trust to commitment, can depend on borrowed power, the power of God Himself. And even the gates of hell, or all the forces of Pharaoh, cannot prevail against that power.

DEATH AND LIFE

Having moved through the chapter in a sweeping way, let's narrow our focus. Throughout this book we will see the purposeful movement of God. Those purposes are not always clear ahead of time, but in retrospect, the hand of God is boldly discernible. The "pillar of cloud" by day and the "pillar of fire" by night, the signs by which God led the people out of Egypt, are overarching symbols of the providence of God, His steadfast care, and His unreserved covenant. But the call is to walk not by sight, but by faith.

It takes a time of reflection to see how remarkable the words in verses 6 and 7 are. "And Joseph died, all his brothers, and all that generation. But the children of Israel were fruitful and increased abundantly."

The book begins with a recapitulation of the names of the sons of Jacob who had come into Egypt. At that time Jacob and his offspring totalled seventy persons. But in four hundred years that seventy had multiplied into almost three million. The statement is so cryptic that it begs attention. "Joseph died. . . . But the children of Israel . . . increased abundantly."

It is a picture of death and life. Need we note the inevitability of death? How desperately we need to note it, because so many of us live our days as though we were going to live forever. "Joseph died, all his brothers, and all that generation." That's as forthrightly as it could be stated. But we try to hide death. Russell Baker, in his Pulitzer-Prize-winning story of growing up in America, has a marvelous description of the fact of death in the little community of his childhood:

> Morrisonville had not developed the modern disgust with death.
> It was not treated as an obscenity to be confined in hospital and
> "funeral homes." In Morrisonville, death was a common part of
> life. It came for the young as relentlessly as it came for the old. To
> die antiseptically in a hospital was almost unknown. In Mor-
> risonville death still made housecalls. It stopped by the bedside,
> sat down on the couch right by the parlor window, walked up to
> people in the fields in broad daylight, surprised them at a bend in
> the stairway when they were on their way to bed.[2]

There's nothing morbid about it, just a conscious awareness of the inevitability of death. Such an awareness gives us perspective on who we are and what we need to be about. Hardly a week passes that I as a pastor do not have a serious conversation with some person who is nearing death. Usually the person confesses regret about how he or she has lived life. Such experiences have led me to suggest a spiritual exercise that has the potential of changing lives.

Set aside a time, at least an hour, for a spiritual retreat. Spiritual retreats don't always require a lot of time. You simply need to be alone, and specifically, alone with God. In that aloneness, ask yourself three questions and take enough time to answer them.

(1) What have I done during the past month that will make a difference in my life or the life of someone else? Will that difference last until next month?

(2) If I died tonight, what would those who know me best remember most about me?

(3) If I knew I was going to die by the end of the week, what would I want to do during these next seven days?

To be preoccupied with death is morbid, but to take death seriously is a mark of wisdom.

LIFE AND CHOICE

The important question is what we place between our living today and our dying tomorrow. That choice is ours. There's no completely satisfactory answer to why we die; some mystery will remain. There is some light on the mystery in a conversation between Asher and his father in the book *My Name Is Asher Lev* by Chaim Potok. When Asher was a little boy, he was walking down the street with his father. There in the street, showing no signs of life, was a little bird. Asher could not bear to look at it, so he asked his father about it.

"Is it dead, Papa?" . . .
"Yes," I heard him say in a sad and distant way.
"Why did it die?"
"Everything that lives must die."
"Everything?"
"Yes."
"You, too, Papa? And Mama?"
"Yes."
"And me?"
"Yes," he said. . . . "But may it be only after you live a long and good life, my Asher." . . .
"Why?" I asked. [Why must everything die?]
"That's the way the Ribbono Shel Olom made His world, Asher."
"Why?"
"So life would be precious, Asher. Something that is yours forever is never precious."[3]

37

That doesn't solve the mystery of the *why* of death, but it is a helpful thought. Life is precious, and something that is ours forever is never precious. So what we do between living today and dying tomorrow is the big question. We have a choice.

The Israelites had it easy in Egypt. The "best of all the land" had been theirs while Joseph was alive and in favor with the Pharaoh. But now a new Pharaoh who didn't know Joseph had arisen; Joseph and all his generation had died. And the expanded number of Israelites was a threat in the mind of the Pharaoh. From life sustained and enriched by the "best of all the land," now the people were made to serve "with rigor"; their lives were made "bitter with hard bondage." They had to choose what was to be placed between their living today and dying tomorrow.

CONFIRMATION AND CERTAINTY

The Hebrew midwives are our great witnesses. Pharaoh commanded them to kill all the boy children born to Hebrew women. The midwives' faithfulness to God gave them strength to refuse the king's bidding. They had no guarantee of the outcome, but they acted out their commitment with a brazen faith. Their faith was confirmed.

"God dealt well with the midwives" (v. 20). This little line of Scripture is a preamble to the way it would be throughout the Exodus experience. The Hebrews would move in confident and exhilarating faith. Then they would back away—sink into despair, be blinded by their trials and difficulties. And God would move in again to confirm their faith and give them certainty. This people who refused to die would make it to Canaan, and they would know the promise "I am the Lord your God, who brought you out of the land of Egypt, out of the house of bondage" (Exod. 20:2).

NOTES

1. Alexander Maclaren, *Expositions of Holy Scripture*, 11 vols. (Grand Rapids: Wm. B. Eerdmans, 1952–59), 1:4.

2. Russell Baker, *Growing Up* (New York: New American Library, Signet Books, 1982), p. 52.

3. Chaim Potok, *My Name Is Asher Lev* (New York: Fawcett Crest Books, 1972), p. 150.

CHAPTER TWO

The Providence of God in Moses' Formative Years

Exodus 2:1–25

The unseen forces of God's providence overshadowed Moses' life from the very beginning. The event of Moses' birth is a moment of suspension, like that moment in the emerging dawn when lingering night and coming day struggle for life. Dawn is brief and its exact moment of birth can't be pinpointed, but though there are only glimmering signs, we know that darkness is doomed and the dim radiance of the East will soon prevail. So, here in Israel's history, hope and despair are in conflict. Israel was sighing in pessimism and moaning in oppression. Then the unseen forces of God's providence took human shape. A baby was born and faith began to emerge, dominant over doubt.

A MIRACLE CHILD

2:1 And a man of the house of Levi went and took *as wife* a daughter of Levi.

2 So the woman conceived and bore a son. And when she saw that he *was* a beautiful *child*, she hid him three months.

3 But when she could no longer hide him, she took an ark of bulrushes for him, daubed it with asphalt and pitch, put the child in it, and laid *it* in the reeds by the river's bank.

4 And his sister stood afar off, to know what would be done to him.

5 Then the daughter of Pharaoh came down to bathe at the river. And her maidens walked along the

riverside; and when she saw the ark among the reeds, she sent her maid to get it.

6 And when she opened *it*, she saw the child, and behold, the baby wept. So she had compassion on him, and said, "This is one of the Hebrews' children."

7 Then his sister said to Pharaoh's daughter, "Shall I go and call a nurse for you from the Hebrew women, that she may nurse the child for you?"

8 And Pharaoh's daughter said to her, "Go." So the maiden went and called the child's mother.

9 Then Pharaoh's daughter said to her, "Take this child away and nurse him for me, and I will give *you* your wages." So the woman took the child and nursed him.

10 And the child grew, and she brought him to Pharaoh's daughter, and he became her son. So she called his name Moses, saying, "Because I drew him out of the water."

Exod. 2:1–10

I never will forget the day a telephone call came from one of our dearest friends, Bonnie Crandall. She wanted to see me immediately. When she walked into my office, the atmosphere was charged with a sense of significance. I knew something very important had happened.

"Another miracle," she said. And then she told me she was pregnant.

Now the announcement of an expected child is not always that charged with elation. Sometimes it is greeted with fear and sorrow, even with anger, because of an unwanted child.

But when the child is wanted, all the angels of heaven stand on tiptoe to join in the rejoicing that is taking place. Bonnie's rejoicing was more intense, and that announcement more electrically charged, because of her past.

When Bonnie was sixteen, a doctor told her that she was "incomplete as a woman" and would never have children. I suppose that was the doctor's way of talking to a sixteen-year-old girl. He communicated to her that normal female functioning was not taking place, and she simply would not be able to bear children.

Bonnie was a popular young woman and dated a lot, but when any serious relationship began to develop, in fairness she shared the fact

40

that she could not have children. Romantic relationships usually ended at that point.

But then she met Ron, a Methodist preacher. They soon loved each other deeply. She shared the news about her inability to bear children. Ron was so much in love with her that that did not change his feelings, and they were married.

One day less than a year later, Bonnie was rushed to the doctor in tremendous pain. The doctors at first thought it was a kidney infection, but it wasn't long before they discovered she was pregnant. Ovaries that had not functioned for years had functioned, and she was going to have a child.

She did. They named him Matthew, a name which means "gift of God."

When Bonnie had surgery three years after Matthew was born, the doctor was mystified. After examining her ovaries he was convinced that the ovaries had never functioned and would never function, and yet there Matthew was!

It was nine years later that Bonnie came to my office to share the news. And now the news that she was pregnant again was made more dramatic and traumatic because she and Ron had adopted a daughter, Sabrina, only a few months before. "Another miracle," she said, and she was right. They named him Joshua, and that name means "God is my salvation."

Two miracle births.

The truth of the matter is that the birth of every child is a miracle—the result of the uniting of male and female to create life. The birth of any child is enough to cause us to be hushed and silent and retreat into ourselves as we contemplate the mystery of it all, and to rejoice greatly when the full impact of it really hits us.

But, there are special cases—when the miracles are very pronounced, when nature and circumstances seem to be defied, and God moves in a mysterious way another wonder to perform.

That was the case with Moses; he was a miracle child.

Let your imagination go as we reflect upon that story. Can you imagine the anxiety that surrounded the birth of that child? The ominous fact was that all male children born to Hebrew women, if discovered, were killed. So, all during pregnancy the mother and the father would know that the death sentence was hanging over the child should the child be a son.

The Hebrew midwives had defied the king, and Moses' mother defied him also and determined that this male child would live. Right from the beginning, a struggle between good and evil swirled around the cradle of a little boy.

God Is the Primary Actor

Note the remarkable fact that all the persons in this narrative are anonymous. Not even the mother and father are named at this particular point; Moses' sister is not named; the daughter of Pharaoh, who played such a significant role in the drama, is not named. We know from the whole story that Moses' father was Amram and his mother, Jochebed (6:20). They had a daughter, Miriam, and a son, Aaron—then came Moses. But at this point, none of these, nor the Pharaoh's daughter, is named.

I believe this says something to us. The reason is not ignorance; so not naming them must have been deliberate. The writer keeps them in the shadow, as it were, in order that the light might shine on the primary actor in the drama—God Himself.

I belong to a small group of twenty-two people, the Ecumenical Institute of Spirituality, which meets once a year for three and a half days. It provides some of the most significant relationships of my life. We share a rare fellowship across Catholic-Protestant lines as we share our spiritual pilgrimages with each other and as we seek to go in depth into a particular theme related to our spiritual growth. For one of our meetings, we gathered in Emmitsburg, Maryland, at the Provincial House of Our Daughters of Charity. This is an order of Roman Catholic nuns founded by Elizabeth Ann Seton.

Mother Seton is the only American-born person canonized as a saint by the Roman Catholic Church. She was married and had three children when her husband died. The Lord laid upon her a burning compassion for the poor, and especially poor children—the education of children, especially poor children. She started her work in New York, but it soon spread all over the world. Those who accepted her call became a part of a community and this community became an order. There's hardly a city in the United States where the work of the Daughters and Sisters of Charity is not felt.

Until I went to this meeting, I had known nothing about Elizabeth Ann Seton. Many of the people in our group are recognized

Christian leaders in this country. One is a Trappist monk whose writings are more popular than almost any other Roman Catholic writer today. Another is an Episcopal priest who is recognized as one of the two or three leaders in the renewal of attention to spiritual formation in our nation today. His books are already becoming classics in the field. These national leaders told the stories of how their lives were impacted by Sisters of Charity who taught them in their elementary schools.

As I sat in a communion service that we celebrated with those nuns at Emmitsburg, and watched them go to take the bread and the wine which sustains their life in deep commitment and community, they were somewhat faceless as they moved about in their old-fashioned habits. While sharing communion with them, I thought about all the anonymous persons that have come through that order since Elizabeth Ann Seton died in 1821, and about the thirty-six thousand of them who are living and working in communities around the world today. The fact of two of our members having been touched profoundly by these anonymous persons caused me to be powerfully struck by the truth of what the writer of Exodus was saying by making those actors in the birth of Moses anonymous. And I remembered what is written on John Wesley's monument in Westminster Abbey: "God buries the workman and carries on His work."

So the light shines on the primary actor in the drama of sacred history—God Himself.

What does that say to us? At least this: We are important. No matter how anonymous we may feel, we are a part of God's drama of covenant and redemption. And we never know how God may use our obedience and faithfulness for His grand purposes.

Let's bring the zoom lens of our minds into close and clear focus on Moses' mother. She was a slave. She had to work in the brickyards or labor in the fields all day. It's hard for us to even imagine what it must have been like to live in that kind of setting and be submitted to that kind of oppression.

It was tough. It was oppressive. It was beyond our imagination to know what went on most intensely in the heart and mind of the mother of Moses during those months she anticipated his birth, knowing the threat that hung over all of them.

Look at her story in verses 2 and 3. *"So the woman conceived and bore a son. And when she saw that he was a beautiful child, she hid him*

three months. But when she could no longer hide him, she took an ark of
bulrushes for him, daubed it with asphalt and pitch, put the child in it,
and laid it in the reeds by the river's bank."

What do we have here? First, there is the natural love of a mother.
But more, there was the faint whisper of providence as the mother
looked upon this *"beautiful child."* Did she know in her heart then
that God was doing something special, very special?

There is a word here for young parents. Do you see your children
as gifts from God? What a gift, and what a responsibility! I am convinced that the godly nurture Moses received during the three years
of his life before he went to live with the princess in the court of
Pharaoh shaped him for receptivity and response to God's call.

Nothing you do for your children, nothing you give them is as
important as making them aware of God's presence in their lives and
their dependence upon God. It is not trite or superficial to say that
the destinies of nations are fashioned on the laps of mothers and
fathers.

But, there is even more here—more than the natural love of a
mother, and that "more" is here to teach us about faith and commitment. Moses' mother hid her child for three months, bravely opposing the edict of the king. When the writer gives his catalogue of faith
in the eleventh chapter of Hebrews, the parents of Moses are there
with Abraham, Isaac, Jacob, Joseph, Gideon, David, and Samuel. The
anonymous ones are now brought into the floodlight, for "by faith"
they hid Moses for three months, because "they were not afraid of
the king's command" (Heb. 11:23).

When she could hide him no longer, she took a boat—an ark or a
chest out of bulrushes—made it waterproof with pitch, and then in
an ultimate act of commitment, put it at the river's edge, in the reeds,
and settled back in faith to wait for God to act.

What challenges are here for us, challenges that judge our faint
faith, yet challenges that stir in the deeps of our souls that longing to
live out there on the edge of mystery—out there where it is tough
and painful, to live out there in the confidence that He who is for us
is greater than all that is against us. What lessons are here for us?

One, *we can reckon completely on God.* Moses' mother had to do
that, to resist Pharaoh's command and risk the threat of death. What
is there in your life that threatens you? Are there lurking fears that
are keeping you from doing what you have already determined is

right for you? Moses' mother's faith tells us that we can reckon completely on God.

There is a second lesson. Not only can we reckon completely on God, *we can relax in trust, and wait for the Lord to do His work.* Moses' mother did everything she could; then she set the little ark that bore the precious cargo, her child, by the river and waited—waited on God.

Is there anything more difficult than to wait? But to wait in trust—ah, there's the secret. Earlier I asked for the attention of young parents; now here is a specific word for parents of older children. Are we willing to trust our children to God? We've done everything we can for them; we've given them everything that has been possible for us to give them, and now they are adolescent or older. We don't have the control we once had. We can't hover over them and attend them as we could when they were children. They now have to make their own decisions, go their own way, establish their own paths. Can we trust them to God?

Can we believe that God will care for our children even as He cared for that little ark in that dangerous river? Oh, for that kind of faith! Oh, for the readiness and the willingness to commit our children into the keeping of a covenant God, who has promised through His word, that if we will "train up a child in the way he should go, . . . when he is old he will not depart from it" (Prov. 22:6).

How much relief and release could come to parents today if we would simply rest in the confidence that God cares for, and is willing to move in the lives of our children as providentially and as precisely as He moved in the life of Moses.

But there is a larger, more general lesson than that here—a lesson for all. *When we have done our best in any task, in any situation, in any circumstance, we can wait and trust that God is in control.*

Look closely at the story. Around that little basket, that frail ark made out of straw, half lost among the reeds, is the mighty shield of God's purpose. Every human act and every circumstance serves that purpose. The reeds prevent the basket from being carried away by the mighty stream. The princess came for her bath at just the right hour. Her idle glance went in precisely the right direction, and the cry of the child came at just the right moment. There was the innocent but brilliant diplomacy of Moses' sister, and there was the shelter of a happy mother's breast as the child was returned to her. Then there was the safety of the palace.

You see, all these and a hundred more trivial and important things combined to paint a picture of God's providential design, His secret purpose being carried out.

Shouldn't that convince us? No matter what the circumstances, no matter how many Pharaohs may rise up against us, no matter how many forces Satan may throw against us, God's will is going to be accomplished eventually.

Do you believe that? Maybe not today, and maybe not even this year, but His will and His purpose are going to prevail. Do you believe that enough to wait—no matter what the situation is—in trust that God is going to intervene and God's will is going to be done, and that in the meantime, He will give you the grace and strength to wait with patience and meaning?

Pharaoh's Daughter

Look at Pharaoh's daughter now (vv. 5–6). The providence of God is at work, bringing the princess to the riverbank at the critical moment. What a role she plays in God's unfolding drama, providing the setting for Moses to be raised in the palace, educated and prepared to be the liberator of his people. But focus on another point for a significant lesson.

When she opened the little ark, she saw the child. The baby was crying, and *"she had compassion on him."* That's what I want to underscore. She had pity on him. *Curiosity was changed to compassion, and her compassion overrode pride of race and station.* She recognized the child as a Hebrew, and she knew that her father wanted all Hebrew baby boys killed. But as soon as the infant cried, her heart was touched and she entered empathetically into the Hebrew experience.

Is anything more needed in our day than empathy? To be able to identify with others, to share their experiences, to laugh with those who laugh and weep with those who weep.

It's not enough to have pity. Our pity must become compassion. Pity is a feeling, an emotion; compassion is rooted in the same feelings, but goes deeper and issues in action.

That's what happened when our congregation gave twenty-two thousand dollars at Christmas for the hungry people in Africa. That's what happened when our government called for sixty volunteers to go to Ethiopia when the famine there came to the attention of the world, and sixty thousand people volunteered.

It's not hard to make the point. Pity for prisoners and their families must issue in compassion as we follow through in specific prison ministry. Pity for people living in hovels for houses must become compassion that gives money, and paints and drives nails to secure a house for some needy family.

Compassion comes from a deliberate identification with another person. It is an identification, an empathy that enables us to see things as Pharaoh's daughter sees them, and feel things as she feels them. That's the place to which God seeks to bring us all, as He brought Pharaoh's daughter.

MOSES GROWS UP

2:11 Now it came to pass in those days, when Moses was grown, that he went out to his brethren and looked at their burdens. And he saw an Egyptian beating a Hebrew, one of his brethren.

12 So he looked this way and that way, and when he saw no one, he killed the Egyptian and hid him in the sand.

13 And when he went out the second day, behold, two Hebrew men were fighting, and he said to the one who did the wrong, "Why are you striking your companion?"

14 Then he said, "Who made you a prince and a judge over us? Do you intend to kill me as you killed the Egyptian?" So Moses feared and said, "Surely this thing is known!"

15a When Pharaoh heard of this matter, he sought to kill Moses.

Exod. 2:11–15a

There is a giant leap in Moses' biography—from the time he was about three years old when he went into the palace to live with Pharaoh's daughter (v. 10) until *"Moses was grown"* (v. 11).

What does *"grown"* mean as a description of Moses here? It's more than chronological and physical, I believe. *"When Moses was grown,*

. . . *he went out to his brethren and looked at their burdens. And he saw an Egyptian beating a Hebrew, one of his brethren."* Had he not *"looked at their burdens"* before? Had his ease and comfort in the palace blinded him to the suffering of his people? Had he pulled the shade down in his mind in order that his heart not be touched by their oppression?

It's easy to do that, isn't it? Easy to pull the shade of our mind so that we will not feel with our hearts the oppression and suffering that's going on around us. It's even easy to be a part of the oppressive system, and not let it get to us.

I've been reading a book that has pronounced its judgment upon me in a searing way. It's a deeply moving and beautiful autobiography of a talented black woman, Maya Angelou. She calls her story, *I Know Why the Caged Bird Sings.* She tells about growing up as a black person in our country. One sentence captures the pathos and tragedy of it all. Listen to her: "If growing up is painful for the Southern black girl, being aware of her displacement is the rust on the razor that threatens the throat."[1]

Isn't that descriptive and powerful? Consciously, or unconsciously, we have been a part of a system that held a rusty razor to the throats of thousands of people like Maya Angelou. For so many years, we pulled the shade of our mind in order that our hearts would not sense and feel the pain of it.

But Moses was *"grown"* now, and when he looked upon the burdens of the people, he saw an Egyptian beating a Hebrew. He intervened and killed the Egyptian. It was an act of undisciplined anger.

We applaud Moses' awareness of his people's suffering, but there is no justification for murder; to debate whether or not the murder was within the will of God is to miss the point of the narrative. What is important here is Moses' identification with his people, the Hebrews, despite the fact that he had lived in the palace and had been trained as an Egyptian. This reveals Moses' sense of justice, his courage, his willingness to act and live decisively.

In our time, most of us hold that violence and killing, even for a good cause, are unjustifiable. The pages of history are stained with the blood of those killed in the name of "good causes," and of religion, even the Christian religion. Minds capable of virtue produce vice also.

There's an interesting twist of irony in the record of this incident. On the day following the murder, which Moses thought was a secret, he intervened in a fight between two Hebrews. Yet, he was impotent in the situation. He had no influence. Worse than that, he was scornfully challenged: *"Do you intend to kill me as you killed the Egyptian?"* This rebuff is the first statement of a continuing motif of Moses' life: although he constantly sought to do good and to follow God's leading, he was the brunt of scorn and ridicule and murmuring. He was often rejected by those he was seeking to liberate.

It was the response of his own kinsman that led to Moses' fleeing Egypt. And the statement *"Moses feared"* gives an authentic ring to the account of Moses' life. He was afraid that Pharaoh was going to find out about his sin, and that his own life would be taken.

Isn't this revealing? Moses is not portrayed as the bold, heroic figure who could slay the Egyptian oppressor and be done with it. The fear which swept over him when he was found out betrays a very human quality, and speaks to us again of God's using us for His cause, despite our foibles and weaknesses.

MOSES' EXILE IN MIDIAN

2:15b But Moses fled from the face of Pharaoh and dwelt in the land of Midian; and he sat down by a well.

16 Now the priest of Midian had seven daughters. And they came and drew water, and they filled the troughs to water their father's flock.

17 Then the shepherds came and drove them away; but Moses stood up and helped them, and watered their flock.

18 When they came to Reuel their father, he said, "How *is it that* you have come so soon today?"

19 And they said, "An Egyptian delivered us from the hand of the shepherds, and he also drew enough water for us and watered the flock."

20 So he said to his daughters, "And where *is* he? Why *is it that* you have left the man? Call him, that he may eat bread."

21 Then Moses was content to live with the man, and he gave Zipporah his daughter to Moses.

> 22 And she bore *him* a son. He called his name
> Gershom, for he said, "I have been a stranger in a
> foreign land."
>
> *Exod. 2:15b–22*

Again, we have Moses intervening on behalf of those who are oppressed. When he arrived in Midian, he sat down at a well, and the daughters of the priest of Midian came to draw water. Shepherds in the vicinity came and drove the women away and used the water that they had drawn for their own flocks. There was no killing here, but Moses delivered the women out of the hands of the shepherds, and then drew water for them. Can we not say that Moses is becoming more "grown-up" as he looks on the oppression of people?

That was Moses' entree into Midian. Though few would have believed it, the providence of God still overshadowed Moses; for God, during this exile from Egypt, was preparing Moses for a heroic task. Moses was probably aware of that himself. Yet, during this period, God revealed Himself to Moses in a fuller way.

The Midianites were distant relatives of the Hebrews. In Genesis 25:2, Midian is described as the son of Abraham by Keturah. So, Moses doubtless learned much that would equip him as a leader of Hebrew tribes later. It's entirely possible that some of the Midianites maintained contact with the Judah tribe. If this was so, some of Moses' insight into the nature of God as Yahweh would have come through the Midianites during the time of his exile.

Moses' father-in-law, Jethro, was a priest (v. 16), who later officiated at, or at least offered, a sacrifice to God (18:12). He also advised Moses about the administration of justice and leadership among the Hebrew people (18:13–27).

The physical details of Midian—geographical terrain, scattered sources of water, oases—and other learnings were accumulated, which served Moses well as he became the nomadic leader of the people in the wilderness.

It's interesting to note here the parallels between the lives of Moses and Jacob. Both fled for their lives to relatives in another country (though Moses was much more distantly related). Both met their future wives at a well where both performed a physical feat in assisting the young women in watering their flocks. Both were taken home to the father of the women they had assisted, and both eventually married the girl met at the well.

"Moses was content to live with the man" (v. 21). When the daughters returned home, they told their father about what had happened at the well. *"An Egyptian delivered us"* (v. 19). Moses had so absorbed his cultural background that he was identified by others as an Egyptian. The father rebuked his daughters for forgetting the customary hospitality that would have required them to invite the stranger into their home. So, Moses came to live with the family, and one of the daughters, Zipporah (a name that means "bird"), was given to him in marriage. Their first-born son was named Gershom. Now the meaning of that name is set against the statement that he was content to dwell there. The name means "a stranger" for Moses said, *"I have been a stranger in a foreign land"* (v. 22).

So, Moses' contentedness in dwelling there does not have the idea of concession about it; it simply shows his willingness. He was pleased to accept the invitation. But the naming of his son was witness to the fact that he was lonely; a restlessness was still burning in his soul. Was the call of God to deliver His people out of bondage being incubated even at that point?

The fact that Moses' father-in-law was a priest, and probably the Midianites were already worshipers of God when Moses arrived to live among them, added additional religious undergirding to that which Moses had received from his mother when he was a child. Is that not another witness to the overshadowing providence of God? For forty years in Midian, Moses was a part of the household of a priest.

When Are We Most Like God

2:23 Now it happened in the process of time that the king of Egypt died. Then the children of Israel groaned because of the bondage, and they cried out; and their cry came up to God because of the bondage.

24 So God heard their groaning, and God remembered His covenant with Abraham, with Isaac, and with Jacob.

25 And God looked upon the children of Israel, and God acknowledged *them.*

Exod. 2:23–25

There was a man who worked downtown in a large city. Each day he rode the commuter train from his lovely suburban home to the inner city. The train went through the impoverished areas of the city, past decaying tenements, dilapidated public housing, dingy streets. When the train slowed down, the fellow could see into the bleak apartments, and when it was especially slow, he could look into the even bleaker faces of those who lived in those drab apartments. He could see the unemployed gathered around a fire in a vacant lot, waiting for someone to come by and pick them up for day labor. He could see the children playing on dusty basketball courts, skipping school, and he wondered who cared about them.

At work he would often catch himself staring into space, thinking about all those people in that desperate environment. It became increasingly difficult for him to fall asleep at night. When he would close his eyes, all he could see were those depressing scenes and those desperate people. He decided he had to do something about it. And he did. Now, when he rides the commuter train, he pulls down the blinds so he doesn't have to look at the depressing environment around him. He now is at peace. Or is he? If he does have peace, what terrible price has he paid for it? How long will it last?

Keep that picture in your mind as we look at these verses that climax the second chapter of Exodus. Here is a description of God that defines God's character. Could more be packed into these verses? Is there a more descriptive passage about the character of God in the whole of the Bible? In four action words, we have a clear picture of God who loves and cares and intervenes in the lives of His people.

God hears: *"God heard their groaning."*

God remembers: *"God remembered His covenant with Abraham, with Isaac, and with Jacob."*

God sees: *"God looked upon the children of Israel."*

God knows: *"God acknowledged them."*

We noted previously that a gap of forty years of silence had occurred between verses 10 and 11 in the biography of Moses. Now another forty years of Moses' life is passed over in silence between verses 22 and 23. The Pharaoh who had oppressed the Israelites so cruelly died after a long reign. This paved the way for Moses to return to Egypt. God had not forgotten His people; neither had He forgotten Moses, who would be their deliverer.

52

The silence of God does not mean that God is unconcerned or inactive. Remember the two most agonizing experiences of Jesus' life: Gethsemane and the Cross. In both of those experiences our Lord was greeted by the silence of God. It is doubtful whether God could ever have been any closer to His Son than on those two occasions.

Even in silence, God is at work on behalf of His people, and Moses would soon learn that when he was confronted by God in the burning bush.

The four verbs describing God express with majestic force God's personal involvement with the burdens of those with whom He has made a covenant.

"God heard their groaning" (v. 24). *"Their cry came up to God"* (v. 23). This was probably not an articulated petition, but something like the "groanings which cannot be uttered" that Paul talked about (Rom. 8:26). It was misery, the deeper voice of humankind, blended with the anguish and pain wrung from these people by their oppression.

There are times when we cannot speak. Our pain and grief cannot be expressed in words. So, in our anguished silence we lay our lives before God. Everything that we are—the riveting pain that tears at our hearts; the foreboding anxiety that renders us impotent; the sorrow for our loved ones who are sick and dying, some of them lost and without God; the emptiness of death. And God hears the voice of our groaning, even though that groaning that stirs within us does not issue in sound. F. B. Meyer has suggested that tears have a voice, and God interprets it.

"God remembered his covenant with Abraham, with Isaac, and with Jacob" (v. 24; see Gen. 12:1–3; 17:1–14; 26:2–5; 28:13ff.). The action of God throughout the Old Testament is focused in His faithfulness to the covenant relationship. This is the primary element that defines Yahweh's nature. So, when we look at various personalities the big issue is not whether they pleased or displeased God, but that God was faithful despite their unfaithfulness. (A dramatic example is King David.)

"God looked upon the children of Israel" (v. 25). "The eyes of the Lord are on the righteous, / And His ears are open to their cry" (Ps. 34:15). The Hebrew verb for "looked upon" in this verse is *rā'âh*. In many instances in Scripture, it has the deeper sense of "knowing." The word may mean to see in such a way as to know (cf. Deut. 33:9);

and it may be synonymous with experiencing something (cf. Jer. 5:12; 14:13; Ps. 89:48). Though they could not be deemed righteous for their own sake, the Israelites were beloved for their forefathers' sake.

"God acknowledged them" (v. 25). The Hebrew verb used here, *yāda‘*, is a word of intimacy. It means to know experientially. It always has the personal experiential dimension in regard to the way in which God knows the condition of His people.

See the added dimension this gives to God's relationship with us. He sees; there's nothing which concerns us that is hidden from Him. That's one thing—but to know that He cannot see without having pity, without feeling and entering into our experience is so heartening. Later, when the children of Israel were assured that Jehovah had seen their affliction, "they bowed their heads and worshiped" (Exod. 4:31) as though they had nothing more to ask; and the result justified their act. "Every blow of the hand that buffets you, every cut of the scourge, every scorching hour under the noon-tide sun, every lonely hour when lovers and friends stand aloof, every step into the valley of the shadow, every moment of sleep beneath the juniper tree, is watched by the eyes that never slumber nor sleep."[2]

Remember the story with which we began this section, of the man pulling down the shade of the commuter train. Remember our emphasis upon Moses' growing up, that when he was grown he saw the affliction of his people. And remember the compassion of Pharaoh's daughter when she looked into the little ark and saw and heard the crying baby. We are "grown-up" as God's people; we are most like Him, when we act as God acts. And how does God act? Look back and reread the Scripture (Exod. 2:23–25) that is printed at the beginning of this section of our discussion.

Here is a picture in one church of people acting as God acts. Bishop Leontine Kelly tells the story. She was elected a bishop of the church in 1984—the first black woman, and only the third woman, to be elected a bishop in the United Methodist Church. She's a powerful preacher.

Bishop Kelly grew up in a parsonage. Her father was a Methodist preacher. When she was a little girl he was assigned to a church in Cincinnati. It had been all white, but the neighborhood had changed and it had become a black congregation. It was the most magnificent church she had ever seen—an awe-inspiring Gothic structure. There was beautiful polished wood and a huge crystal chandelier. The church had been a prestigious and wealthy one in which presidents had worshiped.

Just as impressive as the church was the parsonage. Bishop Kelly says it was so big that each of the children had his or her own room—and that was something new for them. There was a cellar too, a dingy, dark place with a couple of dim light bulbs. There were cobwebs and shadows down there, and she was frightened by it.

One day, when her brothers were down in the cellar, they found a hole behind the furnace which seemed to lead to a tunnel. They asked her to go with them to explore it, but she went to her father and told him about it instead. They all went down to investigate. Her father became very excited. "I think you've found something; let's go over to the church and look." They went over to the church which was next door, down into the cellar, and there behind the furnace they found some old boards, and behind those boards they discovered other tunnels.

That night around the dinner table at the Calvary Church parsonage in Cincinnati, five blocks from the Ohio River, her father told them the story of the underground railroad, a railroad that didn't have tracks or trains, but was a network for helping slaves escape to freedom. The slaves were hunted down like animals, and brutally punished when caught. It was against the law to help them, but the members of the underground railroad accepted risk to themselves in order to help the slaves get to freedom in Canada.

Bishop Kelly says she has never forgotten what her father said that night. "Children, I want you to remember this day as long as you live. We've found a station on the underground railroad. The greatness of this church is not its Gothic architecture, its beautiful furniture, its crystal chandelier. The greatness of this church is below us. We are on hallowed ground. These people dared to risk their lives to become involved and care about the poor, the frightened runaway slaves, and that was the mark of their greatness."

Those Christians in that church were acting as God acts, they were "grown-up." If you want another authority for it, be attentive before that word of Jesus:

> Then the King will say to those on His right hand,
> "Come, you blessed of My Father, inherit the kingdom

prepared for you from the foundation of the world: for I was hungry and you gave Me food; I was thirsty and you gave Me drink; I was a stranger and you took Me in; I was naked and you clothed Me; I was sick and you visited Me; I was in prison and you came to Me." Then the righteous will answer Him, saying, "Lord, when did we see You hungry and feed You, or thirsty and give You drink? When did we see You a stranger and take You in, or naked and clothe You? Or when did we see You sick, or in prison, and come to You?" And the King will answer and say to them, "Assuredly, I say to you, inasmuch as you did it to one of the least of these My brethren, you did it to Me."

Then He will also say to those on the left hand, "Depart from Me, you cursed, into the everlasting fire prepared for the devil and his angels."

Matt. 25:34–41

NOTES

1. Maya Angelou, *I Know Why the Caged Bird Sings* (New York: Random House, 1969; Bantam Books), p. 3.

2. F. B. Meyer, *Devotional Commentary on Exodus* (Grand Rapids: Kregel Publications, 1978), p. 40.

CHAPTER THREE

The Call of Moses

Exodus 3:1–4:17

Moses is an old man now. He had sinned when he had killed an Egyptian, and as a consequence he has suffered forty years of separation from his people and family. But the years have passed and whatever stirrings he once felt are probably now buried in the distant past. He has settled down to a shepherd's life in Midian, content with the family of Jethro the priest. Moses is now eighty years of age. We don't normally look for revolutions in people's lives when they are that age. Nicodemus asked Jesus, "Can a man be born again when he is old?" We know it's possible, but it's highly improbable.

Moses was old. And you remember he'd made an effort to free Israel through his own strength, but that had failed. His had been a very disappointing experience. If as a young boy the dream of liberation of Israel had been conceived in his mind, you can imagine that all during those years in the palace he anticipated when he would be in a position of power and could set his people free.

But God has not forgotten Moses. The phrase "I have come down" (3:8) describes the nature of the God who is soon going to confront Moses. This God does not sit placidly in the heavens, oblivious to history.

In this call of Moses we will find a further revelation of a personal God, working within the framework of history but entering that arena to act purposefully—to name Himself, and to call others by name.

LESSONS FROM THE BURNING BUSH

3:1 Now Moses was tending the flock of Jethro his
father-in-law, the priest of Midian. And he led the

flock to the back of the desert, and came to Horeb, the mountain of God.

2 And the Angel of the LORD appeared to him in a flame of fire from the midst of a bush. So he looked, and behold, the bush was burning with fire, but the bush *was* not consumed.

3 Then Moses said, "I will now turn aside and see this great sight, why the bush does not burn."

4 So when the LORD saw that he turned aside to look, God called to him from the midst of the bush and said, "Moses, Moses!" And he said, "Here I am."

5 Then He said, "Do not draw near this place. Take your sandals off your feet, for the place where you stand *is* holy ground."

6 Moreover He said, "I *am* the God of your father—the God of Abraham, the God of Isaac, and the God of Jacob." And Moses hid his face, for he was afraid to look upon God.

Exod. 3:1–6

One of my favorite plays is *Harvey* by Mary Chase. I've seen it on stage, on TV, and as a movie. It is a delight in any medium. You may recall that this play is about Elwood P. Dowd, an eccentric drinking man whose closest friend is an enormous rabbit called Harvey (who is invisible for the most part to anyone but Elwood). In fact, because Harvey is unseen, yet so real to Elwood, his family hires Dr. Chumley, a psychiatrist, to cure Elwood and rid the family of Harvey's embarrassing presence.

Being a good psychiatrist, and therefore open, Dr. Chumley has a spectacular conversion; not a Christian conversion, but a good conversion nonetheless. In one scene, Dr. Chumley says, "Flyspecks. I've been spending my life among flyspecks while miracles have been leaning on lampposts on Eighteenth and Fairfax." (Eighteenth and Fairfax is where Elwood had originally met Harvey the rabbit.)

Then later, after talking further with Elwood, the doctor bursts out in a magnificent crescendo of joy, exclaiming: "To hell with decency! I've got to have that rabbit."

The dull-minded, unimaginative, dead-spirited will immediately conclude that the psychiatrist was as sick as the patient, that both had lost touch with reality. But wait. Maybe, just maybe, you and I are a lot like Dr. Chumley—living among flyspecks when there are miracles leaning against lampposts right on our own corners.

Moses discovered that—not on a street corner, but in an even more pedestrian place—out in the pasture where he was keeping the sheep of his father-in-law. That's a big part of the meaning of the story of the burning bush: that there are miracles where we have been seeing flyspecks—or whatever matter-of-fact, prosaic part of our lives we have given in to.

Let's move beyond the dramatic, and seek lessons for us, who have not been confronted by any literal burning bushes lately and who have not heard any verbal pronouncement of our name by God. What are those lessons?

God Appears in the Ordinary

Nothing exciting is going on for Moses. What he is doing is matter-of-fact daily work. Look at verse 1: *"Now Moses was tending the flock of Jethro his father-in-law, the priest of Midian. And he led the flock to the back of the desert, and came to Horeb, the mountain of God."* He was just doing his work—nothing out of the ordinary—when God appeared.

Edmund Burke, the eighteenth-century political philosopher, turned a marvelous phrase to express a solid truth: "History is full of momentous trifles." Isn't that a marvelous insight? "Momentous trifles"—ordinary events shot through with extraordinary meaning.

Remember Moses' situation. He had killed an Egyptian and had fled lest Pharaoh take his life. So here he is in Midian, forty years later. Life as a shepherd had become routine, and on this day he is leading the flock *"to the back of the desert,"* and it happens. There it is in verse 2: *"And the Angel of the Lord appeared to him in a flame of fire from the midst of a bush."*

God appears in the ordinary.

There's a beautiful and telling commentary on Moses' life in Midian in the names that he gave his children. The Hebrews gave names with very specific meanings to their children.

Moses called his first child Gershom, which means "a stranger." Moses called him that because he had been "a stranger in a foreign land."

Then came a second child. Moses named him Eliezer ("God is help") because "the God of my father was my help" (Exod. 18:4). The depression and loneliness of being a "stranger" had somewhat lightened. He had found a way to live by faith in that place of sojourn, in that dull, out of the way Midian, far from the excitement and glamour of palace life of Egypt.

The lesson? Be faithful to God where you are. Know with Moses, "My God is my help." And God will come. Probably when you least expect Him, for God comes in the ordinary.

God has to get our attention before He presents Himself to us. Get the picture clearly in your mind. Moses is walking along an old familiar path. He's probably been there hundreds of times. By chance, he lifts his eyes, and he beholds a rather strange sight on the mountainside. He sees a bush there that seems to be on fire. He watches it, expecting it to crumble into gray ashes. But to his amazement, it burns on. That gets Moses' attention. Now comes the important part of the story. Don't stop with the burning bush. Don't let that be the center of your attention. Read verse 3: *"Then Moses said, 'I will now turn aside and see this great sight, why the bush does not burn.'"*

It is now, when God has gotten Moses' attention, that God presents Himself to Moses. We must read verse 4: *"So when the Lord saw that he turned aside to look, God called to him from the midst of the bush and said, 'Moses, Moses!' And he said, 'Here I am.'"*

Now, there are all sorts of ways that God gets our attention. I've known some couples who have given God their attention when their first child was born. The miracle of *birth*, their responsibility as parents, the binding of their lives in the event, all combine to call their attention to the fact of God and their need to be in right relation with God.

I've known a few people—very few and I'm sorry for that—for whom *good fortune* has caused them to see God's spirit moving in their lives. Not long ago, a man in my congregation, through an almost impossible set of circumstances, was offered a job that he had wanted for a long time but had given up on. That got that man's attention, and God presented Himself.

Unfortunately, for most of us it takes *tragedy* to get our attention. But in these tragedies, we may find the face of God. It is as though in these tragedies we are meeting God on the back side of the desert. God does not bring these tragedies, but God uses these tragedies to get our attention. And He often presents Himself in the midst of tragedy.

Friends of mine in California called recently to share the news about their first grandchild, born that morning. They broke into sobs as they shared the fact that the little boy has Down's syndrome.

I immediately started trying to call the father. It was the next night that we made contact. I don't know how much I ministered to him, but he certainly ministered to me. They had had two days and nights of crying and praying and looking at their lives. This young man said, "We've decided that God has entrusted us with a gift—and that He will give us what we need to rear this special child." Through this special child, God got their attention and presented Himself to them.

So you see, God has to get our attention before He can present Himself to us. And the way He gets our attention is so varied, so miraculously varied. He's always looking for that opportunity to present Himself, and it comes when we give Him our attention, when we turn aside to see whatever burning bush is there.

When we are in God's Presence, the ground whereon we stand is always holy; and we'd better take off our shoes. God had to remind Moses of that. Look at verse 5: *"Then He said, 'Do not draw near this place. Take your sandals off your feet, for the place where you stand is holy ground.'"*

This is a beautiful custom still widely practiced in the East. When you enter a temple, a palace, or even a private home, you take off your shoes.

I think I will never forget my first visit to the Dome of the Rock in Jerusalem. That magnificent mosque is built over the rock where tradition holds that Abraham offered his son Isaac as a sacrifice, and where Mohammed is said to have ascended. Everyone takes off his or her shoes on entering. It is a sign of reverence. No one ever enters a Mohammedan mosque with shoes on.

It was a strange feeling for me, but I felt the symbolic power of being barefoot in God's house. This mingled sense of wonder, reverence, and awe is what distinguishes religion from a code of morals.

I see two practical leadings for us here. One, God is not someone you can be "chummy" with. One of the glaring limitations of many modern expressions of the Christian faith is that God is domesticated, reduced to a good friend next door—or upstairs!—who is always there to attend not only our needs but our wants.

Inevitably, this God is pictured as the one who guarantees success and happiness. And when you carry that superficial understanding of who God is to its practical bottom line, you must conclude that only the "healthy, wealthy, and wise" can be on good terms with Him. What does this say to the poor, the desperately ill, the oppressed? The idea of a chummy God who will give us everything we want if we will practice positive and possibility thinking long enough and hard enough is not Christian. It may be good psychology for some—but it's incomplete Christianity.

You can't take the mystery out of faith. You can't chart the workings of God on a computer or with a slide rule. The stance of faith is to live in the tension that comes from the experience of the immanent God, God with us now, as Jesus pictured Him—Abba, Father, and the experience of the mystery of a transcendent God, the Holy other who says, "My ways [are] higher than your ways,/And my thoughts than your thoughts" (Isa. 55:9).

Now, let's consider the second leading. The practical rationale for taking off our shoes when we enter the temple is that they have dirt and dust on them, and the place and presence of God are not to be defiled. This symbolic action points to the powerful reality of God's presence. The relationship God demands with His people is expressed in covenant, "I am the Lord your God. You shall therefore consecrate yourselves, and you shall be holy; for I am holy" (Lev. 11:44).

Here is where the transcendent and immanent come together. In Exodus 29, God calls Moses to the mountaintop and makes one of the most remarkable promises in the Bible: "I will consecrate the tabernacle of meeting and the altar. . . . I will dwell among the children of Israel" (vv. 44–45).

What a staggering thought: *The sovereign God of the universe promises to dwell in the midst of His people.*

That's a central theme throughout the Scripture. John put it this way in his Gospel: "The Word became flesh and dwelt among us" (John 1:14). The Greek word for *dwelt* literally means to "pitch a tent." So now in the new covenant, through Christ, God comes to "pitch His tent" among His people. That's who God is, eternally, beginning with the old covenant in Genesis and Exodus and concluding with the new covenant that He made in Jesus Christ, and going on in that apocalyptic vision in the book of Revelation of how it will be at the end of time. "The tabernacle of God is with men, and He will dwell with them, and they shall be His people" (Rev. 21:3).

By pitching His tent in our midst, God becomes present with us, identifies Himself with us; and the reality is that God is here. But there is a big condition: God demands something in return for His presence among us. If He is to identify with us, we are to identify with Him, so He commands us, "You shall be holy; for I am holy."

Let's review the lessons of the burning bush.

1. God appears in the ordinary.
2. God has to get our attention to present Himself to us.
3. In God's presence, the ground on which we stand is always holy, and we'd better take off our shoes.

We should not be preoccupied with the burning bush itself, but keep our minds on what it teaches. And remember, when God wants to reveal Himself, any old bush will do!

Let's look now at some special aspects of this section of Scripture.

Mount Horeb, the Mountain of God

While leading the flock of his father-in-law, Moses came to the back of the desert, and to Horeb, the mountain of God. Horeb and Sinai are synonymous. At this place Moses received his call to deliver the people out of bondage, here he would return after their deliverance, and on this mountain he would receive the tablets of the law. As we will see later, this would be a place of confirmation which God would give Moses.

The Burning Bush

The tree most characteristic of that locality was the wild acacia, a shaggy thornbush. To find such a bush burning was not absolutely novel. The ashes of some nomad's fire or a flash of lightning sometimes kindled the dry grass of the wilderness and ignited these bushes. So, the remarkable fact in this instance was that though the bush burned with fire, it was not consumed.

There are all sorts of symbolism here. There are those who contend that this burning bush was intended as an emblem of Israel in Egypt, "existing undiminished among their fiery trials." F. B. Meyer reminds us that the fathers of the Presbyterian Church took it to be a symbol of the words "persecuted, but not forsaken; struck down, but not destroyed" (2 Cor. 4:9). Of that suggestion, Dr. Meyer commented,

> Undoubtedly it is a great truth that we may be enwrapped in the flame of acute suffering, and the fire will only consume the canker worms and caterpillars that preyed upon the verdure of our spiritual life, without scorching the tiniest twig, or consuming the most fragile blossom. The burning fiery furnace will not singe a hair of your head, though it will free you from your fettering bonds. But this can hardly be the truth which the Divine Spirit designed to teach, for it would not have been needful to bid Moses unsandal his feet, if the fire had simply stood for pain.[1]

Fire was and continues to be associated with God's presence. Throughout Scripture, fire is the emblem of deity. This was even true with the rites of heathens, but it was distinctly true with Israel. When God entered into His covenant with Abraham, the lamp of fire denoted God's presence. The pledge that God made to the Israelites during the Exodus was that they would be led by a pillar of fire—it would be a cloud of smoke by day, but a fire-cloud by night.

So, the burning bush does symbolize God's presence. And what symbolism is there in its not being consumed? It is that we can know God's presence eternally.

For many years theologians have discussed and debated the identity of the *"Angel of the Lord"* that appeared to Moses *"in a flame of fire from the midst of a bush."* In some passages of Scripture, the angel seems to be different from God (Exod. 23:20–23; Num. 22:22; Judg. 5:23; 2 Sam. 24:16; Zech. 1:12–13). In other places God and the Angel are identical and interchangeable (Gen. 16:7–13; 22:11–12; 48:15–16; Judg. 2:1; 6:11–24; 13:3–22).

It seems most appropriate to perceive the Angel of the Lord as a visible manifestation of God. Such visible manifestations of God in the Old Testament are called theophanies, from a word that means "an appearance of God." They often occur in the midst of natural phenomena: in fire, Exodus 3:2; in a cloud, Exodus 13:21; in a whirlwind, Job 38:1; in an earthquake, 1 Kings 19:11. They also appear in human form: Exodus 33:21–23; Isaiah 6:1; Genesis 18; Ezekiel 1:26–27.

It's interesting that they never appear in animal form. Theophanies are not common to the New Testament because the ultimate theophany is there—incarnation of Jesus Christ, the Word become flesh. However you choose to interpret the burning bush, the profound truth is that Moses experienced God's presence, and God spoke to him, and he spoke to God.

Words from the Burning Bush

Note two power-packed truths here. (1) God called Moses by name. This is a personal God with whom we are dealing. He looks, He sees, He knows. One recalls that vivid word of the prophet Isaiah, when God reminded His people of His personal covenant relationship with them. "But now, thus says the Lord, who created you, O Jacob,/And He who formed you, O Israel:/'Fear not, for I have redeemed you;/I have called you by your name;/You are Mine'" (Isa. 43:1). Moses' response: *"Here I am"* means literally in the Hebrew "Behold me!" The expression is found frequently in the Old Testament to express attentiveness to some call and a readiness to obey (cf. Abraham, Gen. 22:1; Samuel, 1 Sam. 3:4; Isaiah, Isa. 6:8).

(2) God identified Himself in order that Moses would know that He was not meeting an unknown God. This one who spoke was the God of Abraham, Isaac, and Jacob. When God calls us, like Moses, we may respond and hide our face. We may be confused and feel fear as Isaiah did when he cried, "Woe is me, for I am undone!" And like Ezekiel, we may fall to the ground face down when we see the Lord (Ezek. 1:28b). Even so, in our heart of hearts, we need to know that though this one is holy, high, and lifted up, He is the God of Abraham, Isaac, and Jacob. He is the God of our fathers who is a gracious God, slow to anger, abounding in steadfast love, always keeping His covenant with us.

A REDEEMING GOD AND A REDEMPTION THAT IS COMPLETE

> 3:7 And the LORD said: "I have surely seen the oppression of My people who *are* in Egypt, and have heard their cry because of their taskmasters, for I know their sorrows.

8 "So I have come down to deliver them out of the hand of the Egyptians, and to bring them up from that land to a good and large land, to a land flowing with milk and honey, to the place of the Canaanites and the Hittites and the Amorites and the Perizzites and the Hivites and the Jebusites.

9 "Now therefore, behold, the cry of the children of Israel has come to Me, and I have also seen the oppression with which the Egyptians oppress them.

10 "Come now, therefore, and I will send you to Pharaoh that you may bring My people, the children of Israel, out of Egypt."

Exod. 3:7–10

Here is a picture of a redeeming God and a redemption that is complete. God would not forget the promise that He had made to Abraham and confirmed with Isaac and Jacob. God always hears the cries of His people, and He always remembers His covenant.

A big part of the worship of Israel and of our worship today is a rehearsal of this good news about God. The Psalms, especially, rehearse that good news:

Many times He delivered them;
But they rebelled in their council,
And were brought low for their iniquity,
Nevertheless He regarded their affliction,
When He heard their cry;
And for their sake He remembered His
    covenant,
And relented according to the multitude of His
    mercies.

Ps. 106:43–45

In this Psalm, we are carried back to all those occasions when God kept His covenant with Israel. But we are also carried forward to the covenant God made in Jesus Christ, His ultimate covenant which was ratified in Jesus' blood. Jesus Himself stated it on the night that He was betrayed. He took bread and blessed it and gave it to His disciples. Then He took the wine and blessed it and gave to them, saying, "Drink from it, all of you. For this is My blood of the new covenant" (Matt. 26:27–28). The symbol and the reality are powerful.

It won't be long in the Exodus story before God will instruct His people to prepare and eat a special lamb, a lamb without blemish, and to take blood from that lamb and sprinkle it on the lintel and doorposts of their houses as a sign of who they are and of their faithfulness.

I wish I could remember the words of that old gospel hymn we used to sing in rural Mississippi. The haunting chorus of it still sings in my mind:

> When I see the blood,
> When I see the blood,
> When I see the blood,
> I will pass, I will pass over you.

The blood was covenant blood, the sign that God would deliver the children of Israel and for the angel of death to pass over them. No wonder that the first Christians saw Jesus as the Lamb slain from the foundation of the world—"the Lamb of God who takes away the sin of the world" (John 1:29)—and this has been a powerful image for Christians ever since.

This is a picture of a redeeming God who has made an eternal covenant with us.

It's also a picture of a redemption that is complete. See it in verse 8: *"So I have come down to deliver them out of the hand of the Egyptians, and to bring them up from that land to a good and large land, to a land flowing with milk and honey."*

When God redeems, He not only redeems *from* something, He always redeems *to* something. Not only will He deliver His people out of bondage, out of the enslaving *"hand of the Egyptians,"* He will bring them to *"a land flowing with milk and honey."*

The two people God used to redeem His people Israel were Moses and Joshua. Moses led them out of bondage; Joshua led them into the promised land. The complete redemption, out of bondage into the promised land, is through Jesus Christ. But note the connection between Jesus and Moses and Jesus and Joshua. We've already indicated that the New Testament established a significant parallel between Moses and Jesus.

Moses was the primary actor in the Exodus drama. But *Jesus* is from the Greek form of the Jewish name *Joshua. Joshua* means "God saves." So in the naming of Jesus, we are not only taken back to the tradition of the Exodus and Moses, the primary actor in it, but we have in Jesus' name the completion of all that the Exodus was about. To see the connection between Jesus and Moses is to see Jesus as the liberator, the one who has come to release us from bondage. But it was Joshua who finally led his people into the light that was long awaited, most expected, incessantly prayed for—the fulfillment of their lives.

So, when the angel says, "You shall call His name Jesus" (meaning Joshua), the name fully reveals what Jesus is to do. Not only was He to lead us out of bondage as Moses had done, He was to lead us into the fulfillment of life, as Joshua had done.

It is a complete salvation, and this is what Paul was trying to say to the Ephesians: "Even when we were dead in trespasses, [God] made us alive together with Christ (by grace you have been saved), and raised us up together and made us sit together in the heavenly places in Christ Jesus" (Eph. 2:5–6).

Do you see the connection? That picture of God's redemption back in Exodus, out of Egyptian bondage into the promised land, is now complete in Jesus Christ. In Christ, we're brought out of Adam and put into Christ. We've been brought out of darkness into light, out of death into life. Perhaps, the most dramatic of all, we've been brought out of hell, if you please, and put into heaven—a complete redemption.

Here it is in a personal story. I asked a certain friend if I could share his story in this book. His response was, "If it's to the glory of God, you may share it."

One Monday morning, I found his note slipped under the door of my office. He had written it in a time of reflection and dedication after the sermon the preceding day. He signed his name, and then added "The Alcoholic."

> Dear Dr. Dunnam:
> In my forty-four-month battle with alcohol, I tried every-thing the medical profession thought would help. Nothing did: psychiatrists, psychologists, treatment centers, antidepressant medicines, all types of tranquilizers. But nothing did it. Then, in desperation, I sought God. God delivered me.

Isn't that glorious! What an affirmation of faith—"God delivered me." But that's not all. My friend continued:

I promised Him, since He would not let me die, "God, You must have a purpose for me. If You'll let me live a respectable life and free me from this bondage, every day You permit me to live, I'll serve You and I'll never rob You again."

Every day God stays at least ten paces ahead of me. I'm blessed every day in more ways than I can deserve, and nowhere can a happier man be found.

That's an example of the complete salvation that God offers—out of bondage to alcohol into the worship and service of the living God. Jesus does for us what Moses and Joshua did for Israel. He delivers us out of bondage into the promised land.

A Reluctant Prophet

3:11 But Moses said to God, "Who *am* I that I should go to Pharaoh, and that I should bring the children of Israel out of Egypt?"

12 So He said, "I will certainly be with you. And this *shall be* a sign to you that I have sent you: When you have brought the people out of Egypt, you shall serve God on this mountain."

13 Then Moses said to God, "Indeed, *when* I come to the children of Israel and say to them, 'The God of your fathers has sent me to you,' and they say to me, 'What *is* His name?' what shall I say to them?"

14 And God said to Moses, "I AM WHO I AM." And He said, "Thus you shall say to the children of Israel, 'I AM has sent me to you.'"

15 Moreover God said to Moses, "Thus you shall say to the children of Israel: 'The LORD God of your fathers, the God of Abraham, the God of Isaac, and the God of Jacob, has sent me to you. This *is* My name forever, and this *is* My memorial to all generations.'

16 "Go and gather the elders of Israel together, and say to them, 'The LORD God of your fathers, the God of Abraham, of Isaac, and of Jacob, appeared to me, saying, "I have surely visited you and *seen* what is done to you in Egypt;

17 "and I have said I will bring you up out of the affliction of Egypt to the land of the Canaanites and the Hittites and the Amorites and the Perizzites and the Hivites and the Jebusites, to a land flowing with milk and honey."'

18 "Then they will heed your voice; and you shall come, you and the elders of Israel, to the king of Egypt; and you shall say to him,'The LORD God of the Hebrews has met with us; and now, please, let us go three days' journey into the wilderness, that we may sacrifice to the LORD our God.'

19 "But I am sure that the king of Egypt will not let you go, no, not even by a mighty hand.

20 "So I will stretch out My hand and strike Egypt with all My wonders which I will do in its midst; and after that he will let you go.

21 "And I will give this people favor in the sight of the Egyptians; and it shall be, when you go, that you shall not go empty-handed.

22 "But every woman shall ask of her neighbor, namely, of her who dwells near her house, articles of silver, articles of gold, and clothing; and you shall put *them* on your sons and on your daughters. So you shall plunder the Egyptians."

4:1 Then Moses answered and said, "But suppose they will not believe me or listen to my voice; suppose they say, 'The LORD has not appeared to you.'"

2 So the LORD said to him, "What *is* that in your hand?" He said, "A rod."

3 And He said, "Cast it on the ground." So he cast it on the ground, and it became a serpent; and Moses fled from it.

4 Then the LORD said to Moses, "Reach out your hand and take *it* by the tail" (and he reached out his hand and caught it, and it became a rod in his hand),

5 "that they may believe that the LORD God of their fathers, the God of Abraham, the God of Isaac, and the God of Jacob, has appeared to you."

6 Furthermore the LORD said to him, "Now put your hand in your bosom." And he put his hand in his bosom, and when he took it out, behold, his hand *was* leprous, like snow.

7 And He said, "Put your hand in your bosom again." So he put his hand in his bosom again, and drew it out of his bosom, and behold, it was restored like his *other* flesh.

8 "Then it will be, if they do not believe you, nor heed the message of the first sign, that they may believe the message of the latter sign.

9 "And it shall be, if they do not believe even these two signs, or listen to your voice, that you shall take water from the river and pour *it* on the dry *land*. The water which you take from the river will become blood on the dry *land*."

10 Then Moses said to the LORD, "O my Lord, I *am* not eloquent, neither before nor since You have spoken to Your servant; but I *am* slow of speech and slow of tongue."

11 So the LORD said to him, "Who has made man's mouth? Or who makes the mute, the deaf, the seeing, or the blind? *Have* not I, the LORD?

12 "Now therefore, go, and I will be with your mouth and teach you what you shall say."

Exod. 3:11–4:12

In response to God's call, Moses makes a series of excuses.

Excuse One: Not Capable to Do the Task (3:11–12). The confidence of Moses' youth is gone. The awesome responsibility to which he was being called overwhelmed him. Was it a genuine humility or a lack of faith in God's ability or wisdom? The best promise that God could give, He gave Moses, *"I will certainly be with you."* This promise of presence is echoed throughout the Bible (cf. Gen. 28:15; Josh. 1:5; Jer. 1:8; Hag. 1:13; Matt. 28:20). Need we ask for more? It was not enough for Moses. So God gave an additional sign, promising Moses that he and his liberated people would come back to that very mountain, and there they would worship God. Enough assurance? No, Moses had only begun his excuses.

But we know Moses' feelings, don't we? We have felt personally as Moses did—inferior for such a holy and difficult task to which we are being called.

Excuse Two: No Knowledge of God's Name (3:13–22). Moses' second excuse seemed reasonable enough. He didn't know God's name.

71

So what would he tell the people if they asked the name of the deity he claimed to represent? Every deity in those ancient times had his own personal name. People believed it was necessary to know his name in order to approach him in prayer or to ask his help. Also, the name revealed something of the deity's character. To know the name of the deity was to enjoy a privileged relationship with that god. This excuse of Moses' suggests two possibilities: Moses' own acceptance of these popular beliefs; or, his concern that the Israelites in Egypt had forgotten the God of their fathers and were worshiping the Egyptian deities. We do know from instances like that recorded in Joshua 24:14 that Israel did worship Egyptian deities and continued to worship them even after they occupied the promised land.

But we know Moses' feelings too. He felt he had no answer or message to give to the Israelites. And isn't that true with us, too? We don't think that we know enough, or that we've experienced enough, or that we feel deeply enough. We just don't think that we have anything to say. God's answer to Moses excuse was to reveal to him His personal name. And here is great mystery because the name that God gave Moses was "I AM WHO I AM."

"Say to the children of Israel, '*I AM has sent me to you.*'" The meaning of this name has occupied the attention of Bible scholars for centuries. It is the name that identifies God as the covenant God of His people. It is spelled YHWH (or JHVH), appearing without vowels because for centuries the Hebrew language was written without vowels. The pronunciation of words was transmitted orally from generation to generation. But there was also another ingredient here: this name of Israel's God was so sacred that the people would not speak it; therefore the original pronunciation was eventually forgotten.

Most linguists believe that with vowels added, the name is *Yahweh*. In English Bibles, it is translated as "the Lord" and sometimes as "Jehovah." F. B. Huey, Jr., has given us an interesting insight into the name *Jehovah*. He tells us that the pronunciation "Jehovah" that began in medieval times grew out of a misunderstanding by the Masoretes of the vowels of the name *Adonai* ("Lord") written with the consonants JHVH. (The Masoretes were the scholars who supplied the vowels for the consonantal text around the sixth century A.D.) This combination of vowels and consonants produced the hybrid *Jehovah* in English. However, the vowels were intended to instruct the reader to substitute the name *Adonai* for the sacred unpronounceable name.[2]

The name, as God shared it with Moses, comes from the Hebrew word for "to be" and that's the reason that it's translated "I AM THAT I AM." It's clearly related to the self-existence of God, and it has been understood to mean not only "I AM WHAT I AM," but "I AM BECAUSE I AM," and "I WILL BE WHAT I WILL BE" (or "WHAT I CAUSE TO BE"). In his *Expositions of Holy Scripture*, Alexander Maclaren beautifully connects this word of introduction to the burning bush.

> That is to say, the fire that burns and does not burn out, which has no tendency to destruction in its very energy, and is not consumed by its own activity, is surely a symbol of the One Being, whose being derives its law and its source from itself, who only can say—"I AM THAT I AM"—the law of his nature, the foundation of his being, the only conditions of his existence being, as it were, enclosed within the limits of his own nature. You and I have to say, "I AM THAT WHICH I HAVE BECOME," or "I AM THAT WHICH I WAS BORN," or "I AM THAT WHICH CIRCUMSTANCES HAVE MADE ME." He says, "I AM THAT I AM." All other creatures are links; this is the staple from which they all hang. All other being is derived, and therefore limited and changeful; this being is un-derived, absolute, self-dependent, and therefore unalterable forevermore. Because we live, we die. In living, the process is going on of which death is the end. But God lives forevermore, a flame that does not burn out; therefore his resources are inexhaustible, his power unwearied. He needs no rest for recuperation of wasted energy. His gifts diminish not the store which he has to bestow. He gives and is none the poorer. He works and is never weary. He operates unspent; he loves and he loves forever. And through the ages, the fire burns on, unconsumed and undecayed.[3]

Excuse Three: People Will Not Believe (4:1–9). Moses had every reason to expect that the people would not believe him, so there was legitimacy in his excuse. Unbelief in respect to the works of the prophets is found in every period of Israel's history. So we get to a point that really touches home. What Moses is actually saying is, "Lord, is there anything in my life that would verify what I'm saying? They won't believe that You've spoken to me." We know the feeling, don't we? We're always burdened with the awful fact that our lives do not measure up to our testimonies.

God provided Moses with three signs in order that he might be able to convince the skeptical.

One was a rod that would become a serpent when cast to the ground. The second was his hand that would become leprous when touched to the breast. The third was water from the Nile that would become blood when poured on dry land. We will talk more about signs later when we discuss the plagues and Moses' dramatic signs connected with those plagues. The truth is that the sign does not have meaning within itself. The interpretation given the sign is the important thing, and beyond that, the credibility of the one performing the sign.

This remarkable gift of God to Moses should have been enough to melt his doubts, but Moses had another excuse.

Excuse Four: Inability to Speak Eloquently (4:10–12). This was Moses' last bastion to hide behind—and it's usually ours. When we're urged to witness, to share our faith, we insist that we're not eloquent enough. We can't talk easily to others. God's answer to this reluctant prophet was *"I will be with your mouth and teach you what you shall say."* Can we believe that even the words that we need to say at any particular time will be given us if we operate in faith and commitment to our Lord?

Lessons from This Reluctant Prophet

Having rehearsed these excuses of Moses, there are two truths we can learn. The first may surprise you, because most of us concentrate on all of the excuses Moses made and really do not get down to the heart of the matter. The first truth is this: *In the Christian life, in our response to and relationship with God, most of us do not arrogantly aspire for too much, we sheepishly settle for too little.* So we're onlookers to God's activity in history, spectators and recipients, but not actors and participants. Have we forgotten that word of Jesus, one of the most amazing words in the Bible: "Most assuredly, I say to you, he who believes in Me, the works that I do he will do also; and greater works than these he will do, because I go to My Father" (John 14:12)?

But there's a second lesson here, as well. On the surface it may seem to be directly opposite from the first, but that's not so. *Only when we know we can't do it, can we do it by the grace and power of God.* The bottom line of all this was that Moses was saying to God, "Who am I? *I* can't do what You're asking me to do." I believe that's the point to which God wants to bring us. That's His way of bringing us to the place where we know we're completely dependent upon Him.

It happened to David too. David could slay a giant, but God put him into the caves and dens of the earth. He was hunted like a bird, and he found out how weak he was. Then God made him a king.

It was the case with Elijah also. He was the prophet brave enough to walk right into the court of Ahab and Jezebel and tell them that "there shall not be dew nor rain these years, except at my word" (1 Kings 17:1).

But Elijah was not as brave as he seemed. God sent him into the desert for his training. Elijah drank from a brook, and there was a drought that caused the brook to dry up and Elijah got the lesson. He watched the brook grow smaller and smaller and said, "My life is no more than a dried-up brook." He was right. Then you remember the other chapter—Elijah spent some time eating from a flour bin that should have been empty. He found out that he was nothing and that God was everything; and when he realized this, God used him to face the prophets of Baal and bring down fire from heaven.

Paul learned it also, over a long period of time—until he came to the place where he could say, "Therefore I take pleasure in infirmities, in reproaches, in needs, in persecutions, in distresses, for Christ's sake. For when I am weak, then I am strong" (2 Cor. 12:10).

It's a paradox, a puzzling one. But what God was teaching Moses, He wants to teach us. Only when we know we can't do it, can we do it by the grace and power of God.

MOSES' REFUSAL AND GOD'S ANGER

4:13 But he said, "O my Lord, please send by the hand of whomever *else* You may send."

14 So the anger of the LORD was kindled against Moses, and He said: "Is not Aaron the Levite your brother? I know that he can speak well. And look, he is also coming out to meet you. When he sees you, he will be glad in his heart.

15 "Now you shall speak to him and put the words in his mouth. And I will be with your mouth and with his mouth, and I will teach you what you shall do.

16 "So he shall be your spokesman to the people. And he himself shall be as a mouth for you, and you shall be to him as God.

17 "And you shall take this rod in your hand, with which you shall do the signs."

Exod. 4:13–17

After Moses had given all of his excuses and God had responded to them, he simply laid the truth out: "I don't want to go, send somebody else."

Now this refusal made God angry. Still He would not let Moses off. He gave him a spokesman, his brother Aaron.

Up to this point, we know nothing about Aaron's existence or whereabouts. It is assumed that he lived in Egypt all the years that Moses was living in Midian. He will become a primary actor in the drama of God's deliverance of the people out of bondage and their sojourn through the wilderness.

Moses would be the leader of the Israelites, and God would still speak directly to him and teach him what he should do. But there would be a mediator between him and the people. He would speak to Aaron God's word, and Aaron in turn would share it with the people.

There's something great about that. God always gives us what we need to do His work. But there's something sad about it also. Because of his stubborn reluctance, Moses forfeited the privilege of being the spokesman of God before the people.

NOTES

1. F. B. Meyer, *Devotional Commentary on Exodus* (Grand Rapids: Kregel Publications, 1978), pp. 46–47.

2. F. B. Huey, Jr., *Exodus: A Study Guide Commentary* (Grand Rapids: Zondervan, 1977), p. 30.

3. Alexander Maclaren, *Expositions of Holy Scripture*, 11 vols. (Grand Rapids: Wm. B. Eerdmans, 1952–59), 1:23–24.

CHAPTER FOUR

The Testing of Faith

Exodus 4:18–5:21

Vernard Eller is a Church of the Brethren pastor and professor. He has an unusual ability to capture your imagination and to communicate ideas in fresh and gripping ways. He has written a book, *In Place of Sacraments*, in which he describes in a whimsical yet profound manner two different models for the church.

One model he calls the "Commissary." This is the model for an institution which passes out graces from its stock on the shelves to people who come to it only when they have need for them. They come to the Commissary with the proper coin of exchange to get what they need. Their only responsibility to the Commissary is to obtain the coins so they may obtain the "graces"—the goods, services, and benefits from the Commissary. The other model is that of a "Caravan," a walking caravan, "a group of people banded together to make a common cause in seeking a common destination." Meaning is found in moving toward the destination, following the dream, in Exodus terminology, pursuing "the pillar of cloud by day [and] the pillar of fire by night." Eller says, "A Caravan has its existence only in a continual becoming, a following of its Lord on his way toward the kingdom."[1]

Professor Eller draws another analogy. He likens the way the Commissary Church acts to the Royal Vienna String Quartet, while he likens the Caravan Church to a barbershop quartet. Both are dedicated to making music, but with the Royal Vienna Quartet, the emphasis is on the quality of the performance, while the emphasis of the barbershop quartet is on having a satisfying experience of singing. The Commissary Church "puts great value upon the value of its performance, whereas the caravan—which is the people gathered for fellowship with God—puts its value upon the joy of participation."[2]

There's no doubt where Professor Eller gets his image of the caravan. That image is established before the Israelites begin their journey out of Egyptian captivity; it starts with Moses' return to Egypt, following the Lord's command to go and deliver His people. He says: "Momentous events in history often have obscure beginnings. An aged shepherd, a lonely spot in a desolate wasteland, a desert plant in flames, and the voice of God are the ingredients that are about to emerge in a hitherto unheard of happening—a bold demand for freedom made to the mightiest ruler of the then-known world: 'Let my people go!' It is a cry for recognition of human dignity that has echoed down to the present time."[3]

Even as the journey begins Moses' faith is tested. And this entire section of Scripture is one huge event after another testing his faith.

FAITH TESTED ON THE JOURNEY BACK TO EGYPT

4:18 So Moses went and returned to Jethro his father-in-law, and said to him, "Please let me go and return to my brethren who *are* in Egypt, and see whether they are still alive." And Jethro said to Moses, "Go in peace."

19 Now the LORD said to Moses in Midian, "Go, return to Egypt; for all the men who sought your life are dead."

20 Then Moses took his wife and his sons and set them on a donkey, and he returned to the land of Egypt. And Moses took the rod of God in his hand.

21 And the LORD said to Moses, "When you go back to Egypt, see that you do all those wonders before Pharaoh which I have put in your hand. But I will harden his heart, so that he will not let the people go.

22 "Then you shall say to Pharaoh, 'Thus says the LORD: "Israel *is* My son, My firstborn.

23 "So I say to you, let My son go that he may serve Me. But if you refuse to let him go, indeed I will kill your son, your firstborn."'"

24 And it came to pass on the way, at the encampment, that the LORD met him and sought to kill him.

25 Then Zipporah took a sharp stone and cut off the foreskin of her son and cast *it* at *Moses'* feet, and said, "Surely you *are* a husband of blood to me!"

26 So He let him go. Then she said, *"You are* a husband of blood!"—because of the circumcision.

27 And the LORD said to Aaron, "Go into the wilderness to meet Moses." So he went and met him on the mountain of God, and kissed him.

28 So Moses told Aaron all the words of the LORD who had sent him, and all the signs which He had commanded him.

29 Then Moses and Aaron went and gathered together all the elders of the children of Israel.

30 And Aaron spoke all the words which the LORD had spoken to Moses. Then he did the signs in the sight of the people.

31 So the people believed; and when they heard that the LORD had visited the children of Israel and that He had looked on their affliction, then they bowed their heads and worshiped.

Exod. 4:18–31

Moses has been commissioned; he is to go to Egypt. God has given him a mouthpiece, Aaron, who will meet him in the wilderness, and God has made his shepherd-staff the rod "with which you shall do the signs." Now Moses obeys. But he first returns to his father-in-law, Jethro. Jethro was both Moses' father-in-law and his employer. Deference to the head of the family had to be observed, because Moses was still under Jethro's authority.

There's a marvelous dynamic at work here. There are some calls upon our lives that transcend family loyalty, and this was one of them. Yet it's a beautiful thing to see Moses returning to his father-in-law, asking permission to leave. It is not really known why he did not reveal to Jethro the real reason for his return to Egypt, but only expressed the desire to visit his kinsmen there. Those visions and possibilities God had laid out before him were secrets he kept locked in his own heart.

It is not wise in our Bible study and teaching to exalt all the coincidences that are there that seem to point to some expressed prediction. To do that is to dilute the genuine promises that are there throughout the Scripture. Yet there is an observation to be made here that teaches a profound truth. *"The Lord said to Moses in Midian, 'Go, return to Egypt; for all the men who sought your life are dead'"* (v. 19). You can hardly keep from comparing this to the words with which the infant Jesus is recalled from exile—there's such a close verbal resemblance. *"Go to the land of Israel, for those who sought the young Child's life are dead"* (Matt. 2:20).

G. A. Chadwick has made the point of the truth of that observation so well. *"One can scarcely venture to speak of the death of Herod when Jesus was to return from Egypt as being deliberately typified in the death of those who sought the life of Moses. But it is quite clear St. Matthew intentionally points the reader back to this narrative, for, indeed, under both there are to be recognized that God does not thrust His servants into needless or excessive peril; and that when the life of a tyrant has really become not only a trial, but a barrier, it will be removed by the King of kings. God is prudent for His heroes."*[4]

And the journey itself—Moses' journey back to the land of his people—is paralleled by that journey of Joseph and Mary in the New Testament. The life of faith is one of pilgrimage, and the people of God have their life *"in caravan."* Like Jacob before him, Moses returned to his fathers' land with his family. This is the motif of faith for the nation Israel in the Old Testament.

Hardening of the Heart

As Moses moved out toward Egypt, God rehearsed with him what he was to do when he got to Egypt. He was to perform all of the wonders that God had placed at his disposal and then demand the release of the Israelites from slavery. Then God added a very perplexing word. It must have been as perplexing to Moses as it is to the modern reader: *"But I will harden his heart, so that he will not let the people go"* (v. 21b).

References to the hardening of Pharaoh's heart are found eighteen times in the chapters that follow. And the thought is expressed three different ways. (1) God hardened Pharaoh's heart, (2) Pharaoh hardened his own heart, and (3) Pharaoh's heart was hardened.

There are shades of meaning in these phrases. One of them means "to be strong," hence, stubborn. The second means "to be heavy," thus, dull or unresponsive. The third means "to be hard, severe," therefore, obstinate. Put all of these together and you have a description of how Pharaoh is going to respond to Moses' demands that he let Israel go free.[5]

To begin to understand this perplexing notion, we need to remember that in Hebrew thought the heart was understood to be the seat of the intellect or will, not the emotions. It was the seat of volitional action and did not carry with it the emotional tones with which we identify it in the twentieth century. Also, Hebrew thought did not deal with secondary causes—causes standing between an event and God. We might say "The circumstances hardened Pharaoh's heart." But that would not fit into the Hebrew pattern of thought. God was sovereign, and His action was direct and everything could be traced to Him. So, the Israelites could only say, "Pharaoh hardened his heart," or "God hardened Pharaoh's heart," and they would see no difference or contradiction in it.

But how do we grapple with this? Did Pharaoh have no choice in his action, since "God hardened his heart"? If that was the case, how could he be punished for what he could not control? We can more easily understand the phrase "Pharaoh hardened his heart"—he refused to release the Israelites; that was a willful decision.

But how do we reconcile all those different expressions? The only satisfactory answer, I think, is in the biblical paradox of the sovereignty of God set against the freedom of man. While a person is free to accept or to reject the will of God for his or her own life, God's purposes are going to be accomplished regardless of that person's decision. In that context, of the sovereignty of God and the freedom of man, people are responsible and accountable for what they do.

In his commentary, Alexander Maclaren has provided a helpful word on the result of the plagues with Pharaoh.

> God hardens no man's heart who has not first hardened it himself. But we do not need to conclude that any inward action on the will is meant. Was not the accumulation of plagues, intended as they were to soften, a cause of hardening? Does not the gospel, if rejected, harden, making consciences and wills less susceptible? Is it not a "savior of death unto death" as our fathers recognized in speaking of "gospel-hardened sinners"? The same fire softens wax and hardens clay. Whosoever is not brought near is driven farther off by the influences which God brings to bear on us.[6]

I've known a number of people throughout my ministry who seemed to be impervious to the gospel. In the old days, it would be said of them, "Their hearts are hardened." I remember a dramatic example of this in the first church I served in rural Mississippi. A seventy-two-year-old man went through some terrible ordeals—the breakup of the family of one of his sons, the imprisonment of another son for bootlegging, the terminal disease of a grandchild, and finally his own broken health. One would have thought that all of this would have brought him to his knees, that there would be some opening for the Spirit of God to get through to him, but not so. I remember so vividly those times that I would spend with him, seeking to share the grace of the gospel. It wasn't as though he turned me off with a deaf ear or that he was obstinate toward me personally, but there seemed to be a barrier there that couldn't be penetrated. Because I never shared an experience with that man in which he confessed any faith in God, I always wondered if his heart was not so hardened by his continual refusal of the gospel that he could not now respond.

There is a mystery in all of this, but it's the kind of mystery that we need to grapple with, because it has to do with our own eternal destiny.

This is serious business. It is soul business with eternal consequences. Besides that dramatic experience in my first church, I've seen it in varying degrees throughout my ministry. To refuse the gospel call upon our lives at any level is to lay another brick in our wall of resistance to God's grace. That's the reason little decisions—responses to what appear to be minor calls—are important. Our obedience to the everyday calls of God is the discipline that equips us to respond faithfully when the big calls come.

What are those everyday calls?

• to repent; as soon as you sense some sin in your life, repent, come to Christ, be genuinely sorry, beg His forgiveness.

• to give a cup of cold water in Jesus' name.

• to speak up for that colleague or neighbor who is being maligned by gossip.

• to tithe your income as God has called each one of us to do.

• to witness for Christ every time the opportunity arises.

• to live holy lives; to be recognized as set apart, refusing to participate in the immorality that is rampant in our time—cheating, infidelity, deceit, fornication, lying.

God's call comes to us in some form every day. Every day we have the opportunity to respond to Him. Though it may not be noticeable to us, refusing these calls will gradually harden our hearts.

That's the reason the psalmist made this call to his people:

> O that today you would hearken to his voice!
> Harden not your hearts, as at Meribah,
> as on the day at Massah in the wilderness.
>
> *Ps. 95:7b–8, RSV*

We'll come to Meribah and Massah soon in chapter 17. The people have experienced the glorious works of the Lord—the passing over of the death angel and the deliverance out of Egypt, escape through the Red Sea and the drowning of Pharaoh's army, manna from heaven to miraculously feed them daily—glorious acts of God! Yet when they came to Rephidim, and there was no water there, in their thirst they forgot God. They railed against Moses: "Why is it you have brought us up out of Egypt, to kill us and our children and our livestock with thirst?" (Exod. 17:3b).

Years later, the psalmist refers to this:

> O that today you would hearken to his voice!
>   Harden not your hearts, as at Meribah,
>   as on the day at Massah in the wilderness,
> when your fathers tested me,
>   and put me to the proof though they had seen my
>   work.
> For forty years I loathed that generation
>   and said, "They are a people who err in heart,
>   and they do not regard my ways."
> Therefore I swore in my anger
>   that they should not enter my rest.
>
> *Ps. 95:7b–11, RSV*

"The Lord Met Him and Sought to Kill Him"

Here in verse 24 is another puzzling word and a baffling test of faith for Moses as he journeys back to Egypt. Along with his wife Zipporah and his two sons, Moses was camping out on his journey when *"the Lord met him and sought to kill him."*

83

The entire episode is difficult to understand. Zipporah intervenes quickly, circumcising her son (which one, Gershom or Eliezer, we do not know). She took the *"foreskin of her son and cast it at Moses' feet, and said 'Surely you are a husband of blood to me!'"* When this happened, the Lord turned loose of Moses, and Zipporah repeated, *"You are a husband of blood!"* The reason: *"because of the circumcision."*

Numerous explanations have been given for this, but Huey's word seems most plausible: God's "seeking to kill Moses has been explained as a way of saying that Moses became dangerously ill or was being attacked by a desert demon, but it can best be understood as the consequence of Moses' neglect of circumcision for himself or his son. He could not lead the covenant people unless he himself was obedient to the requirements of the covenant. The episode underscores the tremendous importance of circumcision in ancient Israel."[7]

This experience probably played a role in validating the practice of circumcision early in life rather than during adulthood. And since circumcision predominated Israelite thought, this passage is a significant statement on its historical background.

The Brothers Meet and the Proclamation Is Shared

What a grand reunion that must have been in the wilderness. With what joy Aaron must have greeted the Lord's word when the Lord told him to go meet his brother Moses in the wilderness. There's a strange silence here that may teach us something. Nothing is said about any struggle that Aaron had with what the Lord had commanded him to do. There are rare souls like that who never seem to question or struggle, but move out whenever they are clear as to what the Lord wishes.

But there's another thought here as well. Aaron did not go through the struggle through which Moses went; he didn't argue or wrestle with the Lord, yet it was Aaron who yielded to the people's request in the wilderness when they returned to their former idolatry and asked him to forge for them the golden calf.

Those are thoughts worth pondering. Do we sometimes answer too quickly, without knowing what it is that we are being asked? Isn't it appropriate to struggle with the Lord in order to know what the price might be, and what the demands are in responding to His call?

Even so, it must have been a joyful day of meeting. Aaron kissed his brother and listened as Moses shared with him all that the Lord had sent him to do, and all the signs which He had given him, and the miracles that they were going to be able to perform.

Then together they went and shared that news with the people, living out the pattern that would continue throughout their pilgrimage—Moses sharing with Aaron, and Aaron speaking to the people *"all the words which the Lord had spoken to Moses."*

"So the people believed; and when they heard that the Lord had visited the children of Israel and that He had looked on their affliction, then they bowed their heads and worshiped" (v. 31).

Their response is not too unlike Aaron's. They were ready for deliverance, but they had no notion of the sacrifice they would have to make, the self-denial and the self-control, the suffering and oppression that was still ahead.

It is one thing to admire abstract freedom, but a very different thing to accept the austere conditions of the life of genuine freedom. And surely the same is true of the soul. The gospel gladdens the young convert: he bows his head and worships; but he little dreams of his long discipline, as in the forty desert years, of the solitary places through which his soul must wander, the drought, the Amalekite, the absent leader, and the temptations of the flesh. In mercy, the long future is concealed; it is enough that, like the apostles, we should consent to follow; gradually we shall obtain the courage to which the task may be revealed.[8]

FAITH TESTED IN CONFRONTATION WITH PHARAOH

5:1 Afterward Moses and Aaron went in and told Pharaoh, "Thus says the LORD God of Israel: 'Let My people go, that they may hold a feast to Me in the wilderness.'"

2 And Pharaoh said, "Who *is* the LORD, that I should obey His voice to let Israel go? I do not know the LORD, nor will I let Israel go."

3 So they said, "The God of the Hebrews has met with us. Please, let us go three days' journey into the

desert and sacrifice to the LORD our God, lest He fall
upon us with pestilence or with the sword."

4 Then the king of Egypt said to them, "Moses
and Aaron, why do you take the people from their
work? Get *back* to your labor."

5 And Pharaoh said, "Look, the people of the
land *are* many now, and you make them rest from
their labor!"

Exod. 5:1–5

It's rather astonishing, isn't it, that Moses would get an audience
with Pharaoh immediately? But, on second thought, in that day, if
a person who had been a part of the court of Egypt returned after a
long absence with the claim that he had a word from a deity, it's
easy to understand that it would get the Pharaoh's attention. What is
incredible is the brazen courage of Moses and Aaron as they laid that
bold claim before the one who controlled the destiny of the people:
"Thus says the Lord God of Israel: 'Let My people go'" (v. 1). After an
initial response from Pharaoh, the command is not so brazen and
direct. *"The God of the Hebrews has met with us. Please, let us go three
days' journey into the desert and sacrifice to the Lord our God, lest He
fall upon us with pestilence or with the sword"* (v. 3).

Pharaoh's response to all this was, *"Who is the Lord, that I should
obey His voice to let Israel go? I do not know the Lord, nor will I let
Israel go"* (v. 2). Moses' faith is now being tested in his confrontation
with the most powerful of all living men in his day.

It may be insightful here to look at these two men in contrast.
What was Moses like? Jack Finnegan points out that he was a man of
very human traits whose anger, for instance, is not glossed over in
the record (Exod. 2:12; 11:8; 32:19). He was a great prophet. Long
afterward, it was remembered that "by a prophet the Lord brought
Israel out of Egypt" (Hos. 12:13). Also, the promise of a Moses for
the future—"The Lord your God will raise up for you a Prophet like
me" (Deut. 18:15)—was claimed by the early Christians in application to Jesus Christ (Acts 3:22).

Finnegan paints the picture clearly. "What is the difference between Moses and Pharaoh? What did Moses have that Pharaoh did
not? Moses had a concern for human justice; Pharaoh enslaved a

people. Moses liberated a people; Moses had a concern for human relations. Pharaoh ruled a people; Moses led a people. Moses had a knowledge of the will of God; Pharaoh was not unreligious—he was beloved of Ammon and the son of Ra—but this religion gave him privilege. The knowledge of God which came to Moses gave him a task and a service to render to his fellow men."[9]

Moses lives on today as a power in the minds and hearts of two great religions of the world: Judaism and Christianity. Pharaoh, even if he was the great Rameses II, has only a crumbling monument to his name. The Ramesseum, the mortuary temple of Rameses II in western Thebes, records this inscription of the Pharaoh, using the Greek form, Ozymandias: "King of kings am I, Ozymandias. If anyone would know how great I am and where I lie, let him surpass one of my works." Shelley wrote of this in his celebrated poem *Ozymandias:*

> I met a traveler from an antique land
> Who said: "Two vast and trunkless legs of stone
> Stand in the desert. Near them, on the sand,
> Half sunk, a shattered visage lies, whose frown,
> And wrinkled lip, and sneer of cold command,
> Tell that its sculptor well those passions read
> Which yet survive, stamped on these lifeless things,
> The hand that mocked them, and the heart that fed:
> And on the pedestal these words appear:
> 'My name is Ozymandias, King of kings:
> Look on my works, ye Mighty, and despair!'
> Nothing beside remains. Round the decay
> Of that colossal wreck, boundless and bare
> The lone and level sands stretch far away."

But Moses' passion for justice and his powerful faith will continue to be embodied within the lives of those who seek to follow the Lord.

Egyptian Pharaohs were considered by their own people to be gods. What a challenge it must have been to Pharaoh for Moses to confront him with a word from the God of Israel. There was contempt in Pharaoh's reply as well as stubborn anger and hardness of heart. *"Who is the Lord, that I should obey His voice to let Israel go? I do not know the Lord, nor will I let Israel go"* (v. 2).

There is rich food for thought in setting this word of the Pharaoh alongside Paul's words to the Romans when he talked about God's wrath on the unrighteous.

> For the wrath of God is revealed from heaven against all ungodliness and unrighteousness of men, who suppress the truth in unrighteousness, because what may be known of God is manifest in them, for God has shown it to them. For since the creation of the world His invisible attributes are clearly seen, being understood by the things that are made, even His eternal power and Godhead, so that they are without excuse, because, although they knew God, they did not glorify Him as God, nor were thankful, but became futile in their thoughts, and their foolish hearts were darkened. Professing to be wise, they became fools, and changed the glory of the incorruptible God into an image made like corruptible man—and birds and four-footed animals and creeping things. Therefore God also gave them up to uncleanness, in the lusts of their hearts, to dishonor their bodies among themselves, who exchanged the truth of God for the lie, and worshiped and served the creature rather than the Creator, who is blessed forever. Amen.
>
> *Rom. 1:18–25*

Before it was over, the work of Yahweh would be presented to Pharaoh time and time again, even the wrath of God from heaven against his ungodliness, but the pride of Pharaoh's heart would keep his heart hardened.

> When he [Pharaoh] came to know God, he did not give Him glory as God, nor render Him thanks, but yielded himself to his own self-will, so that his senseless heart became darkened; and he refused to have the perfect knowledge which the Divine Spirit endeavored to impart. God, after nine proofs of His power and grace—power towards Egypt and grace towards His shielded people—gave him up to learn in the terror of the Red Sea the lessons which he had refused to learn in an easier school. This pride of heart flamed forth in the vehement outburst of angry

utterance with which he fell on the two brethren. He upbraided them for raising false hopes and hindering [the people's] pride in their toils. They were sedition-mongers, dangerous firebrands, mob-orators, and the like. Instead of dictating to him, let them get back to their own burdens upon the brick-kilns! What were they but insolent bondsmen who thought to conceal their indolence under the plea of religion![10]

FAITH TESTED IN THE RENUNCIATION OF MOSES BY HIS PEOPLE

5:6 So the same day Pharaoh commanded the taskmasters of the people and their officers, saying,

7 "You shall no longer give the people straw to make brick as before. Let them go and gather straw for themselves.

8 "And you shall lay on them the quota of bricks which they made before. You shall not reduce it. For they are idle; therefore they cry out, saying, 'Let us go *and* sacrifice to our God.'

9 "Let more work be laid on the men, that they may labor in it, and let them not regard false words."

10 And the taskmasters of the people and their officers went out and spoke to the people, saying, "Thus says Pharaoh: 'I will not give you straw.

11 'Go, get yourselves straw where you can find it; yet none of your work will be reduced.'"

12 So the people were scattered abroad throughout all the land of Egypt to gather stubble instead of straw.

13 And the taskmasters forced *them* to hurry, saying, "Fulfill your work, *your* daily quota, as when there was straw."

14 Also the officers of the children of Israel, whom Pharaoh's taskmasters had set over them, were beaten *and* were asked, "Why have you not fulfilled your task in making brick both yesterday and today, as before?"

15 Then the officers of the children of Israel came and cried out to Pharaoh, saying, "Why are you dealing thus with your servants?

16 "There is no straw given to your servants, and they say to us, 'Make brick!' And indeed your

servants *are* beaten, but the fault *is* in your *own* people."

17 But he said, "You *are* idle! Idle! Therefore you say, 'Let us go *and* sacrifice to the LORD.'

18 "Therefore go now *and* work; for no straw shall be given you, yet you shall deliver the quota of bricks."

19 And the officers of the children of Israel saw *that* they *were* in trouble after it was said, "You shall not reduce *any* bricks from your daily quota."

20 Then, as they came out from Pharaoh, they met Moses and Aaron who stood there to meet them.

21 And they said to them, "Let the LORD look on you and judge, because you have made us abhorrent in the sight of Pharaoh and in the sight of his servants, to put a sword in their hand to kill us."

Exod. 5:6–21

Moses did not accomplish what he had set out to do—obtain the release of his people; instead he brought greater trouble upon them. Pharaoh is beyond appeal, and he responds by making the burdens of the people even heavier. He assumes that by increasing their labor he will make them forget any foolish notions about freedom.

One of the primary tasks of the children of Israel was the making of bricks. In the Egypt of that day, bricks were made by soaking clay and water, mixing it with straw or some other kind of cohesive matter and shaping it by hand or with a wooden mold, then drying it in the sun. Some of the great monuments of ancient Egypt were made of sun-dried brick, and these monuments still stand.

Straw for the brick had always been provided for the laborers. Now as an added burden upon them, the straw is taken away, and they have to scour the land looking for their own straw. But their quota remains the same, and when the quota is not met, the Israelite foremen are beaten by the Egyptian taskmasters. When the foremen protest to Pharaoh, he repeats his brutal allegation, *"You are idle! Idle!"* And in a kind of cruel sarcasm directed at Moses or possibly Aaron, he adds, *"Therefore you say, 'Let us go and sacrifice to the Lord'"* (v. 17).

In language that verges on cursing, Pharaoh dismisses the Israelite foremen, *"Go now and work; for no straw shall be given you, yet you shall deliver the quota of bricks"* (v. 18). These men are shamed and frustrated, smarting not only under the burden of additional labor, but under the lashing from Pharaoh. As they leave him, they run into Moses and Aaron, and they let loose their own anger and outrage against them. Here Moses' faith is tested by the repudiation of his own people. What they say to Moses and Aaron is, literally, "You have made us stink!"

To be rebuffed by Pharaoh was one thing, to be renounced by their own people is another. Moses and Aaron must have been cut to the core as the venom of the people was poured out upon them: *"You have made us abhorrent in the sight of Pharaoh and in the sight of his servants, to put a sword in their hand to kill us"* (v. 21).

Moses does what we find him doing over and over again in the face of personal bitterness and oppression—he turns to the Lord. We'll look at that in the next chapter. However, there are two general lessons to be drawn at this point. These lessons have to do with barriers to grace. There are two huge barriers that we need to recognize.

One is the *hardening of the heart.* We've already discussed this, but it needs to be underscored. Each time a person is confronted with an opportunity to respond to the truth of God, refusal of that opportunity results in a hardening of the heart. Though God does not arbitrarily decide to pre-set human minds and hearts so they cannot openly and freely respond to Him, in the process of responding (or refusing to respond), our hearts are set and conditioned for other responses in the future. God never deals unjustly or arbitrarily with us; our own free actions are always the cause of our downfall and punishment.

The common illustration Bible teachers use to talk about this difficult phenomenon is that of the sun shining on two different materials such as clay and wax. The heat melts the wax but hardens the clay. The difference is not in the rays of the sun, but in the materials on which they shine.

The day-to-day message for us in this phenomenon of the hardening of the heart is that every decision we make each day has some determining influence on the decisions we will make following that one. In a very real sense, the decisions we make today shape the decisions we will be making tomorrow. To allow our hearts to be hardened in any way by any refusal of God's call upon our lives is a barrier to His grace-full activity in our lives, and can cut us off from the gracious love that He constantly wishes to bestow upon us.

We anticipate the second major barrier to grace by looking forward a bit in Moses' story. When Moses had made his complaint to the Lord following Pharaoh's refusal and the repudiation by his own people, God instructed him to carry a message back to the children of Israel—the message that "I am the Lord; I will bring you out from under the burdens of the Egyptians, I will rescue you from their bondage, and I will redeem you with an outstretched arm and with great judgments" (6:6). Moses took that message to the people, "but they did not heed Moses, because of anguish of spirit and cruel bondage" (6:9). That's one of the biggest barriers to grace—our *refusal to listen.*

This is a barrier to grace in relation to God. But not only is a failure to listen a barrier to grace in relation to God, it is a barrier to grace in our interpersonal relationships. In our relation to God, our refusal to listen is usually rooted in the mistaken notion that we are in control, that we can do it ourselves. And the emphasis is upon doing it ourselves—a works-righteousness idea that supposes that if we "pull ourselves up by our own bootstraps," if we reform ourselves, if we "do good" and "act right," all will be well, so we put the emphasis on moral reform. In doing so, we address the symptoms of our problems, and not the cause.

Supposedly Noel Coward once sent a picture postcard of the Venus de Milo to a little girl and wrote across the bottom, "This is what will happen to you if you do not stop biting your fingernails." Now that may have been a cruel thing to do to a little girl, because who knows the problems responsible for a little girl's biting her fingernails. But at a superficial level, it's very humorous. And in a humorous way, it makes a point. Moral reform is like that—refusal to listen to God and receive His grace, thinking that we can do it ourselves, leads us into remedies that are always superficial. Such efforts at moral self-reform do not go deeply enough because they are completely dependent on willpower, and we all know that our willpower is flawed and limited.

We need to listen to God, not only at the point of His direction for our lives, but at the point of His constantly offering grace as an alternative to our self-powered efforts to work out our own salvation.

Though you may have never given much thought to the idea that our hearts can be hardened, and a part of the hardening process is our refusal to listen—it's time to do so. We can become dull to the claim of the gospel. We can resist God's call to the point that our ears are insensitive to His voice and we don't even recognize it.

Does that sound too much like doomsday? It may be—but if you are hearing it, it isn't doomsday. You're still listening. It isn't doomsday. It's *your* day to respond to God. The biggest issue is His call for us to yield our lives to Him.

When the writer to the Hebrews was making this call, he went back and called upon the ninety-fifth psalm, quoted earlier. "Therefore, as the Holy Spirit says: 'Today, if you will hear His voice, / Do not harden your hearts as in the rebellion, / In the day of trial in the wilderness, / Where your fathers tested Me, tried Me, / And saw My works forty years. / Therefore I was angry with that generation, / And said, "They always go astray in their heart, / And they have not known My ways"'" (Heb. 3:7–10).

The Holy Spirit speaks. We must listen and respond, that our hearts not be hardened.

NOTES

1. Vernard Eller, *In Place of Sacraments* (Grand Rapids: Wm. B. Eerdmans, 1972), p. 31.

2. Ibid., p. 36.

3. Ibid., p. 33.

4. G. A. Chadwick, *The Book of Exodus,* The Expositor's Bible (London: Hodder & Stoughton, n.d.), p. 81.

5. F. B. Huey, Jr., *Exodus: A Study Guide Commentary* (Grand Rapids: Zondervan, 1977), p. 34.

6. Alexander Maclaren, *Expositions of Holy Scripture,* 11 vols. (Grand Rapids: Wm. B. Eerdmans, 1952–59), 1:37.

7. Huey, *Exodus,* p. 35.

8. Chadwick, *The Book of Exodus,* p. 88.

9. Jack Finnegan, *Let My People Go* (New York: Harper and Row, 1963), pp. 45–46.

10. F. B. Meyer, *Devotional Commentary on Exodus* (Grand Rapids: Kregel Publications, 1978), p. 90.

CHAPTER FIVE

The Triumph of Faith

Exodus 5:22–7:13

When Moses had been rebuffed by Pharaoh and repudiated by his own people, what did he do? It's a marvelous sight that should put us in awe of Moses, and should send us to our knees as we examine our own lives.

It's a very simple description of a crucial movement on the part of Moses: "So Moses returned to the Lord" (5:22a). Here is a pristine picture of an honest relationship with God, and of the triumph of faith. Not all his problems were solved or all his questions answered, but the crucial action was that Moses returned to where he belonged. He went to the only source of life and light.

Now there was no tabernacle or temple or altar at this point in Moses' journey of faith—no visible sign or consecrated place of worship. Still, he returned to the Lord.

This is a picture that can guide us. Any place can be consecrated if the heart bestows upon that place attention to God in the privacy of prayer, if the world is shut out and the soul becomes aware of its dependence upon the Lord.

There is a sense in which we never leave the Lord, therefore we never "return" to Him. Certainly it's true that He never leaves us. But, in another sense, there is the need for direct attention and the centeredness of our will in Him as we enter into His presence. It is in that act of centeredness that we find Him present who is always present in our midst, the One who is everywhere.

Moses returned to the Lord, and his engagement with the Lord was not a typical act of tranquil worship and spiritual renewal.

LIVE THE QUESTIONS

5:22 So Moses returned to the LORD and said, "Lord, why have You brought trouble on this people? Why *is* it You have sent me?

23 "For since I came to Pharaoh to speak in Your name, he has done evil to this people; neither have You delivered Your people at all."

6:1 Then the LORD said to Moses, "Now you shall see what I will do to Pharaoh. For with a strong hand he will let them go, and with a strong hand he will drive them out of his land."

2 And God spoke to Moses and said to him: "I *am* the LORD.

3 "I appeared to Abraham, to Isaac, and to Jacob, as God Almighty, but *by* My name LORD I was not known to them.

4 "I have also established My covenant with them, to give them the land of Canaan, the land of their pilgrimage, in which they were strangers.

5 "And I have also heard the groaning of the children of Israel whom the Egyptians keep in bondage, and I have remembered My covenant.

6 "Therefore say to the children of Israel: 'I *am* the LORD; I will bring you out from under the burdens of the Egyptians, I will rescue you from their bondage, and I will redeem you with an outstretched arm and with great judgments.

7 'I will take you as My people, and I will be your God. Then you shall know that I *am* the LORD your God who brings you out from under the burdens of the Egyptians.

8 'And I will bring you into the land which I swore to give to Abraham, Isaac, and Jacob; and I will give it to you *as* a heritage: I *am* the LORD.'"

9 So Moses spoke thus to the children of Israel; but they did not heed Moses, because of anguish of spirit and cruel bondage.

10 And the LORD spoke to Moses, saying,

11 "Go in, tell Pharaoh king of Egypt to let the children of Israel go out of his land."

12 And Moses spoke before the LORD, saying, "The children of Israel have not heeded me. How then shall Pharaoh heed me, for I *am* of uncircumcised lips?"

13 Then the LORD spoke to Moses and Aaron, and gave them a command for the children of Israel and for Pharaoh king of Egypt, to bring the children of Israel out of the land of Egypt.

Exod. 5:22–6:13

I have to fight hard the sin of covetousness. I admire poets, and I find myself coveting the gift of poetic expression I find in others. Great poets have a double gift—the gift of perception and the gift of expression. The gift of expression is enhanced by the added beauty of rhythm and rhyme and symbol. Great poets seem able to distill the essence of an experience or an idea, and present it as a lovely bouquet, or a fragrant perfume—all in words.

Now, some poets are not easy for me to read, but occasionally I struggle with one because I know that here and there will come a small picture or phrase that will explode with meaning in my mind and heart.

Rainer Maria Rilke is one such writer. In his book *Letters to a Young Poet,* there is an explosive phrase. Ponder this puzzling, probing, profound word: "Be patient toward all that is unsolved in your heart and try to love the *questions themselves* like locked rooms and like books that are written in a very foreign tongue. Do not now seek the answers which cannot be given you because you would not be able to live them. And the point is, to live everything. *Live* the questions now."[1]

The explosive thought for me is: "live the questions." That would have been a good motto for Moses and the people of Israel. When he had been rebuffed by Pharaoh and repudiated by his people, *"Moses returned to the Lord."* He stormed, as it were, into the Lord's presence. *"Lord, why have You brought trouble on this people? Why is it You have sent me? For since I came to Pharaoh to speak in Your name, he has done evil to this people; neither have You delivered Your people at all"* (5:22–23).

Does that startle our notion of reverence? Has Moses' faith utterly given way? Has he forgotten the Lord's word back in Midian—"Do not draw near this place. Take your sandals off your feet, for the place where you stand is holy ground"?

Moses is not alone in coming into the presence of the Lord with questions. It will be a part of all the people coming after him who seek to be faithful. The psalmist reflected their style of prayer and proclamation to the Lord.

> For I was envious of the boastful,
> When I saw the prosperity of the wicked. . . .
> Their eyes bulge with abundance;
> They have more than heart could wish.
> They scoff and speak wickedly concerning
>   oppression;
> They speak loftily.
> They set their mouth against the heavens,
> And their tongue walks through the earth. . . .
> Behold, these are the ungodly,
> Who are always at ease;
> They increase in riches.
> Surely I have cleansed my heart in vain,
> And washed my hands in innocence.
>   *Ps. 73:3, 7–9, 12–13*

So, it is no casual or profane movement on Moses' part when he returns to the Lord and begins to fling questions in His face. If the people were frustrated and confused because of the increased oppression upon them, Moses was even more so.

God spoke again to Moses, reminding him of the covenant that He had made, promising deliverance and repeating the commitment *"I will bring you into the land which I swore to give to Abraham, Isaac, and Jacob."* But when Moses shared this word with the people, they did not listen *"because of anguish of spirit and cruel bondage."*

Listen to the poet Rilke again: "Be patient toward all that is unsolved in your heart and try to love the *questions themselves*. . . . Do not now seek the answers which cannot be given you because you would not be able to live them. . . . *Live* the questions now."[2]

How often in life questions far outnumber answers. Why was our child, among all the children of the world, born retarded? Why, when life-sustaining goods are so plentiful in the world, do millions die of starvation? Why was that father taken in death at so young an age when his family needed him so desperately? Why is it that I suffer when I've sought to be so faithful to God? Why have my children been so heartless and hurt me so much? Why have they become the victims of drugs? Why have they been caught in the clutches of this sin-sick society? Why was it Mary whose marriage broke up? She's such a committed Christian, so alive in the faith. Why does she now have to bear the awful pain of loneliness and the burdensome task of rearing children alone?

"Lord, why have You brought trouble on this people? Why is it You have sent me?" (5:22).

We know it's true—so often our questions far outnumber answers. And how often our questions are so deep and pervasive that they make us impotent, drain us of energy, and bring us to a state of passive numbness. Our wills are frozen. The wish to be other than we are is so diminished that it no longer stirs dissatisfaction and action. We're like the Hebrews who didn't listen to Moses. Our spirits are broken.

Just before I left Southern California back in the early 1970s, there was a story in the newspaper which is hard to forget. A young soldier killed in the Asian war was brought back and buried in Van Nuys, which is a part of the huge San Fernando Valley. The boy's father was deeply grieved by the loss of his son. One day, buried deep in the extremity of his sorrow, he went out to the cemetery. There at the grave which symbolized all the dark losses of his life, he pulled a pistol out of his pocket and killed himself.

Now, we're not apt to respond to our situations in such drastic, destructive ways. But in our heart of hearts, we have empathy, for we know how a person could come to that point. A big question mark hangs like an ominous cloud over our lives—a cloud holding the snow that may freeze our spirits, or holding the rain that may drench our whole lives, drowning out all we had hoped for and worked for and prayed for and trusted God for.

The psalmist put those feelings in these words: "For Your arrows pierce me deeply, / And Your hand presses me down. . . . / I am feeble and severely broken; / I groan because of the turmoil of my heart. . . . / My heart pants, my strength fails me; / As for the light of my eyes, it also has gone from me" (Ps. 38:2, 8, 10).

Lofton Hudson describes times like these that try men's souls: "They hit like a hurricane or creep up and grab one's leg like an alligator, or pierce from within like a leg cramp or a charley horse, or dawn on a person like a sudden realization to a hunter that he is lost one hour before dark."[3]

So where does that put us? "Live the questions!" And where does *that* put us? Some will not like what I'm about to say, because it's not an easy answer. Some may think it's no answer at all. But if we're not going to be dishonest and if we don't want to be superficial, we must state it bluntly: *There is no life apart from suffering.*

I don't know why that is. But strangely enough, most of our deepest learning and much of our best growth is a result of suffering or conflict—or at a more surface level, misunderstanding, confusion, trying times, hardships, difficult relationships. The question mark is a more piercing stimulus for growth than the exclamation point.

So where are we? "Live the questions." And how do we live the questions? *We can live the questions when we remember who God is.*

That's one of the biggest questions of Exodus. Over and over again, Moses and Aaron and the Hebrews had to be reminded of who the Lord is.

When Moses flung his questions into the Lord's face, God didn't answer the questions. He simply reminded Moses of who He is. So many things happen for which no clear explanation is possible—the deep spiritual meaning cannot be expressed in words. We have to wait, wait for experience.

Experience is the true communicator of God. If only we can live the questions, and wait and listen and keep returning to God, then we will experience deliverance and the clearing away of the shades over our understanding.

God's reminder of who He is is power-packed. Someone has designated these the seven "I wills" of redemption (6:6–8):

"I will bring you out."

"I will rescue you from their bondage."

"I will redeem you with an outstretched arm and with great judgments."

"I will take you as My people."

"I will be your God."

"I will bring you into the land which I swore to give."

"I will give it to you as a heritage."

The absurd extravagance, the staggering nature of this promise of God is seen best only as contrasted with the condition of Israel at that time. Nothing could have been more unlikely than that these promises would be fulfilled. The nation had descended into the valley of the shadow of death. The dread sentence of destruction and extinction was hanging over them.

Pharaoh's heart was being hardened more and more. You can imagine how strange it seemed to them that they were told by God that He was going to deliver them, that He was going to bring them out of that land of bondage into freedom. It seemed absolutely incredible that they could rise from that low level of degradation and move to a land that was "flowing with milk and honey."

We can live the questions if we remember who God is. God has brought to pass what He has promised. Later, when God has brought the Israelites out of Egypt as He promised, His word of reminder is a beautiful picture. "You have seen what I did to the Egyptians, and how I bore you on eagles' wings and brought you to Myself" (19:4).

Isn't that sublime imagery? It's a picture of a parent bird bearing the young fledglings on his mighty wings. How magnificent and effortless—how incomparable that flight! So, God spread His wings abroad, took His people, and bore them out—outstretched His mighty arm and freed them, bringing them to a land of milk and honey.

Now some may not think that's much of an answer. But if you live with the questions, remembering who God is, then it will be a saving answer. When we remember who God is, we know that He is faithful. His name and character are on the line when He promises to deliver us.

J. Vernon McGee has told a very simple story that expresses the depth of this truth. There was a little Scottish lady who worked hard taking in washing in order to send her son to the university. When he came home for vacation, his mind was filled with doubts about God from the modern teaching he had received. He did not want his mother to know about the change in his thinking. But she kept telling him how wonderful it was of God to save her, and how she knew she was saved. Finally, he could not listen to more of her talk and said, "Mother, you do not seem to realize how small you are in this universe. If you lost your soul, God would not miss it at all. It would not amount to anything."

She didn't reply right away, but kept putting dinner on the table. Finally she said, "I've been thinking about what you said. You're right. My little soul does not amount to much; I would not lose much and God would not lose much. But if He does not save me, He will lose more than I will. He promised if I would trust Jesus, He would save me. If He breaks His word, He will lose His reputation and mar His character."[4]

Do you see that as crude or too simple? Not so. God's reputation is at stake. He has promised to deliver us. When we remember that, we can live the questions.

It needs to be noted parenthetically that much of the material in Exodus is a part of the worship life of Israel. B. Davie Napier reminds us that the moving words of God in 6:2–8 should be read aloud.

> Its form suggests strongly that it had existed for generations as a spoken liturgy or confession of faith, habitually recited from memory in the rhythm of formalized worship. Note also in the reading that this is the *Word*, it is what God *said* to Moses; that the quality of divine compassion and mercy and grace here comes through as it has not previously in Exodus; that this is a recital of faith in the nature and purpose of God (see the emphasis upon the divine "I", even more pronounced in Hebrew, and compare the same feature in Josh. 24); and that all of this is an expansion of the single, simple, eloquent theme which opens and closes the recital "I am the Lord," conveying in the very name all the essential meaning of the divine life.[5]

THE FAMILY TREE

> 6:14 These *are* the heads of their fathers' houses: The sons of Reuben, the firstborn of Israel, *were* Hanoch, Pallu, Hezron, and Carmi. These are the families of Reuben.
>
> 15 And the sons of Simeon *were* Jemuel, Jamin, Ohad, Jachin, Zohar, and Shaul the son of a Canaanite woman. These *are* the families of Simeon.
>
> 16 These *are* the names of the sons of Levi according to their generations: Gershon, Kohath, and Merari. And the years of the life of Levi *were* one hundred and thirty-seven.

17 The sons of Gershon *were* Libni and Shimi according to their families.

18 And the sons of Kohath *were* Amram, Izhar, Hebron, and Uzziel. And the years of the life of Kohath *were* one hundred and thirty-three.

19 The sons of Merari *were* Mahli and Mushi. These *are* the families of Levi according to their generations.

20 Now Amram took for himself Jochebed, his father's sister, as wife; and she bore him Aaron and Moses. And the years of the life of Amram *were* one hundred and thirty-seven.

21 The sons of Izhar *were* Korah, Nepheg, and Zichri.

22 And the sons of Uzziel *were* Mishael, Elzaphan, and Zithri.

23 Aaron took to himself Elisheba, daughter of Amminadab, sister of Nahshon, as wife; and she bore him Nadab, Abihu, Eleazar, and Ithamar.

24 And the sons of Korah *were* Assir, Elkanah, and Abiasaph. These are the families of the Korahites.

25 Eleazar, Aaron's son, took for himself one of the daughters of Putiel as wife; and she bore him Phinehas. These *are* the heads of the fathers' houses of the Levites according to their families.

26 These *are the same* Aaron and Moses to whom the LORD said, "Bring out the children of Israel from the land of Egypt according to their armies."

27 These *are* the ones who spoke to Pharaoh king of Egypt, to bring out the children of Israel from Egypt. These *are the same* Moses and Aaron.

Exod. 6:14–27

The narrative breaks with the insertion of this genealogy. In chapter 2, the names of Moses' parents were omitted. Now they are named. *"Amram took for himself Jochebed, his father's sister, as wife; and she bore him Aaron and Moses."*

The genealogy begins with the three oldest sons of Israel (Jacob): Reuben, Simeon, and Levi. It lists the names of the sons of each. Up until this point, it duplicates the genealogy of all the sons of Israel that we find in Genesis 46:9–27. However, the *Interpreter's Bible* reminds us that its real concern is with the priestly tribe of Levi. Of the three sons of Levi, Kohath is the bearer of the line. Two of Kohath's sons are considered significant: Izhar, who becomes the father of Korah; and Amram, who becomes the father of Aaron and Moses. Through Aaron, the line carries to Eleazar and through him to Phinehas. In Numbers 3, the same pattern is elaborated to show the role of various branches of the family in the service of the tabernacle. Aaron and Moses are four generations removed from Jacob. It is significant that the line does not carry on through Moses but through Aaron. The genealogist is concerned to show that the priest has played an active role in the founding of the nation; his list symbolizes the legitimacy and authority of the priesthood in his own day. Moses is the prophet by whom God spoke in the foundation of the nation, and who instructed the priests. But he has no extant continuation. The priests build on the foundation he laid long ago. . . . Without attacking the priority of Moses it asserts the present priority of Aaron, the first-born of Amram.[6]

Though this genealogy interrupts the scene which breaks off at 6:13 and resumes at 6:28, it has its place and should not be seen as a real interruption. It is necessary to know who Moses and Aaron and the Levites are. To know who they are, we have to know who they were. Perhaps more important than anything else, the ancient authority and legitimacy of the institution of the priesthood is established.

AARON'S MIRACULOUS ROD

6:28 And it came to pass, on the day the LORD spoke to Moses in the land of Egypt,

29 that the LORD spoke to Moses, saying, "I *am* the LORD. Speak to Pharaoh king of Egypt all that I say to you."

30 But Moses said before the LORD, "Behold, I *am* of uncircumcised lips, and how shall Pharaoh heed me?"

7:1 So the LORD said to Moses: "See, I have made you *as* God to Pharaoh, and Aaron your brother shall be your prophet.

2 "You shall speak all that I command you. And Aaron your brother shall tell Pharaoh to send the children of Israel out of his land.

3 "And I will harden Pharaoh's heart, and multiply My signs and My wonders in the land of Egypt.

4 "But Pharaoh will not heed you, so that I may lay My hand on Egypt and bring My armies *and* My people, the children of Israel, out of the land of Egypt by great judgments.

5 "And the Egyptians shall know that I *am* the LORD, when I stretch out My hand on Egypt and bring out the children of Israel from among them."

6 Then Moses and Aaron did *so;* just as the LORD commanded them, so they did.

7 And Moses *was* eighty years old and Aaron eighty-three years old when they spoke to Pharaoh.

8 Then the LORD spoke to Moses and Aaron, saying,

9 "When Pharaoh speaks to you, saying, 'Show a miracle for yourselves,' then you shall say to Aaron, 'Take your rod and cast *it* before Pharaoh, *and* let it become a serpent.'"

10 So Moses and Aaron went in to Pharaoh, and they did so, just as the LORD commanded. And Aaron cast down his rod before Pharaoh and before his servants, and it became a serpent.

11 But Pharaoh also called the wise men and the sorcerers, so the magicians of Egypt, they also did in like manner with their enchantments.

12 For every man threw down his rod, and they became serpents. But Aaron's rod swallowed up their rods.

13 And Pharaoh's heart grew hard, and he did not heed them, as the LORD had said.

Exod. 6:28–7:13

Verses 6:28–7:7 retell the story of Moses' call, adding the specific ages of Moses and Aaron.

Here are two aged men. Moses is eighty, having spent his first forty years in Egypt and his next forty years in Midian before he was brought back to Egypt by God to deliver his people. And his brother Aaron was eighty-three.

Two aged men pitted against all the power of Egypt! What overwhelming odds against them! And can't you imagine how Pharaoh at this point would chuckle sneeringly as he saw them coming? But his sneering laughter would become dry cotton in his throat as his confrontation with these two men continued.

God was on the side of Moses and Aaron, and Pharaoh was going to learn that it doesn't matter how few there are; if they have the Lord on their side, they are enough.

Dwight L. Moody has been quoted as saying, "Moses spent forty years in Pharaoh's court thinking he was somebody, forty years in the desert learning that he was nobody, and forty years showing what God can do with a somebody who found out he was a nobody."

When Moses repeats the criticism that he has made earlier—his inability to speak well—he uses an interesting phrase, *"I am of uncircumcised lips"* (6:30). The Lord's response to this is a bit shocking: *"See, I have made you as God to Pharaoh, and Aaron your brother shall be your prophet"* (7:1).

Whatever else that means, it certainly means this: God had endowed Moses and Aaron with supernatural power far greater than their own native facility to express. In their weakness, they were made strong. The less Moses tried to assert himself over Pharaoh, the more dependent he would be upon the Lord—and the greater the victory for the Lord when he prevailed. No wonder Dwight L. Moody would put it so picturesquely: "Forty years showing what God can do with a somebody who found out he was a nobody."

With God with him, Moses would be *"as God"* to Pharaoh. Moses would not be acting in his own strength, and the power of God would be visible in him—so much so that Pharaoh, who boasted, "I do not know the Lord," would wither before Moses, the Lord's agent.

This mighty ruler who had contemptuously added insult upon injury and burden upon burden to the people of Israel would cower before Moses in abject prayer: "Please forgive my sin only this once, and entreat the Lord your God, that He may take away from me this death only" (10:17).

What lessons are here for us. Every person has at least one talent. The possession of that talent is a gift from God, and therefore a commission from Him is implied. It is possible for all of us to "do all to the glory of God" (1 Cor. 10:31) even though some of our actions may not be seen as acts of God. Seeking to live in obedience to Him produces a total effect which may be seen as a holy and sacred life. Fruitful reflection can come from our looking at this word of God to Moses, *"I have made you as God to Pharaoh,"* and at that word of Jesus to His followers, "Most assuredly, I say to you, he who believes in Me, the works that I do he will do also; and greater works than these he will do, because I go to My Father" (John 14:12).

It is Aaron now, not Moses, who has the rod. God had given three signs to Moses to overcome the unbelief of the Israelites who might question whether God had really appeared to him. One of these signs was a rod that turned into a serpent when it was thrown to the ground. Now, this same sign is to be used again for the benefit of an unbelieving Pharaoh.

In the ancient world, one's legitimacy was often established through the working of a sign. So, the rod was a source of that sign. It was thrown down in the presence of the Pharaoh and it became a serpent. Pharaoh called his own wise men and magicians and they did the same thing. Then an amazing thing happened. When they all threw their rods down and all of them turned into serpents, Aaron's serpents swallowed all the rest.

This was not enough. *"Pharaoh's heart grew hard."* Later on, the magicians would learn their lesson. After the third great plague, they would cry, "This is the finger of God," and retreat from the conflict (Exod. 8:19; 9:11).

Even though Pharaoh's heart was hardened, the scenario could now be defined: There was no reasonable doubt that there was no god like the Lord. There was no god in heaven or on earth that could do the works that He was doing.

NOTES

1. Rainer Maria Rilke, *Letters to a Young Poet* (New York: W. W. Norton and Co., rev. ed. 1954, 1962), p.35.
2. Ibid.

3. R. Lofton Hudson, *Persons in Crisis* (Nashville: Broadman Press, 1969), p. 120.

4. J. Vernon McGee, *Genesis–Deuteronomy,* Thru the Bible with J. Vernon McGee (Nashville: Thomas Nelson, 1981), 1:27.

5. B. Davie Napier, *Exodus,* Layman's Bible Commentary (Richmond, VA: John Knox Press, 1963), 3:39.

6. J. Coert Rylaarsdam, "Exodus," *The Interpreter's Bible* (New York: Abingdon-Cokesbury Press, 1952), 1:891–92.

CHAPTER SIX

The Plagues: Revelations of God's Power

Exodus 7:14–10:29

"The Plagues," as they are popularly designated, are at the heart of the Lord's redemption of Israel. Those who seek to discount the miraculous dimension of these plagues by presenting evidence that they all fall into events of nature that might appear spontaneously in Egypt miss a crucial point. God uses His own creation, that which occurs in nature—either natural and orderly or that which we might consider to be an aberration or evil—to achieve divine purpose; in this case, to deliver Israel and make God's power known in Egypt and throughout the world.

This is confirmed by the fact that the Egyptians themselves were said to have duplicated the first two events or "plagues." Parenthetically, isn't this a special token of honesty and veracity, that the Bible records the success of the magicians in doing what Moses and Aaron did? Otherwise, would it not have been easier to discredit the story? God was not prevented from using authentic prophets just because fraudulent ones worked the same miracles.

No matter how we may explain them, we must agree that this series of historical catastrophes served as the instrument of God to give His people exodus from Egypt. The point is that within the providence of God, even natural events may occur at such a time as to meet a particular need. However, this is not to be described, as some would tend to do, as "mere chance." H. H. Rowley incisively makes this point. "To regard this timely help as a chance coincidence offers no explanation of the return of Moses to Egypt, or the confidence he had known that Yahweh would deliver the people. There was more than the chance coincidence of help in the nick of time. There was also the strange fact that this timely help vindicated the prior faith of a man who profoundly believed that he was the mouthpiece of God."[1]

So we return to the assertion that the plagues are crucial to biblical faith. They represent the working of God's purposive will through the created order. Other sections of Scripture refer to these plagues as God's activity in history. Moses appealed to Israel on the basis of these plagues (Deut. 4:34). Jeremiah reminded seventh-century Israel that the Lord "set signs and wonders in the land of Egypt" (32:20). Two of the psalms, 78 and 105, review the Exodus events and deal with them historically. Psalm 78 lists seven of the ten plagues; Psalm 105 lists eight.

These plagues testify to the power and redemptive action of the Lord and provide evidence that nothing is too hard for the Lord, not even the deliverance of an enslaved people out of Egypt. The plagues were more than crucial events in the Exodus experience; they provided a continuing affirmation of God's power which gave abiding confidence to succeeding generations.

In this chapter, we're going to look at the first nine plagues, and then in the next chapter we will look at the plague of death and the institution of passover. The first nine plagues are divided into three triads, each triad severer than the preceding one. In the first triad— the Nile, the frogs, and lice—all the land was smitten indiscriminately. But in the last two triads the land of Goshen was not harmed, showing that these strokes of destruction were not the result of mere chance, but were directed by God.

It wasn't long before those in Pharaoh's inner circle of advisors were certain that he was engaged in a conflict with a greater power than they had known. This was proven to them in that though they were able to perform a couple of miracles, they were soon "driven from the field." Also, it became painfully obvious that everything Moses said would happen *did* happen.

As we begin to look at each of these plagues, we need to note their manifold purpose. First, they provided a public manifestation of the mighty power of the Lord God. God stated it: "But indeed for this purpose I have raised you up, that I may show My power in you, and that My name may be declared in all the earth" (Exod. 9:16). The magicians themselves were made to acknowledge this: "Then the magicians said to Pharaoh, 'This is the finger of God'" (8:19).

Second, the plagues were a divine visitation of wrath and punishment upon Pharaoh and the Egyptians for their cruel treatment of the Hebrews. Pharaoh himself admitted this: "Then Pharaoh called for Moses and Aaron in haste, and said, 'I have sinned against the Lord your God and against you'" (10:16).

Third, the plagues were a judgment from God upon the gods of Egypt, and demonstrated that the Lord was above all gods.

Fourth, these miraculous plagues served as a time of testing for Israel. Moses put this in perspective, asking Israel, "Did any people ever hear the voice of God speaking out of the midst of the fire, as you have heard, and live? Or did God ever try to go and take for Himself a nation from the midst of another nation, by trials, by signs, by wonders, by war, by a mighty hand and an outstretched arm, and by great terrors, according to all that the Lord your God did for you in Egypt before your eyes?" (Deut. 4:33–34).

The outcome of these testings was expressed in Exodus 15:11 when Moses and the children of Israel sang a song to the Lord after crossing the Red Sea: "Who is like You, O Lord, among the gods? / Who is like You, glorious in holiness, / Fearful in praises, doing wonders?"

So we look at each of these plagues with these manifold purposes of God in mind.

THE FIRST PLAGUE: THE NILE TURNED TO BLOOD

7:14 So the LORD said to Moses: "Pharaoh's heart *is* hard; he refuses to let the people go.

15 "Go to Pharaoh in the morning, when he goes out to the water, and you shall stand by the river's bank to meet him; and the rod which was turned to a serpent you shall take in your hand.

16 "And you shall say to him, 'The LORD God of the Hebrews has sent me to you, saying, "Let My people go, that they may serve Me in the wilderness"; but indeed, until now you would not hear!

17 'Thus says the LORD: "By this you shall know that I *am* the LORD. Behold, I will strike the waters which *are* in the river with the rod that *is* in my hand, and they shall be turned to blood.

18 "And the fish that *are* in the river shall die, the river shall stink, and the Egyptians will loathe to drink the water of the river."'"

19 Then the LORD spoke to Moses, "Say to Aaron, 'Take your rod and stretch out your hand over the waters of Egypt, over their streams, over their rivers, over their ponds, and over all their pools of water, that they may become blood. And there shall be blood throughout all the land of Egypt, both in *buckets of* wood and *pitchers of* stone.'"

20 And Moses and Aaron did so, just as the LORD commanded. So he lifted up the rod and struck the waters that *were* in the river, in the sight of Pharaoh and in the sight of his servants. And all the waters that *were* in the river were turned to blood.

21 The fish that *were* in the river died, the river stank, and the Egyptians could not drink the water of the river. So there was blood throughout all the land of Egypt.

22 Then the magicians of Egypt did so with their enchantments; and Pharaoh's heart grew hard, and he did not heed them, as the LORD had said.

23 And Pharaoh turned and went into his house. Neither was his heart moved by this.

24 So all the Egyptians dug all around the river for water to drink, because they could not drink the water of the river.

25 And seven days passed after the LORD had struck the river.

Exod. 7:14–25

In this first plague, the river Nile is turned to blood. God instructs Moses to go out to the river in the morning to meet Pharaoh there. Pharaoh may be coming to bathe, or to offer his devotions to the Nile, or perhaps to see if the river was beginning to rise, signaling the beginning of the flood season. It may very well be that Pharaoh was going there for religious devotion because the Nile was considered to be a deity. It was regarded with profound veneration by the Egyptians, its waters being held sacred as is the Ganges to Hindus.

The first plague, like many of the others, was a frontal assault on the gods of Egypt. But this assault was not convincing. Yahweh's sovereignty over Egypt was not yet proven absolute because Pharaoh's magicians were able to do the same kind of miracle that Moses and Aaron could do. So, during these initial stages of confrontation, Moses recorded that neither side prevailed. There is, in the record of these plagues, a movement that begins at the point of a total lack of the desired response from Pharaoh to the eventual and climactic capitulation of Pharaoh.

Pharaoh and his pagan friends had gods almost without number, and they felt that somehow their gods were bound to them by bonds of self-interest, depending upon their service and gifts for the gods' welfare. The plagues demonstrated God's sovereignty over all these other gods.

Even though Pharaoh hardened his heart and he and his circle of friends resisted this show of God's power, certainly those who worshiped the Nile as a beneficent deity must have been at least challenged to begin to think that some other power might be greater.

The Second Plague: Frogs

8:1 And the LORD spoke to Moses, "Go to Pharaoh and say to him, 'Thus says the LORD: "Let My people go, that they may serve Me.

2 "But if you refuse to let *them* go, behold, I will smite all your territory with frogs.

3 "So the river shall bring forth frogs abundantly, which shall go up and come into your house, into your bedroom, on your bed, into the houses of your servants, on your people, into your ovens, and into your kneading bowls.

4 "And the frogs shall come up on you, on your people, and on all your servants." ' "

5 Then the LORD spoke to Moses, "Say to Aaron, 'Stretch out your hand with your rod over the streams, over the rivers, and over the ponds, and cause frogs to come up on the land of Egypt.' "

6 So Aaron stretched out his hand over the waters of Egypt, and the frogs came up and covered the land of Egypt.

7 And the magicians did so with their enchantments, and brought up frogs on the land of Egypt.

8 Then Pharaoh called for Moses and Aaron, and said, "Entreat the LORD that He may take away the frogs from me and from my people; and I will let the people go, that they may sacrifice to the LORD."

9 And Moses said to Pharaoh, "Accept the honor of saying when I shall intercede for you, for your servants, and for your people, to destroy the frogs from you and your houses, *that* they may remain in the river only."

10 So he said, "Tomorrow." And he said, *"Let it be* according to your word, that you may know that *there is* no one like the LORD our God.

11 "And the frogs shall depart from you, from your houses, from your servants, and from your people. They shall remain in the river only."

12 Then Moses and Aaron went out from Pharaoh. And Moses cried out to the LORD concerning the frogs which He had brought against Pharaoh.

13 So the LORD did according to the word of Moses. And the frogs died out of the houses, out of the courtyards, and out of the fields.

14 They gathered them together in heaps, and the land stank.

15 But when Pharaoh saw that there was relief, he hardened his heart and did not heed them, as the LORD had said.

Exod. 8:1–15

Seven days after the plague of the Nile turning to blood, God told Moses to return to Pharaoh with the same demand, *"Let My people go."* This time, Pharaoh's refusal was to be greeted with a plague of frogs loosed upon the land. These frogs would fill the Nile, enter the houses, ovens, kneading bowls, and even the beds of Pharaoh and all his people.

In ancient Egypt the frog was associated with the goddess Heka[2] (and a frog-headed deity has been discovered on monuments in Egypt). The goddess Heka was thought to assist women at childbirth, and so was a symbol of life-giving power to the Egyptians.

Pharaoh had easily resisted giving in to Moses' demands under the pressure of the first plague; he could not have cared less about the inconvenience the pollution of the Nile caused his people. But when the swarming frogs overcame all the efforts of his slaves to keep them out of his palace, you can imagine what his response was. Here was one who was able to summon any and all of the luxuries of Egypt—with frogs in his bed! He was willing to promise anything to get rid of the frogs. But as soon as they were gone he dug his heels in and refused to be forced to do what he didn't want to do—he *"hardened his heart."*

THE THIRD PLAGUE: LICE

8:16 So the LORD said to Moses, "Say to Aaron, 'Stretch out your rod, and strike the dust of the land, so that it may become lice throughout all the land of Egypt.'"

17 And they did so. For Aaron stretched out his hand with his rod and struck the dust of the earth, and it became lice on man and beast. All the dust of the land became lice throughout all the land of Egypt.

18 Now the magicians so worked with their enchantments to bring forth lice, but they could not. So there were lice on man and beast.

19 Then the magicians said to Pharaoh, "This *is* the finger of God." But Pharaoh's heart grew hard, and he did not heed them, just as the LORD had said.

Exod. 8:16–19

When Pharaoh refused to yield to God's command following the first two plagues, God ordered Moses to have Aaron *"strike the dust of the land, so that it may become lice throughout . . . Egypt."* The exact identity of the insect which the New King James Version translates as "lice" is uncertain. The word has been translated as gnats, mosquitoes, fleas, sand flies, maggots, and gadflies. Whatever the precise identity of the insect, it filled the land. The frogs had invaded the homes of the Egyptians; the lice now invaded their bodies.

A new aspect enters here. The magicians had been able to counteract the effect of the miraculous work of God through Moses and Aaron in the first two plagues by reproducing the same phenomenon with the use of their magical arts. But they are not able to do so with the phenomenon of the lice. It is to their everlasting credit that they acknowledge this to Pharaoh. *"This is the finger of God,"* they say.

Here again, the freedom of God in His sovereignty is demonstrated. He has allowed these magicians to counterfeit His miracles earlier, but He will do so no longer, and the magicians recognize what Pharaoh is unwilling to admit. This God of Moses and Aaron is obviously more powerful than the gods to whom they have been giving themselves.

The expression *"finger of God"* is a symbol of divine power. The law that God gave to Moses was written by "the finger of God" (Exod. 31:18). Jesus also used the expression: "And if I cast out demons by Beelzebub, by whom do your sons cast them out? Therefore they will be your judges. But if I cast out demons with the finger of God, surely the kingdom of God has come upon you" (Luke 11:19–20).

Still Pharaoh was unconvinced; his heart remained hardened; he would not even listen to the appeals of his own magicians (v. 19).

H. L. Ellison has made an interesting observation that provides fruitful reflection related to Pharaoh's magicians. He suggests that the use of a capital letter to spell God when the magicians say, "This is the finger of God,' is misleading. He contends that the magicians were not confessing that this was the work of Yahweh, but that the plague was supernatural and caused by some deity. "Had they acknowledged the power of Yahweh, it might conceivably have weighed with the Pharaoh, but their half-hearted confession simply discredited them and 'Pharaoh's heart was hard.'" Ellison's conclusion is one we need to take to heart. "Today, also, men are far too ready to say 'supernatural' when they should say 'God', and so spare themselves the trouble and duty of taking events seriously."[3]

How ready are we to name the name of God when some miraculous event takes place in our lives—when there is a divine intervention or our lives are broken in two, forever changing who we are and the direction in which we go?

THE FOURTH PLAGUE: FLIES

8:20 And the LORD said to Moses, "Rise early in the morning and stand before Pharaoh as he comes out to the water. Then say to him, 'Thus says the LORD: "Let My people go, that they may serve Me.

21 "Or else, if you will not let My people go, behold, I will send swarms *of flies* on you and your servants, on your people and into your houses. The houses of the Egyptians shall be full of swarms *of flies*, and also the ground on which they *stand*.

22 "And in that day I will set apart the land of Goshen, in which My people dwell, that no swarms *of flies* shall be there, in order that you may know that I *am* the LORD in the midst of the land.

23 "I will make a difference between My people and your people. Tomorrow this sign shall be."'"

24 And the LORD did so. Thick swarms *of flies* came into the house of Pharaoh, *into* his servants' houses, and into all the land of Egypt. The land was corrupted because of the swarms *of flies*.

25 Then Pharaoh called for Moses and Aaron, and said, "Go, sacrifice to your God in the land."

26 And Moses said, "It is not right to do so, for we would be sacrificing the abomination of the Egyptians to the LORD our God. If we sacrifice the abomination of the Egyptians before their eyes, then will they not stone us?

27 "We will go three days' journey into the wilderness and sacrifice to the LORD our God as He will command us."

28 So Pharaoh said, "I will let you go, that you may sacrifice to the LORD your God in the wilderness; only you shall not go very far away. Intercede for me."

29 Then Moses said, "Indeed I am going out from you, and I will entreat the LORD, that the swarms *of flies* may depart tomorrow from Pharaoh, from his servants, and from his people. But let Pharaoh not deal deceitfully anymore in not letting the people go to sacrifice to the LORD."

30 So Moses went out from Pharaoh and entreated the LORD.

31 And the LORD did according to the word of Moses; He removed the swarms *of flies* from Pharaoh, from his servants, and from his people. Not one remained.

32 But Pharaoh hardened his heart at this time
also; neither would he let the people go.
Exod. 8:20–32

The first three plagues failed to convince Pharaoh, but God would
give him no escape. God instructs Moses to arise early and meet
Pharaoh on his way to the river and again repeat the demand, *"Let
My people go, that they may serve Me."* If Pharaoh will not give in,
then *"swarms of flies"* will be sent to cover the king and his servants,
the people and their houses, even *"the ground on which they stand."*

There are different ways of looking at particular aspects of this
plague. Some scholars believe that this plague was designed to destroy the trust of the people in Beelzebub. Beelzebub was the fly
god—reverenced as the protector of Egypt from visitation by the
swarms of flies which commonly infested the land. The people had
depended upon Beelzebub to be their guard against ravenous flies,
but this plague convinced them of the impotence of Beelzebub, caus-
ing them to look elsewhere for relief.

Others believe that the *"swarms"* are not of flies, but of the sacred
scarab, a beetle which was an emblem of the sun and of the abiding
life of the soul. Innumerable monuments, mummy chests, amulets,
and charms in ancient Egypt bore the effigy of this revered symbol.
But now it became a symbol of death rather than a symbol of life.
And so, another *"god"* in the army of gods was laid low.

Two new dynamics are introduced with this fourth plague. One, a
part of Egypt, the land of Goshen, in which most of God's people
dwelt, was not affected. Flies were so common in Egypt that it would
have been easy for Pharaoh and his circle of advisors to rationalize
this plague and see it as a natural phenomenon. The setting apart of
Goshen witnessed that God was in control, and could plague whom
He chose.

Two, Pharaoh begins to weaken a bit. Moses asks permission for
the people to go into the wilderness to make sacrifice. Pharaoh offers his first concession: *"Go, sacrifice to your God in the land"* (v. 25).
Pharaoh is willing for them to go, but he doesn't want them to go
very far. He needs to keep an eye on them. Though Pharaoh is
weakening, Moses rejects the concession he offers.

When Moses will not accept the concession, Pharaoh proposes a
second one. He will let the people go into the wilderness out of sight

of the Egyptians to sacrifice, *"only you shall not go very far away."* Also, he requests of Moses, *"Intercede for me"* (v. 28).

Moses agrees to this second concession, agrees to pray for the removal of the flies and to intercede for Pharaoh, but he warns Pharaoh not to change his mind. Though Pharaoh is cracking, he still cannot give in. As soon as the flies disappear, Pharaoh hardens his heart and will not let the people go.

It's important to remember what Pharaoh was wrestling with. He was supposedly a god himself, a god in the eyes of his people. He had been told that; he believed it. How could he give in to a God that was going to diminish him in the eyes of his people and reduce his power?

That's a far-fetched question for us on the surface. But it's not far-fetched in terms of the struggle that goes on within. Isn't our struggle the struggle of who is going to be in control? Isn't this the reason we continue to hold on tenaciously to the reins of our lives? Isn't this the reason we continue to sit proudly on the thrones of our hearts? We don't want to give up our control.

THE FIFTH PLAGUE: PESTILENCE UPON THE CATTLE

9:1 Then the LORD said to Moses, "Go in to Pharaoh and tell him, 'Thus says the LORD God of the Hebrews: "Let My people go, that they may serve Me.

2 "For if you refuse to let *them* go, and still hold them,

3 "behold, the hand of the LORD will be on your cattle in the field, on the horses, on the donkeys, on the camels, on the oxen, and on the sheep—a very severe pestilence.

4 "And the LORD will make a difference between the livestock of Israel and the livestock of Egypt. So nothing shall die of all *that* belongs to the children of Israel." '"

5 Then the LORD appointed a set time, saying, "Tomorrow the LORD will do this thing in the land."

6 So the LORD did this thing on the next day, and all the livestock of Egypt died; but of the livestock of the children of Israel, not one died.

7 Then Pharaoh sent, and indeed, not even one of
the livestock of the Israelites was dead. But the heart of
Pharaoh became hard, and he did not let the people go.
Exod. 9:1–7

This fifth plague is designated in verse 3 as *"a very severe pestilence."* The cattle, horses, donkeys, camels, oxen, and sheep of the
Egyptians are going to be struck down, but the livestock of the children of Israel will be delivered. God not only judged Pharaoh and
the gods of Egypt; God spared His own people in the process.

The degree of Pharaoh's hardness of heart is underscored in this.
Not only were cattle necessary for life in Egypt; in Egyptian theology, there was a sanctity to animals. A word from Pharaoh could
have spared the cattle, but Pharaoh's heart was hard as steel and he
still *"did not let the people go."*

THE SIXTH PLAGUE: BOILS UPON MAN AND BEAST

9:8 So the LORD said to Moses and Aaron, "Take for
yourselves handfuls of ashes from a furnace, and let
Moses scatter it toward the heavens in the sight of
Pharaoh.

9 "And it will become fine dust in all the land of
Egypt, and it will cause boils that break out in sores
on man and beast throughout all the land of Egypt."

10 Then they took ashes from the furnace and
stood before Pharaoh, and Moses scattered *them* toward heaven. And *they* caused boils that break out in
sores on man and beast.

11 And the magicians could not stand before Moses
because of the boils, for the boils were on the magicians and on all the Egyptians.

12 But the LORD hardened the heart of Pharaoh;
and he did not heed them, just as the LORD had spoken to Moses.
Exod. 9:8–12

It's an awful picture. Moses takes ashes, stands before Pharaoh,
and throws the ashes into the heavens. These ashes multiply, settle
on *"man and beast,"* become *"boils that break out into sores."*

Here comes a new aspect to the plagues. Not only are the representatives of Pharaoh, the magicians, unable to duplicate the deeds of Moses; they themselves now become the victims. *"And the magicians could not stand before Moses because of the boils, for the boils were on the magicians and on all the Egyptians."*

In graphic terms, the unlimited power of Yahweh is underscored. It wasn't that the magicians could not stand before Moses because the boils were on their feet; they could not stand before Moses because they knew their impotence. They withdrew from the struggle, unable to resist further, and appealed to Pharaoh, but he still would not give in.

THE SEVENTH PLAGUE: HAIL

9:13 Then the LORD said to Moses, "Rise early in the morning and stand before Pharaoh, and say to him, 'Thus says the LORD God of the Hebrews: "Let My people go, that they may serve Me,

14 "for at this time I will send all My plagues to your very heart, and on your servants and on your people, that you may know that *there is* none like Me in all the earth.

15 "Now if I had stretched out My hand and struck you and your people with pestilence, then you would have been cut off from the earth.

16 "But indeed for this *purpose* I have raised you up, that I may show My power *in* you, and that My name may be declared in all the earth.

17 "As yet you exalt yourself against My people in that you will not let them go.

18 "Behold, tomorrow about this time I will cause very heavy hail to rain down, such as has not been in Egypt since its founding until now.

19 "Therefore send now *and* gather your livestock and all that you have in the field, for the hail shall come down on every man and every animal which is found in the field and is not brought home; and they shall die."'"

20 He who feared the word of the LORD among the servants of Pharaoh made his servants and his livestock flee to the houses.

21 But he who did not regard the word of the LORD left his servants and his livestock in the field.

22 Then the LORD said to Moses, "Stretch out your hand toward heaven, that there may be hail in all the land of Egypt—on man, on beast, and on every herb of the field, throughout the land of Egypt."

23 And Moses stretched out his rod toward heaven; and the LORD sent thunder and hail, and fire darted to the ground. And the LORD rained hail on the land of Egypt.

24 So there was hail, and fire mingled with the hail, so very heavy that there was none like it in all the land of Egypt since it became a nation.

25 And the hail struck throughout the whole land of Egypt, all that *was* in the field, both man and beast; and the hail struck every herb of the field and broke every tree of the field.

26 Only in the land of Goshen, where the children of Israel *were,* there was no hail.

27 And Pharaoh sent and called for Moses and Aaron, and said to them, "I have sinned this time. The LORD *is* righteous, and my people and I *are* wicked.

28 "Entreat the LORD, that there may be no *more* mighty thundering and hail, for *it is* enough. I will let you go, and you shall stay no longer."

29 So Moses said to him, "As soon as I have gone out of the city, I will spread out my hands to the LORD; the thunder will cease, and there will be no more hail, that you may know that the earth *is* the LORD'S.

30 "But as for you and your servants, I know that you will not yet fear the LORD God."

31 Now the flax and the barley were struck, for the barley *was* in the head and the flax *was* in bud.

32 But the wheat and the spelt were not struck, for they *are* late crops.

33 So Moses went out of the city from Pharaoh and spread out his hands to the LORD; then the thunder and the hail ceased, and the rain was not poured on the earth.

34 And when Pharaoh saw that the rain, the hail, and the thunder had ceased, he sinned yet more; and he hardened his heart, he and his servants.

121

35 So the heart of Pharaoh was hard; neither would
he let the children of Israel go, as the LORD had spoken by Moses.

Exod. 9:13–35

A key word relating to this plague is verse 14: *"For at this time I
will send all My plagues to your very heart, and on your servants and on
your people, that you may know that there is none like Me in all the
earth."* The purpose of the plague is the recognition of Yahweh's
uniqueness—there is none like Yahweh in all the earth.

Hailstorms were quite rare in Egypt. The infrequency of such a
phenomenon and the severity of the storm begin to create a response in Pharaoh. A distinct break in his attitude is expressed. He
confesses that he has sinned, that the Lord is in the right, and that
he and his people have been wrong. He also appeals to Moses to
pray to the Lord to end the storm. More importantly, he agrees to an
unconditional release of the Hebrews: *"I will let you go, and you shall
stay no longer"* (v. 28).

But once again Pharaoh breaks his word. It is important to see that
Pharaoh was no accidental obstacle, but a God-willed means to
demonstrate God's power. H. L. Ellison relates this to a constant
theme of Scripture. "Israel would not be eliminated (v. 19), for God's
purpose was to show His power in deliverance, not in destruction.
This is an ever-recurring theme in Scripture. It recurs in a strikingly
different form in Isaiah, chapters 40–49, where God declares that
He has raised up Cyrus, who does not know Him, to be His instrument for Israel's second exodus. We find it also in the apocalypse,
where even the powers of evil are called forth by the Lamb to accomplish His purpose for the church and Israel."[4]

History is replete with examples. The ultimate expression of it
came from Jesus Himself in His word to Peter: "On this rock I will
build My church, and the gates of Hades shall not prevail against it"
(Matt. 16:18).

THE EIGHTH PLAGUE: LOCUSTS

10:1 Now the LORD said to Moses, "Go in to Pharaoh;
for I have hardened his heart and the hearts of his

servants, that I may show these signs of Mine before him,

2 'and that you may tell in the hearing of your son and your son's son the mighty things I have done in Egypt, and My signs which I have done among them, that you may know that I *am* the LORD.

3 So Moses and Aaron came in to Pharaoh and said to him, "Thus says the LORD God of the Hebrews: 'How long will you refuse to humble yourself before Me? Let My people go, that they may serve Me.

4 'Or else, if you refuse to let My people go, behold, tomorrow I will bring locusts into your territory.

5 'And they shall cover the face of the earth, so that no one will be able to see the earth; and they shall eat the residue of what is left, which remains to you from the hail, and they shall eat every tree which grows up for you out of the field.

6 'They shall fill your houses, the houses of all your servants, and the houses of all the Egyptians— which neither your fathers nor your fathers' fathers have seen, since the day that they were on the earth to this day.'" And he turned and went out from Pharaoh.

7 Then Pharaoh's servants said to him, "How long shall this man be a snare to us? Let the men go, that they may serve the LORD their God. Do you not yet know that Egypt is destroyed?"

8 So Moses and Aaron were brought again to Pharaoh, and he said to them, "Go, serve the LORD your God. Who *are* the ones that are going?"

9 And Moses said, "We will go with our young and our old; with our sons and our daughters, with our flocks and our herds we will go, for we must hold a feast to the LORD."

10 Then he said to them, "The LORD had better be with you when I let you and your little ones go! Beware, for evil is ahead of you.

11 "Not so! Go now, you *who are* men, and serve the LORD, for that is what you desired." And they were driven out from Pharaoh's presence.

12 Then the LORD said to Moses, "Stretch out your hand over the land of Egypt for the locusts, that they

may come upon the land of Egypt, and eat every herb of the land—all that the hail has left."

13 So Moses stretched out his rod over the land of Egypt, and the LORD brought an east wind on the land all that day and all *that* night. When it was morning, the east wind brought the locusts.

14 And the locusts went up over all the land of Egypt and rested on all the territory of Egypt. *They were* very severe; previously there had been no such locusts as they, nor shall there be such after them.

15 For they covered the face of the whole earth, so that the land was darkened; and they ate every herb of the land and all the fruit of the trees which the hail had left. So there remained nothing green on the trees or on the plants of the field throughout all the land of Egypt.

16 Then Pharaoh called for Moses and Aaron in haste, and said, "I have sinned against the LORD your God and against you.

17 "Now therefore, please forgive my sin only this once, and entreat the LORD your God, that He may take away from me this death only."

18 So he went out from Pharaoh and entreated the LORD.

19 And the LORD turned a very strong west wind, which took the locusts away and blew them into the Red Sea. There remained not one locust in all the territory of Egypt.

20 But the LORD hardened Pharaoh's heart, and he did not let the children of Israel go.

Exod. 10:1–20

Tension is building now. An invasion of locusts is probably the most terrible pest that a land can suffer. Pharaoh's advisors knew that whatever had survived the hail would perish before these voracious hordes. These advisors become more aggressive in their relationship to Pharaoh. When they hear Moses and Aaron say that this visitation of locusts will be more destructive than anything their fathers or father's fathers have heard or seen from the earliest days of man's history, they are profoundly moved. So, they plead, *"Let the men go, that they may serve the Lord their God. Do you not yet know that Egypt is destroyed?"* (v. 7).

Pharaoh weakens a bit more and tries to make an arrangement with Moses and Aaron. He is willing for the men to go, but wants the young to stay, but Moses refuses. Not only is he going to take the men, his plan is also to take the old and the young, the sons and the daughters, the flocks and the herds.

This exasperates Pharaoh—that mere men would take issue with him, a "god-man." So he drives Moses and Aaron from his presence, unable to bow down to any god but himself, and the plague comes. The locusts darken the ground with their brown bodies, destroying every green thing, and leaving the land a waste. Again Pharaoh repents, confessing his sin not only against the Lord, but against Moses and Aaron. He asks their forgiveness, and begs them to intercede on his behalf. But when the plague is removed, he returns to his former hardness of heart.

THE NINTH PLAGUE: DARKNESS

10:21 Then the LORD said to Moses, "Stretch out your hand toward heaven, that there may be darkness over the land of Egypt, darkness *which* may even be felt."

22 So Moses stretched out his hand toward heaven, and there was thick darkness in all the land of Egypt three days.

23 They did not see one another; nor did anyone rise from his place for three days. But all the children of Israel had light in their dwellings.

24 Then Pharaoh called to Moses and said, "Go, serve the LORD; only let your flocks and your herds be kept back. Let your little ones also go with you."

25 But Moses said, "You must also give us sacrifices and burnt offerings, that we may sacrifice to the LORD our God.

26 "Our livestock also shall go with us; not a hoof shall be left behind. For we must take some of them to serve the LORD our God, and even we do not know with what we must serve the LORD until we arrive there."

27 But the LORD hardened Pharaoh's heart, and he would not let them go.

28 Then Pharaoh said to him, "Get away from me! Take heed yourself and see my face no more! For in the day you see my face you shall die!"

29 So Moses said, "You have spoken well. I will never see your face again."

Exod. 10:21–29

This ninth plague struck at the very foundation of Egyptian theology. That theology gave priority to the sun god, Ra, and the Pharaoh was himself believed to be the embodiment of that god. What could be a more dramatic climax than for the encounter between Moses and Pharaoh to bring about a darkness that triumphed over the sun for three days?

The plagues had begun by striking a blow at the prestige of the Nile, one of Egypt's two leading deities. Now it is the other leading deity, the sun, which is shown to be powerless in withstanding the power of Yahweh. This is the crowning insult for Pharaoh. And the darkness does not come to the people in Goshen; further proof for Pharaoh that Moses' God is responsible for the plagues.

Once again, Pharaoh is reduced to making concessions to the Israelites. He agrees to let them go and worship God, taking their families with them, but he insists that they leave their flocks and herds behind. Had Moses been waging a political battle, he would have accepted this compromise. But this is no political argument; it has to do with the sovereignty of God. Pharaoh is God's enemy, and therefore must make an unconditional surrender.

Isn't it true that people always like to bargain with God? Jacob did it at Bethel (Gen. 28:20–22). "If God will be with me, and keep me in this way that I am going, and give me bread to eat and clothing to put on . . . then the Lord shall be my God." But by the time Jacob returned from Paddan Aram, God had done far more for him than he ever expected and he realized the need for a complete surrender. So, he wrestled with the Lord's emissary; all night long he wrestled, until the Lord gave him a new name and blessed him.

We can't bargain with God, and there's no need to. What He has in store for us is far greater than we can imagine.

LET GOD BE GOD

There is another plague yet to come, and we'll give that our attention in the next chapter. For now, let's reflect in a general way on the revelation of God's power as seen in the plagues.

John Newton once wrote, "If you think you see the ark of the Lord falling, you can be quite sure that it is due to a swimming in your head." The richness of that statement is understood when we remember a biblical story from the book of Samuel. It's one of the most difficult, yet one of the most significant stories in the Old Testament.

David had been made king and had captured Jerusalem. He sought to bring the Ark of the Covenant up to the Holy City. The ark was a chest in which was kept the law that God gave Moses. David and his men placed the sacred ark on a cart drawn by oxen. As the cart moved along, carrying the sacred ark, it was accompanied by a host of people singing and dancing as they journeyed to Jerusalem, the Holy City.

At one place on the journey, the oxen drawing the cart stumbled and it looked as though the ark might fall off. Uzzah, a man walking alongside the cart, saw what was about to happen and put out his hand to steady the ark and keep it from falling. And immediately he fell dead.

That tragedy made a great impression on the people. They believed that Uzzah was stricken by the Lord for putting his hand on this holy object. The Hebrews believed that since the ark was so holy, to touch it, even with the best of intentions, was to invite death. They were certain that Uzzah was the victim of God's wrath. Trying to protect God, as it were, trying to ensure His good character, many people would say that Uzzah simply slipped and fell, and that the writer of the story jumped to the conclusion that he was smitten dead because of what he had done.

There are many ways to interpret the story, but I like the way my friend, Bishop Gerald Kennedy was able to cut through the stereotypical efforts to explain away mystery and to solve the problem of the sovereignty of God. He said the story was saying that there are some things "which are not to be manipulated, or interfered with by human beings." There are some things in life which are not for us to adjust, and not for us to arrange to suit our wishes. In that story, we're being told that not every reality is amenable to our desires, and that "if a generation assumes it has the right to arrange everything to its convenience, that generation will die. There are eternal truths which cannot be amended."[5]

So when we remember that story, Newton's word takes on more meaning, "If you think you see the ark of the Lord falling, you can be quite sure that it is due to a swimming in your head." God's ark does not fall. God is God. God's sovereignty cannot be violated. God has an ultimate and an unchanging will which we humans cannot manipulate.

That's the heart of what the plagues teach us. God is God. When we refuse to recognize that, sooner or later some plague will do us in.

From that general truth, let's outline some specific lessons.

The first is that God is sovereign, and we cannot presume upon His grace. The plagues provide a horrible picture, a picture of judgment.

I remember being in Stuttgart, Germany, a few years ago, and visiting the marvelous statue of Dietrich Bonhoeffer, the young German theologian who was imprisoned for his opposition to Hitler and was eventually put to death. As I looked at that statue and moved about it, it seemed as though Bonhoeffer's eyes were following me wherever I moved. It was as though his piercing eyes were questioning me about one of the big ideas that he sought to communicate, an idea about cheap grace.

"Cheap grace," Bonhoeffer said, "is the preaching of forgiveness without requiring repentance, baptism without church discipline, Communion without confession, absolution without personal confession. Cheap grace is grace without discipleship, grace without the cross, grace without Jesus Christ, living and incarnate."[6]

We fall into the snare of cheap grace. Because we know that at the heart of the gospel is forgiveness, we presume upon God's grace and begin to act as though God is obligated to show us favor. We forget that God does not owe it to anyone to stop justice from taking its course. He is not obliged to pity and pardon. If He does so, it is an act of His own free will, and nobody forces His hand.

This is what Paul was saying when he wrote to the Romans, tying his own New Testament message to the message of the Book of Exodus.

What shall we say then? Is there unrighteousness with God? Certainly not! For He says to Moses, "I will have mercy on whomever I will have mercy, and I will have compassion on whomever I will have compassion." So then it is not of him who wills, nor of him who runs, but of God who shows mercy. For the Scripture says to the Pharaoh, "For this very purpose I have raised you up, that I may show My power in you, and that My name may be declared in all the earth." Therefore He has mercy on whom He wills, and whom He wills He hardens.

Rom. 9:14–18

So, grace is free; that is, free in the sense that you and I don't originate it or deserve it. However, we need always to remember that this grace comes from God, who is free not to be gracious if He chooses not to be gracious. So we remember God is sovereign and we cannot presume upon His grace.

A second general lesson from the plagues is that God is sovereign and jealous. We've said that the significant factor about these plagues is the evidence that they not only were designed to break the Egyptian grip on Israel, but also to expose and discredit the gods of Egypt. Through the plagues, God showed Egyptian and Hebrew alike that there is one true God, a sovereign Lord of the gods, who alone deserves worship and obedience.

Time after time, the Egyptians were tortured by the very things whose images they had turned into gods to worship. Time after time, they saw themselves suffer incredible disease and disorder while the Hebrews remained untouched. Was not God making it clear that it does matter what we believe about God? It matters what we call God. And this God, the God Yahweh, is sovereign. He is jealous because He alone deserves to be worshiped and obeyed.

The third general lesson from the plagues has to do with the whole idea of the hardening of the heart. We said earlier that the Hebrews did not deal with secondary causes. For them, all that transpired ultimately was traceable to God. While those observations are correct, at the same time we must not diminish the power and the awful reality of this idea by trying to psychologize it. The writer of Exodus was convinced, as we should be, that the Lord is sovereign, even to the point of being directly responsible for Pharaoh's stubbornness if He chose to be.

The other side of that coin is that this sovereign God has given us free will. To be sure, in God's hands we are as clay in the hand of the potter, but God has given us free will. God could crush that, but then man would cease to be fully man. That free will is ours in the context of a sovereign God whose will is going to prevail.

Pharaoh was free to act as he would, to harden his heart, or to have his heart hardened by his actions. But he was not free to thwart completely God's will to deliver His people out of bondage.

A fourth lesson from a general observation of these plagues has to do with the tendency of all humankind to make vows to God in the midst of affliction, but not to keep them when the affliction is over. Pharaoh is the personification of that tendency.

In the midst of the havoc wrought by the hail, he called for Moses and Aaron and made what must have been for him an extremely difficult confession: "I have sinned this time. The Lord is righteous, and my people and I are wicked" (9:27). He appealed to Moses to stop the hail with the promise that he would let the Israelites go immediately. Even as Moses expected, when the hail ceased, Pharaoh returned to his hardened-heart position against the Exodus of Israel.

How much of Pharaoh is in us? "Lord, if You'll get me out of this situation, I'll serve You the rest of my life." How quickly do we make vows in the midst of darkness and difficulty, only to go back on those vows when the sun begins to shine and the roads of our lives smooth out!

The fifth lesson is centered in that word the Lord commanded Moses to speak to Pharaoh. It's repeated over and over again: "Let My people go, that they may serve Me" (9:1). This needs to be etched indelibly upon our minds. "Let My people go"—not so that they may be free from a master, but *that they may serve.*" Let them go, because having been redeemed by Christ, they're not their own, they belong to Christ. Their deliverance from sin, which God works, changes them from one devotion to another, from one service to another. It changes them from serving sin, which is bondage, to serving God, which is freedom.

When Christopher Parkening was thirty years old, he was at the top of his profession as a concert guitarist. His recitals were booked years in advance, and his albums were best sellers. Then he stopped.

For three years he was nowhere to be seen. He stopped recording or performing, saying he had burned out.

Having been successful, he had enough money to buy a small ranch in Montana with a trout stream running through it. A champion fly-caster, as well as a musician, he thought that would be the answer to his problems. He thought he'd find what he was looking for. He did, but not the way he expected. In Montana, you can fish from May to October, but the rest of the time, the other six months, there's no fishing. You have to stay inside. Christopher did; he read books; he read the Bible.

A neighbor asked him one day if he wanted to go to church, and he responded. The minister preached a sermon on the Christian life and the ways we try to avoid living it. That struck a chord in Parkening. "That was for me," he said. And from that point on he began to see things differently.

He doesn't use the term "born-again," but he says what happened to him was the renewal of his faith. The result was that he got a sense of mission in his life. He went back to his guitar, returned to the stage, started recording again, but as a different man. He says now that he burned out earlier because there was no other purpose in his life than his own fame. "And now," he says, "my music has a purpose. Now I can give voice to what I believe through what I play."

He was delivered out of bondage to self. It was as though he had heard the call of God, "Let My people go, that they may serve Me."

NOTES

1. H. H. Rowley, *The Faith of Israel* (London: SCM, 1956), p. 42.

2. H. D. Spence and T. S. Exell, eds., *Exodus,* The Pulpit Commentary, vol. 1 (New York: Funk & Wagnalls, n.d.).

3. H. L. Ellison, *Exodus,* Daily Study Bible Series (Philadelphia: Westminster Press, 1982), p. 47.

4. Ibid., p. 53.

5. Gerald H. Kennedy, *Fresh Every Morning* (New York: Harper and Row, 1966), p. 2.

6. Dietrich Bonhoeffer, *The Cost of Discipleship,* trans. R. H. Fuller, rev. ed. (New York: Macmillan, 1960), p. 30.

CHAPTER SEVEN

The Passover

Exodus 11:1–13:16

Bible students and teachers have always connected the Old and New Testaments by using types. That is, seeing in the Old Testament a "type" of what is really revealed in the New Testament. This began with those who wrote the New Testament. Paul saw Jesus as "the new Adam." Matthew saw him as a Moses. The writer of the Epistle to the Hebrews interpreted at length the tabernacle of the Old Testament as a type for the ministry and mission of Jesus.

In the Introduction to this book, we talked about Exodus as a pattern for the Christian pilgrimage. Israel in bondage to Pharaoh represents the picture of human beings in bondage to sin and evil. The account of Israel's being delivered by God out of bondage, wandering in the wilderness, and at last reaching the promised land, provides a striking picture of the spiritual history of the individual—by the power of Christ, moving out of bondage and by His grace and mercy finding that promised life of fullness and joy in a life in Christ, and at death, eternal life.

The Passover is one of the most vivid types in Old Testament literature. What the crucifixion is for Christians, the Passover was for Israel. So, we look now at this pivotal event in Jewish/Christian history.

THE TENTH PLAGUE: DEATH

11:1 And the LORD said to Moses, "I will bring one more plague on Pharaoh and on Egypt. Afterward he will let you go from here. When he lets *you* go, he will surely drive you out of here altogether.

2 "Speak now in the hearing of the people, and let every man ask from his neighbor and every woman from her neighbor, articles of silver and articles of gold."

3 And the LORD gave the people favor in the sight of the Egyptians. Moreover the man Moses *was* very great in the land of Egypt, in the sight of Pharaoh's servants and in the sight of the people.

4 Then Moses said, "Thus says the LORD: 'About midnight I will go out into the midst of Egypt;

5 'and all the firstborn in the land of Egypt shall die, from the firstborn of Pharaoh who sits on his throne, even to the firstborn of the female servant who *is* behind the handmill, and all the firstborn of the animals.

6 'Then there shall be a great cry throughout all the land of Egypt, such as was not like it *before*, nor shall be like it again.

7 'But against none of the children of Israel shall a dog move its tongue, against man or beast, that you may know that the LORD does make a difference between the Egyptians and Israel.'

8 "And all these your servants shall come down to me and bow down to me, saying, 'Get out, and all the people who follow you!' After that I will go out." Then he went out from Pharaoh in great anger.

9 But the LORD said to Moses, "Pharaoh will not heed you, so that My wonders may be multiplied in the land of Egypt."

10 So Moses and Aaron did all these wonders before Pharaoh; and the LORD hardened Pharaoh's heart, and he did not let the children of Israel go out of his land.

12:29 And it came to pass at midnight that the LORD struck all the firstborn in the land of Egypt, from the firstborn of Pharaoh who sat on his throne to the firstborn of the captive who *was* in the dungeon, and all the firstborn of livestock.

30 So Pharaoh rose in the night, he, all his servants, and all the Egyptians; and there was a great cry in Egypt, for *there was* not a house where *there was* not one dead.

31 Then he called for Moses and Aaron by night, and said, "Rise, go out from among my people, both you and the children of Israel. And go, serve the LORD as you have said.

32 "Also take your flocks and your herds, as you have said, and be gone; and bless me also."

33 And the Egyptians urged the people, that they might send them out of the land in haste. For they said, "We *shall* all *be* dead."

34 So the people took their dough before it was leavened, having their kneading bowls bound up in their clothes on their shoulders.

35 Now the children of Israel had done according to the word of Moses, and they had asked from the Egyptians articles of silver, articles of gold, and clothing.

36 And the LORD had given the people favor in the sight of the Egyptians, so that they granted them *what they requested*. Thus they plundered the Egyptians.

37 Then the children of Israel journeyed from Rameses to Succoth, about six hundred thousand men on foot, besides children.

38 A mixed multitude went up with them also, and flocks and herds—a great deal of livestock.

39 And they baked unleavened cakes of the dough which they had brought out of Egypt; for it was not leavened, because they were driven out of Egypt and could not wait, nor had they prepared provisions for themselves.

40 Now the sojourn of the children of Israel who lived in Egypt *was* four hundred and thirty years.

41 And it came to pass at the end of the four hundred and thirty years—on that very same day—it came to pass that all the armies of the LORD went out from the land of Egypt.

42 It *is* a night of solemn observance to the LORD for bringing them out of the land of Egypt. This *is* that night of the LORD, a solemn observance for all the children of Israel throughout their generations.

Exod. 11:1–10; 12:29–42

There remained one more plague in store for Egypt. The word for "plague" in 11:1 means literally "a stroke" or "a blow." This one will crack the stone-hard resistance of Pharaoh, pierce his hardened heart, and bring the freedom God has promised Israel.

As the plagues draw to a close, several points are worth reflecting upon.

Why was more than one plague necessary? We might answer that this was an affirmation of the long-suffering of God. Pharaoh had opportunity after opportunity to avoid the plague of death. He could have believed God and spared the Egyptians all the pain and suffering that came upon them in the plagues. The long-suffering God gave him numerous opportunities.

Another explanation is that Pharaoh needed convincing that Moses and Aaron represented a God who was really at work. If only one or two things had happened, they might have been labeled coincidence. But ten convinced even the most skeptical, even the most hard-hearted, that God was responsible for these calamities.

What was the real purpose of the plagues? There is more than one answer. God's primary purpose was to deliver Israel from Egyptian bondage. But there were other issues at stake. The plagues served to make Egypt know that Yahweh was truly God: "And the Egyptians shall know that I am the Lord, when I stretch out My hand on Egypt and bring out the children of Israel from among them" (7:5).

Another purpose of the plagues often gets a negative response. The Egyptians were being punished for their sins. Even Pharaoh recognized this. After the plague of hail struck throughout the whole land of Egypt, he called for Moses and Aaron, and said to them, "I have sinned this time. The Lord is righteous, and my people and I are wicked" (9:27).

Certainly an objection might be raised to this last purpose—that it was Pharaoh who sinned and not the Egyptian people. It might be argued that they were innocent bystanders to the contest that swirled around them. But what does that say to us about social sin? The Egyptians passively stood by and watched the enslavement and mistreatment of the Israelites. Did they not therefore share in the responsibility for Israel's oppression? We think about the German people, and even the church, standing by as Adolph Hitler and his circle of friends did the work of the Holocaust. The question is, isn't passivity or failure to stand up for justice a part of the sin that is actively committed?

Let's look specifically at this tenth plague and the Passover event.

I said earlier that what Calvary is to the Christian, the Passover was to the Jew. The intimate connection between the two must never be forgotten because the Passover informs Christians about the heart of our faith. It was the Passover that Jesus was celebrating with His disciples on the eve of His crucifixion when He announced to them that He was the Passover Lamb to be slain for the sins of the whole world. And when Paul called the Corinthians to a life of sincere Christianity, challenging them to put away all immorality and uncleanness and be that people set apart by Christ, he used language recalling the Passover. "Therefore purge out the old leaven, that you may be a new lump, since you truly are unleavened. For indeed Christ, our Passover, was sacrificed for us. Therefore let us keep the feast, not with old leaven, nor with the leaven of malice and wickedness, but with the unleavened bread of sincerity and truth" (1 Cor. 5:7–8).

We'll come back to the connection between Passover and Calvary, but let's look a bit more at the plagues. God had dealt with Pharaoh through the plagues—sending nine plagues of judgment against Pharaoh's rebellion, and now sending a tenth and final one. The Lord is going to come and is going to claim the firstborn of all the land. Those will be delivered who do what the Lord calls them to do; that is, slay a lamb that is without blemish and mark their households with the blood of that lamb.

Someone has put it crudely, perhaps harshly, but truthfully: In every house of Egypt that night, there was either a dead lamb or a dead firstborn. It is a picture, an awful picture, of judgment.

Divine Judgment

Try to put yourself in the place of Pharaoh. Moses told him that at midnight the Lord would go through the land, bringing death to every firstborn. Even the firstborn of Pharaoh would not be spared; it would begin there, and would include the firstborn of the lowliest servant, and even the firstborn of the animals. Pharaoh was looked upon as a god. If he could not protect his firstborn, his impotence would be exposed. Even the announcement of that possibility, however, did not melt his hardened heart.

Judgment could not have been stated more dramatically. *"Then there shall be a great cry throughout all the land of Egypt, such as was not like it before, nor shall be like it again. But against none of the children of Israel shall a dog move its tongue, against man or beast, that you may know that the Lord does make a difference between the Egyptians and Israel"* (11:6–7).

Israel had cried to God and to Pharaoh—now it was the Egyptians' turn to cry out in anguish at God's judgment on them. What we said previously about one of the purposes of the plagues—that of punishment for sins—is obviously a part of the plot.

There can be no covering up or diminishing the reality of divine judgment. The fact is set forth on page after page of Bible history. God judged Adam and Eve, expelling them from the garden and pronouncing curses on their future earthly life. God judged the corrupt world of Noah's day, sending a flood to destroy humankind. God judged Sodom and Gomorrah, engulfing them in a volcanic catastrophe (Gen. 19:24). And God judged Pharaoh and the Egyptians just as He had foretold He would (Gen. 15:14), unleashing against them the terrors of the ten plagues.

There are "big judgments" about which we all know. Apart from these, the pages of the Bible are literally filled with judgment. Those who don't study the Bible seriously nonchalantly suggest that when you leave the Old Testament and come to the New, the theme of divine judgment fades almost to nothing. That isn't so. Even a cursory reading of the New Testament reveals God's action as judge. In fact, the entire New Testament is overshadowed by the certainty of a coming day of universal judgment which was set forth by Jesus Himself. It's not easy to forget that picture, the powerful imagery of it—the sheep separated from the goats, the righteous on the right hand of God and the unrighteous on the left, the righteous invited into the presence of the Lord, the unrighteous condemned to eternal punishment where there is "weeping and gnashing of teeth" (Matt. 8:12).

The picture in the New Testament is that the world's Savior, Jesus Christ, is also the world's judge. Listen to Jesus Himself:

> "For the Father judges no one, but has committed all judgment to the Son, that all should honor the Son just as they honor the Father. He who does not honor the Son does not honor the Father who sent Him.

"Most assuredly, I say to you, he who hears My
word and believes in Him who sent Me has everlasting
life, and shall not come into judgment, but has passed
from death into life. Most assuredly, I say to you, the
hour is coming, and now is, when the dead will hear
the voice of the Son of God; and those who hear will
live. For as the Father has life in Himself, so He has
granted the Son to have life in Himself, and has given
Him authority to execute judgment also, because He is
the Son of Man. Do not marvel at this; for the hour is
coming in which all who are in the graves will hear
His voice and come forth—those who have done good,
to the resurrection of life, and those who have done
evil, to the resurrection of condemnation.'

John 5:22–29

There is no way to cover up or diminish the reality of divine judgment.

God's Grace in Light of God's Sovereignty

And that leads to a second major point. God's grace must be seen
in light of His sovereignty and His position as judge.

It's an awful picture, a severe one—the Lord moving over the land
claiming the firstborn of the land, but passing over those houses
marked with the blood of the Passover lamb, identifying them as
those who had heard God's call and were faithful.

One of the general observations with which we closed the last
chapter is that we must not presume upon God's grace. How it happens I don't know, but it happens: We get the notion that God is
obliged to love us. Now God does love us. That is God's most identifying characteristic: love. However, we are far afield in our thinking
when we make this a central notion—that God is somehow obliged
to love us, little though we deserve it.

It follows then that since we have sinned, we need to know and
keep in mind that God is not obliged to show us favor. We deserve
only justice, and for us that means certain condemnation. God does
not owe it to anyone to stop justice from taking its course. God is not
obliged to pity and pardon. If God does so, it is an act done of His
own free will, nobody forces God's hand.

We must not presume upon God's grace. We must see His gracious mercy in the context of His being sovereign judge. Grace is free in the sense that you and I don't originate or deserve it. However, we need to always remember that this grace comes from God who is free to be gracious or not as He chooses.

I am struggling to express a profound truth. God's grace and mercy is a free decision of a sovereign God who is our judge. Only when we see that our destiny is dependent upon whether or not God resolves to save us from our sins, and that that is a decision God makes, and that He doesn't have to make it—only then can we grasp the biblical view of grace, the extravagant, undeserved mercy of God extended to us.

The Blood Shall Be a Token

Now let's look specifically at that grace as seen in the tenth plague and the Passover. We see it in the Lord in the form of the Angel of Death sweeping over the land with piercing eyes, looking hither and yon, and finding occasionally a door on which there was sprinkled the blood of an unblemished lamb. When that blood was seen, the Lord passed over and that household was saved. We see it ultimately and radically in a frail man, hanging from an ugly cross, every drop of blood and life drained from Him.

The Lord had said, "The blood shall be a sign for you, on the houses where you are. And when I see the blood, I will pass over you" (12:13). The blood is the sign—the "token" as some translations say. It was the token of redemption at the Passover—and how much more so is the crucifixion for us Christians.

Three things are present in this token: protection, cleansing, and substitution.

The first word is *protection*. The Hebrew word that is translated "Passover" in 12:11 is really inadequately rendered, according to Arthur W. Pink. The word is *pesaḥ*, and it seems to have no connection with any other Hebrew words. It closely resembles the Egyptian word *pesh*, which means "to spread the wings over" or "to protect," thus suggesting such "sheltering and protection as is found under the outstretched wings of the Almighty God. . . . It was not merely that the Lord passed by the houses of the Israelites, but that He stood on guard *protecting* each blood-sprinkled door."[1] Ponder the richness of that image. Protected—protected by the blood. And now we are everlastingly protected by the blood of the cross.

Some talk casually, even glibly, about "eternal security" as though the burden were upon the Lord to keep us safe once we accept Him as Savior. Remember what we said earlier: don't presume upon God's grace. God has done His part. Christ has paid the awful price for our salvation, paid the price in His own blood. We are protected only as long as we continually claim the power of the blood.

> The hands of Christ seem very frail
> For they were broken by a nail.
> But only they reach heaven at last,
> Whom those frail broken hands hold fast.
> —*Anonymous*

The second word is *cleansing*. The lamb was to be an unblemished lamb, and the bread was to be unleavened. In Scripture, "leaven" symbolizes evil. So the lesson here is of vital importance. It is captured in this verse: "That you may know that the Lord does make a difference between the Egyptians and Israel" (11:7).

Don't forget this. The Lord accepts us as we are, but He does not leave us there. He makes a distinction between us and those who are not yet delivered. In New Testament language it is stated thus: "The blood of Jesus Christ His Son cleanses us from all sin" (1 John 1:7). I used to have trouble with that image. In Mississippi during my childhood, we sang a spirited gospel song, attributed to Elisha A. Hoffman. The chorus went like this:

> Are you washed in the blood,
> In the soul-cleansing blood of the Lamb?
> Are your garments spotless?
> Are they white as snow?
> Are you washed in the blood of the Lamb?

Now that's not easy symbolism for a child to grasp, not even easy for an adult. And the words of the verses were even stronger. One verse said:

> When the Bridegroom cometh will your robes be
> white,

Pure and white in the blood of the Lamb?
Will your souls be ready for the mansions bright
And be washed in the blood of the Lamb?

That's not easy to grasp: "The blood of Jesus Christ . . . cleanses." Many people still don't like that language. If you don't like the language, you'll have to argue with God. It's the language of the Bible, both the Old and the New Testaments.

It is only when we are cleansed from what is repugnant to divine holiness that we can really be one with Christ. As long as we continue indulging in sin, there can be no communion with Him. It is only as we "walk in the light as He is in the light" that the blood of Christ "cleanses us from all sin," and "we have fellowship with one another" (1 John 1:7).

The last word that helps us understand the meaning of the blood as a token is *substitution*. Here we come to a type again as a revealing symbol.

The lamb is the clearest representative type of Christ in the Old and New Testaments. The beloved disciple John called Jesus "the Lamb slain from the foundation of the world" (Rev. 13:8). John the Baptist designated Him "the Lamb of God who takes away the sin of the world" (John 1:29).

The Passover in the Book of Exodus, according to the apostle Paul, was a type, a shadow of the great substance, our Lord Jesus Christ. Israel was saved by a lamb, the best and most perfect of its kind. The lamb was slain, and its blood was applied to their houses. Entering through blood-sprinkled doors, protected by the blood of the lamb, they then feasted on the lamb which had been slain for them.

See how clear the connection is between the Passover lamb and the "Lamb slain from the foundation of the world"?

Now, I hope we are wise enough and humble enough to know that no simple theory of the atonement can adequately contain the full meaning and mystery of what Christ did for us at Calvary. But I also pray with Spurgeon that "we do not subscribe to the lax theology which teaches that the Lord Jesus did something or other which, in some way or other, is in some degree or other, connected with the salvation of men."[2]

We are more certain than that. With faith we hold that Christ died for us, and had He not died, eternal damnation would be our lot. He paid our debt, died in our stead, was a substitution for our punishment. Mercy and grace are the key—unmerited, undeserved, extravagant grace.

So, we are confident with the poet Philip Doddridge that,

> Grace first inscribed my name,
> In God's eternal Book:
> 'Twas grace that gave me to the Lamb,
> Who all my sorrows took.

INSTITUTION OF THE PASSOVER

12:1 Now the LORD spoke to Moses and Aaron in the land of Egypt, saying,

2 "This month *shall be* your beginning of months; it *shall be* the first month of the year to you.

3 "Speak to all the congregation of Israel, saying: 'On the tenth of this month every man shall take for himself a lamb, according to the house of *his* father, a lamb for a household.

4 'And if the household is too small for the lamb, let him and his neighbor next to his house take *it* according to the number of the persons; according to each man's need you shall make your count for the lamb.

5 'Your lamb shall be without blemish, a male of the first year. You may take *it* from the sheep or from the goats.

6 'Now you shall keep it until the fourteenth day of the same month. Then the whole assembly of the congregation of Israel shall kill it at twilight.

7 'And they shall take *some* of the blood and put *it* on the two doorposts and on the lintel of the houses where they eat it.

8 'Then they shall eat the flesh on that night; roasted in fire, with unleavened bread *and* with bitter *herbs* they shall eat it.

9 'Do not eat it raw, nor boiled at all with water, but roasted in fire—its head with its legs and its entrails.

142

10 'You shall let none of it remain until morning, and what remains of it until morning you shall burn with fire.

11 'And thus you shall eat it: *with* a belt on your waist, your sandals on your feet, and your staff in your hand. So you shall eat it in haste. It *is* the LORD'S Passover.

12 'For I will pass through the land of Egypt on that night, and will strike all the firstborn in the land of Egypt, both man and beast; and against all the gods of Egypt I will execute judgment: I *am* the LORD.

13 'Now the blood shall be a sign for you on the houses where you *are*. And when I see the blood, I will pass over you; and the plague shall not be on you to destroy *you* when I strike the land of Egypt.

14 'So this day shall be to you a memorial; and you shall keep it as a feast to the LORD throughout your generations. You shall keep it as a feast by an everlasting ordinance.

15 'Seven days you shall eat unleavened bread. On the first day you shall remove leaven from your houses. For whoever eats leavened bread from the first day until the seventh day, that person shall be cut off from Israel.

16 'On the first day *there shall be* a holy convocation, and on the seventh day there shall be a holy convocation for you. No manner of work shall be done on them; but *that* which everyone must eat— that only may be prepared by you.

17 'So you shall observe *the Feast of* Unleavened Bread, for on this same day I will have brought your armies out of the land of Egypt. Therefore you shall observe this day throughout your generations as an everlasting ordinance.

18 'In the first *month*, on the fourteenth day of the month at evening, you shall eat unleavened bread, until the twenty-first day of the month at evening.

19 'For seven days no leaven shall be found in your houses, since whoever eats what is leavened, that same person shall be cut off from the congregation of Israel, whether *he* is a stranger or a native of the land.

20 'You shall eat nothing leavened; in all your dwellings you shall eat unleavened bread.'"

21 Then Moses called for all the elders of Israel and said to them, "Pick out and take lambs for yourselves according to your families, and kill the Passover *lamb*.

22 "And you shall take a bunch of hyssop, dip *it* in the blood that *is* in the basin, and strike the lintel and the two doorposts with the blood that *is* in the basin. And none of you shall go out of the door of his house until morning.

23 "For the LORD will pass through to strike the Egyptians; and when He sees the blood on the lintel and on the two doorposts, the LORD will pass over the door and not allow the destroyer to come into your houses to strike *you*.

24 "And you shall observe this thing as an ordinance for you and your sons forever.

25 "It will come to pass when you come to the land which the LORD will give you, just as He promised, that you shall keep this service.

26 "And it shall be, when your children say to you, 'What do you mean by this service?'

27 "that you shall say, 'It *is* the Passover sacrifice of the LORD, who passed over the houses of the children of Israel in Egypt when He struck the Egyptians and delivered our households.'" So the people bowed their heads and worshiped.

28 Then the children of Israel went away and did *so;* just as the LORD had commanded Moses and Aaron, so they did.

Exod. 12:1–28

This section of Scripture describes the institution of the Passover. Directions are given for the annual celebration of this event which would be a vivid reminder of the Lord's deliverance of Israel out of bondage. *"So this day shall be to you a memorial; and you shall keep it as a feast to the Lord throughout your generations"* (v. 14).

The practice continues today as faithful Jews remember. *"And it shall be, when your children say to you, 'What do you mean by this service?' that you shall say, 'It is the Passover sacrifice of the Lord, who passed over the houses of the children of Israel in Egypt when He struck the Egyptians and delivered our households'"* (vv. 26–27).

The symbolic and actual richness of the Passover for Christians can hardly be exaggerated. *"Take a bunch of hyssop, dip it in the blood that is in the basin, and strike the lintel and the two doorposts with the blood that is in the basin"* (v. 22). In his book *Gleanings in Exodus*, Arthur Pink suggests that this is a marvelous picture of the suffering of our blessed Lord upon the cross. The picture is marred a bit, he suggests, by the weak translation of the Hebrew word for "basin." The word rendered "basin" is really an old Egyptian word for the step before a door, or the threshold of a house.[3] That's the way the word is translated in other sections of Scripture. In Judges 19:27, it is translated as "threshold"; in 2 Kings 12:9, it is translated as "door."

No direction was given for putting blood upon the threshold. The reason is that the blood was already there. The lamb was evidently slain at the door of the house that was to be protected by its blood. This point is not simply one of academic interest, but it concerns the accuracy of type in terms of rich symbolism. The door of the house wherein the Israelite was protected had blood on the lintel (the crosspiece), on the sideposts, and on the step. With vivid imagination, Pink sees this as a marvelous picture of Christ on the cross with blood above, where the thorns pierced His brow, blood at the sides from His nail-pierced hands, blood below from nail-torn feet![4]

Some may think that theory too imaginative, straining too far for a type. Yet there is no question about the connection between Passover and Calvary, and again, we cannot exaggerate the symbolic and actual richness of the Passover for Christians.

Let's look at some of the detailed instructions in the institution of the Passover.

A Beginning of Months

"This month shall be your beginning of months; it shall be the first month of the year to you" (v. 2).

Passover month was to begin Israel's year. This served as a reminder of their coming into being as God's delivered people. The Passover occurred during the month of Abib, later called Nisan, which is comparable to the period March–April. Passover, therefore, was both a spring festival and a New Year festival. In the ancient Near East, the Babylonian New Year was observed in the spring; in Canaan, it occurred in the fall. Many scholars believe that early in Israel's history, before the Exile, the Israelites followed the Canaanite method of reckoning their New Year in the fall, but changed it to the Babylonian calendar after the Exile. Today in modern Judaism, Passover is observed in the spring, and New Year (Rosh Hashana) in the fall.

The symbolism for Christians is rich also. As already indicated, the Passover Lamb is a type of Christ; and the calendar we use is dated back to the birth of Christ. *Anno mundi* (in the year of the world) has given place to *anno Domini* (in the year of the Lord). As the Passover marked the beginning of months for the Hebrews, so the coming of Christ into the world marks the changing of our world; and the entrance of Christ into our lives marks the beginning of our lives.

Sometimes we witness this in a dramatic fashion. Tom, a preacher friend, shares such a dramatic witness. One night he was called by a church member to an accident on a major thoroughfare near his home. When he got there, one young fellow was in the ditch near his smashed car, his face so muddy and bloody that Tom didn't recognize him. In the other ditch was a member of Tom's church, not seriously injured. Tom inquired as to who the other fellow was. When told that his name was Jim Bob, Tom remembered him. His mother was a member of Tom's church, and occasionally Jim Bob had attended. Tom had visited him in jail on a couple of occasions, because he'd lived the kind of life that often got him into trouble with the law.

Tom knelt down beside Jim Bob in the ditch and visited with him as they awaited the ambulance. "Wouldn't you like to pray?" Tom asked.

"Preacher, I don't know how to pray."

The ambulance was coming, but Tom prayed with Jim Bob before he was put in the ambulance. During the following time of hospitalization, Tom visited often with Jim Bob, sharing his love and concern, seeking to share the life that Christ could give with this one who seemed so far removed from that possibility. Then the medical verdict came: Jim Bob was permanently paralyzed from his waist down.

Tom moved away from that city about a month after the accident. But his successor in the congregation he had served told him the rest of the story. About three months later, a wheelchair came down the aisle one Sunday morning at the close of the worship service, and Jim Bob made a public profession of faith in Jesus Christ and asked to be baptized. After the service, the preacher asked him, "Jim Bob, how do you feel? What are you thinking? How are you handling being paralyzed for the rest of your life?"

"Preacher, I'd rather be paralyzed and in this wheelchair for the rest of my life, than to be walking around without Jesus Christ."

For the Jews, Passover was the beginning of months. For any one of us, Jesus Christ, the Lamb of God who takes away the sins of the world, is the beginning of beginnings.

A Family Affair

"On the tenth day of this month every man shall take for himself a lamb . . . a lamb for a household" (v. 3).

Moses and Aaron were instructed to tell the *"congregation"* (12:3)—this is the first occurrence of the word that would become the technical term for Israel as an organized religious community—to take a lamb for each household. If the household was too small to eat an entire lamb, next-door neighbors would be invited to share the lamb. Later in the development of this ritual, a regulation fixed ten as the number of persons for each lamb. To be noted here is the fact that Passover was instituted as a family observance, and it is still celebrated in the home.

There are some words which, though made trite by casual use, still express profound truth. "The family that prays together stays together." "The hand that rocks the cradle guides the world." Now the scriptural admonition is a truth upon which we can depend, the hope to keep us going as parents: "Train up a child in the way that he should go, and when he is old he will not depart from it" (Prov. 22:6). Faith is a family affair!

A Lamb without Blemish

"Your lamb shall be without blemish" (v. 5). Does that remind you of the word of Peter? ". . . but with the precious blood of Christ, as of

a lamb without blemish and without spot. He indeed was foreordained before the foundation of the world" (1 Pet. 1:19–20).

"Without blemish" suggests what was present in the Old Testament law—the perfect sacrifice. "And whoever offers a sacrifice of a peace offering to the Lord, to fulfill his vow, or a freewill offering from the cattle or the sheep, it must be perfect to be accepted; there shall be no defect in it" (Lev. 22:21). Nothing but a perfect sacrifice could satisfy the requirements of God, who Himself is perfectly righteous. However, in the religious history of humankind, it became very clear that no sacrifice was adequate. For that reason, God had to provide something else, something altogether different; He had to provide the perfect Lamb without blemish, God's only Son, Jesus Christ. That's the reason Peter refers to Christ as "a lamb without blemish and without spot."

Earlier in this chapter, we talked about the cleansing and protecting aspects of the blood of the lamb. This is undergirded in the specific narrative that we are now considering. For instance, the blood was to be sprinkled with hyssop. Hyssop was a small, bushy plant often used in purification rights. It appears many times in Old Testament context. It was used to sprinkle blood (Exod. 12:22), or other ritual mixtures (Num. 9:18). It was also used as an ingredient in ritual cleansing of leprosy (Lev. 14:4, 6, 49, 51, 52), and the purification of the unclean (Num. 19:6).

One of the most dramatic usages of "hyssop" is in David's agonizing cry: "Purge me with hyssop, and I shall be clean" (Ps. 51:7). Here, hyssop is associated with the cleansing of sin, and certainly that became the primary meaning of blood sacrifice in Old Testament law, and is at the heart of Christ's redeeming work in our lives.

The blood represented not only cleansing, but also protection. The doorposts and the lintel had the blood spread upon them. In primitive times, doorposts were uniquely holy, seen as the residence of both good and evil spirits. The Old Testament reflects practices that support this. The sanctity of the threshold of the people of God is seen in the command that Israel write the commandment "on the doorposts of your house" (Deut. 6:9).

This note of protection is seen in the way the Scripture is written. The Lord says, "I will pass through the land. . . . and when I see the blood, I will pass over you" (vv. 12–13).

Later, in verse 23, it says, *"the Lord will pass over the door and not allow the destroyer to come into your houses to strike you."* There is a distinction here that invites reflection. The Hebrew verb meaning "pass over" is *'ābar*, distinct from *pesaḥ* (the noun for Passover). It is from this latter word that we derive the English word "paschal" to designate the paschal lamb in our Christian celebrations of Lent and Easter.

Honeycutt reminds us that the phrase "when I smite the land of Egypt" (v. 13, RSV) suggests that the writer presupposed no secondary agent through which the Lord operated. "He Himself smote Egypt, and as the source of destruction, He passed over the Hebrews."[5] However, when you get to the next reference, "the Lord will pass over the door and not allow the destroyer to come into your houses to strike you" (v. 23), another interpretation becomes possible, and commendable. This verse suggests that the Lord will pass over the threshold, enter the house, and prevent the destroyer from coming in to destroy the residents there who have faithfully put the seal of blood on their doors.

Here it is possible to see as the destroyer of the firstborn of Israel, not God, but some other power whom the Lord opposes and from whom He protects the Israelites. Putting these two together, the Feast of the Passover became a festival to celebrate the visiting and redeeming God—the One who comes to dwell among us, not only as protector but as sustainer and giver of life.

One other note that suggests a relevant truth is in the simple instruction that the lamb be killed and eaten. The lamb was to be killed, and the blood placed as a token on the lintels and the doorposts. Inside, where the family gathered, the lamb was to be eaten. In Scripture, eating signifies two things: *appropriation* and *fellowship.* Of course, a journey lay ahead for Israel, and food was needed to strengthen them, but by eating the lamb, more was being said. Israel was *appropriating* the power God alone provided, and they were sharing in a *fellowship,* an identity, a covenant, that thenceforth would give them their characteristic sense of being. It is not a long leap in our minds from this lamb that was to be eaten by ancient Israel, to the "Lamb of God who takes away the sins of the world" and refers to Himself as "the bread of life" (John 6:48).

With Sandals on Your Feet

"And thus you shall eat it: with a belt on your waist, your sandals on your feet, and your staff in your hand" (v. 11).

What a picture of the joy of anticipation and readiness for the Exodus! Can you put yourself in the picture? You are standing around the table, fully clothed, sandals on your feet, staff in hand, ready with your family to start off on the most exciting journey of your life. The light of hope is burning brightly in your eyes. Years of oppression are coming to an end. The faithfulness of God will come to a climax at any moment when, through the silence of the night, you will hear the sound of a trumpet, calling you to join your comrades in the faith to make that momentous march to Canaan, the promised land of God.

"Your sandals on your feet, and your staff in your hand" is suggestive of the journey that lies ahead, the long pilgrimage. It is going to be a forty-year struggle marching through the wilderness, though Israel is not aware of it at the moment. In Deuteronomy 29:5, there is an interesting reflection on that journey which harks back to this night of nights. Moses says, "And I have led you forty years in the wilderness. Your clothes have not worn out on you, and your sandals have not worn out on your feet."

In another passage, he reminds them, "Your garments did not wear out on you, nor did your foot swell these forty years" (Deut. 8:4).

The Lord who was taking them on this journey would sustain them in it, for the Lord is sufficient at every stage of our pilgrimage.

So, it is also for Christians: our life is a pilgrimage. As the Israelites journeyed to the promised land, they passed through a wilderness in which they were strangers and pilgrims. Paul reminds us that our home is not here, but "our citizenship is in heaven" (Phil. 3:20), and we too are just passing through.

Not only does the staff in our hand remind us that life is a journey, it also signifies that we can lean on something outside ourselves. That's the witness of God's word. The person who knows God and is dependent upon God learns early what the psalmist knew, "Your rod and your staff, they comfort me" (Ps. 23:4).

I have some friends who have learned this lesson well. John and Jo Walt are in China at the time of this writing. John is a lawyer and

Jo is a homemaker; both are faithful Christians. Jo is teaching English and John is teaching law in a university in Xi'an. But that's not the reason that they've gone to China for a year. They've gone to make their witness for Christ in these days when a door is being slightly opened for the word to be shared.

Miracle after miracle has taken place in their life there. Prior to his going, John had had a threatened detached retina with great pressure building up in his eye; there was a possibility of loss of sight. Such a traumatic experience would have caused a person with less commitment, a more timid soul, to call off this year-long journey. But not John and Jo. In a recent letter, they talked about life there.

> "Shang de" (that's Chinese for the God) has blessed our every step. One miracle after another made it possible for us to get here, and still we're carried in the palm of His hand. Daughter Mary Minor suggested we read the twenty-third Psalm six times a day, which we have joyously done. And the verse, "You prepare a table before me in the presence of my enemies; / You anoint my head with oil; / My cup runs over" (v. 5) so well describes how God cares for His own. It seems as though every one of the three million people in Xi'an has heard how God provided a doctor in this provincial city to make my eye pressure better and how the doctor was not only an ophthalmologist, but she had recently returned from a year-and-a-half training in New York City with a specialty in retina. "My cup runs over" in that she is very kind and takes my matter very personally. I better understand what the psalmist meant by "for His name's sake." God seems to be saying, "I did not bring you over here to abandon you. I will glorify Myself in You." Please pray we will not get in the way, and will let Him glorify His name.

You shall eat in haste," verse 11 continues. They did not know when the signal would be given or when it would be time to depart. At any moment they might be called to rise and go out of the land of bondage. Doesn't this suggest a style for the Christian? Always be ready. We don't know when the trumpet shall sound and the call of judgment be sent forth across the earth.

The call is to *"eat in haste,"* to live each day as though the Lord might return on that day.

Unleavened Bread and Bitter Herbs

The instruction was that the lamb was to be eaten *"with unleavened bread and with bitter herbs* (v. 8). The significance of bitter herbs is not explained here, but later it would remind the Israelites of their bitter experience as slaves. Also, it would be the sign of repentance and sorrow over the breaking of God's law.

In the later celebrations of the Feast of the Passover, the Israelites would eat unleavened bread for seven days. The instruction was stern: *"For whoever eats leavened bread from the first day until the seventh day, that person shall be cut off from Israel"* (v. 15).

In Scripture, leaven symbolizes evil; so the lesson taught here is of vital importance. The bread of our life must be unleavened. That is, we must separate ourselves from all that which is repugnant to God in His holiness. We cannot have communion with Christ when our lives are leavened with sin.

Unleavened bread played a uniquely sacred role in Israel's sacramental life, a role dependent upon the removal of evil (leaven) from the bread associated with various worship and ceremonial acts. In addition to the Feast of Unleavened Bread, it was also used at sacrificial meals such as the ritual peace offerings (Lev. 2:4–5), the consecration of the priesthood (Exod. 29:2, 23), the peace offering of a Nazarite (Num. 6:15). Not only was unleavened bread to be eaten, all leaven was to be removed from their houses. Later in Judaism, a very specific list of items indicated what should be removed from the house during the Passover time.

In the New Testament, Paul picks up on this image to give us direction for life: *"Therefore purge out the old leaven, that you may be a new lump, since you truly are unleavened. For indeed Christ, our Passover, was sacrificed for us. Therefore let us keep the feast, not with old leaven, nor with the leaven of malice and wickedness, but with the unleavened bread of sincerity and truth"* (1 Cor. 5:7–8).

Just As the Lord Commanded

This section closes with the response of Israel: *"Then the children of Israel went away and did so; just as the Lord had commanded Moses and Aaron, so they did"* (v. 28).

Faith is a personal thing, but it's also a matter of the community. If either fails to do *just as the Lord . . . commanded,"* fellowship is broken, and life with God is interrupted.

The temptation to be inactive about matters of faith is a strong one, and perhaps universal. C. S. Lewis, the great English writer and Christian, first came to prominence in our country with a book called *The Screwtape Letters.* These were imaginary letters from a devil to one of his representatives on earth. In one letter the devil gave advice on how to handle a person who was a prospective follower of Christ: "The great thing is to prevent his doing anything. . . . Let him do anything but act. No amount of piety in his imagination and affections will harm us if we can keep it out of his will. . . . The more often he feels without acting, the less he will be able ever to act, and, in the long run, the less he will be able to feel."[6]

Faith which is denied in practice soon erodes. The call, always, is to do *"just as the Lord . . . commanded."*

PASSOVER REGULATIONS

12:43 And the LORD said to Moses and Aaron, "This *is* the ordinance of the Passover: No foreigner shall eat it.

44 "But every man's servant who is bought for money, when you have circumcised him, then he may eat it.

45 "A sojourner and a hired servant shall not eat it.

46 "In one house it shall be eaten; you shall not carry any of the flesh outside the house, nor shall you break one of its bones.

47 "All the congregation of Israel shall keep it.

48 "And when a stranger dwells with you *and wants* to keep the Passover to the LORD, let all his males be circumcised, and then let him come near and keep it; and he shall be as a native of the land. For no uncircumcised person shall eat it.

49 "One law shall be for the native-born and for the stranger who dwells among you.'

50 Thus all the children of Israel did; as the LORD commanded Moses and Aaron, so they did.

51 And it came to pass, on that very same day, that
the LORD brought the children of Israel out of the land
of Egypt according to their armies.

Exod. 12:43–51

The Passover was to be a distinctively Israelite celebration. No foreigner, sojourner, or hired servant could participate in it. Circumcised slaves who had been purchased could share in the meal, but
no uncircumcised person could participate in it. This meant that
strangers among the Israelites who wanted to observe the Passover
were required to submit to circumcision.

Passover is still observed each year in Jewish homes and is their
most important home festival. It is celebrated for eight days (seven
days by reformed Jews) during March or April. The big point to be
noted here is that the distinction between those who might or
might not partake of the Passover was based on religious rather
than racial or ethnic grounds. Participation in the feast was dependent upon whether a person was fully identified with Israel
through circumcision, not upon whether that person was of "foreign" extraction.

This priority of circumcision is grounded in the fact that it was the
external sign of the covenant relationship. Later on, "circumcision of
the heart" (Rom. 2:29) was to be the identifying mark of those who
followed Yahweh.

DEDICATION OF FIRSTBORN

13:1 Then the LORD spoke to Moses, saying,

2 "Consecrate to Me all the firstborn, whatever
opens the womb among the children of Israel, *both* of
man and beast; it is Mine."

3 And Moses said to the people: "Remember this
day in which you went out of Egypt, out of the house
of bondage; for by strength of hand the LORD brought
you out of this *place*. No leavened bread shall be
eaten.

4 "On this day you are going out, in the month
Abib.

5 "And it shall be, when the LORD brings you into the land of the Canaanites and the Hittites and the Amorites and the Hivites and the Jebusites, which He swore to your fathers to give you, a land flowing with milk and honey, that you shall keep this service in this month.

6 "Seven days you shall eat unleavened bread, and on the seventh day *there shall be* a feast to the LORD.

7 "Unleavened bread shall be eaten seven days. And no leavened bread shall be seen among you, nor shall leaven be seen among you in all your quarters.

8 "And you shall tell your son in that day, saying, '*This is done* because of what the LORD did for me when I came up from Egypt.'

9 "It shall be as a sign to you on your hand and as a memorial between your eyes, that the LORD's law may be in your mouth; for with a strong hand the LORD has brought you out of Egypt.

10 "You shall therefore keep this ordinance in its season from year to year.

11 "And it shall be, when the LORD brings you into the land of the Canaanites, as He swore to you and your fathers, and gives it to you,

12 "that you shall set apart to the LORD all that open the womb, that is, every firstborn that comes from an animal which you have; the males *shall be* the LORD's.

13 "But every firstborn of a donkey you shall redeem with a lamb; and if you will not redeem *it*, then you shall break its neck. And all the firstborn of man among your sons you shall redeem.

14 "So it shall be, when your son asks you in time to come, saying, 'What *is* this?' that you shall say to him, 'By strength of hand the LORD brought us out of Egypt, out of the house of bondage.

15 'And it came to pass, when Pharaoh was stubborn about letting us go, that the LORD killed all the firstborn in the land of Egypt, both the firstborn of man and the firstborn of beast. Therefore I sacrifice

to the LORD all males that open the womb, but all the
firstborn of my sons I redeem.'

16 'It shall be as a sign on your hand and as front-
lets between your eyes, for by strength of hand the
LORD brought us out of Egypt."

Exod. 13:1–16

In this passage, Moses reminds the people that after they escape
from bondage and enter the promised land, they are to continue this
practice of Passover celebration *"because of what the Lord did for me
when I came up from Egypt."* This word is to be passed from generation to generation *"as a sign . . . and as a memorial"* before their
eyes, *"that the Lord's law may be in your mouth; for with a strong hand
the Lord has brought you out of Egypt"* (v. 9).

The section begins with a new commandment from the Lord:
*"Consecrate to Me all the firstborn, whatever opens the womb among the
children of Israel, both of man and beast; it is Mine"* (v. 2).

At the time death was being visited upon the firstborn of the
Egyptians, Moses was saying to the Israelites, "Your firstborn belongs to God." F. B. Huey, Jr., reminds us that "the firstborn occupied a place of special privilege among ancient Semites. Many of
them believed that the firstborn belonged to the deity and had to
be sacrificed to Him; child sacrifice was widely practiced and was
not unknown in early Israel (Gen. 22:2–3; Judg. 11:34–39; 2 Sam.
21:8–9)."

In the Old Testament, "firstborn" (defined as that which first
opens the womb) is most frequently used to designate the eldest son.
His privileges and responsibilities included succession to the head-
ship of the family, and responsibility for the continuation and well-
being of the family. He received preferential treatment (Gen. 43:33),
a double portion of the family inheritance (Deut. 21:17), and the
family blessing (Gen. 27:1–4, 35–37).[7]

In Israel, the firstborn now had a special place—the firstborn was
to be dedicated to God. While the firstborn animals were to be sacrificed to the Lord, the firstborn son was to be redeemed. This was an
important reminder that human sacrifice was never sanctioned by
God (Deut. 18:10; Lev. 18:21; 20:2–5).

The Israelites themselves did sacrifice their children, even as did
their pagan neighbors. Yet the prophets spoke out angrily against

this abhorrent practice (cf. Isa. 57:4–5; Jer. 7:30–34; 19:4–9; Ezek. 16:20–21).

The price of redemption for a firstborn is not given in Exodus 13:13, but in Numbers 18:15–16 the price is fixed at five shekels of silver. Sometimes, instead of redeeming a son in that fashion, Israelite parents devoted their son to the Lord for service as a priest. This was the case with Samuel (1 Sam. 1:11, 22).

For us, not just our firstborn, but all our children should be dedicated to God. It is the role of parents to be priests to their children, guiding them in making their lives sacrificial offerings to the Lord. That is best done as the parent, himself or herself, demonstrates that sacrificial offering.

NOTES

1. Arthur W. Pink, *Gleanings in Exodus* (Chicago: Moody Press, 1981), p. 93.

2. Charles H. Spurgeon, "The Sacred Love Token," *Sermons of C. H. Spurgeon* (New York: Funk & Wagnalls, n.d.), p. 247.

3. Pink, *Gleanings*, p. 93.

4. Ibid.

5. Roy L. Honeycutt, Jr., *The Broadman Bible Commentary* (Nashville: Broadman Press, 1969), 1:356.

6. C. S. Lewis, *The Screwtape Letters* (New York: Macmillan, 1960), pp. 68–69.

7. F. B. Huey, Jr., *Exodus: A Study Guide Commentary* (Grand Rapids: Zondervan, 1977), p. 61.

CHAPTER EIGHT

The Crossing of the Red Sea

Exodus 13:17–14:31

An eight-year-old boy was reporting to his folks at Sunday dinner what he had learned at church school that morning. "Boy, was it exciting!" he exclaimed to his parents. "Moses organized all the Hebrews into a resistance group. They planned real carefully, and finally they broke loose from their Egyptian slave masters. They moved as fast as they could toward Canaan. They drove every kind of vehicle they could get hold of—jeeps, half-tracks, sixteen-wheelers—everything.

"But Pharaoh's army wouldn't quit. They tracked down the Israelites with color radar. They exploded missiles all around them and shot at them from jet planes in the sky. When Moses and his people reached the Red Sea, they thought they were finished. There was raging water in front of them and Egyptians behind them. Suddenly, though, the Corps of Engineers came to the rescue and built a pontoon bridge over the Red Sea and all the fugitives crossed over to freedom. Then, just as Pharaoh's forces were about to go across the bridge, the Hebrews blew it up with dynamite and saved all the people. Then they lived happily ever after in the promised land. What a terrific story!"

The youngster's mom and dad were more than just a little concerned about their child's overactive imagination. "Is that really what they told you at church this morning?" they inquired. "Well, not exactly," their son replied. "But if I told you what they told me, you'd never believe it!"

The little boy may have been right, yet this dramatic story of the crossing of the Red Sea has stood on its own for thousands of years. In Jewish history, the Exodus is paramount. It is the high tide of

God's power moving on the ocean of Israel's corporate history. Their crossing of the Red Sea, escaping from the death clutches of Pharaoh's army, was a pivotal event. In the previous chapter, we said that the Passover is to Jews what Calvary is to Christians. Likewise, there is a sense in which the crossing of the Red Sea is to Jews what Easter is to Christians.

It is this pivotal event we will examine in this chapter.

THE WILDERNESS WAY

13:17 Then it came to pass, when Pharaoh had let the people go, that God did not lead them by way of the land of the Philistines, although that *was* near; for God said, "Lest perhaps the people change their minds when they see war, and return to Egypt."
18 So God led the people around *by* way of the wilderness of the Red Sea. And the children of Israel went up in orderly ranks out of the land of Egypt.
19 And Moses took the bones of Joseph with him, for he had placed the children of Israel under solemn oath, saying, "God will surely visit you, and you shall carry up my bones from here with you."
20 So they took their journey from Succoth and camped in Etham at the edge of the wilderness.
21 And the LORD went before them by day in a pillar of cloud to lead the way, and by night in a pillar of fire to give them light, so as to go by day and night.
22 He did not take away the pillar of cloud by day or the pillar of fire by night *from* before the people.
Exod. 13:17–22

When Pharaoh let the people go, God did not lead them by way of the land of the Philistines, which would have been very near. He had other things in mind for them, things necessary for their total salvation. There were two reasons for the decision to move southeastward across Sinai, rather than along the Mediterranean Sea. First, had Israel followed the traditional coastal route, they would have encountered numerous Egyptian fortifications. That's why we see this word in the text, *"Lest perhaps the people change their minds when they see war."*

The second reason centered in Moses' determination to lead the people to the mountain of God, in response to the call of God in the burning bush experience. God had said to him, "I will certainly be with you. And this shall be a sign to you that I have sent you: When you have brought the people out of Egypt, you shall serve God on this mountain" (3:12). He had not secured Israel's release soon enough for them to celebrate the Festival of Passover at the mountain of God, so they celebrated the feast in Egypt. Still, he was determined to bring Israel to the holy mountain.

So he led them around by way of the wilderness toward the Red Sea. They went *in orderly ranks* out of Egypt, *and Moses took the bones of Joseph with him* (v. 19). What a marvelous little detail that carries huge meaning! Moses remembered to take the bones of Joseph. This was the fulfillment of a pledge that Joseph had gotten from the Israelites before his death (Gen. 50:25).

Joseph knew, even in his lifetime, that Egypt was not the permanent abode of God's people. He remembered the covenant—the promise of the land of Canaan that God had given to Abraham, and renewed with his grandfather Isaac, and then his father Jacob. That was the land in which Joseph desired to be buried. Finally, when the Exodus was coming to a close and the Israelites had entered Canaan and occupied it under Joshua, he was laid to rest at Shechem (Josh. 24:32).

It is a beautiful affirmation of how God moves even in the most minute fashion to honor the covenant that He made. It's also a confirmation of the faith of so many, personified in the faith of Joseph who wanted to be taken to the land God had promised His people—even if he could only be taken after death.

Here is confirmation of the confidence that God fulfills His promises, not only to one man—but to all of Abraham's descendants. We can count on it. God is faithful; God's covenant is dependable.

"And the Lord went before them by day in a pillar of cloud to lead the way, and by night in a pillar of fire to give them light, so as to go by day and night" (v. 21).

So, from the very beginning, the central truth is underscored: God led Israel in a unique and personal way. The living presence of God became a vital experience. This passage speaks of more than a cloud and a fire that were with them constantly. It speaks of a divine providence that overshadows and guides God's people in every generation, in every wilderness through which we must go.

In 1984, Louise Degrafinreid of Branden, Tennessee, astounded the nation when she persuaded an escaped convict from a Tennessee prison to surrender. The prisoner, brandishing a gun, surprised Louise's husband, Nathan, outside their modest home and forced him inside at gunpoint. Louise was not afraid of the gun. Amazingly, this grandmotherly woman with a confidence that had to be from God, began to talk to the prisoner and convinced him that he should put his gun down while she fixed him some breakfast. Surprisingly, the prisoner responded. She spoke to him about her faith in Jesus, and how a young man like him could have a better life if he accepted Jesus also.

When the breakfast was ready, they had grace together and Louise prayed for the young man. They ate together, and by a miraculous working of the Spirit, the young man telephoned authorities, and before long, he was on his way back to a Tennessee prison.

Responding to questions about that, Louise Degrafinreid talked about the confidence that was hers in God—how she trusted God as ultimate authority, and therefore could overcome her fears. She was secure in the "pillar of cloud by day" and the "pillar of fire by night" that guided her life.

It is everlastingly true. The cloud and the fire do not depart. The guiding and sustaining presence is ours always if we put our trust in God. The pillar of cloud by day and the pillar of fire by night were the constant presence that guided Israel throughout their journey.

WHAT TO DO WHEN YOU ARE IN A FIX

14:1 Now the LORD spoke to Moses, saying:

2 "Speak to the children of Israel, that they turn and camp before Pi Hahiroth, between Migdol and the sea, opposite Baal Zephon; you shall camp before it by the sea.

3 "For Pharaoh will say of the children of Israel, 'They *are* bewildered by the land; the wilderness has closed them in.'

4 "Then I will harden Pharaoh's heart, so that he will pursue them; and I will gain honor over Pharaoh

and over all his army, that the Egyptians may know that I *am* the LORD." And they did so.

5 Now it was told the king of Egypt that the people had fled, and the heart of Pharaoh and his servants was turned against the people; and they said, "Why have we done this, that we have let Israel go from serving us?"

6 So he made ready his chariot and took his people with him.

7 Also, he took six hundred choice chariots, and all the chariots of Egypt with captains over every one of them.

8 And the LORD hardened the heart of Pharaoh king of Egypt, and he pursued the children of Israel; and the children of Israel went out with boldness.

9 So the Egyptians pursued them, all the horses *and* chariots of Pharaoh, his horsemen and his army, and overtook them camping by the sea beside Pi Hahiroth, before Baal Zephon.

10 And when Pharaoh drew near, the children of Israel lifted their eyes, and behold, the Egyptians marched after them. So they were very afraid, and the children of Israel cried out to the LORD.

11 Then they said to Moses, "Because *there were* no graves in Egypt, have you taken us away to die in the wilderness? Why have you so dealt with us, to bring us up out of Egypt?

12 *Is* this not the word that we told you in Egypt, saying, 'Let us alone that we may serve the Egyptians?' For *it would have been* better for us to serve the Egyptians than that we should die in the wilderness."

13 And Moses said to the people, "Do not be afraid. Stand still, and see the salvation of the LORD, which He will accomplish for you today. For the Egyptians whom you see today, you shall see again no more forever.

14 "The LORD will fight for you, and you shall hold your peace."

15 And the LORD said to Moses, "Why do you cry to Me? Tell the children of Israel to go forward.

16 "But lift up your rod, and stretch out your hand

over the sea and divide it. And the children of Israel
shall go on dry *ground* through the midst of the sea.

17 "And I indeed will harden the hearts of the
Egyptians, and they shall follow them. So I will gain
honor over Pharaoh and over all his army, his chariots, and his horsemen.

18 "Then the Egyptians shall know that I *am* the
LORD, when I have gained honor for Myself over
Pharaoh, his chariots, and his horsemen."

Exod. 14:1-18

It's always good to review the story because it is so revealing of
human nature. Pharaoh, fickle man that he was, was bent on power.
Though the plagues had eventually gotten to him, especially the
death angel claiming the firstborn of the land, still he had not
learned his lesson. Though he thought he had had enough of God's
intervention in his life—to the point that he summoned Moses and
Aaron in the middle of the night and commanded them to take the
people and leave the land and go serve the Lord—still his stubborn
trust in self prevailed. God knew that was the way it would be. He
had directed Moses as to where the children of Israel were to camp,
saying that Pharaoh would think, *"They are bewildered by the land;
the wilderness has closed them in"* (v. 3). And again, we have that
word that can be confusing, *"Then I will harden Pharaoh's heart, so
that he will pursue them; and I will gain honor over Pharaoh and over
all his army, that the Egyptians may know that I am the Lord"* (v. 4).

Remember our earlier discussion of the hardening of Pharaoh's
heart? Here it is again. When Israel had gone from the land, Pharaoh
and his servants changed their mind. *"Why have we done this, that we
have let Israel go from serving us?"* It's hard to give up a place of
privilege and position. It was impossible for Pharaoh and the Egyptians to give up having all those servants and slaves around to fulfill
their every need. So, the army of Pharaoh made itself ready, and
with all its leading officers and with its mighty chariots, went in hot
pursuit of the Israelites.

Here we come to a recurring practice on the part of Israel—the
loss of faith, the murmuring against Moses, and the murmuring
against God. When the Israelites saw the dust of Pharaoh's army
coming, naturally they were terrified. They turned on Moses and
accused him of bringing them into the wilderness to die. They

reminded him that they had told him in Egypt to leave them alone. How veiled were their eyes, how dull their minds! For them, slavery in Egypt was preferable to death in the wilderness—and those were the only alternatives they could see.

Throughout the forty years that lay ahead, Moses and God would hear this murmuring complaint of the Israelites, who would often sink into despair, constantly vascillating between trust and doubt. Two opposing positions are reflected in the attitude of the Israelite people throughout their history: a rebellious people versus a faithful people committed to the covenant God.

Time and time again, some of them followed by faith while others rebelled against God; some trusted, and others did not. They had not heard a New Testament lesson they sorely needed, that the best remedy for a complaining spirit is thanksgiving: "In everything give thanks; for this is the will of God in Jesus Christ for you" (1 Thess. 5:18).

Rather than rebuking the people for their murmurings and lack of faith, Moses sounded a note that has given direction to people ever since: *Do not be afraid. Stand still, and see the salvation of the Lord, which He will accomplish for you today"* (v. 13).

Here is direction for any of us when we are in a fix. There's a saying that describes the sort of experience Israel was having. We talk about being "between a rock and a hard place." Certainly that metaphor is descriptive of many of life's dilemmas. The same thing is expressed in the picturesque phrase, "between the devil and the deep blue sea."

The Israelites were there, almost literally. Pharaoh (the devil) and his army were in hot pursuit and the sea was raging before them. They were between a rock and a hard place—in a fix. What were they to do? God taught them through Moses. And He teaches us.

We can identify with the Hebrews, can't we? Because we've all experienced it—being in a fix, between a rock and a hard place. If we haven't experienced it thus far, we will. Maybe not to the degree of the Hebrews, caught between the Egyptians and the Red Sea, but we all know what it's like to be in a fix nonetheless.

What God sought to teach the Israelites, He teaches us. His lessons are profound and redemptive. Let's look at them.

Don't Fear

Through Moses, God's word to the Hebrews was *"Do not be afraid"*—don't fear.

Did you hear the story of the 747 jetliner taxiing down the runway, with the passengers all buckled up for takeoff? A voice came over the speakers in the plane's cabin, "Good morning, ladies and gentlemen, this is your captain speaking. Welcome aboard Flight 22 for London's Heathrow Airport. We will climb to a cruising altitude of 30,000 feet and will travel at an air speed of 660 miles per hour. Our flight plan will take us across Canada, Greenland, Iceland, and over the tip of Ireland. Our flying time will be about nine hours. As soon as we are airborne the flight attendants will be serving you breakfast. We'll take off . . . just as soon as I can get up the nerve!"

To be human is to know fear, to be scared. So, you can imagine how skeptically those words *"Do not be afraid"* were received by the Israelites. Can you feel with them? There they were on the brink of a raging Red Sea. They looked back and Pharaoh's army was drawing near; the chariots and marching soldiers were pressing in upon them. And the Scripture says in remarkable understatement: *"So they were very afraid, and the children of Israel cried out to the Lord"* (v. 10). Of course they were afraid. It was hard, almost impossible for them to hear God's word through Moses: *"Do not be afraid."*

As difficult as it may be for us to hear, God's word to us when we're in a fix is don't fear; keep your eyes open, because I'm going to show you My salvation.

Fear plays havoc with our lives. It leads us to *find fault,* and *falsely condemn.* That's what happened to the Hebrews. They cried out against the Lord and against Moses. *"Because there were no graves in Egypt, have you taken us away to die in the wilderness? Why [did] you . . . bring us up out of Egypt? . . . It would have been better for us to serve the Egyptians than that we should die in the wilderness"* (vv. 11–12).

Not only does fear lead us to find fault and falsely condemn, it *blinds us to a healthy perspective.* In the midst of fear we forget all that God has done. That's what happened to the Hebrews. They had forgotten the plagues; they had forgotten how they had been miraculously delivered from death; they had forgotten how God was guiding them now. And so it is with us. Fear blanks our mind to what God does, and blinds us to what He is seeking to do.

Fear also *paralyzes our spirits, our wills.* When we give in to fear, we are incapacitated. We don't think, and we can't act. We're frozen in our dilemma.

So the word is, "Don't fear."

Stand Still

The second direction God gave to the Israelites through Moses was *"Stand still"* (v. 13).

Another translation of this admonition is "stand firm." Both meanings are in what Moses is trying to communicate. When we are in a fix, we need to do both; we need to stand firm, and we need to stand still.

When we're in a fix, there comes a time when we simply need to *stand firm* and wait for *"the salvation of the Lord"* (v. 13).

I never will forget a visit to Estonia a few years ago, and a man named Alexander Koom. Alexander Koom is the father, the patriarch, of the Methodist church in Estonia. During the time of Stalin, when the church was being savagely oppressed and persecuted, governmental leaders came to him one day and told him that the Methodist church had to either be dissolved or be united with another denomination. Alexander Koom refused to agree to that, and the officer of the government told him that it would be easier for him to give in and merge the church with another than to have the government force the church to close. Brother Koom stood firm and refused to give in.

The government official pressed him, "What difference will it make whether you take the easy way without raising a lot of questions and allow the church to be merged, or we force the issue and banish the church?"

Brother Koom painted a beautiful picture in his response. "There's all the difference in the world. If you give me a rope and tell me to hang myself and I do so, then I'm responsible. But if you take a rope and hang me, you're responsible."

Brother Koom stood firm. They sent him into Siberian exile for a twenty-five year sentence. While he was in prison, the church grew even stronger because of the powerful witness of his faith. He was willing to risk imprisonment, even death, to stand firm for his faith. And after five years, he was miraculously released from prison.

The situation may not be so dramatic for us, yet when forces are pressing in upon us—when we can't see any evidence of God's work in our lives or any light at the end of the dark tunnel through which we are passing, when we're in a fix—we need to remember this word of the Lord through Moses: Stand firm.

Stand still! There is an added nuance in this translation—just stand still, wait awhile.

One of our problems is that we want to act too quickly. When we're in a fix, we look frantically for the nearest escape. Many times we act foolishly, doing things we shouldn't do, taking advice we shouldn't take, spending our energy in futile efforts. We need to stand still, to wait awhile.

That's one of the most difficult calls in our lives, because most of us want to act. We don't want to wait. I've discovered that it's only in being still, in waiting for a while, that I gain the perspective I need before taking action in whatever trying circumstance I find myself.

When we're confronted with a problem, most of us amplify that problem, making it much bigger than it is by anticipating the worst that could come from it. So, we add depression to our dilemma. Whereas if we would stand still and wait awhile, we would gain a healthy perspective to deal with our problems in a healing, redemptive, wholesome way.

It's a shame that many people don't learn this lesson until they are forced to learn it. Yet when they do learn it, their witness is worth listening to. I had a minister friend out in California who died of cancer. About a month after receiving the diagnosis that the cancer was inoperable and probably would not respond very well to treatment, he wrote a letter to his congregation. He shared this letter with me.

> Dear Christian Friends:
>
> It has taken me fifty-one years of living, and thirty-three years of Christian life to learn the real meaning of Jesus' words in the Sermon on the Mount, "Do not worry about tomorrow."
>
> I've been a very ambitious man, and I've abhorred the mediocre. Always within me has been the desire to excel. And living this way, I've been impatient and anxious, inattentive and often unkind. My goals have been long-distance and compulsive. In

167

consequence I've given less than my best to the person in front of me because I was thinking way ahead to the plans and goals beyond.

Now all is different. My anxieties are gone. I have no idea how long I shall live, but, then, there is today. Each day is meaning more to me than ever before. Each person I meet can have all there is of me for those moments we're together. I may not get as much done from here on out, but life is far more peaceful. I have at last come to accept these words of Jesus as being for me, "Do not worry about your life."

My friend had heard God's word, *"Stand still."*

Go Forward

The third word of the Lord to us when we are in a fix is to *"go forward"* (v. 15).

One of my heroes, and for eight years my bishop in Southern California, was Gerald Kennedy. He was the most remarkable preacher I've ever known. He concluded his autobiography, *While I'm on My Feet*, with the observation that "we can assume only two positions in the presence of God. One is on our knees, saying, 'God, be merciful to me a sinner!'; the other is on our feet, saying, 'Here am I! Send me.'" [1]

What a picture of the Christian life—on our knees, or on our feet, in response to God's call; being still, holding our peace before Him to gain perspective and strength, or going forward at His command. These two positions in the presence of God are put clearly in verses 14 and 15 of our text. *"The Lord will fight for you, and you shall hold your peace. And the Lord said to Moses, 'Why do you cry to Me? Tell the children of Israel to go forward.'"*

Sometimes we must stand still before we go forward, but we can't stay on our knees forever. God's ultimate call is to go forward.

You really can't get the full impact of this command unless you put yourself into the picture.

The Israelites are bewildered. Can you imagine their bewilderment? The Red Sea is stretching out before them, high mountain ranges are on either side, and Pharaoh's army is pressing in from behind. They seem to have only one choice—to surrender to Pharaoh and a fate almost worse than death. How disillusioned about the whole affair they are becoming. Our Scripture indicates that. Better to be in slavery, they conclude, than to endure the trying anxieties of freedom, the frustration and despair of this arduous exodus.

The alternative Moses gives them is a strange one: *"Go forward!"* How astonished they must have been. How could they go forward? The Red Sea was stretching out before them.

The story of the Red Sea is not recorded simply to tell us what happened to the Hebrews long ago. It is to teach us, also. At that point, history made a new beginning, and everything had to be reevaluated in light of it. There in that mighty act of God and the response of Moses and the Hebrew people, faith was anchored, and a new people was born. As they face an apparently impossible barrier, they are told to *"go forward."*

Here, we come to one of the toughest lessons any of us will ever learn. Prayer is essential, prayer is good, but unless we rise from our knees to obediently follow the Lord, prayer is a farce.

This is the lesson: It is only as we take that step forward, only as we act obediently, that the power we need to do what God calls us to do is given. God's power is given to us in proportion to our obedience. That power is given, not ahead of time, but only as we need it. Likewise, light for our path. The light is given only as we need the light. God doesn't shine the light a mile down the road. He shines it far enough ahead for us to take the next step.

Suppose that Moses had not believed that divine intervention would happen? God had commanded him, *"Stretch out your hand over the sea,"* so that a path will be made for them. Just as He promised, it happens. A strong east wind arises and drives back the waters of the sea, even drying out the land for the crossing.

Now here's the point. Many a miracle has never occurred because there was no one who believed it would. You can't find anywhere in the Scripture a record of God's people walking with Him and seeking His will and being told to retreat. He always calls us to go forward. Someone has suggested that the waters did not part until the Israelites began to press forward, putting their feet into the water. Now that's stretching the point a bit, but the right idea is there. God provides His miracles as we expect those miracles; He gives us power according to our obedience; and He lights our path as we move ahead.

A preacher of another generation has given us the most succinct guideline that I know for our journeying through life in faith. Go forward, he said: (1) from the point to which God has conducted us; (2) along the path God bids us take; (3) by the light which God affords; (4) with the staff which God provides; and (5) to the land which God prepares. That is powerful advice.

The Israelites should have known, as we should know, that our presence here at all is a miracle of God and that our way forward will be as providentially guided as has been our journey thus far. The child of God is a traveler, a pilgrim, and the Christian should never pitch his tent in the same place twice. Old things get further and further behind, recede in significance, but new things continue emerging.

The poet Theodore Roethke wrote a line that is packed with meaning: "I learn by going where I have to go." How true. That's the way the Christian and the church learn, by going where we have to go because God is calling us to go there. His call is clear: Don't be afraid; stand still; and go forward!

CROSSING THE RED SEA

14:19 And the Angel of God, who went before the camp of Israel, moved and went behind them; and the pillar of cloud went from before them and stood behind them.

20 So it came between the camp of the Egyptians and the camp of Israel. Thus it was a cloud and darkness *to the one,* and it gave light by night *to the other,* so that the one did not come near the other all that night.

21 Then Moses stretched out his hand over the sea; and the LORD caused the sea to go *back* by a strong east wind all that night, and made the sea into dry *land,* and the waters were divided.

22 So the children of Israel went into the midst of the sea on the dry *ground,* and the waters *were* a wall to them on their right hand and on their left.

23 And the Egyptians pursued and went after them into the midst of the sea, all Pharaoh's horses, his chariots, and his horsemen.

24 Now it came to pass, in the morning watch, that the LORD looked down upon the army of the Egyptians

through the pillar of fire and cloud, and He troubled the army of the Egyptians.

25 And He took off their chariot wheels, so that they drove them with difficulty; and the Egyptians said, "Let us flee from the face of Israel, for the LORD fights for them against the Egyptians."

26 Then the LORD said to Moses, "Stretch out your hand over the sea, that the waters may come back upon the Egyptians, on their chariots, and on their horsemen."

27 And Moses stretched out his hand over the sea; and when the morning appeared, the sea returned to its full depth, while the Egyptians were fleeing into it. So the LORD overthrew the Egyptians in the midst of the sea.

28 Then the waters returned and covered the chariots, the horsemen, *and* all the army of Pharaoh that came into the sea after them. Not so much as one of them remained.

29 But the children of Israel had walked on dry *land* in the midst of the sea, and the waters *were* a wall to them on their right hand and on their left.

30 So the LORD saved Israel that day out of the hand of the Egyptians, and Israel saw the Egyptians dead on the seashore.

31 Thus Israel saw the great work which the LORD had done in Egypt; so the people feared the LORD, and believed the LORD and His servant Moses.

Exod. 14:19–31

At the brink of the Red Sea, just prior to what is to be one of the mightiest acts of God in history, the transition is a very enlightening one. *"The Angel of God,"* which literally means *"messenger of God,"* who previously had gone before the camp of Israel, *"moved and went behind them."* Also, *"the pillar of cloud went from before them and stood behind them."* It was as though God was acting in another very specific way to give witness of His presence to the Hebrews.

Then comes this remarkable word in verse 20: *"So it* [the pillar of cloud] *came between the camp of the Egyptians and the camp of Israel. Thus it was a cloud and darkness to the one, and it gave light by night to the other, so that the one did not come near the other all that night."*

Isn't it remarkable how a thing can be a blessing to God's people while it may be a curse to others?

We all know the story well. Moses extends his rod, the waters of the sea separate, the Israelites walk through on dry land. Then when the Egyptians in hot pursuit come into the midst of the sea, the waters close in, and Pharaoh's horses and charioteers are all drowned.

Nothing in Israel's history provides a more remarkable example of God's intervention on their behalf. It interests me that even a so-called liberal scholar like Martin Noth comes to this event and says, "It is extremely questionable whether it is appropriate to look for a natural parallel for the events."[2]

What happened is rather clear. The water completely disappeared from the middle of a sea of perhaps quite moderate size, only to reappear later in the same fashion. It disappeared in order that the people of Israel might be delivered, and it reappeared in order that God's judgment might come upon Pharaoh.

In a situation of impossible desperation, God acted mightily to deliver His people.

We might appropriate the meaning of this event by looking at four practical lessons here.

None of Us Escapes the Trying Circumstances of Life

How vividly this has been brought home to me. A few months preceding this writing, my dearest friend, Buford Dickinson, died of cancer just six weeks after the diagnosis was made. It has been one of the most painful times in my life. Buford had always been a picture of health. He worked at being healthy in as intentional a way as anybody else I know. He had been my dearest friend. We've shared so much of our lives together. Now, at fifty-one, he is dead.

It happens all the time. None of us escapes the trying circumstances of life. I see it in people who are reaching the prime of their career, or just reaching retirement, filled with anticipation of dreams yet to come. Then, a malignancy—often quiet and lethal—appears in the body, and everything stops dead in its tracks.

And not just cancer, but other diseases and tragedies can invade our lives and bring everything to a jolting halt. And it can happen in a low-key manner as well as dramatically.

Most of us have lived long enough, or have had enough experience to affirm the truth: None of us is going to escape the trying circumstances of life. Somewhere along the way, a Red Sea is going to be stretching out before us, and a Pharaoh's army will be in hot pursuit.

In Times of Trial We Are Most Vulnerable

This is the second lesson. Put another way, the trying circumstances of life give Satan his greatest opportunity to divert us from our journey of faith. We even see this demonstrated in those closest to Jesus.

Look at what happened during the last week of Jesus' life. Boisterous, seemingly courageous Peter had jerked out his sword in the Garden of Gethsemane and cut a guard's ear off trying to protect the Master. Later, in the courtyard of Pilate's palace where Jesus was on trial, he denied that he ever knew Jesus. His own life was at stake, and denial was his way out.

We need always to remember that the power of sin in us is great. Satan never ceases to seek control of our lives. Habits that have been years in the making may be put aside by a transforming experience of Christ. Yet, these habits sometime have a residual hold on us. When we are on trial, when things become tough, and it seems as though we're not going to make it, we are tempted to turn back to those old ways for the false security they offer.

Walker Railey is the pastor of First Methodist Church in Dallas, Texas. The church is located in the heart of that exploding city. Walker says that one of the nicest things that has happened during the past few years has been the construction of the Dallas Museum of Art across the street from the church. In the museum's plaza, there is a huge piece of art by Rodin, called "The Gates of Hell." Taking his inspiration from Dante's *Inferno* and Michelangelo's "Last Judgment," the sculptor sought to depict the pathos of the human condition: our sufferings, struggles, despairs, temptations.

Shortly after the sculpture was set in place, a reporter called Walker to ask what it felt like to have "The Gates of Hell" across the street from the church. Walker was very perceptive, and thought quickly on his feet as he made his response. He told the reporter that the gates of hell have always been across the street from the church; that was not the museum's doing! Then, in sharing that with the congregation one Sunday morning, Walker said, "No matter which

173

door we exit today, we will see the gates of hell: always tempting us to love less than God demands, to live less than Christ expects, to be less than the church we were called to be and more like the world than we can afford to be." [3]

It's always true, isn't it? In life the choice is always before us: the wide gates of hell or the narrow gate of heaven. In our trying circumstances we are most vulnerable, and Satan takes advantage of our suffering and despair to divert us from the journey of faith through the narrow gate.

It happened over and over again with the Israelites as they fled the Egyptians and wandered in the wilderness prior to their arrival in the promised land. "Why did you bring us out here to die?" they groaned to Moses. Even though they had been in slavery there, they looked with longing eyes back to the security of Egypt, and they were confused and frustrated in their journey of faith.

We need to remember that no matter how trying the circumstance, we must resist the temptation to turn back to false supports. We must continue to trust in the Lord, knowing that while deliverance may not come today, deliverance *is* on the way. What God promised, He will provide. And that leads to a third lesson.

God Wants to Use All Circumstances for Our Good and God's Glory

Though it may be hard to grasp, we need to hang on to this truth: God wants to use all circumstances for our good and God's glory.

That was one of Alexander Solzhenitsyn's greatest discoveries in the Soviet gulag where he was a political prisoner. Like other prisoners, Solzhenitsyn worked in the fields. His days followed a pattern of back-breaking labor and slow starvation.

> One day the hopelessness became too much to bear. Solzhenitsyn felt no purpose in fighting on; his life would make no ultimate difference. Laying his shovel down, he walked slowly to a crude work-site bench. He knew at any moment a guard would order him up and, when he failed to respond, bludgeon him to death, probably with his own shovel. He'd seen it happen so many times.
>
> As he sat waiting, head down, he felt a presence. Slowly he lifted his eyes. Next to him sat an old man with a wrinkled,

174

utterly expressionless face. Hunching over, the man drew a stick through the sand at Solzhenitsyn's feet, deliberately tracing out the sign of the cross.

As Solzhenitsyn stared at that rough outline, his entire perspective shifted. He knew he was merely one man against the all-powerful Soviet Empire. Yet in that moment, he knew that the hope of all mankind was represented by that simple cross—and through its power, anything was possible. Solzhenitsyn slowly got up, picked up his shovel, and went back to work—not knowing that his writings on truth and freedom would one day inflame the whole world.[4]

But those writings have!

God wants to use all circumstances for our good and His glory. Solzhenitsyn discovered that and now he unequivocally thanks God for that prison experience.

In the Struggle between Good and Evil, Victory Is with God

Now we come to the final truth: In the struggle between good and evil, victory is with God. That's what Israel's miraculous crossing of the Red Sea teaches us.

Nothing is more obvious than the presence of evil in the universe. We may debate the *origin* of evil, but there's no question about the stark, grim, colossal *reality* of evil in the world—whatever its origin. Yet, there is a checkpoint against evil—a time when evil plays itself out, digs its own grave as it were, and God's righteousness and justice prevail.

The dramatic picture of this truth is seen in verse 30: *"And Israel saw the Egyptians dead on the seashore."* God demonstrated His power, parted the Red Sea, and His covenant people passed through on dry land. But when the Egyptians were in *"the midst of the sea,"* seeking to block the Hebrews' escape and return them to Pharaoh's bondage, God released the parted waters and the Egyptian army was drowned. When the Israelites looked back, all they could see was here and there a poor drowned body, beaten upon the seashore. This was a great moment for Israel, the end of a frightful period in their history, a joyous daybreak that had come at the end of a long night of oppressive captivity.

Now, the meaning of the story is not found in the drowning of the Egyptian soldiers. No one should rejoice at the death or defeat of another human being. Rather, the story symbolizes the death of evil—God's victory in the struggle between good and evil. That's the connection between Easter and Exodus, which we mentioned earlier. Easter gives universal and eternal meaning to the particular experience of Exodus. Here is God's ultimate act of both love and power, shattering the tomb, pulling out the fangs of death, announcing the triumph of eternal life.

I experienced it more powerfully than ever before in the death of my friend Buford, whom I mentioned earlier. I was in the room with Buford's wife, Jean, and her two children when Buford died. Of course it was painful, heart-wrenchingly painful. The day before, he had struggled to verbalize the meaning of our friendship, and only a little while before he died, the last word that he spoke was to Jean, telling her he loved her. It was painful, so painful—but oh, so meaningful—exactly as it should have been. Jean and the children and I were holding him in love as he died.

Buford loved to sing. When our families were together, we almost always gathered around the piano and sang those old gospel songs he and I grew up on back in Mississippi. I'm sure Jean was remembering that and a lot more. There in Buford's room, when we knew he had announced his own "it is finished," Jean said, "I feel like singing the doxology."

And we did—holding each other and holding Buford. It was the worst singing we've ever done, for our voices were cracking with tears, but it was the most meaningful singing we've ever done. And it was the most significant affirmation of faith in which I've ever participated: "Praise God from whom all blessings flow; / Praise Him, all creatures here below; / Praise Him above, ye heavenly host; / Praise Father, Son, and Holy Ghost."

No one can ever convince me that Buford was not singing with us. What were we saying? In the struggle between good and evil, victory is with God. Exodus and Easter were connected in the death room that day, and I'll never forget it. No wonder Moses closed this section of Scripture: *"Thus Israel saw the great work which the Lord had done in Egypt."*

NOTES

1. Gerald Kennedy, *While I'm on My Feet* (Nashville: Abingdon, 1963), p. 204.

2. Martin Noth, *Exodus, a Commentary*, Old Testament Library (Philadelphia: Westminster Press, 1962), p. 116.

3. Walker Railey, "Plundering the Egyptians" (sermon delivered at First Methodist Church, Dallas, TX, August 26, 1984).

4. Charles W. Colson, *Loving God* (Grand Rapids: Zondervan, 1983), p. 172.

CHAPTER NINE

The Gospel of Marah

Exodus 15:1–27

Somewhere along the way I heard a sermon entitled "Detours, Dead Ends, and Dry Holes." It was a dramatic and vivid account of Israel's wandering in the wilderness and the up-against-it-experiences they shared. The entire wandering was a kind of detour—a forty-year detour. Certainly the Red Sea was a dead end. Three days away from their deliverance through the Sea, the Israelites were threatened by thirst. They found bitter water in Marah and later, in Rephidim, no water at all.

So, it is a graphic picture: detours, dead ends, and dry holes. That captures the wilderness saga of the Israelites, and their response was a kind of seesaw in prevailing mood. At one time, they felt exhilarated, celebrating God's merciful deliverance. At another time, they were down in the mouth, murmuring, protesting to Moses, "Why is it you have brought us up out of Egypt, to kill us and our children?" (Exod. 17:3).

Songs Celebrating Victory

15:1 Then Moses and the children of Israel sang this
song to the LORD, and spoke, saying:
"I will sing to the LORD,
For He has triumphed gloriously!
The horse and its rider
He has thrown into the sea!
2 The Lord *is* my strength and song,
And He has become my salvation
He *is* my God, and I will praise Him;
My father's God, and I will exalt Him.

3 The LORD *is* a man of war;
   The LORD *is* His name.
4 Pharaoh's chariots and his army He has cast
     into the sea;
   His chosen captains also are drowned in the
     Red Sea.
5 The depths have covered them;
   They sank to the bottom like a stone.
6 Your right hand, O LORD, has become glorious
     in power;
   Your right hand, O LORD, has dashed the
     enemy in pieces.
7 And in the greatness of Your excellence
   You have overthrown those who rose against
     You;
   You sent forth Your wrath;
   It consumed them like stubble.
8 And with the blast of Your nostrils
   The waters were gathered together;
   The floods stood upright like a heap;
   The depths congealed in the heart of the sea.
9 The enemy said, 'I will pursue,
   I will overtake,
   I will divide the spoil;
   My desire shall be satisfied on them.
   I will draw my sword,
   My hand shall destroy them.'
10 You blew with Your wind,
   The sea covered them;
   They sank like lead in the mighty waters.
11 "Who *is* like You, O LORD, among the gods?
   Who *is* like You, glorious in holiness,
   Fearful in praises, doing wonders?
12 You stretched out Your right hand;
   The earth swallowed them.
13 You in Your mercy have led forth
   The people whom You have redeemed;
   You have guided *them* in Your strength
   To Your holy habitation.
14 "The people will hear *and* be afraid;
   Sorrow will take hold of the inhabitants of
     Philistia.

179

15 Then the chiefs of Edom will be dismayed;
   The mighty men of Moab,
   Trembling will take hold of them;
   All the inhabitants of Canaan will melt away.
16 Fear and dread will fall on them;
   By the greatness of Your arm
   They will be *as* still as a stone,
   Till Your people pass over, O LORD,
   Till the people pass over
   Whom You have purchased.
17 You will bring them in and plant them
   In the mountain of Your inheritance,
   In the place, O LORD, *which* You have made
   For Your own dwelling,
   The sanctuary, O LORD, *which* Your hands have
      established.
18 "The LORD shall reign forever and ever."
19 For the horses of Pharaoh went with his chari-
ots and his horsemen into the sea, and the LORD
brought back the waters of the sea upon them. But
the children of Israel went on dry *land* in the midst of
the sea.
20 Then Miriam the prophetess, the sister of Aaron,
took the timbrel in her hand; and all the women went
out after her with timbrels and with dances.
21 And Miriam answered them:
   "Sing to the LORD,
   For He has triumphed gloriously!
   The horse and its rider
   He has thrown into the sea!"

                                        Exod. 15:1–21

Verses 1–19 of this chapter comprise "The Song of Moses"; verses
20–21, "The Song of Miriam." The Hebrews had triumphed over
Pharaoh; God had delivered them across the Red Sea and had
drowned their enemies. There on the seashore they celebrated.

Many scholars believe that Moses' song grew through the years as
people reflected upon the mighty acts of God and, in retrospect,
praised God. But Miriam's song captured the essence of praise—the
brief, pungent, joyous spontaneity of a delivered people rejoicing.
You can see them in your mind. Miriam took a timbrel in her hand,

began to beat it joyously, dancing to its rhythm, with all the people following in circles of ecstatic thanksgiving.

Whether Moses' song as we have it actually dates from the seashore as does Miriam's is not a significant issue. The theology of the two is the same. Moses' hymn became a part of the worship of Israel, probably used in Passover celebration.

There are three movements in the song.

First, it *celebrated* God's mighty deeds. From beginning to end it was *praise of God.*

It is helpful to note that the word "to thank" does not exist in biblical Hebrew. In his book *The Praise of God in the Psalms*, Claus Westermann reminds us that "thanksgiving" is a relatively modern development. He suggests that "where a worshiper in the Psalms says, 'I will praise the Lord . . . ,' he does not mean 'I will be thankful to God,' but rather 'I will respond to him for what he has done for me.'"[1]

This is the celebration that is present here—the praising of God, meaning that responsive action is called for. Jesus' warning supports this kind of praise: "Not every one who says to Me, 'Lord, Lord,' shall enter the kingdom of heaven, but he who does the will of My Father in heaven" (Matt. 7:21).

The second movement in the song is a *claiming* of strength. *"The Lord is my strength and my song, / And He has become my salvation"* (v. 2).

These words occur three times in the Bible: here, in Isaiah 12:2, and in Psalms 118:14. They teach us three lessons:

(1) God's universal grace and mercy must be a personal possession. That is the work of true faith in our lives.

(2) Every act of mercy we experience should confirm the claim "The Lord is *my* strength."

(3) The circle is complete only as it leads back to praise. The Lord has become my *song*. And remember, praise means "I will respond to what the Lord has done." The circle begins again as we personally claim God's mercy and grace.

When I said that there were three movements in this song, I did not mean *successive* movements, or one movement built on another. *Celebration* of God's mighty deeds recurs throughout, and the personal *claiming* of strength and salvation takes place in the midst of that celebration.

181

There is a third movement: *confidence* in God's continuous triumph, and joyous anticipation of the future. Not only has God delivered, He has *brought out* the people from bondage. (*"You will bring them in and plant them in the mountain of your inheritance"* v. 17).

Our song of praise is incomplete without this final movement of *confidence.* Are we willing to trust our future to God?

THE BITTER WATERS OF MARAH

15:22 So Moses brought Israel from the Red Sea; then they went out into the Wilderness of Shur. And they went three days in the wilderness and found no water.

23 Now when they came to Marah, they could not drink the waters of Marah, for they *were* bitter. Therefore the name of it was called Marah.

24 And the people complained against Moses, saying, "What shall we drink?"

25 So he cried out to the LORD, and the LORD showed him a tree. When he cast *it* into the waters, the waters were made sweet. There He made a statute and an ordinance for them, and there He tested them,

26 and said, "If you diligently heed the voice of the LORD your God and do what is right in His sight, give ear to His commandments and keep all His statutes, I will put none of the diseases on you which I have brought on the Egyptians. For I *am* the LORD who heals you."

27 Then they came to Elim, where there *were* twelve wells of water and seventy palm trees; so they camped there by the waters.

Exod. 15:22–27

The Songs of Moses and Miriam are marvelous pictures of joy and praise, the celebration of God's mighty deeds, and the people's hallelujah to God's delivering mercy. Three days have passed now, and they have come to Marah. They are weary, despite the exhilaration they have so recently experienced. They are thirsty, but the water they have found is bitter.

Again there is a seesaw of prevailing moods, from celebrating to complaining and condemning Moses.

Sometimes in our Bible study and in our preaching and teaching, we need to look for truth that is not so obvious, for opaque meaning, lessons to which we may be blinded by the dramatic. Not so, I think, in this passage. The lessons are neither subtle nor subdued. They are right on the surface, hard to miss even by those who try. You may find other lessons in this passage, but don't miss these.

In Life We Come Often to Marah

Marah is not only the designation of a geographical location three days' journey from the Red Sea in the wilderness of Shur; it is a place on the life-map of each of us. It's not geographical, but circumstantial.

The Hebrew adjective *mar,* from which the name Marah comes, means "bitter." In the Old Testament, this adjective is seen clearly in two verses from Proverbs. First, Proverbs 27:7: "A satisfied soul loathes the honeycomb, / But to a hungry soul every bitter thing is sweet."

Clearer yet is the picture in verses 3 and 4 of Proverbs 5: "For the lips of an immoral woman drip honey, / And her mouth [speech] is smoother than oil; / But in the end she is bitter as wormwood, / Sharp as a two-edged sword."

"Bitter as wormwood." Do you have any notion about that metaphor? Remember the lines from Edward Perronet's great hymn "All Hail the Power of Jesus' Name":

> Sinners, whose love can ne'er forget
> The wormwood and the gall,
> Go spread your trophies at his feet,
> And crown him, crown him, crown him,
> Crown him Lord of all.[2]

Wormwood is the bitterest of all wood—bitter as gall. In C. S. Lewis's delightful and provocative book *The Screwtape Letters,* Screwtape was the major devil commissioned to tempt us. The lesser devil was Wormwood. No wonder C. S. Lewis named him that.

You get the picture. The Hebrew word *mar* is an adjective meaning "bitter"—so Marah is not only a geographical designation, it is a place of circumstances, events, and experiences to which we often come in our life journey.

Don't let that word "bitter" mislead you into seeking literal pictures. Let it be a metaphor to designate any place, any circumstance, any experience, any painful or estranged relationship through which you may be passing. Let it refer to the illness that has ominously been designated "terminal." Let it describe that difficult situation to which you've come with your children. Someone has said that a parent is as happy as his unhappiest child. The fact that we parents love our children makes us vulnerable to our children's hurts. The fact that we want the best for them causes us to be deeply sorrowful when things are not working out for them. Certainly, there are those times when our children bring us far more pain than pleasure.

So, let the word designate whatever place it is in your experience to which you've come but don't want to be. In *Pilgrim's Progress,* Bunyan referred to "the slough of despondency." That may be what Marah is all about. We become despondent because of the circumstances of our lives.

No one has described the feeling better than the psalmist: "Why are you cast down, O my soul?" (Ps. 42:5a).

It's true, isn't it? If you haven't had sorrow or bitterness, just wait—your turn will come. In life we come often to Marah, and we get to the point where we want to cry with Martin Luther, "I'm sick of life, if that is what you call it."

God Comes to Us at Marah

Note a second truth: God comes to us at Marah. In fact, it may be true that God brings us to Marah. God was leading the Hebrews when they came to Marah.

This is a hard truth to reckon with, and there are no easy answers. Look at what happened to the Hebrews. They moved from *triumph to trouble*. They came through the Red Sea dry-shod, led by God. And there on the shore, safe from Pharaoh's army, they sang joyfully: "The Lord is my strength and my song, / And He has become my salvation" (v. 2).

Three days later, their triumph had turned to trouble. There they were in Marah, a place not of *blessedness* but of *bitterness*. And the

Lord had led them there. Now that's hard to take, hard to reckon with. Somewhere between the extreme notion that a severe providence plots every step of our lives and that everything that happens to us is planned and decreed by God, and the other extreme position that all is capricious, happenstance, and whim, we must find our place to stand. William Cowper put it in a hymn:

> God moves in a mysterious way
> His wonders to perform;
> He plants His footsteps in the sea,
> And rides upon the storm.
>
> Deep in unfathomable mines
> With never-failing skill,
> He treasures up His bright designs
> And works His sovereign will
>
> Judge not the Lord by feeble sense
> But trust Him for His grace;
> Behind a frowning providence
> He hides a smiling face.[3]

When you feel that the Lord has led you to Marah, when the searing question, "Why?" smolders in your mind, reach back for Paul's word to the Romans, "We know that in everything God works for good with those who love Him" (8:28, RSV).

The third stanza of Cowper's hymn, partially quoted above, is my favorite:

> Ye fearful saints, fresh courage take;
> The clouds you so much dread
> Are big with mercy, and shall break
> In blessings on your head.

That's really the big point. Whether God brings us to Marah or not, He will come to us in Marah. Look again at the Israelites. They moved from *triumph* to *trouble*. Now they move from *trouble to testing*. Look at verse 25: *"So he cried out to the Lord, and the Lord showed him a tree. When he cast it into the waters, the waters were made sweet. There He made a statute and an ordinance for them, and there He tested them"* (v. 25).

The phrase to which I call your attention is the last one: "He tested them." The big question is not whether we can sing in our triumph at the Red Sea, but whether we can sing in our troubles at Marah. The proof of faith, the testing, always comes in the barren desert at Marah, not in the oasis at Elim, where there were twelve springs of water and seventy palm trees. The testing comes when nothing makes sense, except to God. It's the kind of testing that came to Job, and his faith lights our way: "Though He slay me, yet will I trust Him."

But there is more insight to be gained from the Hebrews. They went from *triumph to trouble,* from *trouble to testing,* and from *testing to teaching.* Look at verse 26 again: *"If you diligently heed the voice of the Lord your God and do what is right in His sight, give ear to His commandments and keep all His statutes, I will put none of the diseases on you which I have brought on the Egyptians. For I am the Lord who heals you."*

There it is, the big point: "I am the Lord who heals you." Don't lose this point. God will come to us in Marah, and He will say, "I am the Lord who heals you."

What a gospel!—and in the Old Testament: the Lord is our ultimate Healer. We go to a lot of different places for healing, and we give ourselves to all sorts of would-be "healers." Yet it is the Lord who is our ultimate Healer.

Morris Abram, an Atlanta lawyer who wrote an autobiography after his recovery from cancer, discovered this. He entitled the book *The Day Is Short.* The title is taken from a Talmudic saying:

> The day is short, the work is great. . . .
> It is not thy duty to complete the work,
> but neither art thou free to desist from it.

Morris Abram learned that wisdom in fighting the disease of cancer. He did all he could. He fought vigorously and strenuously. He never desisted from fighting, but he knew that, in the end, it was something other than his own efforts that brought the healing. This is what he wrote: "The tendency of the cancer to recur was held at bay or perhaps even wiped out by my will to live, by a new love, by new interests, by immunotherapy, maybe by hepatitis, maybe by good fortune, maybe by God. . . . I give respectable scientific methods the credit due and reserve for the unknown factors the awesome name of the mystery which I refuse to confuse with science."[4]

The Lord is our ultimate Healer.

Note also that His healing is perpetual. "I AM the Lord who heals you." His healing never ceases.

And note finally that it is universal; it is available to all, and it is encompassing.

We see it, and we know it; but it's easy to forget. The Healing Lord who continues to transform circumstances and persons always amazes us. We know that this happens, but when we see the miracle of it dramatically and transparently present in a particular situation, it always staggers and challenges our too-weak faith.

I remember being in a city in another state several years ago, and following a Sunday preaching service, I was visiting with a group of people at lunch time in a home. I knew the hostess from a conference I had led, but not the host—I'd never met him before. He was a hard-driving business man, the stereotypical workaholic who placed work above everything. The dream of the good life was the magnet that pulled him on.

It was also a situation I see so often. The wife is the religious one; the husband goes to church but is only present in body for the sake of the family. The wife is genuinely seeking a vital spirituality; the husband is too preoccupied with the so-called "real world," caught in the phony idea that spiritual things are not masculine. But for some mysterious reason, John and I hit it off that Sunday afternoon. We found ourselves alone out on the balcony of his beautiful home. He talked honestly as I dared to probe a bit, and listen. By a miracle of the Spirit, soul touched soul. Only a short time before, the huge manufacturing business that he headed was swallowed up in a conglomerate, and he had lost his prestigious and powerful position. His world had crumbled and the "good life" that he had finally grasped was now fading. It was like sand running out of his fingers. This towering man was now feeling impotent, no longer in control.

He wrestled with this "lost dream" for over a year before he began to get a grip on things and move toward a degree of wholeness. Then something big happened in his life. He attended an Emmaus Weekend retreat and had a life-changing experience—life-changing in the sense that it gave him a whole new direction, but also a whole new approach to life and resources to deal with it. This was proven dramatically not long ago when his youngest son came "out of the closet" and shared the fact that he was a homosexual. I can only imagine how John would have dealt with this shattering experience, this Marah, back where he was when he and I first met. Now, having something new and dynamic going on within him—a Power not his own—he invited his wife and son to sit together and talk about this new situation. The conversation began, "Son, I want you to know there are four persons here—you, your mother and me, and the Holy Spirit. The Holy Spirit is here because I've invited Him. I want you to know I love you and I believe the Holy Spirit is going to give us the wisdom and the power to deal with this situation."

What could have been the most destructive estrangement a son and father could experience had been short-circuited by the power of the Lord who comes to us in Marah as the healing One. Grace, explained only by Christ's Presence, was working in that situation that otherwise would have destroyed an entire family.

Not long ago as I was traveling through John's city, I had a two-hour layover and we met for dinner. I could feel the Power stirring in him, and I could see it in the light on his face as he shared the healings taking place in his family.

I look back on the difference between John when I first met him and John as I know him now, and I can only exclaim: There is a gospel in Marah; the Lord comes to us there. And the Lord who comes is our Healer.

NOTES

1. Claus Westermann, *The Praise of God in the Psalms*, trans. Keith R. Crim (Richmond, VA: John Knox Press, 1965), p. 25.

2. Edward Perronet, "All Hail the Power of Jesus' Name," 1779.

3. William Cowper, "God Moves in a Mysterious Way," 1774.

4. Morris B. Abram, *The Day Is Short: An Autobiography* (New York: Harcourt Brace Jovanovich, 1982), pp. 222, 223.

CHAPTER TEN

Fresh Every Morning

Exodus 16:1–36

The distinguished French author Albert Camus once described a fellow writer who kept searching for the right word. Because he could never find it, he was last seen sitting motionless before a blank piece of paper.

I feel like that sometimes in my sermon preparation. Sitting motionless before a blank piece of paper, I am overwhelmed with the importance of what I want to communicate. I feel the powerful impact of the Scripture, and I know I must not fail. The truth of it is so crucial, and I'm so committed to being faithful in preaching God's word, that I will often sit for an hour without putting anything down.

I did that often in the course of writing this commentary, for I kept always in mind that I was writing for the teacher or preacher, the one for whom Sunday or Bible class time comes with demanding regularity.

I also wrestled with space, and I pray I have been wise. Some of the passages in Exodus are such signal ones and so awesome that they demand concentrated attention. This chapter contains a case in point—the miracle of the manna given by God to the Israelites, *fresh every morning*.

We're going to look at this chapter by dividing it into two sections. Our concentration will be on the first section: the miracle of the manna.

THE MIRACLE OF THE MANNA

16:1 And they journeyed from Elim, and all the congregation of the children of Israel came to the

Wilderness of Sin, which is between Elim and Sinai, on the fifteenth day of the second month after they departed from the land of Egypt.

2 Then the whole congregation of the children of Israel complained against Moses and Aaron in the wilderness.

3 And the children of Israel said to them, "Oh, that we had died by the hand of the Lord in the land of Egypt, when we sat by the pots of meat *and* when we ate bread to the full! For you have brought us out into this wilderness to kill this whole assembly with hunger."

4 Then the LORD said to Moses, "Behold, I will rain bread from heaven for you. And the people shall go out and gather a certain quota every day, that I may test them, whether they will walk in My law or not.

5 "And it shall be on the sixth day that they shall prepare what they bring in, and it shall be twice as much as they gather daily."

6 Then Moses and Aaron said to all the children of Israel, "At evening you shall know that the LORD has brought you out of the land of Egypt.

7 "And in the morning you shall see the glory of the LORD; for He hears your complaints against the LORD. But what *are* we, that you complain against us?"

8 Also Moses said, "This *shall be seen* when the LORD gives you meat to eat in the evening, and in the morning bread to the full; for the LORD hears your complaints which you make against Him. And what *are* we? Your complaints *are* not against us but against the LORD."

9 Then Moses spoke to Aaron, "Say to all the congregation of the children of Israel, 'Come near before the LORD, for He has heard your complaints.'"

10 Now it came to pass, as Aaron spoke to the whole congregation of the children of Israel, that they looked toward the wilderness, and behold, the glory of the LORD appeared in the cloud.

11 And the LORD spoke to Moses, saying,

12 "I have heard the complaints of the children of Israel. Speak to them, saying, 'At twilight you shall

eat meat, and in the morning you shall be filled with bread. And you shall know that I *am* the LORD your God.'"

13 So it was that quails came up at evening and covered the camp, and in the morning the dew lay all around the camp.

14 And when the layer of dew lifted, there, on the surface of the wilderness, was a small round substance, *as* fine as frost on the ground.

15 So when the children of Israel saw *it*, they said to one another, "What is it?" For they did not know what it *was*. And Moses said to them, "This *is* the bread which the LORD has given you to eat.

16 "This is the thing which the LORD has commanded: 'Let every man gather it according to each one's need, one omer for each person, *according to the* number of persons; let every man take for *those* who *are* in his tent.'"

17 Then the children of Israel did so and gathered, some more, some less.

18 So when they measured *it* by omers, he who gathered much had nothing left over, and he who gathered little had no lack. Every man had gathered according to each one's need.

19 And Moses said, "Let no one leave any of it till morning."

20 Notwithstanding they did not heed Moses. But some of them left part of it until morning, and it bred worms and stank. And Moses was angry with them.

21 So they gathered it every morning, every man according to his need. And when the sun became hot, it melted.

Exod. 16:1–21

I sat a long while with this passage in prayer and reflection, struggling not for the right words, but for the right dynamic of development that would provide a framework to grasp and to be grasped by its monumental truths.

Let's pick up where we left off in the last chapter. The Israelites had come to Marah, a place in the wilderness of Shur, three days' journey from the triumph of the Red Sea. We have learned that Marah means place of bitterness, and we have looked at it not only as a geographical location but as a place on the life-map of each of us.

The water at Marah was bitter. The people were unable to drink it, and they murmured against Moses, because their thirst was overwhelming. Again God intervened. He gave Moses a tree to throw into the water, and instantly the water became sweet.

It's interesting to note that the next stop in the wandering of the Israelites was at Elim. At Elim, there were twelve springs of water, and seventy palm trees. It was a welcome resting place after the difficult days in the wilderness. F. B. Meyer once suggested that God does not multiply our Elims, for He cannot trust us there: "He gems the earth with them, to teach us that it is not all blasted, and that we are not a cursed race in a cursed world. He sets them before our eyes as witnesses that there are worlds where there is no bitterness in the fountains of life. He causes us to lie down in them, only that we may be better able to tread in the paths of righteousness in which He leads us."[1]

It is my observation that the Lord never allows us to linger too long in Elim. He summons us to go forth, and our going forth sometimes takes us into the desert. Our journey really is a pilgrim's journey. Now and then we may rest in Elim, but we can't pitch our tent for a long season there. In our lives, there will appear a cloud by day and a light by night which is God's summons for us to move on.

The Israelites moved away from Elim, led by the Lord, traveling along the brink of the Red Sea, through the wilderness of Sin. Though that's the name of the wilderness, it also indicates the state of their souls. As they got into the wilderness, again they showed themselves for what they were—faithless people who had not yet learned to trust the Lord.

Within a month the Hebrews forgot the Red Sea. They had struck their timbrels and sung their lyrics of praise there in their triumph over Pharaoh as they looked back and saw his army drowned on the seashore—but now, they were hungry. Though God had delivered them out of the bony hands of death, they could not believe that He could satisfy today's hunger.

Unbelief has a short memory, and discontent perverts our perspective. The Hebrews began to wish for the fleshpots of Egypt. They could remember and savor in their minds the security of food and shelter and clothing that they had had back in Egypt, but they had forgotten their affliction—the affliction of slavery.

Isn't this a picture of human nature? When the Hebrews were back in Egypt, they cried out in their oppression and were ready to give up everything for liberty. Yet when they got liberty, they were ready to put their necks back in the yoke again in order that their stomachs might be filled. Alexander Maclaren put it well: "Men do not know how happy they are until they cease to be so. Our present miseries and our past blessings are the themes on which unbelief harps. Let him that is without similar sin cast the first stone at those grumbling Israelites."[2]

So as the Israelites moved into the wilderness away from the Red Sea, it was a toilsome journey. They had been threatened by thirst and now they were facing famine. Again, Moses and Aaron were assailed by the anger of the people. But then came the miracle of the manna, which is the focus of this chapter: *"Then the Lord said to Moses, 'Behold, I will rain bread from heaven for you. And the people shall go out and gather a certain quota every day, that I may test them, whether they will walk in My law or not'"* (v. 4). Here was a distinct act of God, a supreme act of grace.

Let's look from three angles at this mighty act of God, this miracle of the manna. Let see it (1) as a token, (2) as a test, and (3) as a truth.

A Token

If you want a picture of the Israelites, you will find it in the Scripture's continuous reference to their murmurings. They were constantly complaining; their faith was shallow; their trust was superficial; they were selfish, their stomachs prevailing over their minds and hearts. What a token of the Lord's loving patience and long-suffering grace is provided in this picture. No doubt the hearts of the Hebrews would quake when they were summoned to hear the voice of God—and His voice would ring out, "I have heard your moaning, I know your affliction, and I hear your murmuring."

And how they must have trembled in their souls, how wide-eyed must have been their amazement when the glory of God flashed above them in a Shekinah cloud by day and a burning fire by night, guiding them on in their journey. But, here the message is different, for here the heart of God is clearly revealed. It comes in the sweet gentleness of the Lord as He promises manna because they have murmured about their hunger and have complained against Moses and God. So, in order that they may know He is the Lord, He performs the miracle of manna.

I can't help seeing in this picture a mother soothing her crying infant by feeding it from her own breast. You see, it would have been easy for God to take the rod to His crying children, but rather He sought to win them by His loving patience and His long-suffering love. He answered their whimpering unbelief and their sneering complaints with an expression of love.

We find the same expression in a story about Joy Davidman, a brilliant writer, who, at the time of her death, was the wife of C. S. Lewis. She was raised by parents who were militant nonbelievers. She graduated with top honors from Hunter College and began her adult life with a kind of cynical sophistication and skepticism that expects the worst and believes the least. She disdained religion and morality. In her arrogant, intellectual pride, she conceived of them as havens for the neurotic, ideas on which only the untutored would depend. Peak experiences of poetic insight were dismissed as some glandular disturbance that science would in time explain.

Then one day her husband, who had been growing more and more depressed, called from another city and told her that he was losing his mind, that life no longer mattered to him, and then sent her into shock and despair by abruptly hanging up and saying no more. Joy Davidman was in the country with her children. She didn't know where her husband was in the city, so she was desperate, hopeless. All she could do was telephone some friends in the city to help, and then wait in quiet desperation and despair.

Then something happened. In her words, "There was another person with me in the room—a presence so real that all my previous life was by comparison mere shadowplay. . . . I think I must have been the world's most astonished atheist. My awareness of Christ's presence was not conjured up to bolster me about my husband. No, it was terror—terror, and ecstasy, repentance and rebirth."

Even in the life of a supposed atheist, as in the life of whimpering unbelievers whom God had chosen to be in covenant with Him, God works with loving patience and long-suffering grace to reveal Himself as the one who cares for each one of us, who is concerned about our coming out and our going in, who notes the fall of a sparrow. We can see that in this miracle of manna, a token of God's loving patience and long-suffering grace.

A Test

The second angle from which we see the miracle of manna is that of a test. *"That I may test them, whether they walk in My law or not"* (v. 4).

How did the manna become a test? It became a test because it was given daily, and only enough of it for the day's needs could be gathered.

What lessons are here! The overarching one, suggested by the title of this chapter, is that God's provisions are fresh every morning. The manna as a test teaches us about *habitual* dependence. God could have provided it once; He could have given the Israelites everything they needed for their wilderness wandering. But He didn't. He gave them only enough for the day. *"So they gathered it every morning, every man according to his need. And when the sun became hot, it melted"* (v. 21).

Jesus was telling us the same thing when He taught us to pray, "Give us this day our daily bread." So, the gift of the manna was a continual training, and therefore a continual test of faith—disciplining us to be habitually dependent upon the Lord.

I believe that the Lord, joyful in His giving, gives because "infinite love loves infinitely to be loved." Have you ever thought of God in that fashion? He loves because He loves to be loved. The ongoing expressions of His love call forth our love, and that makes the heart of God happy. That's a part of the reason He provides for us "fresh every morning." He does it for His own sake. But more, He does it for our sakes, that we may know the peace and strength that come from continual dependence upon Him, the joyful life that is ours when we trust Him and see the truth of our trusting.

The happiest people I know are not people who don't have any needs, but people who experience the meeting of their needs by God. That happened to a single parent I know. Left alone to rear her children, she had just taken a new job and had been working only one month when she became ill. With no sick leave and no savings, she was in crisis to be without income for two weeks. I wish you could have been with me when I gave her $250. "It's manna from heaven," she said. "The Lord provides."

Now I know that woman's commitment, and this was no pious response to momentary relief. She lives daily in dependence upon God. She works hard and prays earnestly. She spends herself for her children and for others. Hers is a tough lot—not just where money is concerned, but also in the daily pressure of rearing three children, the daily pain of loneliness for a young woman without a marriage partner, the temptations of singleness, and the moral pressures. But she's happy. Her face radiates a sort of transparent joy. I hardly ever see her without thinking of Jesus' first beatitude: "Blessed are the poor in spirit, for theirs is the kingdom of heaven." No wonder Jesus put that one first. The poor in spirit are those who know they are dependent upon God, and they are the happy ones. Have you noticed it? The happiest people I know are not those who have no needs, but those people who experience having their needs met by God.

There's another category of happy people I know. They're the ones who seem to have been extravagantly blessed with material resources, but know that what they have is indeed a blessing—a gift. It could be gone tomorrow, and so they accept it as manna, "fresh every morning."

The $250 I gave to the woman who is happy in her dependence upon God is a good example of such "manna." The Christmas before, a man gave me $6,000 and told me to use it to be a blessing for people as I saw fit. I put it into what I call an Agape Fund, and I use it as the giver asked me to use it. This generous man is not wealthy. He tithes to the church, and this money was over and above— probably equal to—his tithe. It was his way of expressing his gratitude, of saying that what he has is a gift and that he, too, is dependent upon the Lord.

So, that's one big lesson as we look at the miracle of manna as a test. It teaches us about habitual dependence.

There's another lesson in this test. It is the vivid reminder that there are some things that we *cannot* store up for tomorrow. Yesterday's manna cannot be used as food for today. It cannot be hoarded. It is there in the morning, and we can use it until evening; but tomorrow we'll have to gather it again. There is no laying in of a supply, then sleeping late the rest of the week. Some things are a day-to-day affair.

Love in the family is like that. Oh, I know that love is half history and half intuition, that there is power in ritual and memory, that we gain strength from the residual experience of love. But I also know that expressions of love, keeping love powerfully alive in our families and in other relationships, is a "daily manna" affair. We have to make it fresh every morning. I recently talked to a man who lost his wife about a month ago. He was sharing his heart-tearing pain. He said something I've never heard before: "I know the pain will lessen. Everybody tells me it will. But I'm not sure I want it to. The lessening of the pain will mean distance from the love."

When we think about it, we know what he is feeling—the loss of a love that is fresh every morning. That ought to teach us something. Don't think you can store up love. Love must be kept alive in word and deed daily. It must be fresh every morning. Marriages fail because we don't give attention to this. Children are not nurtured to love, because we don't give attention to this. Children grow up unable to be the marriage partners and the parents they need to be, because we do not see love in the family as daily manna which we gather and share together.

We could catalog a number of things that cannot be gathered in advance and stored up for tomorrow: democracy, education, character. Think about it. Character is on trial every day. Even civilization and culture are tenuous; they must be attended to every day. Arnold Toynbee, the eminent historian, reminds us that "the jungle, like a beast, waits to spring on a careless civilization."

Let's focus particularly on one other way in which the Christian faith is a daily manna affair. When we come to Christian experience, yesterday's manna won't keep. As the veteran housemaid told the young bride: "Child, housework won't get you if you make up your mind in advance that you're not going to get caught up. Anytime you look around and think things look nice, just remember that even when you're gloatin', sheets are wrinklin', dust is settlin', and stomachs are getting ready all over again."

Though homespun, that's an apt warning for the soul. Faith can't coast. It's a daily thing. With faith, as with housework, we need to make up our minds that we're never going to get caught up.

Think about that in terms of God's forgiveness. Last month's forgiveness—even yesterday's forgiveness—is inadequate for today. We can't store up forgiveness. Forgiveness must be appropriated for every sin of our life. I remember an experience I had following a preaching service. A woman at least seventy years old asked for an appointment. When we met, she told me a very sad story. Many years before, she and her husband had had a dog that had bitten a little child, tearing up his face and disfiguring him for life. This couple was sued by the parents of the child. A court trial took place. On the stand, this woman had been asked whether the dog ever frightened other people by growling at them and threatening to bite them. The lawyer, according to this woman, short-circuited her response, and she felt that she had not been able to tell the whole truth. She had been plagued by guilt ever since, because she had felt through these years that she had lied on the stand. She was in a quandary as to what she should do. Should she contact the lawyer again? Should she seek the family and make amends? Should she send the family a check? Should she leave something in her will to that little boy? Though the incident had taken place at least twenty years before, the burden of guilt was devastating her life.

An overall blanket of forgiveness is not extended to us by God. Forgiveness must be fresh every morning. It has to be appropriated for every sin, every shortcoming of life.

Manna as a test teaches us habitual dependence on God, that there are some things in life we can't store up for tomorrow. Yesterday's manna can't be used as food today.

A Truth

The third angle from which we want to look at our Scripture is that the miracle of manna is given by God for a truth. In miraculous and transient form, the manna speaks God's eternal word. The God who sent manna sends our daily bread and we are dependent upon Him. That daily bread cannot be stored up and hoarded. It is fresh every morning. But equally deep in the meaning of this truth is the explanation Jesus gave in His wilderness hunger: "It is written [Deut. 8:3], 'Man shall not live by bread alone, but by every word that proceeds from the mouth of the Lord'" (Matt. 4:4). God humbled the Israelites, suffered them to be hungry and fed them manna, that He might make them know that man does not live by bread alone, but by every word that comes from the mouth of God.

Some commentators make much of the manna's being a *natural* product of the land. Although the provision of food included both quail and manna, only ten words are given to the quail. Scripture is full of reference to manna, in this account and elsewhere. The Hebrew word actually translates as, "What is it?" Some scholars have pointed out that several desert plants, notably the tamarisk tree, exude a sweet sticky substance that drips to the ground, turns white as it crystallizes, and tastes like honey. Others believe that it is the excretion of certain insects. (The substance is still called *mann* by Arabs living in the region.)

I agree with Alexander Maclaren:

> No doubt, we are to recognize in the plagues of Egypt, and in the dividing of the Red Sea, the extraordinary action of ordinary causes; and there is no objection in principle to doing so here. But that manna is an exudation from the bark of a shrub, . . . seems a singular (natural) "substratum" on which to build the feeding of two millions of people, more or less exclusively and continuously for forty years. . . . Whether we admit connection between the two, or not, the miraculous character of the manna of the Israelites is unaffected. It was miraculous in its origin—"rained from heaven," in its quantity, in its observance of times and seasons, in its putrefaction and preservation—as rotting when kept for greed, and remaining sweet and preserved for the Sabbath. It came straight from the creative will of God, and whether its name means "What is it?" or "It is a gift," the designation is equally true and appropriate, pointing in one case, to the mystery of its nature; in the other, to the love of the Giver, and in both referring it directly to the hand of God.[3]

There is a deeper truth yet. The manna in the wilderness is also a "type" of Christ. Throughout the Old Testament, but especially in the Book of Exodus, types are used to express eternal truth. The whole Exodus journey is a type of the Christian's pilgrimage. Here we come to a magnificent expression of truth in a type—the manna being a type of Christ.

This is a type that was claimed by Jesus Himself. You no doubt remember the story of the feeding of the 5,000 in the sixth chapter of John's Gospel. But do you remember what followed that? Crowds of people followed Jesus across the Sea of Galilee. Jesus confronted them with the shallowness of their curiosity. "You seek me, not because you saw signs, but because you ate the fill of the loaves," He said. Then He challenged them, "Do not labor for the food which perishes, but for the food which endures to everlasting life" (John 6:27, RSV).

Still, the truth had not come through clearly to them, and they asked, "What sign do you do that we may see, and believe you? What work do you perform? Our fathers ate the manna in the wilderness; as it is written, 'He gave them bread from heaven to eat'" (v. 31, RSV).

Listen to Jesus' revealing word: "Most assuredly, I say to you, Moses did not give you the bread from heaven, but My Father gives you the true bread from heaven. For the bread of God is He who comes down from heaven and gives life to the world" (vv. 32–33).

Their spiritual appetites had been whetted, and they said, "Lord, give us this bread always." And then came Jesus' remarkable and revealing claim, "I am the bread of life. He who comes to Me shall never hunger, and he who believes in Me shall never thirst" (v. 35).

The Jews couldn't take that; they couldn't appropriate that truth. It was too much for them. They couldn't see the connection between the bread they had eaten on the mountaintop that had fed their gnawing hunger and Jesus' claim to be the Bread of Life. So, what did they do? It's interesting. Verse 41 of the sixth chapter says: "The Jews then complained against Him." Does that take you back to the wilderness—to the complaining of the unfaithful, of those who can see only as their stomachs fill? "The Jews then murmured at Him, because He said, 'I am the bread which came down from heaven.'" The story continues:

> And they said, "Is not this Jesus, the son of Joseph, whose father and mother we know? How is it then that He says, 'I have come down from heaven'?" Jesus therefore answered and said to them, "Do not murmur among yourselves. No one can come to Me unless the Father who sent Me draws him; and I will raise him up at the last day. It is written in the prophets, 'And

they shall all be taught by God.' Therefore everyone
who has heard and learned from the Father comes
to Me. Not that anyone has seen the Father, except
He who is from God; He has seen the Father. Most
assuredly, I say to you, he who believes in Me has
everlasting life. I am the bread of life. Your fathers
ate the manna in the wilderness, and are dead. This
is the bread which comes down from heaven, that
one may eat of it and not die. I am the living bread
which came down from heaven. If anyone eats of
this bread, he will live forever; and the bread that I
shall give is My flesh, which I shall give for the life
of the world.'

John 6:42–51

The Jews continued to murmur among themselves as to how it
could be that He was the bread of life. Jesus again responded to
them and gave us the truth of what we celebrate in Holy Communion. They argued among themselves, 'How can this man give us his
flesh to eat?'

Then Jesus said to them, 'Most assuredly I say to
you, unless you eat the flesh of the Son of Man and
drink His blood, you have no life in you. Whoever
eats My flesh and drinks My blood has eternal life,
and I will raise him up at the last day. For My flesh
is food indeed, and My blood is drink indeed. He
who eats My flesh and drinks My blood abides in
Me, and I in him. As the living Father sent Me, and I
live because of the Father, so he who feeds on Me
will live because of Me. This is the bread which
came down from heaven—not as your fathers ate
the manna, and are dead. He who eats this bread
will live forever.'

John 6:53–58

The manna as a type of Christ shows us that through Jesus Christ
God provides for our deepest needs—daily. This provision of God in
Jesus Christ is a *satisfying* provision. It is the only thing that will
satisfy our eternal need. It is a *sufficient* provision. It is the only

thing that can give us the salvation we desperately cry for. It is a *sustaining* provision—sustaining not only today and every day, but sustaining for eternity. "He who eats this bread will live forever."

A man in prison wrote to author Robert A. Raines. He described his setting. "There's a high chain-link fence below my second-story window, and on the top of the fence, there are huge coils of barbed wire. A dozen or so little sparrows were flitting about in the barbed wire, and they reminded me of that scriptural verse about God caring even for the sparrow that falls." This man shared with Dr. Raines a poem he had written about the satisfying, sufficient, sustaining provision of God. Though it's not great poetry, it expresses deep faith and great hope.

> My prison house is cold and gray
> And made of rock and steel.
> It's filled with tears both night and day,
> There's little love to feel.
>
> The sick and sad and broken men
> Who suffer here with me
> Cannot recall the joys of when
> They last were gay and free.
>
> Yet I am happy and I'm free
> Though tombed within this Hell,
> For mighty acts of God I see
> Through cold bars of my cell.
>
> For sparrows play outside my wall
> And flit from fence to tree
> I know He grieves their every fall
> And He is here with me.[4]

If a prisoner can feel God's providential care in a cold stone tomb cell behind barbed wire, can we find it and feel it where we are today?

MANNA FOR THE SABBATH

16:22 And so it was, on the sixth day, *that* they gathered twice as much bread, two omers for each one.

And all the rulers of the congregation came and told Moses.

23 Then he said to them, "This *is what* the LORD has said: 'Tomorrow *is* a Sabbath rest, a holy Sabbath to the Lord. Bake what you will bake *today,* and boil what you will boil; and lay up for yourselves all that remains, to be kept until morning.'"

24 So they laid it up till morning, as Moses commanded; and it did not stink, nor were there any worms in it.

25 Then Moses said, "Eat that today, for today *is* a Sabbath to the LORD; today you will not find it in the field.

26 "Six days you shall gather it, but on the seventh day, the Sabbath, there will be none."

27 Now it happened *that some* of the people went out on the seventh day to gather, but they found none.

28 And the LORD said to Moses, "How long do you refuse to keep My commandments and My laws?

29 "See! For the LORD has given you the Sabbath; therefore He gives you on the sixth day bread for two days. Let every man remain in his place; let no man go out of his place on the seventh day."

30 So the people rested on the seventh day.

31 And the house of Israel called its name Manna. And it *was* like white coriander seed, and the taste of it *was* like wafers *made* with honey.

32 Then Moses said, "This *is* the thing which the LORD has commanded: 'Fill an omer with it, to be kept for your generations, that they may see the bread with which I fed you in the wilderness, when I brought you out of the land of Egypt.'"

33 And Moses said to Aaron, "Take a pot and put an omer of manna in it, and lay it up before the LORD, to be kept for your generations."

34 As the LORD commanded Moses, so Aaron laid it up before the Testimony, to be kept.

35 And the children of Israel ate manna forty years, until they came to an inhabited land; they ate manna until they came to the border of the land of Canaan.

36 Now an omer *is* one-tenth of an ephah.
Exod. 16:22–36

Here is the earliest passage in the Old Testament that mentions the Sabbath day. Obviously, the Sabbath was already observed in Israel before it became one of the Ten Commandments.

Moses instructed the people to gather enough manna on the sixth day to feed them also on the seventh, because no manna was to be gathered then. The people who did as Moses commanded discovered another miracle. Whereas on other days when they had tried to hoard for tomorrow, the manna spoiled, this was not so with the manna gathered for the Sabbath.

Others were slow to believe. But when they went out on the Sabbath to get their daily manna, it was as Moses had told them. There was no manna.

At the conclusion of this chapter of Exodus, the experience of the provision of God was tangibly memorialized. An *omer* (twenty-four dry quarts) of manna was placed in a jar and kept as a testimony of God's provision for the needs of His people. This omer of manna was a reminder to the Israelites of the meaning of the experience: a token, a testing, and a truth—a time of discipline. That's the way Deuteronomy interpreted it. "So He humbled you, allowed you to hunger, and fed you with manna which you did not know nor did your fathers know, that He might make you know that man shall not live by bread alone; but man lives by every word that proceeds from the mouth of the Lord" (Deut. 8:3). And much later, as already indicated, Jesus responded to the manna experience with His claim to be the "true bread which came down from heaven."

In time, this testimony, this omer of manna, would be in the tabernacle with Israel's holiest and most treasured objects. It would be the mute but telling reminder to all generations of the grace by which Israel was so marvelously nurtured. It would remind Israel that she was who she is because of what she was, alive as a people *now* because of God's sustaining grace.

Let us remember that the Sabbaths of our lives also should be living reminders of this grace.

NOTES

1. F. B. Meyer, *Devotional Commentary on Exodus* (Grand Rapids: Kregel Publications, 1978), p. 186.

2. Alexander Maclaren, *Expositions of Holy Scripture*, 11 vols. (Grand Rapids: Wm. B. Eerdmans, 1952–59), 1:66.

3. Ibid., 1:70–71.

4. Robert Raines, *To Kiss the Joy* (Waco, TX: Word Books, 1973), pp. 88–89.

CHAPTER ELEVEN

Lessons from Rephidim

Exodus 17:1–16

The Hebrew word *Rĕphîdîm* signifies "resting place." One can imagine that the Israelites, tired, weary, and on edge, were looking forward to arriving there. A mass of people compelled to try to stay in some sort of order, barely subsisting in the wilderness, would not be ready to contain themselves in calmness and amiability. No doubt nerves were raw and tempers were flaring. The scorching of the sun, its glare reflecting from the granite rocks, and now the failure of the water supply all threatened to drive the whole camp into a frenzy.

At Marah the water had been bitter. Now at Rephidim, there was no water at all. The brook which at times watered the valley was dry. So again, the people turned against Moses with outcries of anger, and against God with their blatant lack of trust. There are lessons here at Rephidim.

BEING THE LORD'S INSTRUMENT

17:1 Then all the congregation of the children of Israel set out on their journey from the Wilderness of Sin, according to the commandment of the LORD, and camped in Rephidim; but *there was* no water for the people to drink.

2 Therefore the people contended with Moses, and said, "Give us water, that we may drink." So Moses said to them, "Why do you contend with me? Why do you tempt the LORD?"

3 And the people thirsted there for water, and the people complained against Moses, and said, "Why *is*

it you have brought us up out of Egypt, to kill us and our children and our livestock with thirst?"

4 So Moses cried out to the LORD, saying, "What shall I do with this people? They are almost ready to stone me!"

5 And the LORD said to Moses, "Go on before the people, and take with you some of the elders of Israel. Also take in your hand your rod with which you struck the river, and go.

6 "Behold, I will stand before you there on the rock in Horeb; and you shall strike the rock, and water will come out of it, that the people may drink." And Moses did so in the sight of the elders of Israel.

7 So he called the name of the place Massah and Meribah, because of the contention of the children of Israel, and because they tempted the LORD, saying, "Is the LORD among us or not?"

Exod. 17:1-7

Over and over again, the Israelites challenged Moses' leadership, and it was no different when they got to Rephidim. No water was there. The people were thirsty. They began to find fault with Moses. It didn't help that he put the whole matter in the perspective that it should have been put by asking, "Why do you put the Lord to the proof?" Because that's what they were doing, and that's what we often do. We test the Lord. We want Him to prove Himself over and over again. We won't be content and accept God's grace and intervention in our life in the "big picture." We want Him to move down into the smallest, minute details of our living, to prove Himself over and over again.

The people didn't get Moses' message. He couldn't get them to think about God. Moses was there with them, therefore he became the focus of their anger. "Why did you bring us out of Egypt, to kill us and our children and our cattle with thirst?" they screamed.

Moses did what you and I would have done. He cried to the Lord: "What shall I do with this people? They're almost ready to stone me."

And here we come to one of three big lessons of Israel's experience in Rephidim—what it means to be the Lord's instrument.

Notice that again God uses Moses' shepherd's staff—the rod. You recall the significant role that Moses' rod played in his leadership of the people. How many sermons have you heard on the question, "What is that in your hand?" (4:2). That's the question God had asked Moses back in chapter 4 when Moses was trying to resist God's call, making all sorts of excuses, finally concluding, "Suppose they will not believe me or listen to my voice: suppose they say, 'The Lord has not appeared to you'" (4:1).

It was in response to that statement that the Lord had asked: "What is that in your hand?" and Moses had said, "It's a rod." "Cast it to the ground," God said. When Moses did, it became a serpent from which Moses fled. But God commanded him to pick up the serpent, and when he did, it became a rod again. And God used that rod of Moses and then continued to use it throughout the wilderness wandering. It's a powerful symbol. Every life has some capacity, and to all of us God is constantly saying, "What is that in your hand?"

God takes for granted that each of us has something that is useful for Him and in ministry on His behalf. We're all given gifts, according to the measure of the grace of God, as Paul would put it. One of the hardest lessons that we can learn is to believe that *while there may not be any equality among our gifts and our talent, at the same time every person is of intrinsic worth in the economy of the Kingdom.* Our usefulness to God is not measured by the character or the capacity of our gifts, but by our willingness to use those gifts.

So the lesson here is for us to be the Lord's instrument, as Moses was.

There are at least two things necessary if we are going to be the Lord's instrument. One is that we have to have a sense of our own uniqueness. As Charlie Brown would say, "Even the two of clubs wins a trick now and then." How different were Moses and Aaron. Yet they both became the Lord's instruments in their uniqueness.

Central in my theology is the conviction that each one of us is a unique, unrepeatable miracle of God. There are no carbon copies in God's family.

Maya Angelou is a black woman, a poet, playwright, and singer. She's been a writer-producer for Twentieth Century Fox and now teaches at Wake Forest University in Winston-Salem. Her book *I Know Why the Caged Bird Sings* is the moving and beautiful autobiography of this talented woman. It's been called a sort of "biblical study of life in the midst of death." She talks about growing up in the South, and she celebrates uniqueness, the uniqueness of the unrepeatable miracle of God that each one of us is. She dedicated her book to her son, Guy Johnson, and to "all the strong blackbirds of promise who defy the odds and gods and sing their song." Isn't that phrase beautiful? "All the strong blackbirds of promise who defy the odds and gods and sing their song." That's an expression of the realization of uniqueness essential if we are to be the Lord's instrument.

Jesus made it plain. Even the hairs on your head are numbered, He said. You are special. Dr. Mouzon Biggs, pastor of Boston Avenue United Methodist Church in Tulsa, has shared that when he was a child his mother would whisper in his ear as she tucked him into bed, "You're such a special child, I think God must have sent you to do something special. I hope you find out what it is." He said, "I didn't know until years later that she was whispering the same thing to my sister and little brother."

Once he told that story in a sermon at a church, and later as he started to back his car out of the parking lot, a fellow tapped on his window. Mouzon rolled it down and the fellow said with tears in his eyes, "What if you didn't have a mother to do that for you?"

Every child needs to hear that kind of affirmation, and if the child doesn't hear it from his or her own parents, then God sends us to speak that word. Every child is special, every person is special, and God has something for every one of us to do no matter who we are.

Not only were Moses and Aaron unique; all of Israel were reminded of how they had been especially chosen by God.

> For you are a holy people to the Lord your God;
> the Lord your God has chosen you to be a people for
> Himself, a special treasure above all the peoples on
> the face of the earth. The Lord did not set His love
> on you nor choose you because you were more in
> number than any other people, for you were the least
> of all peoples; but because the Lord loves you and
> because He would keep the oath which He swore to
> your fathers, the Lord has brought you out with a
> mighty hand, and redeemed you from the house of
> bondage, from the hand of Pharaoh king of Egypt.
> *Deut. 7:6–8*

Then there is this second thing: to be the Lord's instrument, we have to have a sense of our usefulness.

Stradivarius is a monumental name among violins. Antonio Stradivari had a sense of uniqueness and a sense of usefulness in relation to God. George Eliot has him saying

> When any master holds
> 'twixt chin and hand a violin of mine,
> He will be glad that Stradivari lived,
> made violins, and made them of the best.
> . . . For while God gives them skill
> I give them instruments to play upon.
> [God] could not make
> Antonio Stradivari's violins
> Without Antonio.[1]

But that's Stradivari, you say, an exceptionally gifted individual. And implicit in those words "exceptionally gifted" is the suggestion that you are not gifted, resulting in the question then of how you can be useful.

Perhaps the answer lies in another story. A few years ago, fourteen hundred Chicagoans met in the Grand Ballroom of a large hotel to honor a person selected as Chicago's Mother of the Year. She turned out to be a woman no one had ever heard of. She was Mrs. Dominic Salvino, an Italian immigrant, a housewife, and extremely poor. Mrs. Salvino lived on Erie Street. She had many neighbors who were poorer than she. Most families had eight or ten children in them, and she had only four; her neighbors were old, she was only forty-nine; they were sick, she was healthy; they were tired, she was full of energy; they had problems like alcoholism, and she was steady emotionally, and so was her husband. Mrs. Salvino appointed herself to care for the people of Erie Street. She visited the sick, she collected money from the comparatively poor, and gave it to the desperately poor. She did the housework of the bed-ridden, cooked for the motherless, and spread smiles the length and breadth of Erie Street. Although she put about 1600 hours a year into her personal mission, she did it quietly and without fanfare. But in a place of blighted hopes, she was an argument for dreams; in a place of failure, she inspired dignity and courage; in a place of empty arms and lonely rooms, she promoted love and caring.

Erie Street was a better and more beautiful place because Mrs. Dominic Salvino made a difference. She saw herself as God's instrument, *unique* and *useful*.

There is a third fact to be noted. To be the instrument of God, some of us will have to radically break our life-pattern, while others will simply have to add to, or deliberately act out in our daily lives what God is calling us to.

Fred and Mabel Mills have been active Christians for years. Several months ago, Fred began to talk to me about God's call upon his life. He was not clear about it in specific terms but he felt it so keenly that he was thinking about early retirement, and the possibility of giving his life totally in ministry.

Well, Fred has done that. Our Staff-Parish Relations Committee has appointed Fred to be a staff member of our church—without pay, mind you, but a full staff member. In that position he now coordinates the ministry of our church in seeking to meet the housing and employment needs of the poor in our city. He spends fifteen to twenty hours each week working on roofs, plumbing, winterizing houses, trying to do something practical for those Jesus called "the least of these." He spends the rest of his time recruiting and training others to do this work, serving as a presence of love to those who need that sign. Fred is being God's instrument by a radical commitment and a break in the pattern of ordinary life.

Not all of us are called to radically break the pattern of ordinary life. Most of us can deliberately act out in our routine life what God is calling us to do by intentionally being about His business day in and day out. A friend of mine tells one of the loveliest and most inspiring stories about how this happened with one woman.

Three years ago in his church, during the singing of the invitation hymn "Just As I Am," a young woman named Mary came down the aisle to accept Jesus Christ as her Savior and Lord. Mary was in her early thirties, a divorcee who worked as a cocktail waitress at a local lounge. She'd met a woman at the beauty parlor, and her new friend had invited her to her church. She had come several Sunday evenings and now was presenting herself for membership in this holy flock.

After the service was over, people were visiting in the pastor's study, and they suddenly discovered that Mary had never been baptized. They decided that several Sunday evenings later Mary would be baptized in the First Baptist Church. The woman who had invited her did an interesting thing. She sent out engraved invitations to the baptismal service—invitations like those you would send out for a wedding or a graduation. She sent them to every person in Mary's social network—fellow workers, friends from the bowling alley, the beauty parlor, the cocktail lounge, neighborhood friends, and so on, and by the time that evening rolled around, the first three rows were filled with friends from Mary's social web. Her former husband was sitting on one row, and her current boy friend was sitting on another row.

Afterwards they had a reception in which they had a great time simply singing songs . . . it was a celebrative evening. Very briefly, the pastor shared with the people what had been happening in Mary's life, and simply announced to them that all the resources and ministry of that church were available to them, as well as the friendship of Christ Himself.

To make a long story short, for the next eight Sunday evenings, Mary once again walked the aisle during the singing of an invitational hymn. But this time, rather than bringing herself to the faith, she was bringing one or more of her friends.

You see, someone brought Mary to Christ by sharing her witness intentionally at the beauty parlor. Then Mary, by simply adding to her everyday routine a self-conscious decision to be Christ's witness, brought scores of others to Christ.

We can be the Lord's instruments only as we sense our uniqueness and as we sense our usefulness. Sometimes we are to be the Lord's instruments by radically breaking our routine, while at other times, in a deliberate way, we simply add on to the ministry to which Jesus calls us all, that of being His servants and His witnesses where we are.

One man, Moses, was faithful. When God told him what to do, he did it. He used the rod of God, struck the rock in the presence of the elders, as God instructed him, and the water gushed out to satisfy the thirsty Israelites.

Some make "rational" explanations for the supply of water, citing instances when water has poured out of certain desert rock formations when the surface of the rock was broken. Moses would laugh at that. He called the place Massah (from *nâsâh*, "to test") and Meribah (from *rîb*, "to strive" or "to argue"). That's what was taking place— *testing* and *striving*. The supplying of water was the demonstration that the Lord was with His people. God never abandons God's people, but provides them life-giving water. Paul pointed to this fact and the wilderness confirmation of it when he wrote to the Corinthians: "Moreover, brethren, I do not want you to be unaware that all our fathers were under the cloud, all passed through the sea, all were baptized into Moses in the cloud and in the sea, all ate the same spiritual food, and all drank the same spiritual drink. For they drank of that spiritual Rock that followed them, and that Rock was Christ" (1 Cor. 10:1–4).

This reminds us, too, of the connection of Christ with the water incident in Marah. The Lord gave Moses a tree to cast into the bitter, undrinkable water, and the waters were made sweet (Exod. 15:25). The faith framed in this story is a "foreshadowing" of the crucifixion "tree" of love which God redemptively threw into the world for the healing of the bitterness of all human life.

God made the point in that incident at Marah, "I am the Lord who heals you" (Exod. 15:26), but centuries later, in the Cross, the point was blazoned unforgettably and eternally. The line first spoken of the Servant of the Lord, "By His stripes we are healed" (Isa. 53:5) is etched before us forever by the Cross, the tree that heals all bitterness.

BEING THE LORD'S INTERCESSOR

17:8 Now Amalek came and fought with Israel in Rephidim.

9 And Moses said to Joshua, "Choose us some men and go out, fight with Amalek. Tomorrow I will stand on the top of the hill with the rod of God in my hand."

10 So Joshua did as Moses said to him, and fought with Amalek. And Moses, Aaron, and Hur went up to the top of the hill.

11 And so it was, when Moses held up his hand, that Israel prevailed; and when he let down his hand, Amalek prevailed.

12 But Moses' hands *became* heavy; so they took a stone and put *it* under him, and he sat on it. And Aaron and Hur supported his hands, one on one side,

and the other on the other side; and his hands were steady until the going down of the sun.

13 So Joshua defeated Amalek and his people with the edge of the sword.

14 Then the LORD said to Moses, "Write this *for* a memorial in the book and recount *it* in the hearing of Joshua, that I will utterly blot out the remembrance of Amalek from under heaven."

15 And Moses built an altar and called its name, The-LORD-Is-My-Banner;

16 for he said, "Because the LORD has sworn: the LORD *will have* war with Amalek from generation to generation."

Exod. 17:8–16

This story is a dramatic one. It was Israel's first battle. They met the Amalekites at Rephidim. Joshua commanded the forces of Israel, while Moses, Aaron, and Hur went up on the mountain to pray. Moses had the rod of God in his hands.

The encounter was a dramatic seesaw of prevailing power. At times Israel would appear to be winning, and then the Amalekites; then Israel, then the Amalekites. Finally the issue of battle was decided. When Moses lifted up his hands in prayer, Israel prevailed. When he lowered his hands, the Amalekites prevailed. The soldiers on the field of battle were not determining the issue of victory by themselves, but the intercessors on the mountain were playing an integral role. See that beautiful picture of those intercessors on the mountain in your imagination? Moses, an old man, held up his hands with the rod of God in them but he grew weary. His friends Aaron and Hur took a stone and put it under him so that he could sit down on it; then they stood on either side and held up Moses' hands so that they would be steady. They did that all day long, *"until the going down of the sun."* And Joshua prevailed in that battle.

It's a stirring picture—a picture of the Lord's intercessor. In the twelfth chapter of Acts there is a marvelous story that demonstrates the power of intercessory prayer. The villain in this story of the persecution of the church is King Herod, the grandson of the infamous King Herod who presided over the slaughter of the innocent children when Jesus was born. This Herod not only inherited his grandfather's name but also seems to have inherited his violent nature. A cruel and brutal man, he ruled with an iron fist. The Bible says that he "laid violent hands upon some who belonged to the church." One of those on whom he laid violent hands was James. James was the elder brother of the apostle John and was the son of Zebedee. Herod arrested him and ordered his execution. When there was no great public outcry against this execution, Herod decided to do the same with Peter, the leader of the Christian community in Jerusalem. Peter was scheduled for the same sort of execution that James experienced. But on the very night that he was to meet his death something wonderful happened. As he was sleeping in a prison cell with four guards keeping watch over him, two at the door of the cell and two outside, an angel appeared. A sudden bright, unearthly light flooded the dingy, dark prison of Peter. The angel called for Peter to get up, and when Peter did, mysteriously the chains fell from his wrists and his ankles. The angel told him to put on his sandals, wrap his cloak around him, and follow him.

Peter thought he was dreaming or having some sort of vision. However, he soon became convinced it was real. The cell door was opened, and he followed the angel down a corridor. At the end of the corridor there was an iron gate that was kept locked at all times. But Peter and the angel passed the first guard post and then the second, and when they reached the iron gate, it swung open. As the Bible puts it, it "opened to them of its own accord" (Acts 12:10).

When Peter was finally out on the street, he realized what was happening. He said to himself, "Now I know for certain that the Lord has sent His angel and has delivered me from the hand of Herod."

Now that's the miracle—and some people have problems with such a happening and try to explain it in a logical fashion. You may do what you will with it, but remember that the Bible doesn't have problems with that sort of thing. It simply accepts the fact that people are miraculously delivered from desperate circumstances. You see this throughout Scripture. The Hebrew people crossed safely through the Red Sea. Daniel spent a night in the lions' den, with the king who put him there discovering the next morning that "an angel had come to shut the lions' mouths." The young Hebrews were thrown into the fiery furnace, but another Presence was seen to be in the furnace with them, and they emerged unsinged. We could go

215

on with more examples, but that's really not the purpose of telling this story about Peter.

To continue, when Peter got through the iron gate and found himself out on the street, the angel disappeared. Peter knew immediately where he was to go. His friends had gathered in the house of one of the believers and were holding an all-night prayer vigil for him. They knew how desperate the situation was, but there didn't seem to be much they could do about it. They were no match for Herod and the authorities. The one thing they could do, though, was pray.

Then suddenly, Peter himself was knocking at their door. It's a marvelous story. A young woman named Rhoda went to the door and asked who it was. When Peter identified himself, she was so overjoyed that she left him standing there while she went to tell the other people that he was alive. And here comes the interesting thing: they didn't believe her. They had been praying all night for the deliverance of Peter, and yet they didn't believe that Peter had been delivered. You can imagine their surprise when Peter kept on knocking and Rhoda returned and opened the door for him and brought him into the presence of those who had prayed for his deliverance.

How much does that tell us about prayer? We do learn about the effectiveness of prayer, but we are also reminded that many, many times we pray, not expecting anything to happen. It tells us also that many of us think of prayer as a last resort, a kind of last-ditch effort when everything else fails. We conclude so many times, "I guess there's nothing left to do but pray."

But what would happen if we put prayer first? Prayer may be the greatest resource we have.

I want to focus this lesson from Rephidim—the lesson about being the Lord's intercessor—on a form of prayer that may best be described with the word "wrestle." Great teachers in prayer have often referred to prayer as a battleground. In his classic book on prayer, Harry Emerson Fosdick has a chapter entitled "Prayer as a Battleground." He reminds us that prayer has often been the place where people rediscover faith and reestablish confidence in God and themselves. It's a battlefield where struggles for right desire are fought, because in prayer all desires are known and no secrets are hidden.

Prayer is also the battlefield on which is addressed the issue between two conflicting motives that most master human life—the praise of the world on the one side and the approval of God on the other. And on this battlefield we learn to wrench our way out of the hands of the praise of the world and struggle to put our lives under the scrutiny of God. Prayer is a battlefield in which we fight for the power to see and seek the courage to do the will of God.[2]

David Brainerd was a great missionary to India. He came out of one of his own Gethsemanes, one of his own great wrestling periods in prayer, saying, "My joints were loosed; the sweat ran down my face and body as if it would dissolve." That confession of Brainerd calls to mind Jesus wrestling in Gethsemane.

Sure, we know with Bishop Jeremy Taylor, author of *Holy Living* (1650) and *Holy Dying* (1651), that "prayer is the peace of our spirits, the stillness of our thoughts." But we also know prayer is *wrestling*.

None of us is going to escape struggle and conflict if we're seeking to achieve integrity that cannot be bought or sold, if we're seeking a courage that will not bend in the face of the gravest fear. Dr. Fosdick says, "The best guarantee of a character that is not for sale is this battlefield of prayer, where day by day the issue is settled that we shall live 'not as pleasing men, but God who proveth our hearts'" (1 Thess. 2:4).[3]

Do you remember the word with which Paul closed his letter to the Ephesians? "Finally, my brethren, be strong in the Lord and in the power of His might. Put on the whole armor of God, that you may be able to stand against the wiles of the devil. For we do not wrestle against flesh and blood, but against principalities, against powers, against the rulers of the darkness of this age, against spiritual hosts of wickedness in the heavenly places" (Eph. 6:10–12).

Then after naming the armor of God the Ephesians are to put on, Paul begged them: "Pray at all times in the Spirit, with all prayer and supplication. To that end keep alert with all perseverance, making supplication for all the saints" (v. 18, RSV). It is the language of struggle, of wrestling, of warfare.

So prayer is often a battlefield, where we *fortify ourselves to endure*, where we *deal with our temptations*, where we *engage the devil and fight his efforts to divert us from God's way*, where we *link ourselves with God and "struggle for clear vision to see and strength to do the will of God."*

Wrestling, then, is a good image of a kind of praying, especially a good image for intercession.

We must realize that the idea that God can do all that He wishes to do without any help from us is false. The experience of the race is clear that some things God can never do until He finds a person who prays.

That ought not to seem outrageous to us. Meister Eckhart, the mystic, put the truth with extreme boldness: "God can as little do without us, as we without Him." And Fosdick reminds us:

> If at first this seems a wild statement, we may well consider in how many ways God's will depends upon man's cooperation. God himself cannot do some things unless men think. He never blazons His truth on His sky that men may find it without seeking. Only when men gird the loins of their mind and undiscourageably give themselves to intellectual toil, will God reveal to them the truth even about the physical world. And God Himself cannot do some things unless men work. Will a man say that when God wants bridges and tunnels, wants the lightnings harnessed and cathedrals built, He will do the work Himself? That is an absurd and idle fatalism. God stores the hills with marble, but he never built a Parthenon; He fills the mountain with ore, but He never made a needle or a locomotive. Only when men work can some things be done. . . . Now if God has left some things contingent on man's *thinking* and *working*, why may He not have left some things contingent on man's *praying*? The testimony of the great souls is a clear affirmation of this: Some things never without thinking; some things never without working; some things never without praying![4]

Isn't the battle at Rephidim a marvelous picture? Can't you see Aaron and Hur bringing a stone for Moses to sit upon as he grows weary standing there with his lifted rod, interceding for the people? Then when his hands grow weary, even while he is seated, they get on either side of him and they hold his hands up in order that he can continue wrestling on behalf of his people. It's a marvelous picture of the connection, or interconnection, of God's people, and this act is so vivid at the point of our prayer.

In a mysterious way that we can never understand, we are connected with one another. And when we pray, the beautiful image that Clarence Jordan gives us as he translates 2 Corinthians 5:14 in his *Cotton Patch Epistles* becomes a reality: "God was in Christ putting His arms around the world and hugging it to Himself."[5] That's what we do when we pray.

But we do it in other ways also, because we are interconnected. There is no solitary Christian. Paul is right when he calls us to "bear one another's burdens, and so fulfill the law of Christ" (Gal. 6:2).

In a sermon entitled "The Story of the Iron Gate," Clarence J. Forsberg recounted the following:

> Many years ago, Bishop McConnell told a story of something that happened in a little fishing village on the New England coast. One winter's day a storm came up suddenly while the boats were out at sea. The men rowed desperately to reach the safety of the harbor. Everybody made it except for one old man named John. He had almost reached the mouth of the harbor when a great wave came along and dashed his tiny boat up against a rock. He managed to pull himself up on a tiny ledge and hang there for dear life.
>
> His friends saw what happened. There wasn't anything they could do about it. It was growing dark, and the seas were high. All they could do was wait. They built a bonfire on the shore and kept it burning all night. Every once in a while, someone would throw his cap up in the air, hoping that the old man would see it. At last dawn began to break, and the winds began to die down. They put out their boats and were able to get close enough so they could bring him safely back to shore.
>
> When the old man had been warmed by the fire and had been given something to eat, they asked what it was like out there. "Well," he said, "it was the longest night of my life. I made out pretty well at first, but then a big wave came along and flattened me out and I felt myself slipping. I was worn out. I was ready to give up. My old father went down at sea, and I had decided my time had come. But just as I was ready to let go, I looked through the darkness and saw somebody's cap going up in the air. I said to myself, 'If there's somebody who cares enough about old John to stay out on a night like this, I guess I'm not going to quit yet.' Just then the winds seemed to ease up, and I got a fresh hold, and well, here I am.[6]

That's the picture. Connect that picture with Aaron and Hur holding up the hands of Moses, and know that that's a picture of being interconnected with the Lord's people. We hold them up in our prayers in the kindness that we show by simply being with them, by joining them sympathetically when they enter the dark night of their soul. And we pray, and we pray, and we keep on praying. We're being the Lord's intercessors and we're being interconnected with the Lord's people.

The chapter closes with the Lord instructing Moses to write. This is the first time that command comes. *"Write this for a memorial in the book."* The purpose was to confirm the promise the Lord had made, *"I will utterly blot out the remembrance of Amalek."*

Then Moses built an altar. The combination—the book and the altar, instruction and worship—remains at the heart of a growing faith. The altar was called The-Lord-Is-My-Banner (Heb. [*Yahweh*] *nissî*). The Hebrew word from which *nissî* is formed means "standard" or "ensign," such as a battle flag. Two meanings emerge. (1) The Lord was the rallying point of Israel. (2) *Nissî* may refer to Moses' rod, the instrument of the Lord in the hand of the one who had truly become the Lord's instrument in person.

NOTES

1. Harry Emerson Fosdick, *The Meaning of Prayer* (New York: Association Press, 1917; repr. Folcroft, 1976), p. 61.

2. Ibid., pp. 155–62.

3. Ibid., p. 162.

4. Ibid., pp. 60–61.

5. Clarence Jordan, *The Cotton Patch Version of Paul's Epistles* (Piscataway, NJ: New Century, 1968).

6. Missouri United Methodist Church, Columbia, MO, February 3, 1985.

CHAPTER TWELVE

Family Reunion

Exodus 18:1–27

In Hebrew historical writing, chronological order takes second place to the flow of the story. This family reunion, recorded in chapter 18, the reunion of Moses with his father-in-law, his wife Zipporah, and his two sons, is probably out of place in terms of time sequence. Deuteronomy 1:9–18 suggests that Moses chose able men as leaders shortly before Israel left Sinai. Israel's arrival at Mount Sinai, the experience there, and the departure are one compact story, and the writer wanted to keep it that way. Therefore, he had the choice of either interrupting the story with this family reunion, or putting it at the beginning or end of the story. He chose the former.

The fact that the Hebrew historical writer practiced this style is confirmed even in this one section of Scripture. There is no earlier mention of Moses having sent his wife and sons back to her father. Zipporah was last mentioned in 4:24–26, when she was on her way to Egypt with her husband. It's obvious that she must have been sent back sometime after that, but the story is not recorded.

You may recall that Zipporah had spoken some very harsh words to Moses on the occasion of the circumcision of their sons (4:25, 26). Some have even supposed that Moses was angered by his wife's harshness, and that's the reason he sent her back. It's far more likely that his sending his family back to his father-in-law was a very sensible precaution. It could well have been that Pharaoh would vent his wrath on Moses by killing his wife and family. Also, Moses wasn't at all certain as to how long he would be in Egypt exercising the ministry to which God had called him—the deliverance of God's people from bondage.

So, here they are now, in a family reunion.

A Joyful Reunion

18:1 And Jethro, the priest of Midian, Moses' father-in-law, heard of all that God had done for Moses and for Israel His people—that the LORD had brought Israel out of Egypt.

2 Then Jethro, Moses' father-in-law, took Zipporah, Moses' wife, after he had sent her back,

3 with her two sons, of whom the name of one *was* Gershom (for he said, "I have been a stranger in a foreign land")

4 and the name of the other *was* Eliezer (for *he said*, "The God of my father *was* my help, and delivered me from the sword of Pharaoh");

5 and Jethro, Moses' father-in-law, came with his sons and his wife to Moses in the wilderness, where he was encamped at the mountain of God.

6 Now he had said to Moses, "I, your father-in-law Jethro, am coming to you with your wife and her two sons with her."

7 So Moses went out to meet his father-in-law, bowed down, and kissed him. And they asked each other about *their* well-being, and they went into the tent.

Exod. 18:1–7

It was with a bit of reservation that I titled this section "A Joyful Reunion." No mention is made here of Moses' reunion with his wife and his children, and that certainly seems strange. Our immediate response may be that the omission means alienation between the two marriage partners, or it may have signified inconsideration on Moses' part. That would be interpretation based on silence, and in relation to Scripture, that can sometimes be misleading. Especially in Hebrew literary style, writers frequently did not record events not deemed central to the story that they were telling. I believe this is the case here, and the reunion must have been a joyful one.

I can't imagine a mother and two sons, knowing the mission on which their husband and father had gone, not being joyful on being reunited with him. I can't imagine a husband and father, involved in the intense and demanding work in which he had been involved, not rejoicing in being back in the family circle with his wife and children.

So here they were. Jethro, the priest of Midian, Moses' father-in-law, had heard of all that God had done for Moses and for Israel, so he came with his daughter and his grandsons to the reunion with his son-in-law. Looking ahead, we see his excitement expressed in verse 9: "Then Jethro rejoiced for all the good which the Lord had done for Israel." "Rejoiced" is a rare word in the Old Testament; in fact, it is found in only two other places: Job 3:6 and Psalm 21:6.

While the focus of the Scripture here is on Moses and Jethro, the mention of Moses' sons and the meaning of their names invite our attention immediately. Gershom and Eliezer were the names.

Hebrew parents often gave expression to their hopes or their emotions in the names they gave their children. Certainly this was the case with Moses. The meaning of each name is recorded in the text. Gershom means "I have been a stranger in a foreign land" and Eliezer means "The God of my father was my help."

Can you feel the depths of soul revealed here? These two names relfect Moses' feelings during his exile from Egypt. The naming of the first child indicates his inner struggle and feeling of alienation. The naming of the second child witnesses to the spiritual pilgrimage he had made in the meantime.

You can imagine the shock Moses experienced after he fled from Egypt into Sinai. There was a vast difference between the glittering life of Pharaoh's court and the drudgery of a shepherd's lot. There was also a marked and depressing difference between the gaunt peaks of Sinai with its blazing, fierce sunshine, and the cool, luscious vegetation of Egypt, especially Goshen, the land for cattle. You can imagine the kind of thoughts that went through Moses' mind: "What have I done? What am I doing here? How did it all happen? How could I have been so stupid? And where is God? I was seeking to respond to Him, but now, where am I?"

One interpretation of the name Gershom is "banishment." Certainly Moses felt that. He had been banished from a life of ease, and from an important place in the king's court, even the possibility of being an heir to the kingdom.

But, God did not leave Moses alone nor did Moses cease seeking God. During those years of being alone, there was nothing in his shepherd's life to interfere with communion with God, and his faith was restored. So when the second child was born, he witnessed to the confidence of his faith. He called that son "Eliezer," for he said, "The God of my father was my help, and delivered me from the sword of Pharaoh."

There is fruitful reflection here. It's not all bad to say, "I am a stranger here." Moses' witness related to his exile from a posh life in Pharaoh's court and to the strangeness and drabness of Midian as compared to Egypt. But for the Christian, there is a sense in which that is our true lot: "Here we have no continuing city." Isn't it at the heart of our spiritual discipline to resist the temptation to become too much "at home" in our environment? Jesus warned about this: "Be in the world, but not of the world."

John Fowles, in his novel *The Magus*, even though he was not speaking specifically to this issue, captures the Christian stance:

> It poured rain the day I left. But I was filled with excitement, a strange sense of taking wing. I didn't know where I was going, but I knew what I needed. I needed a new land, a new race, a new language; and although I couldn't put it into words then, I needed a new mystery.[1]

We too experience this condition. It's our badge of being. We are homesick for a future. There is a sense in which Gershom is also our name, and will always be. I have been a stranger in a foreign land.

But our name is also Eliezer, for "God is our helper." The psalmist said, "I am a stranger *with You*, a sojourner, as all my fathers were" (Ps. 39:12). Alexander Maclaren reminds us:

> It is the secret that takes away all the mourning, all the possible discomfort and pain out of the thought "Here we have no continuing city," and makes it all blessed. It does not matter whether we are in a foreign land or not, if we have that Companion with us. His presence will make blessedness in Midian or in Thebes. It does not matter whether it is Goshen or the wilderness, if the Lord is by our side. So, sweetness is breathed into the thought, and bitterness is sucked out of it, when the name of the second child is braided into the name of the first; and we can contemplate quietly all else of tragic and limiting and sad that is involved in the thought that we're sojourners

and pilgrims, when we say, "Yes! We are; but the Lord is my helper."[2]

JETHRO WORSHIPS YAHWEH

18:8 And Moses told his father-in-law all that the LORD had done to Pharaoh and to the Egyptians for Israel's sake, all the hardship that had come upon them on the way, and *how* the LORD had delivered them.

9 Then Jethro rejoiced for all the good which the LORD had done for Israel, whom He had delivered out of the hand of the Egyptians.

10 And Jethro said, "Blessed *be* the LORD, who has delivered you out of the hand of the Egyptians and out of the hand of Pharaoh, *and* who has delivered the people from under the hand of the Egyptians.

11 "Now I know that the LORD *is* greater than all the gods; for in the very thing in which they behaved proudly, *He was* above them."

12 Then Jethro, Moses' father-in-law, took a burnt offering and *other* sacrifices *to offer* to God. And Aaron came with all the elders of Israel to eat bread with Moses' father-in-law before God.

Exod. 18:8–12

Two basic concerns emerge in Jethro's visit to Moses. First, he had heard of all the victorious deeds God had performed on behalf of Israel. In an unusual expression of praise, he shouted, *"Blessed be the Lord, who has delivered you out of the hands of the Egyptians, and out of the hand of Pharaoh, and who has delivered the people from under the hand of the Egyptians"* (v. 10).

The second concern related to the way Moses was dispensing justice, and Jethro's reordering of that system. Our focus in this section is on the first concern.

Jethro was a priest of Midian, and the Midianites were worshipers of another deity. Yet, Jethro is "beyond himself" in enthusiasm and praise for what Yahweh has done for Israel.

The question is: was this a conversion experience for Jethro, or had he already become a worshiper of Yahweh? Some interpret his word in verses 10–11 as the word of a true polytheist, and others, as the word of a true monotheist.

Whether this was a time of initial conversion or not, it was certainly a time of a deeper commitment of one who already believed in God.

The exciting thing for me is in what went on in the tent between Moses and Jethro. Certainly everything is not recorded in the scriptural account. I think of the story of Jesus going home with Zacchaeus. What was said in that visit is not recorded in the Gospels, but the crucial thing is: "Today salvation has come to this house" (Luke 19:9a). And also recorded is a life-style commitment on the part of Zacchaeus: "I [will] give half of my goods to the poor" (v. 8a).

So, what went on in the tent was important, so important that Jethro rejoiced, and concluded, "Now I know the Lord is greater than all the gods" (Exod. 18:11). He went even further than that. He made a burnt offering to the Lord. Though a priest of Midian, he acts now as a priest of Yahweh. When the change that needs to come in our lives comes, when the Lord becomes our God, our vocation is directed to the service and praise of God.

Also note this: Moses showed us what the right kind of witnessing will do. The witness that is effective is our sharing what the Lord has done for us. So what goes on in the tent is important—how you entertain and what you talk about. Many a person in the balance would be turned in favor of God if only you and I would begin to tell of God's dealings in our own lives. You remember what Jesus said to the man from whom he cast out a legion of demons? "Go home to your friends, and tell what great things God has done for you . . ." (Mark 5:19).

One other thing is to be noted about Jethro's worship of Yahweh. Aaron and the elders of Israel joined Moses to eat bread with Jethro when Jethro made his burnt offering and sacrifice. Is this a foreshadowing of Isaiah's prediction?

> Now it shall come to pass in the latter days
> That the mountain of the Lord's house
> Shall be established on the top of the mountains,
> And shall be exalted above the hills;
> And all nations shall flow to it.
> Many people shall come and say,

226

"Come, and let us go up to the mountain of the
Lord,
To the house of the God of Jacob;
He will teach us His ways,
And we shall walk in His paths."
For out of Zion shall go forth the law,
And the word of the Lord from Jerusalem.

Isaiah 2:2–3

SHARING THE LOAD

18:13 And so it was, on the next day, that Moses sat to
judge the people; and the people stood before Moses
from morning until evening.

14 So when Moses' father-in-law saw all that he
did for the people, he said, "What *is* this thing that
you are doing for the people? Why do you alone sit,
and all the people stand before you from morning
until evening?"

15 And Moses said to his father-in-law, "Because
the people come to me to inquire of God.

16 "When they have a difficulty, they come to me,
and I judge between one and another; and I make
known the statutes of God and His laws."

17 So Moses' father-in-law said to him, "The thing
that you do *is* not good.

18 "Both you and these people who *are* with you
will surely wear yourselves out. For this thing *is* too
much for you; you are not able to perform it by yourself.

19 "Listen now to my voice; I will give you counsel,
and God will be with you: Stand before God for the
people, so that you may bring the difficulties to God.

20 "And you shall teach them the statutes and the
laws, and show them the way in which they must
walk and the work they must do.

21 "Moreover you shall select from all the people
able men, such as fear God, men of truth, hating covetousness; and place *such* over them *to be* rulers of
thousands, rulers of hundreds, rulers of fifties, and
rulers of tens.

22 "And let them judge the people at all times. Then it will be *that* every great matter they shall bring to you, but every small matter they themselves shall judge. So it will be easier for you, for they will bear *the burden* with you.

23 "If you do this thing, and God *so* commands you, then you will be able to endure, and all this people will also go to their place in peace."

24 So Moses heeded the voice of his father-in-law and did all that he had said.

25 And Moses chose able men out of all Israel, and made them heads over the people: rulers of thousands, rulers of hundreds, rulers of fifties, and rulers of tens.

26 So they judged the people at all times; the hard cases they brought to Moses, but they judged every small case themselves.

27 Then Moses let his father-in-law depart, and he went his way to his own land.

Exod. 18:13–27

We indicated earlier that the visit of Jethro to Moses revolved around two basic concerns. We've discussed one of those concerns already, Jethro's response to the Lord's victorious deeds on behalf of Israel. The second basic concern is Jethro's advising Moses in adopting a better method of dispensing judgment. Our present section of Scripture focuses on this concern.

One can imagine the amazement of Jethro when he saw Moses sitting as the judge of the people, settling their disputes by appeal to the statutes of God and God's laws. It may be hard for us to get that picture in mind. The people inquired of God through Moses—that is, they sought specific answers through the mouth of Moses. It was a theocratic form of government where God was the ultimate judge, but in this case, his oracle was Moses. So, the people stood before Moses from morning until evening as he dealt with their cases one by one.

Whether Jethro was aware of it or not, Moses had fallen into the trap that victimizes many charismatic leaders. Moses allowed himself to be responsible for all the people, and the problems that might rise among them. How often do we see that in leadership? In our modern day, some have made the case that this was the failure of President Jimmy Carter. He wanted to deal with too many details of government himself, and did not delegate responsibility to capable people. History has yet to write that story, but whether true of President Carter or not, we know it's a common one.

People fall into the snare of not only thinking that they are responsible, but that they are capable.

The mistake of Moses, and Jethro's assessment of the situation, provide good guidance for would-be leaders. Three bad results flowed from Moses' style: (1) he was overworked and simply could not cope with all he had to do; (2) the people were deprived of immediate attention and the swift justice they needed; (3) the elders and other competent individuals were not given the opportunity to use their talents. It is to Jethro's everlasting credit that he was sensitive to this. It was also a sign of his wisdom that he recognized the fact that there were situations with which only Moses would be capable of dealing. So it wasn't a matter of taking leadership from Moses; it was a matter of reordering and dispensing leadership in such a way that other people would share the load.

Pastors can learn a lesson from this. There is, in our calling, a built-in priority. The ultimate priority is that which Jethro defined for Moses. He was to concentrate on the "higher branches of his great calling." He was to be the people-mediator in relation to God, their overseer in relation to God, and his task was to be for the people *Godward*. Many pastors have failed in their high calling because they've not been able to keep that perspective. They lose themselves in trivia, even at a higher level, allowing themselves to be swallowed up in administrative duties that could be more effectively done by others, and so they neglect their own spirituality, their preaching, their sharing as pastor to the people.

Jethro's plan freed Moses in order that he might put his emphasis in the right place: *"You shall teach them the statutes and the laws, and show them the way in which they must walk and the work they must do"* (v. 20).

Jethro described the kind of persons that should be selected for leadership. They were, first of all, to be committed to God: *"such as fear God."* There is the secret of strength for any leadership. We need more in the church than organizational skills, and strong intellectual powers, though these are helpful. He who would be a leader within the context of the church, must have a leader himself, that leader being God. Whatever natural leadership gifts we may start with, these must be heightened and deepened and enlarged by the presence in our lives of a deep and vital religious experience.

I've observed a strange anomaly in our times within the church. We've trained pastors and church leaders how to manage by objective, but altogether too many of them have forgotten what the true objective is. We have sent our pastors to management schools where they have been able to learn how to discipline themselves in relation to time, but too many of them do not know what to do with the time they have saved. Christian leadership must be rooted in the faith, in the leader's commitment to God.

The second characteristic of the leader is a commitment to truth: *"men of truth"* is what Jethro said they must be. This calls for openness, flexibility of mind, a willingness to lay aside pre-judgments and prejudices and to act on the truth as God gives it.

The third characteristic of the leader is commitment to others. Jethro put it as *"hating covetousness,"* or, the phrase could be translated, "hating unjust gain." Some scholars believe that this is a reference to the "oiling of the palms" of Eastern judges. We know how that happens in our day. Those who are in positions of leadership and decision-making are often easily swayed by the favors others show them. The Christian leader must be willing to lay aside all personal gain and to work for the sake of the body, with a commitment to others, always having "clean hands" when it comes to decision-making.

It is to Moses' credit that he heeded the voice of his father-in-law, and did all that his father-in-law had advised him to do.

The chapter closes on a note of sadness. "Then Moses let his father-in-law depart, and he went his way to his own land" (v. 27). That's sad, on the surface, but there are two ways to look at it. The first way to look at it is that Jethro, having come to a new commitment to the Lord and rejoicing in a new revelation of Yahweh, shares with Moses a plan that would provide relief for Moses but would involve hundreds of others in meaningful participation in the faith community. The plan would make relationships in the faith community far more meaningful, orderly, and just. That one had done such a thing and then departed to his own country is quite enough to say about a person. That would be a rather commendable epitaph.

The second way of interpreting the motivation for Jethro's departure is somewhat sadder. In Numbers 10:29-30, which amplifies this brief closing word about Jethro, Moses said to his father-in-law, "'We are setting out for the place of which the Lord said, 'I will give it to you.' Come with us, and we will treat you well; for the Lord has promised good things to Israel.'" And Jethro said to Moses, "'I will not go, but I will depart to my *own* land and to my relatives.'"

Does this give some insight into the heart of Jethro? Did he count the ties of nature more important than the blessings of Jehovah? Did he prefer his own land to the wilderness, and his own kindred to the people of God? Was he not willing to walk by faith, but only by sight? Even after experiencing firsthand, by the witness of Moses, what God had done, and sharing in that blessed community that was on the cutting edge of God's thrust into the future, did Jethro have no heart for God?

We'll never know exactly what went on in Jethro's mind when he left Moses and went back to his own land, but it will help us in ordering our own life in relation to the faith and the call of God upon us to remember Jethro.

NOTES

1. John Fowles, *The Magus* (Boston: Little, Brown, and Co., 1965), p. 150.
2. Alexander Maclaren, *Expositions of Holy Scripture*, 11 vols. (Grand Rapids: Wm. B. Eerdmans, 1952-59), 1:85.

CHAPTER THIRTEEN

With the Lord at the Mountain

Exodus 19:1–25

The mountain had been the goal of the people—the mountain of God. Scholars have long debated the location. No archeological evidence has been discovered that would settle the issue for certain. Some suggest a location in northwest Arabia in the vicinity of the Gulf of Aqaba; others suggest the northern Sinai Peninsula in the vicinity of Kadesh. For hundreds of years now, a mountain peak some 7,647 feet high in the southern Sinai Peninsula called Jebel Musa (Mountain of Moses) has found the greatest number of supporters.

Wherever it was, and is, we encounter in this Scripture the Mountain of God, the object of Moses' dream. The arrival of the people at this place is the climactic point of the entire Book of Exodus. Everything else is prelude; what follows is postlude. Sinai is the scene of the sealing of the covenant, and the establishment of a continuing relationship between God and Israel.

Chapters 19 to 24 of Exodus, along with Genesis 3, have often been called the most important chapters in the Old Testament. Here we find the account of the covenant God made with Israel at Mount Sinai. This covenant was conditioned upon Israel's obedience to laws which were given to the people at Sinai. The balance of the Old Testament contains the story of how Israel responded to that covenant relationship. It is largely a story of disobedience, unheeded warnings of the prophets, stormy judgment, and punishment. A "history of failure" is the title often given to the story of Israel in Old Testament times. Clearly, it is the story of a people's failure to be what God wanted them to be.

Of course, there were those high moments in their life as a people, and no one can dare be too hard on Israel. Theirs has been a tough lot, and one cannot imagine that any other people would have been more faithful. Given the story of our own lives, and looking at our own personal pilgrimages, we can only rejoice in the fact that this "no people" responded as faithfully as they did, became the instrument through which God's salvation history would be written, and out of which would come the Savior of the world.

When Ogden Nash wrote his cryptic jingle "How Odd of God to Choose the Jews," he was expressing the sentiment of many Christians, but in that "oddness" of God is a symbol of God's providential movement, the activity of God that is mysterious and beyond our understanding—yet, an activity on which we're all dependent and to which we must all respond.

Here this "odd" people, who've been brought out of Egyptian bondage, have come to the Mountain where they are going to be with the Lord.

The word "theophany" is a compound of the Greek word meaning "God" and the verb "to appear." Here, at the mountain, in a theophany, God appears to the people. Now to be sure, as we see when we read the text, the Scripture makes it clear that God made no visible appearance. In fact, Israel was soundly warned not to come near enough that they might by chance visibly see God's Presence. It is a theophany nonetheless, because here God manifested Himself.

In all probability, the present narrative in chapter 19 was used often in the worship life of Israel. These mighty acts of God in history, connected with the faith of Israel, were recreated in the worship life of Israel. Certainly, central in that worship was the act of law-giving and covenant. Therefore, at least in the annual religious festivals, these events must have been celebrated. Therefore, the call to prepare for the appearance of the Lord, which we find in this chapter, may have been used often in later generations to call others to prepare themselves for the coming of the Lord, for their own theophany.

ISRAEL: A SPECIAL TREASURE TO THE LORD

19:1 In the third month after the children of Israel had gone out of the land of Egypt, on the same day, they came *to* the Wilderness of Sinai.

2 For they had departed from Rephidim, had come *to* the Wilderness of Sinai, and camped in the wilderness. So Israel camped there before the mountain.

3 And Moses went up to God, and the LORD called to him from the mountain, saying, "Thus you shall say to the house of Jacob, and tell the children of Israel:

4 'You have seen what I did to the Egyptians, and *how* I bore you on eagles' wings and brought you to Myself.

5 'Now therefore, if you will indeed obey My voice and keep My covenant, then you shall be a special treasure to Me above all people; for all the earth *is* Mine.

6 'And you shall be to Me a kingdom of priests and a holy nation.' These *are* the words which you shall speak to the children of Israel."

7 So Moses came and called for the elders of the people, and laid before them all these words which the LORD commanded him.

8 Then all the people answered together and said, "All that the LORD has spoken we will do." So Moses brought back the words of the people to the LORD.

Exod. 19:1–8

When Moses had responded to God's call to deliver his people out of bondage, having been confronted by God in the burning bush, God said to him, "I will certainly be with you. And this shall be a sign to you that I have sent you: When you have brought the people out of Egypt, you shall serve God on this mountain" (Exod. 3:12).

God had kept His promise, and the sign was now manifested. Three months after leaving Egypt, the Israelites had finally arrived at Sinai. They pitched their tents at the base of the mountain, and at this mountain they were to be with the Lord. Here the most significant event in Israel's history, the establishment of the covenant, would take place. Immediately upon their arrival, God called Moses up onto the mountain. There He shared that word—the word of covenant: *"If you will indeed obey My voice, and keep My covenant, then you shall be a special treasure to Me above all people"* (v. 5). The etymology of the Hebrew word for "covenant"—*běrît*—is a bit uncertain. It may come from the word *bârâh*, "to eat"—hence, we have that understanding of a covenant being made by eating a meal together. Or it could have come from *birîtu*, meaning "to fetter" or "to bind." So, we would have covenant as a binding of two or more parties.

Another shade of meaning comes from the use of the word *běrît* as signifying an agreement *between* parties. Generally, "covenant" may be defined as a mutual agreement between two or more parties. Some examples of covenants in the Old Testament are the covenants of Noah (Gen. 9:8–17), Jacob and Laban (Gen. 29:15–20), and David and Jonathan (1 Sam. 18:1–4). We discussed the idea of covenant in the first chapter, in our commentary on Exodus 1.

Two words of the Lord, along with the response from Israel, stand out in this section. The first word is God's reminder to Israel of what He had done. There is no more beautiful word in Scripture: *"You have seen what I did to the Egyptians, and how I bore you on eagles' wings and brought you to Myself"* (v. 4). Here is a beautiful picture of God's marvelous grace.

The eagle is actually a bird of prey. Job says: "They pass by like swift ships, / Like an eagle swooping on its prey" (9:26). So, also says Jesus: "For as the lightning comes from the east and flashes to the west, so also will the coming of the Son of Man be. For wherever the carcass is, there the eagles will be gathered together" (Matt. 24:27–28).

Though a bird of prey, the eagle is used as a symbol for God and for deity throughout Scripture. In the Book of Ezekiel, deity is represented by the face of an eagle. In the fourth chapter of the Book of Revelation, deity is pictured by a flying eagle.

The eagle is seen and admired for its strength and its ability to soar to the heights. It is the king of birds. Someone has called the eagle the "jet-plane of the bird family."

So, there is great beauty in the metaphor of Israel's being born on eagle's wings, held aloft by God's grace, carried by Him safely out of the bony hands of death back in Egypt.

Israel could rehearse that symbolism in very specific events: deliverance from Pharaoh's attacking army at the Red Sea, bitter water made sweet at Marah, water brought from the rock at Meribah and Massah, manna throughout their wilderness wandering, and the defeat of the Amalekites. Over and over again God had delivered them; all the way He had born Israel on eagles' wings.

Isn't that the way He bears us today? He leads us by grace, and we walk by faith.

This eloquent figure of the eagles' wings was movingly employed to describe the relationship of Israel to God in the Song of Moses recorded in Deuteronomy.

> "He found him in a desert land
> And in the wasteland, a howling wilderness;
> He encircled him, He instructed him,
> He kept him as the apple of His eye.
> As an eagle stirs up its nest,
> Hovers over its young,
> Spreading out its wings, taking them up,
> Carrying them on its wings,
> So the Lord alone led him. . . ."
>
> *Deut. 32:10–12a*

The second attention-getting word in this section is the Lord's claim to Israel: *"You shall be a special treasure to Me"* (v. 5).

The essential content of this section is encompassed here. There is the invitation to meet the Lord in Sinai, the call to obey His voice, and the opportunity to enter into covenant relationship with Him. There is a sense in which this section of Scripture summarizes the whole of chapters 19 to 24. Everything revolves around this movement of God to Israel, and Israel's response. The theme is repeated over and over again. In Deuteronomy, it is expressed numerous times, but none more specifically than Deuteronomy 7:6: "For you are a holy people to the Lord your God; the Lord your God has chosen you to be a people for Himself, a special treasure above all the peoples on the face of the earth."

The key word is "chosen." And there's nothing quite like it—to be chosen.

I remember how it was growing up in rural Mississippi. We had to manufacture our toys out of tin cans, broomsticks, barrel hoops, and the like. And we had to invent our games or adapt those which had been passed down to us from who knows where, except that they came to us through our older brothers and sisters. Whether playing "stealing sticks" or slow pitch with a string ball, there was nothing quite like the feeling that came when you knew you were chosen for a team.

Can any married person ever forget the joy that came when it was settled—your mate had accepted your proposal of marriage, or your mate had finally gotten the courage to ask and you could respond "yes"? In human relations, this is the ultimate in being chosen. Someone selects you to be the person with whom he or she wishes to spend his or her life. Then the consummation of the choices comes in the marriage when the decision is sealed with a life commitment of love. Chosen!

The teacher or preacher may well keep repeating the theme: chosen. Chosen by God; chosen for a purpose; chosen for privilege.

The claim that one group of people is chosen can be offensive. It is offensive if those who are singled out are singled out for privileges from which everyone else is excluded. We dare not see this in God's selection of Israel. Immediately following His designation of Israel as *"a special treasure to Me,"* God said, *"For all the earth is Mine"* (v. 5). There can be no arrogance on the part of Israel. Her relationship to Yahweh is set in the context of God's universal sovereignty. Let it be very clear that God does not say He is Israel's possession to be used for Israel's benefit. Israel is to be God's own possession, to be used according to God's will.

As "a special treasure," God's chosen one, Israel was to express herself in two ways. One, she was to be a kingdom of priests. This is the only place in the Old Testament where this phrase is found: *"You shall be to me a kingdom of priests."* It's interesting to note that in Isaiah 61, where the good news of salvation is proclaimed, is the same good news that Jesus announced in his first sermon: "The Spirit of the Lord God is upon Me, / Because the Lord has anointed Me / To preach good tidings to the poor. . . ." In that same chapter of Isaiah, a similar notion to what God is saying here to Israel is put forth. "But you shall be named the priests of the Lord, / They shall call you the servants of our God . . ." (Isa. 61:6). This people is to be a people who live wholly to serve God; as priests they are to be mediators for Him, each one enjoying the right of individual access to Him, but also, each one bearing a responsibility of being a bridge (one meaning of "priest") between God and others. The "priesthood of believers" begins here, and not in the New Testament.

The second way God's chosen ones were to express themselves as God's special treasure was that they were to be a holy nation.

To be holy meant that they were to be separated, set apart, unto God from all other nations, to live lives that would reflect the very nature of God. The essence of holiness as we find it in the Bible is "conforming to the character of God." This is the essence of the covenant and is a central theme running throughout Scripture. It is the recurring call of Paul "that we should be holy and without blame before Him in love" (Eph. 1:4).

As in the Hebrew language, so in Greek the word "holy" had in it the idea of difference and separation. The Christian is to be distinctly different—set apart by God for God's purpose. The church has often mistaken the meaning of the word. The separation is not *from* the world, but a difference expressed *in* the world.

So, as God's special treasure, Israel had been chosen, chosen to be a kingdom of priests and a holy nation. Both mean that Israel was chosen for others. It's interesting that Peter uses this same passage to set forth the vocation of the Christian church: "But you are a chosen generation, a royal priesthood, a holy nation, His own special people, that you may proclaim the praises of Him who called you out of darkness into His marvelous light" (1 Pet. 2:9). The vocation of the Christian is the vocation of a priest, to be a bridge between people and God, to be witnesses, proclaiming the acceptable year of the Lord. Specifically as priests, we are to speak to the people for God, and we are to speak to God for the people. Our dual vocation is the vocation of witness and prayer.

Leo Buscaglia is a popular professor at the University of Southern California and a best-selling author. He teaches courses in love, and his classes are packed every semester. He writes books that are very helpful in the hope and guidance they offer. I'm told that at the start of a semester, Professor Buscaglia always assigns a paper asking the students to answer the question: "What would you do if you had only five days to live?" They say the answers are very interesting, and you can imagine what some of them would be. "I'd say I'm sorry." "I'd say I love you." "I'd say thank you to my parents."

The students turn these papers in, but when they get them back, they're not graded. Instead, Dr. Buscaglia writes in bold letters across the top of the paper, "Why don't you do it now? What are you waiting for?"

It's a challenge to us. We know who we are—we know our vocation as God's people. If God gave us only five days to live, what would we do? We'd do those things He has told us to do, chief among them, performing our function as priests, giving our witness, and making our intercession. Well, why don't we do it now?

That leads to the third word that stands out in this section of Scripture, Israel's response to God's offer: *"All that the Lord has spoken we will do"* (v. 8).

Obviously Israel was clear about the character of the word heard at Sinai. Her response was unequivocal: they were ready to enter the covenant on the terms of the One who initiated the covenant.

For Israel to carry out her mission and to keep the covenant required commitment and obedience.

It's interesting to note that the call for commitment was not a prerequisite that the Israelites had to meet in order to qualify for God's choice. God had already chosen them. Now, why He had chosen them is a mystery. They were not a powerful nation. They were not a repository of cultural achievement. Certainly a more promising candidate to be a chosen people would have been mighty Egypt. Yet, the election of Israel was not due to the merit of the people, but to the grace of God. "The Lord did not set His love on you nor choose you because you were more in number than any other people, for you were the least of all peoples; but because the Lord loves you, and because He would keep the oath which He swore to your fathers, the Lord has brought you out with a mighty hand, and redeemed you from the house of bondage, from the hand of Pharaoh king of Egypt" (Deut. 7:7–8).

So it wasn't a matter of being obedient as a prerequisite, rather God would use His people for the sake of the world only when they were obedient and reliable. Obedient response was possible for Israel, and is possible for anyone, only in response to God's prior act of grace.

Here the tension between law and grace begins to be clearly marked. Israel had done nothing to earn their deliverance out of Egypt. God reminded them of that: *"I bore you on eagles' wings and brought you to Myself"* (v. 4). Indeed, they had been untrue to God before He delivered them, and had complained of God's dealings afterward. Even so, in His great love and pity for them, and in fulfillment of His promise to Abraham, God had taken them from Egypt and brought them to Himself.

Now that they were free and brought near to Him, God had a dazzling proposal to make—the offer to enter into covenant with them. As must be underscored over and over again, it was a conditional promise. The covenant would remain in tact as they remained obedient. There is a fine line here. God did not choose them according to their obedience; but for them to be the kingdom of priests, the holy nation, that He was calling them to be, then they must keep the covenant.

PREPARATION FOR MEETING THE LORD

19:9 And the LORD said to Moses, "Behold, I come to you in the thick cloud, that the people may hear when I speak with you, and believe you forever." So Moses told the words of the people to the LORD.

10 Then the LORD said to Moses, "Go to the people and consecrate them today and tomorrow, and let them wash their clothes.

11 "And let them be ready for the third day. For on the third day the LORD will come down upon Mount Sinai in the sight of all the people.

12 "You shall set bounds for the people all around, saying, 'Take heed to yourselves *that* you do *not* go up to the mountain or touch its base. Whoever touches the mountain shall surely be put to death.

13 'Not a hand shall touch him, but he shall surely be stoned or shot *with an arrow*; whether man or beast, he shall not live.' When the trumpet sounds long, they shall come near the mountain."

14 So Moses went down from the mountain to the people and sanctified the people, and they washed their clothes.

15 And he said to the people, "Be ready for the third day; do not come near *your* wives."

Exod. 19:9–15

The Book of Exodus makes it clear that Yahweh is not merely a territorial God; His sovereignty is not restricted to a particular patch of land over which He holds sway, or over a particular people. Already, to this point, Yahweh has demonstrated that He is in control of the forces of nature and the inhabitants of a great world power, Egypt. In verse 5, He asserted that "all the earth is Mine." Even so, there is obviously something special about God and this place, this mountain. Earlier, at the burning bush, God had told Moses he was standing on holy ground, and that He would bring Moses back to this place. Now, the people are warned that the mountain shares to some degree the holiness of God Himself. Only after they have carefully prepared themselves are they to approach this place where they are going to hear God speak. Also, they are to come only at the time and up to the point that is outlined for them by Moses.

Though it is plain in the text, it is easy to miss the point: it is the Presence or the Glory of God, not the Person, that the people are to see. God was going to manifest Himself in a thick cloud, so that when they heard God speaking to Moses, they would forever believe. God's Presence and His Glory would be manifest, but not His Person.

One remembers the call of Isaiah here (Isa. 6). Isaiah says, "I saw the Lord"—but then Isaiah describes all the dynamics of the Presence of the Lord. To see the Lord is not to see the Lord's Person, but to experience the Lord's Presence. God makes that clear: *"You shall set bounds for the people all around, saying, 'Take heed to yourselves that you do not go up to the mountain or touch its base. Whoever touches the mountain shall surely be put to death'"* (Exod. 19:12). In a later encounter between God and Moses, God tells Moses that He will "make all My goodness pass before you," but "you cannot see My face; for no man shall see Me, and live" (Exod. 33:19, 20).

Four things are to be noted here. First, we must not reduce God to any manifestation of Him that we're able to comprehend. Certainly, Christ gives us access to God's Presence, but we must be careful not to confuse Presence with Person. How often we see people reducing God to the lowest common denominator of their experience. One expression of this is our habit of glorifying the outward details of a religious experience rather than the experience itself. We see that in the way people sometimes seek to lead others into the Christian life. They outline entry into the Christian life according to their own experience of it, so that the *how* of the experience becomes more important than the experience itself.

241

Second, there is always a "distance" between us and God. Be careful of any presentation of religion that offers a chummy God with whom we can come and go as we please.

Third, any place is holy that God chooses to be holy. While there was a specialness about Sinai, remember what Jesus said to the woman at the well in Samaria: "Woman, believe Me, the hour is coming when you will neither on this mountain, nor in Jerusalem, worship the Father. . . . But the hour is coming, and now is, when the true worshipers will worship the Father in spirit and in truth . . ." (John 4:21, 23).

Fourth, the Lord requires preparation for Israel to meet Him. He instructed Moses to tell the people that they were to wash their garments and abstain from sexual relations, thus marking the coming occasion as a special one. Now the details of preparation may be alien to us, but the big point is not alien. Yahweh is God, not a human being. We do not approach God casually, on terms of equality. We come as human beings before the Holy One, knowing that God reveals His presence to us only at His initiative.

It is important to recall the words of the psalmist here:

> Who may ascend into the hill of the Lord?
> Or who may stand in His holy place?
> He who has clean hands and a pure heart,
> Who has not lifted up his soul to [vanity].
> *Ps. 24:3–4*

Moments when heaven touches earth and God meets people are not to be taken casually.

This underscores two disciplines of the Christian life: worship and moral purity.

To concentrate on Moses helps us get the impact of this entire nineteenth chapter. If you examine the passage as a mere report of a sequence of events, it's confusing, to say the least. Moses went up to the mountain in verse 3. He has come back down in verse 7. He apparently has gone back up in verse 8, because he is going to be coming down in verse 14. Still another round trip awaits him in verses 20 and 25.

Lester Meyer reminds us that "none of this trudging back and forth would be necessary if Yahweh would only speak directly to Israel and observe Israel's response for Himself. But that is just the point. Yahweh is quite capable of dealing directly with the people, and does so on many occasions. But He has chosen to work through Moses, not only in the deliverance from Egyptian bondage, but also in the establishment of the covenant."[1]

Moses was the "go-between" between God and Israel—the mediator. And it's important to note that Moses had access to God. One of the greatest tributes to Moses in the entire Bible is in the statement from Exodus 33:11. The Lord "spoke to Moses face to face, as a man speaks to his friend." Now that seems to be contrary to what we have been saying about distinguishing between Person and Presence. That statement is a Hebrew overstatement, but the point is made beautifully. Moses had access to God in a way that others did not. The important question is: why?

First of all, God had chosen Moses for a particular task. God granted the access. But a second reason is equally important: Moses was faithful. He remained obedient, despite the disobedience of his people.

Relationship to God, fruitfulness in witness, effectiveness in prayer, influence in discipleship—all are dependent upon our faithfulness. The degree of our obedience to God determines the degree of His empowerment for our living the lives He calls us to live.

THE COMING OF THE LORD

19:16 Then it came to pass on the third day, in the morning, that there were thunderings and lightnings, and a thick cloud on the mountain; and the sound of the trumpet was very loud, so that all the people who *were* in the camp trembled.

17 And Moses brought the people out of the camp to meet with God, and they stood at the foot of the mountain.

18 Now Mount Sinai *was* completely in smoke, because the LORD descended upon it in fire. Its smoke ascended like the smoke of a furnace, and the whole mountain quaked greatly.

19 And when the blast of the trumpet sounded long and became louder and louder, Moses spoke, and God answered him by voice.

20 Then the LORD came down upon Mount Sinai, on the top of the mountain. And the LORD called Moses to the top of the mountain, and Moses went up.

21 And the LORD said to Moses, "Go down and warn the people, lest they break through to gaze at the LORD, and many of them perish.

22 "Also let the priests who come near the LORD consecrate themselves, lest the LORD break out against them."

23 But Moses said to the LORD, "The people cannot come up to Mount Sinai; for You warned us, saying, 'Set bounds around the mountain and consecrate it.'"

24 Then the LORD said to him, "Away! Get down and then come up, you and Aaron with you. But do not let the priests and the people break through to come up to the LORD, lest He break out against them."

25 So Moses went down to the people and spoke to them.

Exod. 19:16–25

Frederick Buechner says that "glory is what God looks like when, for the time being, all you have to look at it with is a pair of eyes." How the Israelites must have experienced the glory of God's Presence. The mountain was completely surrounded in smoke, because the Lord descended upon it in fire. The smoke was like that of a furnace, and the whole mountain began to shake. After that came the blast of the trumpet—a long, long blast that grew louder and louder. Then, Scripture puts it in a magnificent understatement: *"Moses spoke, and God answered him by voice"* (v. 19).

We can't even begin to imagine the awe-inspiring experience of Moses in that conversation with God. You get a feel of it, years afterward, when Moses was making his farewell address just before his death. He referred to this scene and asked if from the beginning of time such a thing had ever been known. "For ask now concerning the days that are past, which were before you, since the day that God created man on the earth, and ask from one end of heaven to the other, whether any great thing like this has happened, or anything like it has been heard. Did any people ever hear the voice of God speaking out of the midst of the fire, as you have heard, and live? . . . Out of heaven He let you hear His voice, that He might instruct you; on earth He showed you His great fire, and you heard His words out of the midst of the fire" (Deut. 4:32–33, 36).

When the writer to the Hebrews listed the glorious company of faith and came to Moses, he said that Moses was so terrified with the experience of God that he said, "I'm exceedingly afraid and trembling" (12:21). The writer of the letter to the Hebrews was quoting Deuteronomy 9:19.

There is no question about this event in terms of what is happening: this is a theophany—an emphatic appearance of God to Israel. And there are questions, of course. Are the natural phenomena to be interpreted as the violent manifestations of storm? Or as erupting volcanos? Or, are these simply intentional metaphors, designed to describe the otherwise indescribable? It would take language like this to communicate the sense of overpowering awe, mystery, and dramatic violent force of the actual presence of God.

From the point of view of understanding the faith of ancient Israel, these are not critical questions. They may be questions to the typical Western frame of mind. We put so much significance upon delineation of fact; there is a sadness about this, which we should regret. When we get beyond the frustration of such questions and leave behind the uncertainties of the external structure, what we have is an uncomplicated, emphatic presentation of a glorious event as internally apprehended by a faithful people. This faithful people remembered and celebrated the memory of that occasion, and they drew upon that memory in subsequent centuries for strength. They knew themselves to be the children of Sinai. The meaning of their life came predominantly from that event.

> What is said in this record is said in faith. It is said categorically; it is put beyond the limits of dispute. It is affirmed colorfully, vividly, in descriptive language appealing to and involving all the senses: to every instrument of human perception, God made known His glory and presence. It is still not Himself that is perceived, but the unqualified fact of His now immediately impinging life and nature and will. [2]

The external signs—the mountains smoking and rocking and quaking, the trumpets sounding louder and louder, and then the word spoken by the Lord—were given by God to confirm His Presence and to validate the covenant which was coming into being. The covenant is the focus, and we're going to be dealing with that from this point on.

The Christian should never read this passage or consider this stage of God's covenantal relationship with His people without also reading that glorious word from the Epistle to the Hebrews, which puts a new covenant in contrast to this one.

> For you have not come to the mountain that may be touched and that burned with fire, and to blackness and darkness and tempest, and the sound of a trumpet and the voice of words, so that those who heard it begged that the word should not be spoken to them anymore. (For they could not endure what was commanded: "And if so much as a beast touches the mountain, it shall be stoned or shot with an arrow." And so terrifying was the sight that Moses said, "I am exceedingly afraid and trembling.")
>
> But you have come to Mount Zion and to the city of the living God, the heavenly Jerusalem, to an innumerable company of angels, to the general assembly and church of the firstborn who are registered in heaven, to God the Judge of all, to the spirits of just men made perfect, to Jesus the Mediator of the new covenant, and to the blood of sprinkling that speaks better things than that of Abel.
>
> *Heb. 12:18–24*

NOTES

1. Lester Meyer, *The Message of Exodus* (Minneapolis: Augsburg Publishing, 1983), p. 115.
2. B. Davie Napier, *Exodus*, Layman's Bible Commentary (Richmond, VA: John Knox Press, 1963), 3:73.

CHAPTER FOURTEEN

Covenant Law at Sinai: The Ten Commandments

Exodus 20:1–26

I doubt if any document has influenced Western culture to the degree that the Ten Commandments have. In Western civilization, they have a position of inescapable significance. For Jews, Romans Catholics, and Protestants, this is the only formulation of religious principles held in common. In many Christian churches, knowledge of the Ten Commandments is a requirement for membership. The civil law of many lands has rootage in this covenant law of God given at Sinai.

It should be noted as we begin this study of the Ten Commandments that the Israelites were not the first, and certainly not the only, people to have a written law. Other ancient law codes included those of Ur-Nammu (Sumerian, *ca.* 2050 B.C.), Lipit-Ishtar (Sumerian, *ca.* 1900 B.C.), Eshnunna (Akkadian, *ca.* 1875 B.C.), and Hammurabi (Babylonian, *ca.* 1690 B.C.).

The fact that there was no written law in Egypt may be explained by the status of the Pharaoh. He was considered a god, and therefore his spoken word at any given moment was law. Law, in ancient times, as well as today, served to regulate and control interpersonal relationships, to maintain the stability of community life, and to guarantee justice as justice was perceived. For Israel, the law bound together a heterogeneous group of slaves into a nation, a community that endures to the present time. The law became the outward expression of the covenant, so we call it Covenant Law. Obedience to the law was Israel's response to covenant. It was the outward and visible sign of their being a "kingdom of priests" and "a holy nation."

The way the Ten Commandments are stated is rare, in fact, hardly found outside of Israel in the ancient world. The laws are in the form of absolutes, "Thou shalt" or "Thou shalt not." A more common expression of law was conditional: "If you do this and that, then I will do this or that."

Eight of the ten commandments are expressed negatively ("Thou shalt not . . ."). This is a second characteristic of their form. This has been partly responsible for criticism leveled against the Jewish and the Christian faith—that it is a way of life based on restrictions. We'll deal with that criticism as we move through the particular commandments.

There is a third characteristic of the commandments to which we are especially called to give heed. They are expressed in the second person singular form. In the old King James Version, the word is "thou," preserving the singular form distinctly, which the modern "you" does not. To be sure, this singular pronoun may be interpreted as speaking to Israel as a community, but what we need to heed is that here is an emphatic reminder, a probing call to each individual within the community, to bear the responsibility of the law and to obey it.

A final characteristic, one which must not go unnoticed, is that the commandments concern our relationship with God and our relationship with each other. The commandments begin with our relationship with God—the first four dealing primarily with that relationship. The remaining six deal with our relationship to each other. So, the vertical and horizontal relationships of life are included here. Implicitly, the law reminds us that neither of these relationships can be ignored, and neither is to receive emphasis to the exclusion of the other.

The question of law and grace is usually raised when we come to a consideration of the Ten Commandments. And, usually, behind our thinking about them is the question: "Are Christians required to keep the Ten Commandments?"

To keep or not to keep the Ten Commandments does not settle the issue of grace. Yes, Christians are to keep the Ten Commandments, and this does not put law above grace. Though we are saved by grace, and are not dependent upon works, the spirit of the Ten Commandments is binding on us all. Jesus said that He did not come to abolish the law but to fulfill it (Matt. 5:17). On one occasion, in two statements Jesus summarized not only the manner in which the Old

Testament law should be kept, but also the impact of the prophets: "Jesus said to him, '"You shall love the Lord your God with all your heart, with all your soul, and with all your mind.' This is the first and great commandment. And the second is like it: "You shall love your neighbor as yourself." On these two commandments hang all the Law and the Prophets'" (Matt. 22:37–40).

In the New Testament, evidence of our love for the Lord is our obedience. The fact that we are under grace instead of the Old Testament legal relationship with God should not lead us to think that the Ten Commandments are not applicable to us. What grace does for us is give us freedom and joy in being obedient. Since we know that the perfect keeping of the law is not the basis for our salvation, we can live boldly in our obedience, knowing that when we stumble over the law, or because of the law, or in keeping the law, our salvation is still intact because of grace.

During the days of the Gold Rush, a young man and his bride set out across the country to make their fortunes. Somewhere along the way, they drank some contaminated water, and the young bride became ill and died before they could reach Fort Kearney in Nebraska. Heartbroken, the young man took her body to the highest hill and buried it, using the wagon bed to make a coffin. He drove down some wooden stakes to mark the grave, thinking that he would go on West and later come back. But the more he thought about it, the more he was certain that he couldn't go on. He said to himself, "I'll forget where this is; I will never remember it." So, he retraced his steps all the way to St. Louis, Missouri. He found a stonecutter and had him prepare a tombstone engraved with the name "Susan Hale" along with the date of her birth and death.

He tried vainly to get someone to haul it back for him, but all the wagons going west were already overloaded, and no one would help him. Finally, he bought a wheelbarrow, put the stone in it, and walked those weary miles back toward Fort Kearney, and set the stone up on her grave.

It's a tender story. The man knew that there was something he must never forget. Here was a sacred spot on earth, and he must always remember where it was.

Thus it is with Mount Sinai and the Ten Commandments. The Ten Commandments have been set up for us so that we will never forget the importance of some things. We keep coming back to them, for they speak to us of eternal truths and values. So we look at them in that fashion.

THE TEN COMMANDMENTS

20:1 And God spoke all these words, saying:

2 "I *am* the LORD your God, who brought you out of the land of Egypt, out of the house of bondage.

3 "You shall have no other gods before Me.

4 "You shall not make for yourself a carved image—any likeness *of anything* that *is* in heaven above, or that *is* in the earth beneath, or that *is* in the water under the earth;

5 you shall not bow down to them nor serve them. For I, the LORD your God, *am* a jealous God, visiting the iniquity of the fathers upon the children to the third and fourth *generations* of those who hate Me,

6 but showing mercy to thousands, to those who love Me and keep My commandments.

7 "You shall not take the name of the LORD your God in vain, for the LORD will not hold *him* guiltless who takes His name in vain.

8 "Remember the Sabbath day, to keep it holy.

9 Six days you shall labor and do all your work,

10 but the seventh day *is* the Sabbath of the LORD your God. *In it* you shall do no work: you, nor your son, nor your daughter, nor your male servant, nor your female servant, nor your cattle, nor your stranger who *is* within your gates.

11 For *in* six days the LORD made the heavens and the earth, the sea, and all that *is* in them, and rested the seventh day. Therefore the LORD blessed the Sabbath day and hallowed it.

12 "Honor your father and your mother, that your
   days may be long upon the land which
   the LORD your God is giving you.

13 "You shall not murder.

14 "You shall not commit adultery.

15 "You shall not steal.

16 "You shall not bear false witness against your
   neighbor.

17 "You shall not covet your neighbor's house; you
   shall not covet your neighbor's wife, nor
   his male servant, nor his female servant,
   nor his ox, nor his donkey, nor anything
   that *is* your neighbor's."

Exod. 20:1-17

Several years ago, on the cover of *The Saturday Evening Post,* there was a painting by Norman Rockwell showing a woman buying her Thanksgiving turkey. The turkey is lying on the scales and the butcher is standing back of the counter, apron pulled tight over his fat stomach, a pencil tucked behind his ear. The customer, a lovely lady of about sixty, is watching the weighing-in. Each of them has a pleased look as if each knows a secret joke. There's nothing unusual about a butcher and a customer watching as a turkey is being weighed, but the expression on their faces indicates that something unusual is going on. Norman Rockwell lets us in on the joke by showing us their hands. The butcher is pushing down on the scales with a big fat thumb. The woman is pushing up on them with a dainty forefinger. Neither is aware of what the other is doing.

Cecil Myers, who reminds us of that painting, says, "Both the butcher and the lovely lady would resent being called thieves. The lovely lady would never rob a bank or steal a car. The butcher would be indignant if anyone accused him of stealing; and if a customer gave him a bad check, he would call the police, but neither saw anything wrong with a little deception that would make a few cents for one or save a few cents for the other."[1]

Rockwell gives us a picture of how we seek to live, trying to manipulate life for our advantage. And that's what the Ten Commandments are all about—they remind us that there are eternal laws in the universe by which we must live if life is going to come out God's way.

251

The issues addressed in the Ten Commandments are acts that are wrong, but not because the Ten Commandments say so. God said they were wrong because the moral law of the universe won't support killing and stealing and committing adultery. It doesn't matter in what period of history we live, it's still wrong to steal—wrong whether we do it by shoplifting or cheating on our income tax or failing to give our employer a full day's work or by manipulating a stock market sale.

It's still wrong to kill, whether it is done in the heat of a domestic argument with a "Saturday night special," or by the outrageous bombing of an innocent population on the "killing fields" of Cambodia.

It's still wrong to commit adultery, though that has become one of the most socially acceptable sins of our day. It portends the tearing apart of the entire family structure and thus the fabric of our culture.

It is still wrong to bear false witness against our neighbor, whether in deliberate lie, or in the sweet morsel of innuendo that makes malicious gossip destructive of character.

Again, the moral law of the universe won't support killing and stealing and adultery and deception. Let's look at each of these Ten Commandments, not just for the sin they warn against, but also for the direction they give us if we're going to live life the way God would have us live it.

No Other Gods

"You shall have no other gods before Me" (v. 3). No other ancient law code has been found that prohibits worship of other gods. This commandment—belief in one God—set the Israelite religion apart from all other Ancient Near East religions and was responsible for shaping the monotheistic faith of Israel. The call is for undivided allegiance, total commitment. *"Before Me,"* literally translated is "against My face," and the phrase expresses God's insistence that He is to be the only God of Israel. In that we have argued all along that Yahweh was not a territorial God but a universal one, claiming "the whole earth is Mine," this commandment is universal.

We noted earlier that the first four commandments have to do with our relationship to God, while the next six commandments have to do with our relationship to others. The first four commandments, plus the introductory word by which God identifies Himself, provide a marvelous framework for looking at God. B. Davie Napier reminds us that these first words have to do with that which is directly related to "the Senior Party of the Covenant": God's (1) identity, (2) nature, (3) name, (4) day, and (5) claim.[2]

To hear what God has to say, and to appropriate the intensely concentrated definition of the covenant stated in these commandments, we begin with the One who initiates the covenant: *"I am the Lord your God who brought you out of the land of Egypt, out of the house of bondage"* (v. 2).

Though we do not list this as one of the Ten Commandments, there is a sense in which a commandment is implicit. We are to know and acknowledge God as the One who has delivered us, and as the first word of the Bible says, as the One who created us. So the commandment is: "Know Me! Acknowledge Me! Remember Me! I am the Lord your God."

This first commandment is affirmed in a remarkable sentence, which for the Jew is the heart of the Torah: "Hear, O Israel, the Lord our God, the Lord is one!" (Deut. 6:4). The Jews called this the Shema, and it is the word most often on their mouths in worship, and to that description of God is added the word, "You shall love the Lord your God with all your heart, with all your soul, and with all your strength" (Deut. 6:5).

There is a sense in which this first commandment is the greatest, because it gives the motivating power for all the rest. The rest of the commandments mean little or nothing unless commitment to God gives an impelling desire to obey Him. Few, if any, readers would confess to breaking this commandment. We need to remember Martin Luther's word: "Whatever thy heart clings to and relies upon, that is properly thy God." Security, position, power, social prestige, love of country, love of family, profession, job—it is not uncommon for any of these to replace God as our first commitment. Jesus put the matter plainly when He named the greatest commandment, "You shall love the Lord your God with all your heart, mind, soul, and strength; and your neighbor as yourself," and when on the basis of that, He told us how to live: "Seek first the kingdom of God and His righteousness, and all these things shall be added to you" (Matt. 6:33).

I called attention earlier to the negative expression of some of the commandments, as well as the criticism of Judaism and Christianity in terms of restrictiveness and removal of much of the pleasure from life. Think of the other side of this commandment. To be sure, it is that—a commandment: "You shall have no thing, or no one before Me," God says. But, "I am your God." That's the other side—that God is a personal God, available to our needs. The Scripture is filled with that witness. "I cried out to the Lord . . . and He answered me!" (Jon. 2:2). "My God shall supply all your need according to His riches in glory . . ." (Phil. 4:19). "Yea, though I walk through the valley of the shadow of death, I will fear no evil, for You are with me" (Ps. 23:4). "Do not fear, little flock; for it is your Father's good pleasure to give you the Kingdom" (Luke 12:32).

The question is not a matter of whether we believe in *a* god, but whether we believe in God—not only whether we believe in Him, but whether we worship Him and commit ourselves to Him without reservation.

No Images

"You shall not make for yourself a carved image—any likeness of anything that is in heaven above, or that is in the earth beneath, or that is in the water under the earth" (v. 4). This second commandment goes a step beyond the first. The first commandment forbids the worship of any but the true God, the second forbids the worship of any representation of the true God. Here is a call, not only not to worship any other god, but not to worship the true God in the wrong way. This is a word about idolatry.

In commenting on the dramatic sin of idolatry, the making of the golden calf, which will soon happen in Israel at the foot of Mount Sinai where this commandment was given, F. B. Meyer said,

> Had anyone suggested that Israel would apostatize from the God of Abraham, they would have stoned him to death. They had no desire to break the first commandment and to have other gods than Jehovah, but they found the demand of the second commandment too vigorous. They must have an image, a visible representation, an idol.[3]

So, they made the golden calf. They had to have a visible image, something they could see and touch.

Now, on the surface there's nothing wrong with that. To have those things that remind us of God, or of that which represents God, may be a tremendous aid to worship for many of us. God is unseen, a Spirit and Power invisible to our eyes. So, we need settings, symbols, places of worship to be vivid reminders of God. The problem comes when the symbol, the reminder, becomes a substitute, when it becomes an idol and takes the place of God.

There's a dramatic story of this in Numbers 21. In their wandering through the wilderness, the people of Israel were attacked and tortured by fiery serpents. Moses, on the instruction of God, made a bronze serpent and set it up on a pole. Those who had been bitten looked at the bronze serpent and were healed. Not much is made of that story as it is found in Numbers 21:6-9, but centuries later we find that bronze serpent making another brief appearance. This time, we find King Hezekiah breaking the serpent in pieces, because the people had been burning incense to it (2 Kings 18:4). What had happened? What Moses had used as a reminder of God's power prevailing over the poison of the serpents, bit by bit, had become a god itself.

This has happened in Christian history in relation to the cross and the crucifix. That which is to be a reminder of the love of the cross, meant to help men and women in looking at it to fix their hearts and minds on the One who bled and died there, becomes regarded with superstitious reverence. The cross, or the crucifix, becomes a holy thing. The symbol is identified and confused with the reality for which it stands.

The core lesson is this: whenever anyone or anything usurps the place that God should have in our lives, we're guilty of idolatry.

For most of us, that would not be a graven image such as a cross or a crucifix. But how easily money becomes an idol. We allow money—how we get it and how we use it—to edge God out of the number one place in our lives.

I've seen love in marriage distorted to the point that it usurps God's place in our lives. I've certainly seen love of country distorted to the point that it blinds people to God's call to justice and righteousness.

The making of idols usually means making the means an end. This happens all the time in the church. I know some people who do that with the Bible. The Bible itself becomes an idol. Listen carefully to people who passionately crusade, in their words, to "save the Bible." Look at their lives. We can angrily wage a war to protect the inerrancy of the Bible, and appear to be righteous in the cause, and still lose our souls. That's the problem Jesus was addressing when He said, "Not everyone who says to Me, 'Lord, Lord,' will enter the Kingdom of Heaven, but those who do the will of My heavenly Father."

In all sorts of ways, we have committed the sin of idolatry by making the means an end. Even in our worship, we turn the liturgy, our means of worshiping God, into an end itself, so that the means and methods of worship become more important than the worship itself. We need to even look at it in terms of our spiritual disciplines. Spiritual discipline is for the purpose of facilitating our relationship to God. We pray and worship and study Scripture, sometimes we fast, to be open to God, to cultivate Christ's presence. But to make these disciplines ends in themselves, to make them the measurement of how holy we are, is making discipline a fetish. Not only are we in danger of turning others off when we zealously exaggerate these disciplines, they become idols.

Isaiah prophesied of the time when idols would be thrown to the moles and bats (Isa. 2:20), and Jeremiah cried about idols:

> "They are upright, like a palm tree,
> And they cannot speak;
> They must be carried
> Because they cannot go by themselves.
> Do not be afraid of them,
> For they cannot do evil,
> Nor can they do any good."
>
> *Jer. 10:5*

Jeremiah was talking about the impotence of idols. The truth of the matter is they do have power in our lives, a negative power, in that they divert us from the God who is Spirit and whom we must worship in Spirit and in Truth.

The basis of this commandment is that God is a jealous God (Exod. 20:5).

The word "jealousy" comes from a Hebrew word that means "to be red in the face." And, in the Old Testament, it does not connect with the human emotion that we associate with envy, pettiness, and suspicion. Rather, it means that God cares for us, and therefore, is not indifferent to what we do and how we live. Jealousy, in this sense, is as much a part of the nature of God as are His love and forgiveness.

Also, this commandment must be seen against the background of the world in which it was given, a world that believed that gods could reside in wood or stone images and that these gods could be controlled to work on behalf of those who worshiped them. Rituals were very important, because these rituals and repeated incantations were the means by which the worshiper controlled his god. Not so with Yahweh, who is sovereign and cannot be controlled by rites or words. Nor can He be represented by any likeness or be contained in any one location.

This commandment against idolatry closes with an awful word about the consequences of sin on future generations: *"visiting the iniquity of the fathers on the children"* (v. 5). This cannot mean that innocent, unborn generations are going to be punished for the sins of their fathers. The doctrine of individual responsibility is stated over and over again in both the Old and New Testaments. However, it does mean that future generations will suffer the consequences of their predecessors, because there is a connection, a solidarity, a unity of the human race. War works its ravaging havoc, not only upon those who participate in it, but upon those who come after them. Drunkenness and drugs affect not only the ones who are immediately victims of it, but their families and even beyond their families. Immoral behavior has that way. It doesn't end with itself. It spreads out to invade the lives of those within its circle. Not only does it invade, it oftentimes destroys, or if it does not destroy, it maims, brings sorrow and sadness, or causes endless pain.

So, we can't think that we can do whatever we desire because our sin will not hurt anyone else. That simply isn't so. Sin is like the pebble that is cast into the water, rippling it with concentric circles that move out to affect every other surface they touch.

The blessing of righteous living is the same way: *"Showing mercy to thousands, to those who love Me and keep My commandments"* (v. 6). This is a Hebrew parallelism which means not a thousand people, but thousands of generations.

The influence of persons committed to God continues for countless generations.

You Shall Not Take the Name of the Lord in Vain

"You shall not take the name of the Lord your God in vain, for the Lord will not hold him guiltless who takes His name in vain" (v. 7).

For the Hebrew, the name could not be separated from the reality. For that reason, the name could not be treated lightly. The name has to do with the very being, the essence of the One whom it identifies.

To know the name is to know the identity and the nature of the one named. Therefore, we can't be guiltless if we deny that name by perverted use.

We must keep this in mind when we think about this commandment, because normally we associate it with profanity or with careless or irreverent use of God's name. Its implications are far deeper than that. To be sure, "in vain" means empty, groundless, without basis, frivolous, insincere. It means the unjustified use of God's name. So, profanity does violate this commandment. Using God's name when there's no genuine faith or commitment is a violation of this commandment. One thinks of the countless politicians who invoke the name of God to support selfish interpretation of their deeds, as well as in the propositions they seek to make. How profane that we would be in a nuclear arms race "in the name of God."

This is a commandment against profanity and obscenity. But what is more profane or obscene? Four-letter words, or starving children who could be fed if we were not so selfish? Pornographic magazines, or thousands dying in Latin America in political wars which our government supports, or thousands suppressed and dying in Afghanistan because of "Soviet protection"?

This commandment is also broken when we use the name of God to fortify a lie.

I believe that Elton Trueblood was right when he said this is a commandment warning against taking God lightly. We break this commandment when we say we believe in God and that we accept the ideals of His Kingdom, but we don't take Him seriously. This is a form of atheism. We're atheists in practice, though we may be Christians in profession. We're atheists when we live much of our lives as though God did not matter.

If you think that's a crazy notion that has no meaning for you, that there's no way you could be a Christian in profession but an atheist in practice, perform this very serious experiment. Sometime during the coming week, set aside maybe thirty minutes, and honestly answer these three questions:

(1) What do I think about most when I'm not thinking about my work?

(2) How do I spend my leisure time, the time not required for my job or my keeping the household going?

(3) How do I spend my money? Get beyond your normal complaints about big grocery bills and high utility rates and huge house payments and doctor bills. Look at those things, but look further at how you spend the rest of your money.

My hunch is that our answers will provide some shocking revelations. We may discover that we think far more about what we don't have that we wish we had, or about how we can get more of what we think will make us happy, than we do in expressing gratitude to God for His gifts and grace. Probably most of us will discover we spend much more time watching TV than reading the Bible, or in prayer or worship. And most of us will be shocked at the things we spend more money on than we spend on the mission of the church and the needs of others. Many will discover that they spend far more time and money on recreation and relaxation than on serving God's children who need us desperately.

Remember the Sabbath Day to Keep It Holy

This commandment begins with a positive word. It's one of the two commandments not stated negatively. *"Remember,"* it begins. In the Hebrew language, the form of this verb is very powerful, far more emphatic than a normal imperative. This commandment, as stated in Deuteronomy 5:12, begins with the word "observe" or "keep."

The word "Sabbath" is from the Hebrew word meaning "cease" or "to rest." It does not come, as sometimes thought, from the word "seven." The Sabbath was in fact the seventh day of the week in the Hebrew calendar.

Two facts justify the observance of a Sabbath day: first, God's rest from His creation activity on the seventh day, and second, the observance of the Sabbath as a commemoration of the exodus from Egypt.

The Sabbath was initiated in Israel as a day of rest, rest that included even the servants and slaves. Almost immediately it became a struggle to maintain the Sabbath as a holy day, and certainly that struggle has continued through Christian history.

The Jews developed thirty-nine classifications of work which were to be avoided on the Sabbath. By the time of Jesus, the original intent of the Sabbath had been completely distorted, and the Sabbath had become a burden rather than a blessing.

It is easy to recall the incident when Jesus went through the grain fields on the Sabbath with His disciples. They were hungry and the disciples began to pluck grain and eat it. When the Pharisees saw it, they were amazed and condemned Jesus: "Look, Your disciples are doing what is not lawful to do on the Sabbath!" (Matt. 12:2). When Jesus had taught them about the true meaning of the Sabbath, He concluded, saying, "For the Son of Man is Lord even of the Sabbath."

The principle behind this commandment is twofold. First there must be a rhythm to life, a rhythm of work and rest, certainly a rhythm of worship in the midst of our ongoing life. The second principle is that all time belongs to God. One day out of seven, set aside as a special day, serves to remind us of the sacredness of all our days.

Spiritually, every day should be a Sunday, just as every life should be a saintly life. The purpose of our religion is to make our lives more completely Christian. We know, however, that we're not essentially saintly, but are predominately sinful. We all fall far short of the high ideals of Christian discipleship. Origen, who lived in the third century and was one of the great theologians of the early church, apologized for the common observance of Sunday as a concession to the weaker brethren who, "being either unable or unwilling to keep every day in this manner, require more sensible memorials to prevent spiritual things from passing altogether away from their minds."[4]

In a real sense, all of us are "weaker brethren" in Origen's meaning. We all need a Sabbath day, and for Christians that is Sunday which celebrates Easter and the new creation. But we need more than that. We need a Sabbath rhythm in our lives—a rhythm that includes relaxation and reflection, in order that our souls and bodies may be renewed. Certainly, Sunday as the Sabbath day for Christians is essential because of our gathering as the people of God to celebrate God's mighty acts in history and to recommit ourselves to Him within the Body of Christ, the blessed community.

Honor Your Father and Your Mother

This fifth commandment is the centerpiece of the Ten Command-ments. As already indicated, the first four deal with our relationship with God, the other six with our relationship to each other. It is important to note that when we begin the set of six that deals with our relationship with each other, the first of these deals with rela-tionships within the family. That puts the family where it belongs, in the center. Unless people learn to live together in the family, they aren't likely to learn to get along with anybody anywhere.

I believe one of the primary reasons Judaism has survived across the years is precisely its family structure. The Jews survived the Holocaust and thousands of years of anti-Semitism because the Jew-ish family had a sense of identity and a sense of order. It doesn't matter where the family is on the Sabbath, when the Sabbath comes, they stop and pray. It didn't matter what Hitler and all the powers of Nazism said, when Passover came it was time to tell the story, even if the family was gathered in a concentration camp and there were no candles to light. There was a sense of order and identity that gave them roots and strength and perspective and discipline. At the heart of that family structure was a reverence for parents, a high regard, a respect, an esteem for the older members of the family. The elderly were honored and cared for.

The American Heritage Dictionary defines honor as "esteem; re-spect, reverence." In the Old Testament, the word honor comes from the word meaning "to be heavy." It was the same word that is fre-quently translated "glory." F. B. Huey, Jr. reminds us that the link between "heavy" and "honor" is understood against the background of the ancient world in which a heavy person was obviously afflu-ent, so the verse could be translated "respect your father and your mother."

To Respect Means to Listen

I'm concerned about the extreme to which we have gone with the cult of the child during the past thirty or forty years in the United States. To be sure, we needed to give more attention to children. The adage "Children are to be seen and not heard" was a caricature of children treated as wards and, in the extreme in many cultures, as chattel. So we needed to get away from that. But as is so often the case, the pendulum swung too far. We reared our children to be self-centered. We ordered our worlds around not only their needs, but their whims. Our thinking about discipline was distorted. We spared the rod and spoiled the child. There was no center of authority around which the child could order his life, no clear guidelines or directions, no well-defined values. And so respect was diminished, especially at the point of children listening and being obedient. This was not so much the child's fault as the parent's default.

So, the word here is, "Children, respect your parents by listening to them." There's also a word for parents: Provide the setting in your home where children will be taught to listen and be obedient.

Respect means a second thing. It means to be attentive.

In a retreat I was leading, a 73-year-old woman expressed the joy that she had experienced from all the love and affirmation that had been hers that weekend. She said something that brought tears to my eyes. "This is the first time that I've been hugged and loved since my husband died two years ago." That woman has two children, and those children are failing their mother. They are not honoring her by being attentive to her.

Attentiveness takes place all along the road of life, but there is a particular concern that is pulling at my heart-strings—the attentiveness that older parents need. One of the saddest experiences I have as a pastor is visiting in nursing, retirement, and convalescent homes. I see persons wasting away emotionally, as shriveled in spirit as they are in body in settings like that, because of lack of attention from those who should love them most.

To honor our parents means to be attentive to them. How much they need our attention as they grow older and are removed from the setting of their home and family, or are cut off from places and persons in which they have lived and moved and had their being for so many years.

There is a side for parents in this commandment. How do children learn to listen and be attentive? They learn it in a setting of mutual respect, where every person is counted important, where every person is given the floor to speak and is heard with love and appreciation, where every individual is given an extravagant measure of attention because every person is counted precious.

This is really the pattern of the Christian home that Paul defines in the fifth and sixth chapters of Ephesians. We have distorted those instructions despite the fact that they all hang together: instructions to husbands, to wives, to children, and to parents. He begins it all by saying, "Be subject to one another out of reverence for Christ" (Eph. 5:21, RSV). In that kind of mutual commitment, Paul gives specific instructions: "Wives, be subject to your husbands, as to the Lord. . . . Husbands, love your wives, as Christ loved the church and gave himself up for her. . . . Children, obey your parents in the Lord, for this is right. . . . Honor your father and mother. . . . Fathers, do not provoke your children to anger, but bring them up in the discipline and instruction of the Lord" (Eph. 5:22, 25; 6:1, 2, 4, RSV).

That's the pattern of the Christian home, and that's the foundation for Christian relationships within the family—persons reverencing and respecting each other out of their love and commitment to Christ. Out of homes like that come children who will honor their fathers and mothers.

No Killing

The sixth, seventh, and eighth commandments are expressed in only two words each in Hebrew. They could be translated simply "no killing, no adultery, no stealing."

The foundation for this commandment is in the creation story, in which God made man in His own likeness. Humankind is of infinite value to the Creator. Nothing is more at the heart of the Judeo-Christian tradition than the sanctity of human life.

It is obvious, in the Old Testament, that this was not a prohibition against all killing, only unauthorized killing. According to Genesis 9:6, this commandment did not prohibit the death penalty. Israelite law specifically required taking the life of an enemy during warfare (1 Sam. 15:3) and also the life of an adulterer (Lev. 20:10). We remember how the woman caught in adultery was brought to Jesus and He was reminded that the penalty was death by stoning. What Jesus did in that instance, and what He later taught, expanded this commandment against murder from its narrow definition in Old Testament law. He said to the woman, "Neither do I condemn you, go your way, and sin no more" (John 8:11).

263

He addressed the whole issue more fully in the Sermon on the Mount: "You have heard that it was said, 'An eye for an eye and a tooth for a tooth,' but I tell you not to resist an evil person" (Matt. 5: 38–39). And again, "You have heard that it was said, 'You shall love your neighbor and hate your enemy,' but I say to you, love your enemies, bless those who curse you, do good to those who hate you, and pray for those who spitefully use you and persecute you" (Matt. 5:43–44).

Jesus not only expanded the meaning of this commandment, He went beyond it in its implication. "You have heard that it was said to those of old, 'You shall not murder, and whoever murders will be in danger of the judgment.' But I say to you that whoever is angry with his brother without a cause shall be in danger of the judgment" (Matt. 5:21–22).

So, according to Jesus, this command can be violated by the exploitation of another person, by indifference to human need. Not only does Jesus broaden the commandment, he makes it more strict. Destroying the reputation of another is a form of killing. Abortion and euthanasia both raise the question of this commandment. Certainly, when a million babies have been aborted each year in America for the last ten years, it's time that this commandment was revisited, and that we see it in other terms than the stereotype of one individual killing another individual. We need to look at war, abortion, the pollution of the earth, all in light of this command of God.

No Adultery

I believe the four most pressing moral issues of today are: 1) war and peace; 2) racial prejudice; 3) poverty; and 4) sexual immorality. All these issues are addressed in the Ten Commandments. This seventh one addresses the issue of sexual immorality. It commands purity in the marriage state. Adultery violates marriage and is a betrayal of the fundamental respect for one's mate in marriage.

The degree of disregard for this commandment is indicated in the fact that almost half the marriages in our country today end in divorce. Adultery is one of the leading causes for the breakup of families.

As was the case with His interpretation of the other commandments, Jesus' interpretation of this commandment was even more stern than its Old Testament application. He said that whoever looks upon a woman with lust is violating that commandment. Certainly the sex-satiated culture of our day induces the shattering of this commandment in every way. Even our advertising builds upon our carnal lust.

There's only one way to keep this commandment. We must respect the sanctity of the marriage relationship, in our own marriage as well as that of others. We must make a commitment to personal purity as it relates to the expression of our sexuality.

If the historians are right in their warnings that the strength and stability of society are dependent upon the stability of the marriage relationship, then our permissiveness threatens us with doom.

No Stealing

Martin Luther said, "It is the smallest part of the thieves that are hung. If we're to hang them all, where shall we get rope enough? We must make all our belts and straps into halters."

The eighth commandment addresses the issue of property. Theft is taking or keeping what is not ours. The Bible defends the right to own property, but it also pronounces a judgment upon those who injure others in the pursuit of property (Amos 2:6–7; 4:1–2; 6:1–6).

Not only does the Old Testament condemn stealing property, it condemns stealing people (Exod. 21:16). And, get this, it says that withholding tithes and offerings is a form of stealing; it's a matter of robbing God (Mal. 3: 8–10).

One of the tragedies of our day is how the justice system treats crimes of stealing. Poor people, with no money to hire legal defense, waste away in prisons for stealing a car or a television, while officers of huge corporate organizations preside in posh board rooms, though it is proven they have manipulated the stock market. Television gives us almost daily reports of defense contract "cost over-rides" that steal millions of tax dollars, of $600 paid by the government for hammers that should cost $5, and $28 for screws that should cost ten cents. Ours is a society "on the take," and stealing is one of our most blatant sins.

Stealing is a sin against God because it betrays our trust in Him. It is a sin against humankind because it denies love and concern for others.

Apart from the obvious ways of seeing this commandment broken, we should think of the more subtle ways we break it.

• by not giving our employers a full day for the pay we receive
• by stealing the good name of another with malicious gossip
• by remaining silent, thus stealing from another the word that might preserve reputation and/or undergird character
• by failing to give to others the support, praise, and credit they're due.

More of the subtle dimensions of the breaking of this commandment will be seen as we look at the final commandment, "You shall not covet."

You Shall Not Bear False Witness

The broad application of this commandment is as a prohibition against untruthfulness of any kind. However, it originated in the setting of the court where witnesses were under oath to tell the truth.

William Barclay reminds us that though the rendering of this commandment is the same in Exodus and Deuteronomy in the usual English wording (Exod. 20:16, Deut. 5:20), in the Hebrew, they are different. In the Exodus version, the meaning is *lying* or *untruth*, while in the Deuteronomy version, the meaning is *insincere, empty,* or *frivolous.* Though the meaning is not essentially different, the Exodus version is thinking of the nature of the evidence, while the Deuteronomy version emphasizes the spirit in which the evidence is given.

Barclay also reminds us that

> one of the most interesting facts about the Jewish law is that the man who refuses to give evidence, when he has evidence to give, is condemned as severely as the man who gives false evidence . . . (Lev. 5:1). It is an important principle that a cowardly or careless and irresponsible silence can be as senseless a crime as false and lying speech. The sin of silence is as real as the sin of speech.[5]

Barclay lists nine kinds of lies: the lie that comes from malice, of fear, for profit, of silence, of boasting, the lie which is a half-truth, the lie to self, and the lie to God. Seeing the different forms that the lie takes, we immediately realize that the secret is honesty, an honesty that is worked at with all our might, because it's so easy to deceive ourselves, to seek to deceive others, and even to try to deceive God by seeking to conceal things from Him. Yet, God knows our hearts, He searches them and detects our thoughts, as well as our words and our deeds. That's the reason Martin Luther said one of the first principles of prayer is: "Don't lie to God."

The seriousness of the sin which this commandment addresses is seen dramatically in the New Testament, in the way James (3:5, 6) talks about the tongue being a powerful weapon. The tongue can destroy as surely as killing does. A malicious lie, idle gossip, half-truth, insincere flattery, remaining silent, even a raised eyebrow or shrugged shoulders, can be a form of bearing false witness and can violate this command. Certainly it can hurt or even destroy another person.

You Shall Not Covet

"You shall not covet your neighbor's house; you shall not covet your neighbor's wife, nor his male servant, nor his female servant, nor his ox, nor his donkey, nor anything that is your neighbor's" (v. 17). This last commandment has probably received the least attention of all the commandments. A contemporary commentator has confessed that he used to consider this "the weak sister" of the commandments. "It has occurred to me," he said, "that whoever approved the final order of these commandments didn't have much of a sense of suspense or climax. He put all of those dramatic, intriguing sins like stealing, adultery, and murder, first. Then he ended with coveting. It would have seemed more logical to begin with the bland, throw-away sin like coveting, and then work up to the big stuff."

He was actually speaking with tongue in cheek, because it's true that most of us are more guilty of coveting than any of the other sins condemned in the Ten Commandments.

We may not covet our neighbor's wife, or servants, and certainly none of us would covet our neighbor's ox or donkey. But what about position, money, opportunity? Most of us are guilty of looking at others, comparing ourselves to them, and seeing ourselves come out on the short end. We torture ourselves in this fashion, drive ourselves to depression by self-pity, thinking we deserve more. When we find ourselves jealous of what life is for someone else, dreaming of how happy we would be if we were in someone else's situation, it's a dead giveaway that we're falling into the subtle, seductive hands of covetousness.

How often do we convince ourselves that other people always get the breaks and not us? How recently have we thought that we were deprived of opportunity? We look at our peers, friends our own age, and see where they are in life, and we're plagued with the notion that they had far more opportunity than we did.

Do you often find yourself thinking about how unjust the system is? Others have received blessings, grace, talents; luck has been theirs—but not yours?

You probably have not associated that with coveting, but whatever name you give it, it is exactly that, and it is destructive.

Now, not all coveting is wrong. The Hebrew word for "covet," *ḥāmad*, is a neutral word that means "desire" or "take pleasure in." Desire directed in the wrong channel, or desire that causes us to want something that belongs to another, or desire that causes us to go after something to which we have no right—that's covetousness that becomes a sin. Paul reminded us that we ought to "desire earnestly the best gifts" (1 Cor. 12:31).

The Christian remedy for dealing with covetousness is to "be content with such things as you have" (Heb. 13:5).

But let's get back to the popular kind of coveting of which most of us are guilty, the kind that we described above: our desire for what other folks have that we don't, and our almost insatiable desire for more. How do we fall into these snares?

First, we convince ourselves that we have a sort of cosmic right to an equal share of the good things of life. That's a fallacious idea, and it plays folly in our lives. There's no equality in talents, abilities, opportunities. There's not even any equality to being in the right place at the right time.

There is no cosmic right that is ours to have an equal share of what everybody else has. If you're prone to leaning in that direction, consider how you would feel if you were averaged out with the world's two billion starving people. You see, we always want to be averaged up and not down!

But we also fall into a second illusion, and therefore begin to covet. That illusion is the age-old fallacy of thinking that happiness comes from the outside in, rather than the inside out.

Russian writer Alexander Solzhenitsyn has one of his characters in prison say, "The happiness of incessant victory, the happiness of fulfilled desire, the happiness of success, and total satiety—*that* is suffering! That is spiritual death. . . . [People] waste themselves in senseless thrashing around for the sake of a handful of goods and die without realizing their spiritual wealth. . . . It is not our level of prosperity that makes for happiness, but the kinship of heart to heart, and the way we look at the world."[6]

He makes the point, doesn't he? It's not our level of prosperity that makes for happiness, but the kinship of heart to heart, and the way we look at the world.

Happiness is an inside job. It comes from the inner citadel of freedom which belongs to all of us, the inner place where we make our choices. Our problem is that we usually end up coveting that which can never make us happy, failing to realize that what matters most is not what becomes of us, but what we become; we determine that. Someone has suggested that there are at least two ways to be rich. One is to have a lot of possessions; the other is to have few needs. To win the battle over coveting is to put our needs in the proper perspective, and diminish our wants to a manageable level.

So, as one commentator has said, not only is coveting a sin, it's stupid. There is no cosmic right that is ours to have an equal share of what everybody else has, and there is no way of discovering happiness from the outside in. It must always come from the inside out.

THE THICK DARKNESS WHERE GOD WAS

20:18 Now all the people witnessed the thunderings, the lightning flashes, the sound of the trumpet, and the mountain smoking; and when the people saw *it*, they trembled and stood afar off.

19 Then they said to Moses, "You speak with us, and we will hear; but let not God speak with us, lest we die."

20 And Moses said to the people, "Do not fear; for God has come to test you, and that His fear may be before you, so that you may not sin."

21 So the people stood afar off, but Moses drew near the thick darkness where God *was*.

22 Then the LORD said to Moses, "Thus you shall say to the children of Israel: 'You have seen that I have talked with you from heaven.

23 'You shall not make *anything to be* with Me—gods of silver or gods of gold you shall not make for yourselves.

24 'An altar of earth you shall make for Me, and you shall sacrifice on it your burnt offerings and your peace offerings, your sheep and your oxen. In every place where I record My name I will come to you, and I will bless you.

25 'And if you make Me an altar of stone, you shall not build it of hewn stone; for if you use your tool on it, you have profaned it.

26 'Nor shall you go up by steps to My altar, that your nakedness may not be exposed on it.'"

Exod. 20:18–26

This passage, following the Ten Commandments, is reminiscent of chapter 19. The thunderings and the lightning and the sound of the trumpet and the mountain smoking cause the people to cower back in fear and trembling. The Lord has told them that they are not to come too close. I doubt if God needed to give that instruction. These people would not have pushed further even if they were permitted. They want to stand afar off. In fact, they are so frightened that they asked Moses to speak to them, "But let not God speak with us, lest we die." We know from Exodus 19:9 that God has acted to demonstrate to confirm that Moses is His spokesman: "That the people may hear when I speak with you, and believe you forever."

The people, by their own words, confirmed their acceptance of Moses in this role: *"You speak to us, and we will hear you"* (Exod. 20:19). Their saying "We will hear" in Hebrew is equivalent to saying "We will obey." The Hebrew language does not have different words to express these two ideas of hearing and obeying.

There is a lesson in this for us. The Israelites knew that hearing the voice of God required that they obey Him. It is an awesome thing to hear the voice of God, and that voice comes to us. It comes through the written word, the Bible; it comes through direct revelation; it comes through worship; it comes through preaching; it comes in imagination as we meditate with the Lord Himself. It's not enough to hear the word—in fact, there is a sense in which we have not heard the word unless we obey.

It's interesting to note that in this chapter God gives Israel law when He gives them the Ten Commandments, but the Ten Commandments are really only a part of the law. Other aspects of that law are going to be given, and even in this chapter, instructions pertaining to the building of an altar are given. The law and the altar go together. The law reveals that people are sinners needing a Savior. The altar reveals the offer that God makes to us, the offer of sacrifice. In the Old Testament, the altar became the center of the worship life of the community in the Tabernacle. Shedding of blood was the focal point of sacrifice made at that altar. For Christians, that blood has been shed once and for all, and our sacrifice is "the Lamb slain from the foundation of the world," who is now alive making intercession for us.

Let's concentrate now on one big lesson which the people's experience here at Sinai teaches us. Rehearse their situation. They were glad to participate in God's merciful providence, happy for Him to be the sustaining but unseen background of their life. They joyfully sang His praises on the shores of the Red Sea. They had appropriated the bread from heaven in the wilderness. They rejoiced as the shadow of that brooding cloud by day and that light of the pillar of fire by night guided them on their meandering journey through the wilderness. But they wanted it to stay that way: God removed—in the background. They didn't want to expose themselves to the naked beam of His glory, His light unveiled and undiluted. They didn't want Him to speak directly to them. They did not want to come into His Shekinah Glory without some mediator.

The point is this: we do not object to praising and worshiping God in His high heavens, but we shy away from even thinking about each common bush being aflame with divine fire. We relish observing that the heavens declare the glory of God, and the firmament shows forth His handiwork, but we get nervous when the earth begins to tremble, when the skies turn dark, when the solid earth shakes beneath our feet. When those things that we thought would last forever, that we thought would never change—our family, our experience, our ordinary human life—when they begin to change, we worry. Our experiences are like the Israelites, so remarkably described in that one verse *"So the people stood afar off, but Moses drew near the thick darkness where God was"* (v. 21).

We need to appropriate the meaning of this symbol, because this is precisely a description of Israel's history, and our own history.

The Darkness Where God Was

The great Scottish preacher-theologian, James S. Stewart, preached a remarkable sermon on this theme, and he explains it well.

Looking at it from the widest possible angle, as Stewart expresses it, we see *the darkness of history.* And there God is.

Skeptics in every age have told us in books, in plays, in devastating logic, in sarcasm and satire: "There is no living God, certainly no loving Father Almighty." They call our attention to millions of starving people, slave-camps, the colossal shadow of the hydrogen bomb, and they mock us to our face about the darkness of history. We know we can't offer cheap talk. But we can move deeper, and get beyond the glib superficial reading of history. God breaks into history, His light shines in the darkness, and the darkness will never put it out. As James Stewart puts it, the basic fact of history is not the Iron Curtain, but the rent veil, not the devil's strategy, but the divine sovereignty. In history, the thick darkness—that's where God was.

We scale it down to a more narrow focus, more intimate and individual, and we come to *the darkness of human experience.* We could talk about that darkness from the perspective of the devastating trials that occasionally strike us, in natural evil such as a tornado, a hurricane, an earthquake. Then there are other ways to talk about it, the more personal experiences: a failure in business, loss of health, a shattered romance, divorce, desolation and bereavement that comes because of the death of a loved one. In the midst of that kind of darkness we often stand afar off from God. We cry helplessly or we unleash emotional anger. We tremble and usually feel that we have to tread the darkness alone. The witness is that in that darkness, God is.

Bishop Lajos Ordass of the Lutheran Church in Hungary was speaking to a small group. He had protested the Communist regime's confiscation of church schools and was imprisoned for twenty months. Later he was under arrest for six years. Quietly he told his true story: "They placed me in solitary confinement. It was a tiny cell, perhaps six feet by eight feet with no windows and sound-proofed. They hoped to break down my resistance by isolating me from all sensory perceptions. They thought I was alone. They were wrong. The risen Christ was present in that room. And in communion with Him, I was able to prevail."

Our experiences may not be that dramatic, but there are the devastating trials that occasionally strike us, and people like Bishop Ordass are there to remind us that in the darkness of personal tragedy, when the devastating tornado of pain and confusion strikes us, and we must stumble into the darkness, we can find God there.

There are many areas of darkness—the darkness of history, the darkness of human experience, and perhaps the ultimate darkness, *the darkness of death.* This is the last dark valley of all, and that's the darkness where God is.

It is an insult to hurting hearts to talk about death casually, or to assume that we can take it lightly. The New Testament does not do that. It calls death "the last enemy," but the New Testament did something else about death; it proclaimed death as "the thick darkness where God is." It did that, not by talking about immortality and the possible survival of the body, it did it by nullifying the sting of death, breaking the victory of the grave by the shattering glory of the resurrection of Christ.

John Birkbeck, a Scottish preacher friend of mine, once wrote me after I had shared with him the fact that I had lost my dearest friend in death. In his letter, John told about Oliver Cromwell's dying. On his deathbed, Cromwell looked around and noted the glum countenances and the deathly silence of those who had gathered by his bedside, and he bawled out, "Is there no one here who will praise the Lord?"

And John closed his precious letter which brought joy to my heart with a sentence, "Maxie, death is not a period, but a comma in the story of life."

In the darkness of death, God is. Tremble and quake as we may at the darkness, we stride on in confidence, knowing that in the dark as in the light, God was and is . . . and underneath us are His everlasting arms.

NOTES

1. T. Cecil Myers, *Thunder on the Mountain* (Nashville: Abingdon Press, 1965), pp. 119–20.

2. B. Davie Napier, *Exodus*, Layman's Bible Commentary (Richmond, VA: John Knox Press, 1963), 3:78.

3. F. B. Meyer, *Devotional Commentary on Exodus* (Grand Rapids: Kregel Publications, 1978), pp. 423-24.

4. Gardiner M. Day, *Old Wine in New Bottles* (New York: Morehouse-Gorham, 1949), pp. 49–50.

5. William Barclay, *The Ten Commandments for Today* (New York: Harper & Row, 1983), pp. 184–85.

6. Alexander Solzhenitsyn, *The First Circle* (New York: Harper & Row, 1968), p. 34.

CHAPTER FIFTEEN

Covenant Law at Sinai: Civil, Criminal, and Covenant

Exodus 21:1–24:18

There is a sense in which verses 22–26 of chapter 20 are an introduction to the huge body of material we're about to consider. Verse 22 says, "Then the Lord said to Moses, 'Thus you shall say to the children of Israel: 'You have seen that I have talked with you from heaven.'" The fact is declared: Moses is Yahweh's spokesman, and Yahweh considers that role settled. From this point on God will speak to Moses, and Moses will speak to the people.

The material we now consider is known as the book of covenant, which is also a part of God's covenant law. It takes its name from 24:7. "Then he took the Book of the Covenant and read in the hearing of the people." This is also a part of God's covenant law. It includes civil, criminal, and ceremonial laws by which the people are to live. These were rules of life for the "peculiar people" of God.

These laws deal with treatment of slaves, injury to persons, moral and religious duties, and property rights. They are very detailed. There are laws that protect people against being gored by the oxen of other people, laws that describe how slaves are to be treated, laws about fires burning grain, laws about a man seducing a virgin, laws about not returning what one has borrowed from his neighbor.

While most of these laws may appear irrelevant to us, they were the glue that bound this people together as a community. Because they do appear so irrelevant, we are going to look at them in sections, making brief comment on each section. Then at the close of this chapter, I want to suggest three broad lessons which I believe are encompassed in these ordinances, and which have tremendous relevance to our lives. Those three lessons are: 1) a concern for fairness and justice; 2) a compassion for the poor and oppressed; and 3) a consecration of self and resources.

You may wish to move ahead to page 286 and read that section of the chapter first, then return to a consideration of these smaller sections of the ordinances.

THE LAW CONCERNING SERVANTS

21:1 "Now these *are* the judgments which you shall set before them:

2 "If you buy a Hebrew servant, he shall serve six years; and in the seventh he shall go out free and pay nothing.

3 "If he comes in by himself, he shall go out by himself; if he *comes in* married, then his wife shall go out with him.

4 "If his master has given him a wife, and she has borne him sons or daughters, the wife and her children shall be her master's, and he shall go out by himself.

5 "But if the servant plainly says, 'I love my master, my wife, and my children; I will not go out free,'

6 "then his master shall bring him to the judges. He shall also bring him to the door, or to the doorpost, and his master shall pierce his ear with an awl; and he shall serve him forever.

7 "And if a man sells his daughter to be a female servant, she shall not go out as the male servants do.

8 "If she does not please her master, who has betrothed her to himself, then he shall let her be redeemed. He shall have no right to sell her to a foreign people, since he has dealt deceitfully with her.

9 "And if he has betrothed her to his son, he shall deal with her according to the custom of daughters.

10 "If he takes another *wife,* he shall not diminish her food, her clothing, and her marriage rights.

11 "And if he does not do these three for her, then she shall go out free, without *paying* money.

Exod. 21:1–11

It seems strange to even talk about it; it's so foreign to our under-standing of life, but human slavery was a way of life in the ancient world. Slaves were looked upon as property and had no rights. As strange as that may seem to us, it hasn't been too many years since our own nation was plagued by the evil of human slavery.

While it seems so foreign to our minds, it must be recognized that the Mosaic law represented an advancement in the struggle for human rights. It provided safeguards for slaves. Stealing or possessing a stolen person was prohibited by law, but slaves acquired through accepted means such as war or indebtedness were held in Israel, and the significant aspect of the book of the covenant is that laws provided legal safeguards for the slave as well as for the free population.

The laws given here concern only Hebrew slaves. Laws concerning foreign slaves are found in Leviticus 25:44–46.

The picture of Hebrew slavery looked like this: An Israelite could be sold by his parents, and that was a common practice, especially as it related to daughters. A person could be sold for stealing if he could not make restitution (Exod. 22:3) or pay debts (2 Kings 4:1). A poverty-stricken Israelite could sell himself into slavery (Lev. 25:39; Deut. 15:12–17). Here was the most interesting fact: no Israelite could be held as a slave for more than six years (Exod. 21:2).

As we read the book of the covenant, we need to remember that the law codes in Israel were not exhaustive in the sense of setting forth every decision. Rather, when a law was given, selective illus-trative decisions for the guidance of those charged with legal deci-sion were provided. Latitude was given the judge as he sought to determine the will of God concerning the issue at hand. The codes were the guidance he used.

The sense of fairness in the law is indicated in the fact that if a person chose to enter servitude to a master, at the end of his six years he would leave his master's service exactly as he entered it. If he was single when enslaved, he went out single; if married, his wife went with him at the end of the period of their enslavement. If a master had given him a wife during his enslavement and she bore him children, both the wife and the children would belong to the owner at the end of the enslavement.

The purchaser had no right to take advantage of a man's passing need. The Sabbatical year—the seventh year (Deut. 15:12 ff.)—offered a chance for a slave to start anew. It's interesting that even in that inhuman system of slavery, the opportunity of starting over was possible, while in our system, it's not easily afforded.

There is a poignant image in one possibility offered the slave. If, having gotten married while a slave, the slave does not want to leave his wife and children who would have to stay behind with the master, the slave could decide that he would not go free. Then the master would bring him to the doorpost and pierce his ear with an awl, and he would serve his master forever.

Women were in an even lower position in some sense than slaves in the ancient world. Certainly the role of women was unprotected. It is uniquely significant, then, that the covenant law gave specific guidance concerning female slaves. If a master betrothed a woman slave to his son, and the son decided to take another wife, the slave would still retain her marriage rights. If any of her rights were violated, she was to be freed.

THE LAW CONCERNING VIOLENCE

21:12 'He who strikes a man so that he dies shall surely be put to death.

13 'However, if he did not lie in wait, but God delivered *him* into his hand, then I will appoint for you a place where he may flee.

14 'But if a man acts with premeditation against his neighbor, to kill him by treachery, you shall take him from My altar, that he may die.

15 'And he who strikes his father or his mother shall surely be put to death.

16 'He who kidnaps a man and sells him, or if he is found in his hand, shall surely be put to death.

17 'And he who curses his father or his mother shall surely be put to death.

18 'If men contend with each other, and one strikes the other with a stone or with *his* fist, and he does not die but is confined to *his* bed,

19 'if he rises again and walks about outside with his staff, then he who struck *him* shall be acquitted.

He shall only pay *for* the loss of his time, and shall provide *for him* to be thoroughly healed.

20 "And if a man beats his male or female servant with a rod, so that he dies under his hand, he shall surely be punished.

21 "Notwithstanding, if he remains alive a day or two, he shall not be punished; for he *is* his property.

22 "If men fight, and hurt a woman with child, so that she gives birth prematurely, yet no harm follows, he shall surely be punished accordingly as the woman's husband imposes on him; and he shall pay as the judges *determine*.

23 "But if *any* harm follows, then you shall give life for life,

24 "eye for eye, tooth for tooth, hand for hand, foot for foot,

25 "burn for burn, wound for wound, stripe for stripe.

26 "If a man strikes the eye of his male or female servant, and destroys it, he shall let him go free for the sake of his eye.

27 "And if he knocks out the tooth of his male or female servant, he shall let him go free for the sake of his tooth."

Exod. 21:12–27

The laws concerning violence are divided by degree of seriousness. Premeditated murder (vv. 12–14) is to be punished by death. Striking your mother or father also brought the death penalty, as did kidnapping a man and selling him (vv. 15–16).

The reverence with which parents were held is witnessed by the fact that the law prescribed the death penalty for anyone who cursed his mother or father.

Bodily injury, of course, brings less punishment. If striking another person caused enough injury to put that person to bed, then the one who struck him had to provide for him until he was thoroughly healed. Beating a slave also had to be avenged, as was the case with hurting a woman. The rule of thumb was "*if any harm follows, then you shall give life for life, eye for eye, tooth for tooth, hand for hand, foot for foot . . .*" (vv. 23–24).

ANIMAL CONTROL LAWS

21:28 "If an ox gores a man or a woman to death, then the ox shall surely be stoned, and its flesh shall not be eaten; but the owner of the ox *shall be* acquitted.

29 "But if the ox tended to thrust with its horn in times past, and it has been made known to his owner, and he has not kept it confined, so that it has killed a man or a woman, the ox shall be stoned and its owner also shall be put to death.

30 "If there is imposed on him a sum of money, then he shall pay to redeem his life, whatever is imposed on him.

31 "Whether it has gored a son or gored a daughter, according to this judgment it shall be done to him.

32 "If the ox gores a male or female servant, he shall give to their master thirty shekels of silver, and the ox shall be stoned.

33 "And if a man opens a pit, or if a man digs a pit and does not cover it, and an ox or a donkey falls in it,

34 "the owner of the pit shall make *it* good; he shall give money to their owner, but the dead *animal* shall be his.

35 "If one man's ox hurts another's, so that it dies, then they shall sell the live ox and divide the money from it; and the dead *ox* they shall also divide.

36 "Or if it was known that the ox tended to thrust in time past, and its owner has not kept it confined, he shall surely pay ox for ox, and the dead animal shall be his own."

Exod. 21:28–36

Requiring the killing of an ox that gored someone to death confirms the sanctity of human life in Israelite law. But, it's more extreme than that. If a man had an ox and knew that ox to be dangerous yet took no measures to restrain it, and then that ox killed someone, the owner would be put to death.

If relatives of the victim were willing to accept monetary compensation for the life of the killed one, then the owner of the oxen could go free.

Slaves were on a different level; if an ox gored a slave, monetary restitution of 30 shekels of silver was given, and the animal was killed, but there was no provision for the killing of the owner of the animal (30 shekels of silver was the purchase price of the slave).

RESPONSIBILITY FOR PROPERTY

22:1 "If a man steals an ox or a sheep, and slaughters it or sells it, he shall restore five oxen for an ox and four sheep for a sheep.

2 "If the thief is found breaking in, and he is struck so that he dies, *there shall be* no guilt for his bloodshed.

3 "If the sun has risen on him, *there shall be* guilt for his bloodshed. He should make full restitution; if he has nothing, then he shall be sold for his theft.

4 "If the theft is certainly found alive in his hand, whether it is an ox or donkey or sheep, he shall restore double.

5 "If a man causes a field or vineyard to be grazed, and lets loose his animal, and it feeds in another man's field, he shall make restitution from the best of his own field and the best of his own vineyard.

6 "If fire breaks out and catches in thorns, so that stacked grain, standing grain, or the field is consumed, he who kindled the fire shall surely make restitution.

7 "If a man delivers to his neighbor money or articles to keep, and it is stolen out of the man's house, if the thief is found, he shall pay double.

8 "If the thief is not found, then the master of the house shall be brought to the judges *to see* whether he has put his hand into his neighbor's goods.

9 "For any kind of trespass, *whether it concerns* an ox, a donkey, a sheep, or clothing, *or* for any kind of lost thing which *another* claims to be his, the cause of both parties shall come before the judges; *and* whomever the judges condemn shall pay double to his neighbor.

10 "If a man delivers to his neighbor a donkey, an ox, a sheep, or any animal to keep, and it dies, is hurt, or driven away, no one seeing *it,*

11 "*then* an oath of the LORD shall be between them both, that he has not put his hand into his neighbor's goods; and the owner of it shall accept *that,* and he shall not make *it* good.

12 "But if, in fact, it is stolen from him, he shall make restitution to the owner of it.

13 "If it is torn to pieces *by a beast, then* he shall bring it as evidence, *and* he shall not make good what was torn.

14 "And if a man borrows *anything* from his neighbor, and it becomes injured or dies, the owner of it not *being* with it, he shall surely make *it* good.

15 "If its owner *was* with it, he shall not make *it* good; if it *was* hired, it came for its hire."

Exod. 22:1–15

Provisions are made for restitution for loss of livestock or other property by the carelessness of people, through theft, through breach of trust, or anything borrowed.

It's interesting to note that emphasis is put on carelessness, though carelessness is not punished to the degree that intentional negligence is. This is seen in 21:33, with the instance of a man leaving an open pit, allowing an ox or a donkey to fall into it. This is also seen in 22:5, which deals with the man who causes a field or vineyard to be grazed, lets loose his animal, and that animal feeds in another man's field. So, negligence and property loss, as well as liability for the action of one's property, was included in these ordinances.

MORAL AND CEREMONIAL PRINCIPLES

22:16 "If a man entices a virgin who is not betrothed, and lies with her, he shall surely pay the bride-price for her *to be* his wife.

17 "If her father utterly refuses to give her to him, he shall pay money according to the bride-price of virgins.

18 "You shall not permit a sorceress to live.

19 "Whoever lies with an animal shall surely be put to death.

20 "He who sacrifices to *any* god, except to the LORD only, he shall be utterly destroyed.

21 "You shall neither mistreat a stranger nor oppress him, for you were strangers in the land of Egypt.

22 "You shall not afflict any widow or fatherless child.

23 "If you afflict them in any way, *and* they cry at all to Me, I will surely hear their cry;

24 "and My wrath will become hot, and I will kill you with the sword; your wives shall be widows, and your children fatherless.

25 "If you lend money to *any of* My people *who are* poor among you, you shall not be like a moneylender to him; you shall not charge him interest.

26 "If you ever take your neighbor's garment as a pledge, you shall return it to him before the sun goes down.

27 "For that *is* his only covering, it *is* his garment for his skin. What will he sleep in? And it will be that when he cries to Me, I will hear, for I *am* gracious.

28 "You shall not revile God, nor curse a ruler of your people.

29 "You shall not delay *to offer* the first of your ripe produce and your juices. The firstborn of your sons you shall give to Me.

30 "Likewise you shall do with your oxen *and* your sheep. It shall be with its mother seven days; on the eighth day you shall give it to Me.

31 "And you shall be holy men to Me: you shall not eat meat torn *by beasts* in the field; you shall throw it to the dogs.

23:1 "You shall not circulate a false report. Do not put your hand with the wicked to be an unrighteous witness.

2 "You shall not follow a crowd to do evil; nor shall you testify in a dispute so as to turn aside after many to pervert *justice.*

3 "You shall not show partiality to a poor man in his dispute.

4 "If you meet your enemy's ox or his donkey going astray, you shall surely bring it back to him again.

5 "If you see the donkey of one who hates you lying under its burden, and you would refrain from helping it, you shall surely help him with it.

6 "You shall not pervert the judgment of your poor in his dispute.

7 "Keep yourself far from a false matter; do not kill the innocent and righteous. For I will not justify the wicked.

8 "And you shall take no bribe, for a bribe blinds the discerning and perverts the words of the righteous.

9 "Also you shall not oppress a stranger, for you know the heart of a stranger, because you were strangers in the land of Egypt.

10 "Six years you shall sow your land and gather in its produce,

11 "but the seventh *year* you shall let it rest and lie fallow, that the poor of your people may eat; and what they leave, the beasts of the field may eat. In like manner you shall do with your vineyard *and* your olive grove.

12 "Six days you shall do your work, and on the seventh day you shall rest, that your ox and your donkey may rest, and the son of your female servant and the stranger may be refreshed.

13 "And in all that I have said to you, be circumspect and make no mention of the name of other gods, nor let it be heard from your mouth.

14 "Three times you shall keep a feast to Me in the year:

15 "You shall keep the Feast of Unleavened Bread (you shall eat unleavened bread seven days, as I commanded you, at the time appointed in the month of Abib, for in it you came out of Egypt; none shall appear before Me empty);

16 "and the Feast of Harvest, the firstfruits of your labors which you have sown in the field; and the Feast of Ingathering at the end of the year, when you

have gathered in *the fruit of* your labors from the field.

17 "Three times in the year all your males shall appear before the LORD GOD.

18 "You shall not offer the blood of My sacrifice with leavened bread; nor shall the fat of My sacrifice remain until morning.

19 "The first of the firstfruits of your land you shall bring into the house of the LORD your God. You shall not boil a young goat in its mother's milk."

Exod. 22:16–23:19

This next series of laws covers six areas. First, seduction: If a man seduced a maiden who was not betrothed, he was required to pay the marriage price.

Second, capital offenses: Again, we have some listings of crimes punishable by death. These are the practice of sorcery, of having sex with a beast, and of sacrificing *"to any god except the Lord only"* (22:20).

Third, relationships to others: Strangers are not to be mistreated. If widows and the fatherless are afflicted, the wrath of God would *"become hot, and I will kill you with the sword; your wives shall be widows and your children fatherless"* (v. 24).

The poor who were forced to borrow money from neighbors were protected from money-lenders who would charge them great interest. It was against the law of Israel to charge interest to such people.

Fourth, duties to God: Obligations to God under the covenant were certain for every Israelite. Some of these are recorded in verses 28–31. Israelites were not to revile God nor curse a rule of the people. They were to offer the first of their produce as well as the firstborn son to Yahweh. And here again a third duty is a repetition of what had been stated earlier: *"You shall be holy men to Me"* (v. 31).

Fifth, justice for all: Verses 1–9 of chapter 23 contain a number of unrelated regulations, all of which demonstrate the way justice was to be administered in Israel. In the broader commentary that follows, we deal specifically with justice to the poor. It's interesting to note that there is a foreshadowing of that New Testament doctrine of "Love your enemies" (Matt. 5: 44) in verses 4 and 5 here. We also look at that in the next section. The impact of this section on justice is that justice for the poor is not to be perverted or distorted.

Sixth, sabbaths and sacred feasts: The law of the sabbaths is set forth. That law has to do with the land, as well as the people who work the land. Every seventh year, land should lie fallow, in order that it might rest, and that poor people might eat. The seventh day was to be a day of rest, not only that the servants but also the animals might be renewed.

Then come the three feasts of the year: the Feast of Unleavened Bread, the Feast of Harvest, and the Feast of Ingathering. And again, the law of the firstfruits is underscored. The firstfruits belong to the Lord.

Three Lessons for Us

We said earlier that from these ordinances that may appear archaic and irrelevant to us, three very important lessons can be gained.

The first lesson is that there is in these ordinances a *concern for fairness and justice.*

We need to keep in mind the simplicity of the state of civilization which these laws reflect. The ox and the donkey were the primary property of people, one for the toil of agriculture, the other for burden-bearing. There were no fences on the broad pasture land, and there was common land on which all cattle grazed. Therefore, the laws were simple and direct. We have read those laws. If an ox gored a man or a woman to death, the ox would be stoned. But, if the owner had been warned about his ox being dangerous and that ox killed a man or a woman, the ox would be stoned and its owner would also be put to death.

That's very direct and clear. It was an eye for an eye and a tooth for a tooth. But the foundation for these simple and direct laws was an effort for fairness and justice to prevail. Witnesses are warned against inventing untrue tales or circulating them. Judges are warned against being affected by the voices of the multitude. Judges are not to be biased by sentimentality on behalf of the poor or partiality to the rich. Judges are especially charged to see to it that the innocent should not suffer, that the wicked should not escape, and that foreigners get justice. A bribe is not to be entertained, even for a moment. Accusers are also especially exhorted not to slay the innocent by making a false charge, which, even if it is disproved, could blight the defendant's name and soil his character.

Is there a more confused issue in our day? When I was a boy, a word often on our lips at play was, "That's not fair." It wasn't fair for all the big boys to be on the same team, or for someone to try to put more girls on one team than another. It didn't seem fair to me at the time for all the grown folks to eat first when we had company for Sunday dinner. Those were my thoughts about fairness in that day, but it's not so simple anymore.

But fairness has become a manipulative club in the marketplace where salary scales are fought for. Fair trade acts are manipulated selfishly, and usually we think of fairness only when it benefits us. In our complex society, what is fair to one group of people may appear terribly oppressive to another group.

Justice is probably an even more crucial issue. We call the governmental apparatus that deals with crime and punishment, with law and order, with courts and judgment, our *justice system*. That whole system is in trouble because discerning justice is not so simple anymore.

One of the great Christian concerns today is what we refer to as "peace with justice." You see, it's possible to have peace without justice. The fact is, that's what terrorism is all about. People who want more than peace resort to the only warfare available to them: guerrilla and terroristic activity. This doesn't mean that such activity is to be condoned. It simply means that in this complex day in which we live, some persons feel their only way to fight for justice is by killing innocent people in guerrilla tactics that are almost impossible to control.

The earnest desire for fairness and justice has beneath it the need for reconciliation and living together in peace. There's a marvelous picture of it in verses 4 and 5 of chapter 23: *"If you meet your enemy's ox or his donkey going astray, you shall surely bring it back to him again. If you see the donkey of one who hates you lying under its burden, and you would refrain from helping it, you shall surely help him with it."*

Put yourself in that picture. You are a pious Israelite, one who is trying to follow the way of God. You're walking down the trail, and you meet an ox, and you discover it's the ox of a man who has done you wrong; he has brought injury to you. It hits you strongly that your responsibility now is to lead that ox back to the homestead of the owner. You grit your teeth and do that, because it's the law. As you begin to lead that ox back to its owner, you meet the owner coming in search for him. You're forced to confront your enemy, and you confront him in the context of doing something good for him.

The picture can be etched even more clearly than that. You're walking along a path, and you come upon Eli. Eli is your enemy, a person who hates you, and for whom you have little respect. Eli's donkey has fallen down under the burden of his load and can't get up. Eli is struggling to help the donkey to his feet, and you remember the law. You can't pass them by, saying some derisive word, or reminding Eli of what he's done to you, how he hates you and how you hate him. The law commands you to stop and help that enemy lift his beast of burden and get him going again.

You can imagine that in both instances at least a movement toward reconciliation would take place. So, a concern for fairness and justice permeates these ordinances.

A second lesson we learn from these ordinances is a *compassion for the poor and the oppressed.*

Of course we should be horrified at the principle of slavery, unchallenged in that day; the harsh, calloused, unfeeling attitude toward women, the rigorous exacting of the death penalty. There's no justifying of that, and even in the Old Testament we move beyond that understanding of life. When we get to the New Testament, the understanding is boldly communicated in the life and death of Jesus—an ultimate law of love that writes clearly the one big lesson of compassion for the poor and oppressed. Even here in the Old Testament, though, in this primitive civilization, in the midst of what to us is an unenlightened callousness, there is a compassion for the poor and the oppressed.

Even though there were slaves, they were to be treated fairly, as fairly as one could be treated under that kind of oppression. However faint the light might be, it shines through those ordinances and the revelation is there: There must be a concern for all of those who are in less fortunate positions than we.

Isn't that the issue of every age? When Grover Cleveland was President of the United States, he succumbed to the pride of power and success. During the panic of 1893, and the resulting depression with its wide-spread unemployment, Cleveland was confronted with much labor unrest. One day, a lean and hungry man came to the White House. To dramatize the plight of the poor, he got down on his hands and knees and began chewing the grass as the President made an appearance.

"What are you doing?" asked Cleveland.

"I'm out of work, and so hungry, that I have to eat grass," answered the man.

"Why don't you go around to the back lawn?" Cleveland quipped. "The grass is taller there."

What sick humor. What calloused unconcern. The call of God has always been a call to compassion for the poor and the oppressed.

I read recently an interesting exposition of the story of Peter walking on the water when he saw Jesus coming to the boat where they were threatened by the storm. Peter asked, "Lord, if it is You, bid me come." And Jesus responded, "Come."

The exposition centered on this suggestion: There must be a procession of faithful disciples after Peter, who ask, "Lord, is it You?" and then venture into the storms of life. Now that's a perceptive insight. Even if there is uncertainty in our voices, even if our faith is not all that we want it to be, even if we don't have complete assurance, if we're going to walk on the water, we've got to get out of the boat.

So we must continue the procession of those who enter into the storms of life. The storms are all around us and call for us to have compassion for the poor and the oppressed.

And as those storms rage, we ask, "Lord, is it You?"

"Is it You, in the people that are fleeing Latin America, and desiring sanctuary in this country?"

"Is it You in the tent cities of immigrants on our borders?"

"Is it You in our alcoholic parents?"

"Is it You in the middle of the housing projects and crumbling hovels of our city?"

"Is it You in the middle of the poverty of North Memphis?"

"Is it You in the faces of children who must be left alone by parents who cannot afford child care but must go to work to make ends meet?"

"Is it You in the prisons of our state where people are huddled together like animals?"

"If it's You, then bid me come."

And the Lord bids us come. He bids us enter into the storms of life where the only tools we have are compassion and concern. That compassion and concern must become concrete in action.

I like the realism of Mother Teresa of Calcutta. She doesn't theorize about it; she lays her life on the line. She speaks to us:

> If you're preoccupied with people who are talking about the poor, you scarcely have time to talk to the poor. Some people talk about hunger, but they don't come and say, "Mother, here is five rupees; buy food for those people." But they can give a most beautiful lecture on hunger.
>
> I had the most extraordinary experience once in Bombay. There was a big conference about hunger. I was supposed to go to that meeting, and I lost the way. Suddenly I came to that place, and right in front of the door, where hundreds of people were talking about food and hunger, I found a dying man.
>
> I took him out and I took him home. He died there. He died of hunger.
>
> And the people inside were talking about how in fifteen years we'd have so much food, so much this, so much that, and that man died. See the difference?[1]

There is a difference between talking about ministry and doing ministry, between talking about compassion for the poor and putting that compassion to work.

The third lesson suggested by these ordinances is a *consecration of self and resources*: *"You shall not delay to offer the first of your ripe produce and your juices. The firstborn of your sons you shall give to Me. Likewise you shall do with your oxen and your sheep. It shall be with its mother seven days; on the eighth day you shall give it to Me. And you shall be holy men to Me: you shall not eat meat torn by beasts in the field; you shall throw it to the dogs"* (Exod. 22:29–31).

That makes it clear, doesn't it? We are to offer ourselves and our resources, and be persons consecrated to God.

Several months ago, a picture appeared on the front page of our daily paper. It was a picture of an old woman, almost totally blind, standing at the door of her house which was more like a shack. This poor woman was unable to get any help anywhere. Her roof was leaking; therefore her house stayed damp all the time, and for the most part, she stayed sick. That story caught the attention of my wife and some of the lay people in my congregation, and they shared it with me. How could our church not respond to that kind of need?

I preached a sermon the next Sunday, calling for a response. I remember how excited I was when a man called me on the phone the following week and told me he was going to personally pledge $1,000 a month to a housing ministry we wanted to begin as a result of seeing that picture, and he said he'd be responsible for raising another $1,000 monthly. This was the launching of what we call a "Jubilee Ministry" in our city, through which we are seeking to respond to the needs of people like that old woman. We are repairing houses, using unemployed people in the city as well as volunteers from our congregation to do the work, and trying to minister to the total needs of the people in the process.

When that man made his response of pledging $1,000 a month, you can imagine my exhilaration. Then the Lord said something to me that I hope I never forget. He didn't speak in an audible voice, but in my heart I knew what His message was. He said, "Maxie, don't miss the message of this dramatic, generous gift."

I was puzzled by that. "What do You mean, Lord? I'm not missing it. I'm so grateful. This is great!"

"Sure it's great," said the Lord, "and I want you to know it. But that fellow is doing something more than giving money. I want that fellow to be a sign—a sign to you and the whole congregation. I want to teach you, and I want to teach the congregation that there are people all around like that, and I'm going to do a great work through them. What that fellow has done is just the beginning. I'm calling forth other people as well, whose hearts are going to be full of compassion, and who are going to respond joyfully and consecrate themselves and their resources to Me."

That's what the Lord said, and what He said has been coming true in our congregation. The things that have happened during these past months in the lives of our people, the decisions that have been made, the gifts that have been given, have convinced me that what the Lord said is true. At the time of this writing, it's only the beginning, and the Lord is going to do mighty things among us as people continue to consecrate themselves and their resources to Him. Remarkable things happen in congregations and with individuals when there is a consecration of self and resources.

MINISTERING ANGEL

23:20 "Behold, I send an Angel before you to keep you in the way and to bring you into the place which I have prepared.

21 "Beware of Him and obey His voice; do not provoke Him, for He will not pardon your transgressions; for My name *is* in Him.

22 "But if you indeed obey His voice and do all that I speak, then I will be an enemy to your enemies and an adversary to your adversaries.

23 "For My Angel will go before you and bring you in to the Amorites and the Hittites and the Perizzites and the Canaanites and the Hivites and the Jebusites; and I will cut them off.

24 "You shall not bow down to their gods, nor serve them, nor do according to their works; but you shall utterly overthrow them and completely break down their *sacred* pillars.

25 "So you shall serve the LORD your God, and He will bless your bread and your water. And I will take sickness away from the midst of you.

26 "No one shall suffer miscarriage or be barren in your land; I will fulfill the number of your days.

27 "I will send My fear before you, I will cause confusion among all the people to whom you come, and will make all your enemies turn *their* backs to you.

28 "And I will send hornets before you, which shall drive out the Hivite, the Canaanite, and the Hittite from before you.

29 "I will not drive them out from before you in one year, lest the land become desolate and the beasts of the field become too numerous for you.

30 "Little by little I will drive them out from before you, until you have increased, and you inherit the land.

31 "And I will set your bounds from the Red Sea to the sea, Philistia, and from the desert to the River. For I will deliver the inhabitants of the land into your hand, and you shall drive them out before you.

32 "You shall make no covenant with them, nor with
their gods.

33 "They shall not dwell in your land, lest they
make you sin against Me. For *if* you serve their gods,
it will surely be a snare to you."

Exod. 23:20–33

These verses bring to a close the book of the covenant. They are
not what we might have expected to find by way of conclusion. Here
is for Israel a looking forward to the promised land, which was going to be presented as a gift from Yahweh to His people, and which
they would occupy in security and prosperity if they remained faithful to Yahweh and His word.

The demands of the covenant law have been placed upon them,
but now comes the presence of the guiding Providence of God. The
image here is that of a ministering angel, the angel of promises.

We don't talk about angels very much, do we? We think about
them far more than we talk about them. *"Behold, I send an Angel
before you to keep you in the way and to bring you into the place which
I have prepared"* (23:20). The purpose of the angel was to guard and
guide the Israelites. He was to guard them on the way and lead them
to the place which God had prepared for them.

It's easy for us to think in terms of guidance. There have been times
in all our lives when we were certain that we were being guided by a
power not our own. The confusion comes, however, at the point of
the function of the angel to guard us.

There is the aspect of protection in this. God protected the Israelites
against all their enemies, blessed their bread and their water, and as
the Scripture says, "He took sickness away from the midst of them."

Many of us can testify to the protecting hand of God in our lives
and in the lives of our family. But, that's not always the case. Christians die tragic deaths; trouble intervenes in a Christian family and
rips the fabric of that family to shreds. The rain is always falling on
the just as well as the unjust.

So, what is the truth of this guarding, this protecting work of the
angel of God in our lives?

The protection supports our integrity of commitment, our stead-
fastness in the faith. Verse 24 says, *"You shall not bow down to their
gods, nor serve them, nor do according to their works."* Then in verse 25,

"You shall serve the Lord your God." The promise was not that the people would be saved, but that they would be faithful if they depended upon this angel of God.

We need to learn this lesson. God's angels do not always spare us from troubles, but enable us to look at tragedy and trouble through different eyes.

There's the story about the three-year-old child who was visiting his aunt overnight. He begged for the hall light to be left on and his bedroom door ajar when he went to bed. But his aunt reminded him that he was never afraid of the dark when he was at home. To this he responded, "Yes, but there it's *my* dark." That's the protection, the guarding, that the angel of God provides us. He makes the dark our dark because He's with us in it.

We're not protected in the sense of being safe. All the saints have agreed to this. Simone Weil put it well. "If you want a love that will protect the soul from wounds, you must love something other than God."

So, the guarding, guiding ministry of God's angels is the ministry of keeping us faithful, giving us a new way of seeing things.

Then there is this second work of ministering angels. They enable us to be courageous, even joyful, in the midst of our tragedy, trouble, and turmoil.

Do you remember Harper Lee's novel *To Kill a Mockingbird?* Atticus was a wise and generous man in the novel. He tells his son, Jem, about an old woman who is dying of cancer. Her name is Mrs. Dubose. She's been a bitter critic of Atticus for his insistence on equal rights for blacks in that small Southern town. So Jem hates the old woman for criticizing his father. But Atticus wants Jem to see the greatness of this cantankerous old woman. For years she had taken morphine at her doctor's orders to ease her pain. Eventually she became a morphine addict. As she realized that she was coming to the end of her days, she determined to end her addiction to morphine before she died. According to her, she wanted to die "beholden to nothing and to nobody."

Jem reads to her and watches her day by day as she endures the pain of not taking the morphine. After she dies, Atticus says to Jem, "I wanted you to see what real courage is, instead of getting the idea that courage is a man with a gun in his hand; it's when you know you're licked before you begin, but you begin anyway, and you see it through no matter. You rarely win, but sometimes you do. Mrs. Dubose won, all ninety-eight pounds of her. According to her views, she was beholden to nothing and nobody. She was the bravest person I ever knew."[2]

That's what God was saying to the Israelites. They would have nothing between them and Him. They would be beholden to nothing and to nobody. That's the courage the ministering angel provides us.

But the angel of God not only makes us courageous, he makes us *joyously* courageous. That's the reason we can talk about weeping for joy. Joy lies between tears and laughter. Someone has said that the soul would have no rainbows had the eyes no tears.

It's the great gift of the angel of God who enables us to sing with Paul and Silas at midnight in prison, and to claim with Paul, "Nothing, absolutely nothing, can separate us from the love of God in Christ Jesus."

Then there is the third gift of God's angels. They give us peace even in the midst of trouble and turmoil.

Somewhere, Henry Drummond tells the story of two artists who were commissioned to paint pictures that would express peace. The first artist painted a peaceful environment: a mountain lake that was calm, quiet, tranquil, serene; green hills ringed with tall pine trees. It was the picture of peace for those who believe peace comes from the outside in.

The second artist painted a very turbulent scene with a violent waterfall crashing down on jagged chunks of granite rock, but he added something. Alongside the waterfall was a slender birch tree. Its fragile branches reached out just above the crashing foam of the waterfall. In the fork of one of the slim, tender branches of the tree was a bird nest, and in that nest, a bird.

Now the bird was not oblivious to the fragile nature of its security. It could feel the swaying of the branch, but it knew that if the branch broke, it had wings.

That's the picture of the inner peace God's angel gives us. Knowing that even in a turbulent environment we have options. Patrick Overton once put it: "When we walk to the edge of all the light we have and take that step into the darkness of the unknown, we have to believe that one of two things will happen: There will be something solid for us to stand on or we will be taught how to fly."

That was the kind of assurance the angel of promises gave to Israel.

ISRAEL AFFIRMS THE COVENANT

24:1 Now He said to Moses, "Come up to the LORD, you and Aaron, Nadab and Abihu, and seventy of the elders of Israel, and worship from afar.

2 "And Moses alone shall come near the LORD, but they shall not come near; nor shall the people go up with him."

3 So Moses came and told the people all the words of the LORD and all the judgments. And all the people answered with one voice and said, "All the words which the LORD has said we will do."

4 And Moses wrote all the words of the LORD. And he rose early in the morning, and built an altar at the foot of the mountain, and twelve pillars according to the twelve tribes of Israel.

5 Then he sent young men of the children of Israel, who offered burnt offerings and sacrificed peace offerings of oxen to the LORD.

6 And Moses took half the blood and put it in basins, and half the blood he sprinkled on the altar.

7 Then he took the Book of the Covenant and read in the hearing of the people. And they said, "All that the LORD has said we will do, and be obedient."

8 And Moses took the blood, sprinkled *it* on the people, and said, "This is the blood of the covenant which the LORD has made with you according to all these words."

9 Then Moses went up, also Aaron, Nadab, and Abihu, and seventy of the elders of Israel,

10 and they saw the God of Israel. And *there was* under His feet as it were a paved work of sapphire stone, and it was like the very heavens in *its* clarity.

11 But on the nobles of the children of Israel He did not lay His hand. So they saw God, and they ate and drank.

12 Then the LORD said to Moses, "Come up to Me on the mountain and be there; and I will give you tablets of stone, and the law and commandments which I have written, that you may teach them."

13 So Moses arose with his assistant Joshua, and Moses went up to the mountain of God.

14 And he said to the elders, "Wait here for us until we come back to you. Indeed, Aaron and Hur *are* with you. If any man has a difficulty, let him go to them."

15 Then Moses went up into the mountain, and a cloud covered the mountain.

16 Now the glory of the LORD rested on Mount Sinai, and the cloud covered it six days. And on the seventh day He called to Moses out of the midst of the cloud.

17 The sight of the glory of the LORD *was* like a consuming fire on the top of the mountain in the eyes of the children of Israel.

18 So Moses went into the midst of the cloud and went up into the mountain. And Moses was on the mountain forty days and forty nights.

Exod. 24:1-18

Chapter 24 is a kind of transition chapter. Here is a reaffirmation of the covenant. The writer to the Hebrews used this scene as the prototype for the new covenant. When Moses returned to the people and told them all the provisions that God had made for the covenant, they responded with community accord: *"All the words which the Lord has said we will do"* (24:3). To celebrate that, Moses wrote down all the words of the Lord; then he rose early in the morning and built an altar, and there the children of Israel offered burnt offerings and sacrificed peace offerings to the Lord.

Then Moses did a very interesting thing. He read aloud the words of the covenant as he had recorded those words. It was a restatement, an etching again upon their minds and hearts the remarkable thing that had taken place there at Sinai. And again, the people gave their assent. Then Moses took blood, sprinkled it on the people, and said, *"This is the blood of the covenant which the Lord has made with you according to all these words"* (v. 8). The writer to the Hebrews put it, "Therefore not even the first covenant was dedicated without blood" (9:18). And about Jesus the writer to the Hebrews said: "He has appeared to put away sin by the sacrifice of Himself" (9:26). As has been indicated previously, this was a foreshadowing of that new covenant which would be made by the blood of Jesus offered in self-sacrifice on Calvary.

Then God called Moses to come up to the mountain where He would give him the tablets of stone on which the law was written. Moses took Joshua with him, left Aaron and Hur to settle any issues among the people, and as they journeyed to the mountain, a great cloud covered it. The glory of the Lord rested on Mt. Sinai for six days. On the seventh day, God called to Moses out of the midst of the cloud. The sight of God's glory was like a consuming fire on the top of the mountain in the eyes of the children of Israel. Moses left Joshua there and went into the midst of the cloud, up into the mountain, where he communed with God for forty days. It is there that the Lord spoke to him, and gave him instructions about what was to take place next in the history of this covenant relationship.

NOTES

1. Mother Teresa, *Words to Love By* (Notre Dame, IN: Ave Maria Press, 1983), p. 25.
2. Harper Lee, *To Kill a Mockingbird* (Philadelphia: J. P. Lippincott, 1960), p. 105.

CHAPTER SIXTEEN

Camping with God: The Tabernacle and the Priest

Exodus 25:1–31:18

It took God six days to create the world, but it took Him forty days to explain to Moses how to build the tabernacle! I'm not sure who first made that observation, but I know how surprised I was when I discovered that no less than fifty chapters in the Old and New Testaments were devoted to the construction, ritual, and priesthood of the tabernacle. Thirteen of these chapters are in Exodus, eighteen in Leviticus, thirteen in Numbers, two in Deuteronomy, and four in the Epistle to the Hebrews in the New Testament.

In Exodus, the seven chapters which we are going to look at now, chapters 25–31, provide a description of the specifications of the tabernacle. Then in chapters 35–40 of Exodus, these instructions are repeated almost word for word as they were carried out by those who built the tabernacle. No other single aspect of Israel's faith is given as much attention in the Old Testament as the tabernacle, the furnishings of it, and the priests and rituals of its ministry.

We need to get and keep perspective. The tabernacle was not erected in Egypt, nor primarily in Canaan. It was a portable place in the wilderness. This was important. Egypt was a land of idolatry; therefore no place for a sanctuary to Yahweh. Canaan was the permanent dwelling place of the people of God who had been brought out of bondage by God Himself; therefore a permanent place was required there. The tabernacle was stationed in Shiloh for some time, but it remained in Canaan only until Solomon's temple was completed. Primarily, the tabernacle was for the pilgrims in the desert.

There is significance in that. Egypt and bondage under Pharaoh was behind the Israelites; Canaan, the promised land of God, was ahead of them. So, the tabernacle was for a pilgrim people. That has meaning for us, because that's who we are as Christians—a pilgrim people. Here on earth we have no permanent dwelling place, but you remember how Paul affirmed it when he wrote to the Philippians: "Our citizenship is in heaven, from which we also eagerly wait for the Savior, the Lord Jesus Christ" (Phil. 3:20).

Doesn't one of life's primary problems have to do with where we are and what we have? We spend so much time and energy dealing with where we are and what we have that where we are can become an idol and what we have can become a god. We seek meaning for life in these passing things.

A young man had recently lost his father. Though his father was getting on in years, death was unexpected, and I questioned the young man about it. "It causes you to really look at your priorities," he said. "When I stood by that open grave, I had to face again the question, will we ever meet again?"

You see, we're pilgrim people; we have no permanent dwelling, but our common wealth is in heaven.

I know some parents today who would exchange everything they have for a loving relationship with their children. I know parents who would give up everything if their children could have such a deep relationship with Christ that they would cease rebelling, and would have the power to resist seeking happiness and meaning in that which brings only pain and sorrow.

We're a pilgrim people, and where we are and what we have get in the way of our relationship to God.

There's another meaning in this symbol of the portability of this place of worship. The tabernacle was portable like a tent, and whenever and wherever the Israelites camped for a time, the tabernacle was erected. It was always pitched in the sand. Even though it had its rich furnishings, and its ornate decorations, no provision was ever made to cover the floor. There's a powerful symbol in that, too. The priests' and the worshipers' feet were always in the sand, reminding them that they were creatures of the earth and could not escape being in the world.

There is a warning here. Some people become so heavenly minded that they are no earthly good. I've known women to become so involved in Scripture study, prayer groups, efforts at spiritual development, that they neglected the needs of their children and their husbands. I've known men who paid attention to their own spirituality, but ignored that of their wives and their children, failing to be the priests of the household that God called them to be.

Men and women alike need to know that a spirituality that robs husband or wife of emotional support is not what God intends. A spirituality that becomes a substitute for a rich and meaningful sexual relationship with our spouses is not Christian. Paul knew that our sexuality was involved in our spirituality. That's the reason he called husbands and wives to submit to each other out of reverence for Christ. And the same warning must be sounded to parents in relation to their children. Many parents are more intent on developing their own spirituality than they are in being priests to their children.

The bare floor of the tabernacle, the people's feet in the sand, was a reminder that we must never become so heavenly minded that we're no earthly good.

Another lesson is that there is nothing on this earth that can sustain us save the presence of Him who dwells in the tabernacles of our hearts—God Himself.

Stephen F. Olford reminds us that the tabernacle was an object lesson to the children of Israel for nearly five hundred years, from Moses to David. The temple took its place during the reign of Solomon, but even so, its lessons remain today.

Dr. Olford reminds us that a good way to study the tabernacle is in terms of its purpose—its immediate purpose and its ultimate purpose. Its immediate purpose was that of a place of worship, where the established relationship was lived out, and people experienced revelation. It was also a place of witness, a witness to the presence of God, the purity of God, the protection of God, and the provision of God.

The ultimate purpose of the tabernacle was to point to the Christ who was coming, and in whom all of the object lessons of the tabernacle would be fulfilled.

It offers us a type of Christ; that's the meaning of its witness to His Person and His work. This is a huge part of what the book of Hebrews is all about. "But Christ came as High Priest of the good things to come, with the greater and more perfect tabernacle not made with hands, that is, not of this creation. Not with the blood of goats and calves, but with His own blood He entered the Most

Holy Place once for all, having obtained eternal redemption" (Heb. 9:11–12).

So the tabernacle points forward to the completed covenant, the perfect witness of God's redemption, Jesus Christ Himself.

We will see this as we look closely at chapters 25–31 of Exodus.

Overarching all of the understanding about the tabernacle, must be that word of God Himself. "Let them make Me a sanctuary, that I may dwell among them" (25:8). Moses didn't build the tabernacle and invite God to come to it. Rather, God conceived the plan and instructed Moses and the people to build it because of His desire to dwell among them. There is a sense in which this is the overarching purpose of God revealed as we move through Scripture—He purposes to dwell among His people. That comes to ultimate fruition in Jesus Christ, who was God "reconciling the world unto Himself" (2 Cor. 5:19). It is no wonder He was called Emmanuel, "God with us" (Matt. 1:23).

MATERIALS FOR THE SANCTUARY

25:1 Then the LORD spoke to Moses, saying:

2 "Speak to the children of Israel, that they bring Me an offering. From everyone who gives it willingly with his heart you shall take My offering.

3 "And this *is* the offering which you shall take from them: gold, silver, and bronze;

4 "blue, purple, and scarlet *thread,* fine linen, and goats' *hair;*

5 "ram skins dyed red, badger skins, and acacia wood;

6 "oil for the light, and spices for the anointing oil and for the sweet incense;

7 "onyx stones, and stones to be set in the ephod and in the breastplate.

8 "And let them make Me a sanctuary, that I may dwell among them.

9 "According to all that I show you, *that is,* the pattern of the tabernacle and the pattern of all its furnishings, just so you shall make *it.*"

Exod. 25:1–9

"Bring Me an offering," God told Moses to say to the people. At first glance, it would seem ludicrous for such a command to be made. Here was a group of slaves, recently released from captivity in Egypt, now in a barren land. What sort of offering could they bring? God had already anticipated the problem, and had made provision for it. One of the aspects of this Exodus journey is the way God provided, even in the minutest way, for the needs of the people, and for their response to Him.

You will recall that prior to the departure from Egypt, before the Passover, He had instructed the people to ask the Egyptians for their jewels of gold and silver. And so they had all those materials that they had gotten from the Egyptians. Isn't that a kind of irony too? Some of the offerings the people brought they had received from their captors in Egypt.

It's important to note that the materials for the building of the tabernacle came from the people. And it came, according to the request of the Lord, *"willingly with . . . heart."*

Two words are used here that are at the heart of the meaning the tabernacle had for the people. First of all is the word "tabernacle" itself. It is the Hebrew word *miškān,* a word that means "dwelling place," from a root form that may literally mean "pitch a tent." God has made a promise that He is going to "pitch His tent" among us. That's the reason I have titled this chapter "Camping with God."

This is a new and radical intervention in the life of history—that God would choose to dwell among His people. The deep richness of this is seen in the New Testament. In John 15, Jesus uses the word "abide." In the Greek this is the same word from which dwelling place comes in the Hebrew. He talks about our abiding in Him as He abides in the Father, and the Father abides in the Son. The circle is complete. Back in the desert, God took the initiative to pitch His tent among us, to dwell with men, and now through Jesus, He has come to abide among us in the flesh, in order to complete that revelation, but also to provide a way for us to abide, to dwell, in Him.

The Hebrew word translated "sanctuary" literally means "a separated place." The purpose of the tabernacle was that it would be a sanctuary, a holy place, because that was the place where God would dwell.

God gave Moses the exact instructions for the building of the tabernacle, because God alone determines what is acceptable worship.

Those who write most about the tabernacle provide meaning for the rich symbolism that is there. Some of these writers strain at seeing a "type" in everything. We don't want to strain in that fashion, nor do we want to be dogmatic, because the Old Testament itself does not spell out the symbolism. Even so, there is richness of meaning, and in some instances, the types are rather clear. This will especially be so when we look at the furniture in the tabernacle. As to the materials of the tabernacle, there is general agreement that the gold typifies the deity of our Lord Jesus Christ (Rev. 3:18), and also divine righteousness when the gold is connected with the mercy seat (Exod. 25:17). Silver typifies redemption, as seen in the atonement money (Exod. 30:12–16; Num. 18:16). Brass symbolizes the death of Christ as a meeting of man's responsibility toward God. This is seen in the brazen altar (Exod. 27:3; Rev. 1:15).

The main colors of the materials for the tabernacle were blue, purple, and scarlet. These colors occur in this combination and order about twenty-eight times in the Book of Exodus. Blue is the heavenly color, typifying Christ as the spiritual One. The Book of Hebrews described him as "holy, harmless, undefiled, separate from sinners, and has become higher than the heavens" (Heb. 7:26).

Purple typifies Christ as the sovereign One, the King of kings and the Lord of lords.

Churches that use liturgical colors use purple for the period of Lent, recalling that before His crucifixion, they mocked Jesus, "clothed Him with purple; and they twisted a crown of thorns, put it on His head, and began to salute Him, 'Hail, King of the Jews!'" (Mark 15:17–18). Purple is also the kingly color, and this King of kings and Lord of lords is going to reign universally (Rev. 19:16).

Scarlet is the color associated with sacrifice. This sacrificial color embodies the entire thought of redemption, and since the tabernacle is seen as a type of Christ in the Old Testament, all these colors are associated with Him. Christ is the sacrificial One. One remembers that song in the Book of Revelation (see also Num. 19:6; Lev. 14:4; Heb. 9:11–14, 19, 23, 28).

And they sang a new song, saying:

"You are worthy to take the scroll,
And to open its seals;
For You were slain,
And have redeemed us to God by Your blood
Out of every tribe and tongue and people and
      nation,
And have made us kings and priests to our God;
And we shall reign on the earth."

Rev. 5:9–10

There were to be all sorts of fabrics: fine linen, goat skin, ram skin, badger's skin. The wood was to be acacia, or shittim. This was a gnarled and thorny tree that provided a close-grained and durable material for the structure.

However you view these materials, there are big lessons here: This was to be a tabernacle, a dwelling place, because God had chosen to pitch His tent among us. It was to be a sanctuary, literally a separated place, because it is the place where God dwells. The materials for the building of it came from the people, and the exact dimensions for it were given by God, because God alone determines acceptable worship.

The Tabernacle

26:1 "Moreover you shall make the tabernacle *with* ten curtains *of* fine woven linen and blue, purple, and scarlet *thread*; with artistic designs of cherubim you shall weave them.

2 "The length of each curtain *shall be* twenty-eight cubits, and the width of each curtain four cubits. And every one of the curtains shall have the same measurements.

3 "Five curtains shall be coupled to one another, and *the other* five curtains *shall be* coupled to one another.

4 "And you shall make loops of blue *yarn* on the edge of the curtain on the selvedge of *one* set, and

likewise you shall do on the outer edge of *the other* curtain of the second set.

5 "Fifty loops you shall make in the one curtain, and fifty loops you shall make on the edge of the curtain that *is* on the end of the second set, that the loops may be clasped to one another.

6 "And you shall make fifty clasps of gold, and couple the curtains together with the clasps, so that it may be one tabernacle.

7 "You shall also make curtains of goats' *hair*, to be a tent over the tabernacle. You shall make eleven curtains.

8 "The length of each curtain *shall be* thirty cubits, and the width of each curtain four cubits; and the eleven curtains shall all have the same measurements.

9 "And you shall couple five curtains by themselves and six curtains by themselves, and you shall double over the sixth curtain at the forefront of the tent.

10 "You shall make fifty loops on the edge of the curtain that is outermost in *one* set, and fifty loops on the edge of the curtain of the second set.

11 "And you shall make fifty bronze clasps, put the clasps into the loops, and couple the tent together, that it may be one.

12 "The remnant that remains of the curtains of the tent, the half curtain that remains, shall hang over the back of the tabernacle.

13 "And a cubit on one side and a cubit on the other side, of what remains of the length of the curtains of the tent, shall hang over the sides of the tabernacle, on this side and on that side, to cover it.

14 "You shall also make a covering of ram skins dyed red for the tent, and a covering of badger skins above that.

15 "And for the tabernacle you shall make the boards of acacia wood, standing upright.

16 "Ten cubits *shall be* the length of a board, and a cubit and a half *shall be* the width of each board.

17 "Two tenons *shall be* in each board for binding one to another. Thus you shall make for all the boards of the tabernacle.

18 "And you shall make the boards for the tabernacle, twenty boards for the south side.

19 "You shall make forty sockets of silver under the twenty boards: two sockets under each of the boards for its two tenons.

20 "And for the second side of the tabernacle, the north side, *there shall be* twenty boards

21 "and their forty sockets of silver: two sockets under each of the boards.

22 "For the far side of the tabernacle, westward, you shall make six boards.

23 "And you shall also make two boards for the two back corners of the tabernacle.

24 "They shall be coupled together at the bottom and they shall be coupled together at the top by one ring. Thus it shall be for both of them. They shall be for the two corners.

25 "So there shall be eight boards with their sockets of silver—sixteen sockets—two sockets under each of the boards.

26 "And you shall make bars of acacia wood: five for the boards on one side of the tabernacle,

27 "five bars for the boards on the other side of the tabernacle, and five bars for the boards of the side of the tabernacle, for the far side westward.

28 "The middle bar shall pass through the midst of the boards from end to end.

29 "You shall overlay the boards with gold, make their rings of gold *as* holders for the bars, and overlay the bars with gold.

30 "And you shall raise up the tabernacle according to its pattern which you were shown on the mountain.

31 "You shall make a veil woven of blue, purple, and scarlet *thread,* and fine woven linen. It shall be woven with an artistic design of cherubim.

32 "You shall hang it upon the four pillars of acacia *wood* overlaid with gold. Their hooks *shall be* gold, upon four sockets of silver.

33 "And you shall hang the veil from the clasps. Then you shall bring the ark of the Testimony in there, behind the veil. The veil shall be a divider for you between the holy *place* and the Most Holy.

34 "You shall put the mercy seat upon the ark of the Testimony in the Most Holy.

35 "You shall set the table outside the veil, and the lampstand across from the table on the side of the tabernacle toward the south; and you shall put the table on the north side.

36 "You shall make a screen for the door of the tabernacle, *woven of* blue, purple, and scarlet *thread*, and fine woven linen, made by a weaver.

37 "And you shall make for the screen five pillars of acacia *wood*, and overlay them with gold; their hooks *shall be* gold, and you shall cast five sockets of bronze for them."

Exod. 26:1–37

Since the tabernacle is so central in the focus of this chapter, we have moved the material concerning the tabernacle to this point in our commentary. It is interesting to note that instructions for the ark of the covenant, one of the most important pieces of furniture to go in the tabernacle, along with the table for the showbread and the golden lampstand, were the first instructions given (Exod. 25:10–22), and they come at this place in Scripture, following Moses' call to take an offering and get the materials together for the building of the tabernacle. But it seems easier to talk about the tabernacle first, and then to talk about all the furniture in the tabernacle.

When the writer of Hebrews talked about the tabernacle, he spoke of the "shadow of the heavenly things" (Heb. 8:5), "the copies of the things in the heavens" (Heb. 9:23), "copies of the true" (Heb. 9:24), and "a shadow of the good things to come" (Heb. 10:1). There was no question about it: For this writer, the tabernacle was intended to signify spiritual realities, especially those realities that are revealed in Christ.

The plans for the tabernacle are given in intricate detail. Though it may not be easy to visualize without a drawing of the tabernacle to look at as you read the chapter, it's important to remember that the design of the tabernacle served to show that God dwelt among His people, but was separated from them by His holiness, and that He could be approached only in ways that He prescribed.

The tabernacle was actually a tent made of curtains. These curtains hung on wooden frames. These frames were made of acacia wood overlaid with gold. The tabernacle space itself was a rectangular area, ten cubits by thirty cubits, ten cubits high. This structure, in turn, was divided so that there were two rooms: the holy place, and the holy of holies. The significance of this will become clearer as we talk about the furniture of the tabernacle.

As already mentioned, the tabernacle is a type that is rich in meaning, the chief meaning of which the writer to the Hebrews saw as a type of Christ. But the richness of the symbolism goes even beyond that. The tabernacle was *temporary*. It was not a permanent structure, as was the temple of Solomon, but simply a tent that could be moved about from place to place during the journeyings of the children of Israel. God moves with His people, and Jesus "tabernacled" here among us.

The tabernacle was God's dwelling place. It was there in the midst of Israel's camp, that He first made that radical commitment to maintain His tent among us.

Therefore, the tabernacle was the place where God met with men, and it was at the center of Israel's camp.

The tabernacle was the place where the law was preserved. The first piece of furniture built was the ark of the covenant, the container for the law that God had given on Sinai. That word was at the center of the people's life, and that which represented most clearly the covenant was the focus of their worship.

The tabernacle was the place where sacrifice was made. We will talk about that when we talk about the brazen altar where animals were brought and on which they were slain. Certainly, we don't miss the connection between the tabernacle as a type of Christ when we think about its being the center of sacrifice. The body in which Jesus dwelt among us on earth was sacrificed on a cross; so the cross was the altar upon which God's Lamb was slain.

The tabernacle was a place of worship. Within its courts, the priests ministered in their sacred services, and from its door the voice of the Lord was heard.

Interestingly, the tabernacle had only one door. That's unique when you think about such a large building. But that was the instruction of God, and God determines what is acceptable worship. Certainly there is one way into God's presence. That way was described by the prophet, "Who may ascend into the hill of the Lord? / Or who may stand in His holy place? / He who has clean hands and a pure heart, / Who has not lifted up his soul to an idol" (Ps. 24:3–4). But also, one is reminded of the word of Jesus Himself, the One Way, "I am the way, the truth, and the life. No one comes to the Father except through Me" (John 14:6), and His word, "I am the door" (John 10:9).

More of the meaning of the tabernacle will be seen as we discuss the furniture and the space within it.

THE ARK OF THE COVENANT AND THE MERCY SEAT

25:10 "And they shall make an ark of acacia wood; two and a half cubits *shall be* its length, a cubit and a half its width, and a cubit and a half its height.

11 "And you shall overlay it with pure gold, inside and out you shall overlay it, and shall make on it a molding of gold all around.

12 "You shall cast four rings of gold for it, and put *them* in its four corners; two rings *shall be* on one side, and two rings on the other side.

13 "And you shall make poles *of* acacia wood, and overlay them with gold.

14 "You shall put the poles into the rings on the sides of the ark, that the ark may be carried by them.

15 "The poles shall be in the rings of the ark; they shall not be taken from it.

16 "And you shall put into the ark the Testimony which I will give you.

17 "You shall make a mercy seat of pure gold; two and a half cubits *shall be* its length and a cubit and a half its width.

18 "And you shall make two cherubim of gold; of hammered work you shall make them at the two ends of the mercy seat.

19 "Make one cherub at one end, and the other cherub at the other end; you shall make the cherubim at the two ends of it *of one* piece with the mercy seat.

20 "And the cherubim shall stretch out their wings above, covering the mercy seat with their wings, and they shall face one another; the faces of the cherubim *shall be* toward the mercy seat.

21 "You shall put the mercy seat on top of the ark, and in the ark you shall put the Testimony that I will give you.
22 "And there I will meet with you, and I will speak with you from above the mercy seat, from between the two cherubim which are on the ark of the Testimony, about everything which I will give you in commandment to the children of Israel."

Exod. 25:10-22

As already indicated, we moved the material about the tabernacle ahead of its place in Exodus in order to get a picture of the tabernacle before we look at the furniture therein. In the order of Scripture, even before the tabernacle is described and ordered built, God orders the most important piece of furniture that is to go in the tabernacle: The ark of the covenant.

The ark was built of acacia wood, overlaid with pure gold inside and out, with ornamental gold molding around it. It was an oblong chest, two and one-half cubits in length and one and one-half cubits in width and height (25:10). We cannot give the exact size since the cubit measurement in ancient times varied from seventeen to twenty inches, and in practice was based on the distance from the elbow to the tip of the middle finger. The purpose of the ark was to contain the tables of the law, *"the Testimony."* But more than that, it represented the presence of God in a very special way. God promised that He would appear in a cloud upon the mercy seat which was on the ark in the most holy place. Into that holy place, "the holy of holies," the high priest would enter once a year to sprinkle blood on the mercy seat in order that the sins of the people might be atoned (Lev. 16).

The mercy seat was a slab of solid gold the same length and width of the ark and placed on the top of it as a cover.

Two gold cherubim were on either end of the ark, their wings spread out facing each other with their faces toward the mercy seat. Cherubim is from a word meaning "intercessor." They were always associated with the presence of God in the Old Testament. They were made in the shape of winged animals with human faces. The ark, covered with the mercy seat, with the cherubim attached, were the only articles in the holy of holies—standing behind the veil in the holy of holies was the great high priest.

There are three arks mentioned in the Bible: Moses' ark, Noah's ark, and the ark of the covenant. All of these arks are saving arks.

You remember the story of Moses' ark. It is the story of a brave woman trusting God. She already had two children, Aaron and Miriam, when Moses was born. The Pharaoh had put out an edict that all male children were to be killed.

Something even more than a natural mother's love whispered in this mother's heart that this child of hers, Moses, was special to God. So she risked everything, braved the royal edict, and hid her son away for three months.

When the baby was too old to hide any longer—no doubt each day his lungs were stronger, and his infant cries more likely to attract attention—her faith caused her to act in an even riskier fashion. She put all of her trust in God. She built a little "paper boat," an ark, by weaving together strips of papyrus, making it strong and waterproof by repeated coats of vegetable pitch. In an ultimate act of commitment, she placed her baby within that novel cradle, carried it to the riverside and laid it in a thicket of reeds, and then she waited for God to act.

That ark of Moses was a saving ark, keeping the infant child safe until he was rescued by the daughter of Pharaoh. What a miraculous intervention and working out of God's plan.

But a long time before Moses' ark, there was another ark.

> Then the Lord saw that the wickedness of man was great in the earth, and that every intent of the thoughts of his heart was only evil continually. And the Lord was sorry that He had made man on the earth, and He was grieved in His heart. So the Lord said, "I will destroy man whom I have created from the face of the earth, both man and beast, creeping thing and birds of the air, for I am sorry that I have made them." But Noah found grace in the eyes of the Lord.
>
> *Gen. 6:5–8*

Isn't that a marvelous word—that last sentence? "But Noah found grace in the eyes of the Lord." And the Lord commanded him to build an ark. You really have to use your imagination to see what faith Noah had to respond to God. I mean, there he was, out away

from the sea—no water near at hand—and the Lord was command-
ing him to build an ark, a boat, and a big one at that. But Noah
responded. Can't you imagine how crazy his friends thought he
was? Day in and day out, they would pass by and laugh at him as
he worked away at his project. Surely they thought he was crazy.
When they said he was crazy, he responded to them, "The Lord has
commanded me to do this, and I'm doing it." And you know what
happened. Finally the floods came and the water began to rise.
Scripture says the windows of the heavens were opened and rain
fell on the earth for forty days and forty nights. It was in the six-
hundredth year of his life that old Noah led the parade of his sons
and their wives and the beasts and all the things that creep upon the
earth into the ark. And as the waters rose, the ark floated to safety.
It was a saving ark that came into being because one man responded
to God's call.

The ark of the covenant was also a saving ark. Though designated
as two, the ark and the mercy seat formed one piece of furniture.
God instructed Moses to put "the Testimony" given him on the
mountain, for "there I will meet with you." The presence of God is
His word, and His work of pardon in the sacrifice of blood on the
mercy seat was a *saving* word and presence.

Concentrate a moment on "the mercy seat" before we look further
at the ark. Get the setting of the tabernacle clearly in mind. It was a
huge, rectangular tent with one entry way. As you entered the tabernacle, you were confronted by the brazen altar (we'll look at this
later). This was the central place of sacrifice, and therefore great
space surrounded it for the people to gather. At the further end was
the holy place where only the priests went to perform their priestly
functions. And inside the holy place was the holy of holies. A great
thick veil separated the holy of holies from the holy place. Inside the
holy of holies was the ark of the covenant and the mercy seat.

Even when the temple replaced the tabernacle in Jerusalem, there
was still the holy of holies. You remember the dramatic happening
on Good Friday when the veil was rent in twain from the top to
bottom, forever making the "holy of holies" accessible to all through
Jesus Christ.

The mercy seat is the witness of *redeeming pardon*. It was on
the mercy seat that lambs were slain as a sacrifice for the sins of the
people. One can imagine that the mercy seat became encrusted with

the blood of successive years as high priest after high priest sprin-kled there the blood of victims slain on the annual day of atonement.

The word rendered "mercy seat" really means "a covering." This makes special reference to the forgiveness and covering of transgres-sion and sin by the slain blood of the lamb. The same word occurs in the Greek in the New Testament, where we are told by the apostle Paul that the Father sent Christ to be a propitiation through faith, by His blood and in the passing over of sin.

> But now the righteousness of God apart from the law
> is revealed, being witnessed by the Law and the
> Prophets, even the righteousness of God, through
> faith in Jesus Christ, to all and on all who believe.
> For there is no difference; for all have sinned and fall
> short of the glory of God, being justified freely by
> His grace through the redemption that is in Christ
> Jesus, whom God set forth as a propitiation by His
> blood, through faith, to demonstrate His righteous-
> ness, because in His forbearance God had passed
> over the sins that were previously committed. . . .
> *Rom. 3:21–25*

We might translate that 25th verse in this fashion: "The redemp-tion that is in Christ Jesus whom God set forth to be a mercy seat."

Isn't that a beautiful term? A seat of mercy. Is there a more beauti-ful term in our language? Let it hang on your lip—mercy—mercy—mercy. More than that, be immersed in the meaning of it, for that is the constant stream of love flowing from God—abundant mercy. Not wrath, not judgment, not indignation, but mercy is pouring forth from the eternal fountain in the heart of God.

I'm not saying that there's not judgment. I'm not saying that God does not get indignant with our sloppy response to His call. I'm not saying that there isn't the demand of holiness and the expression of wrath in the character of God. I'm saying what the Bible says, that even before we reach that pinnacle of revelation as to who God is—Jesus Christ hanging on a cross—we have the eternal mercy seat to show us God's nature. We also have, even before Jesus, a great prophet of God, breaking through the veil of confusion, the veil of mystery, the veil of unknowing, and reaching a crescendo of praise, exclaiming who God is.

> Who is a God like You,
> Pardoning iniquity
> And passing over the transgression of the
>   remnant of His heritage?
>
> He does not retain His anger forever,
> Because He delights in mercy.
> He will again have compassion on us,
> And will subdue our iniquities.
>
> You will cast all our sins
> Into the depths of the sea.
> You will give truth to Jacob
> And mercy to Abraham,
> Which You have sworn to our fathers
> From days of old.
>
> *Mic. 7:18–20*

So the mercy seat is a witness to redeeming pardon, a witness that was only faintly perceived in the tabernacle, but is now fully revealed in Jesus Christ.

There is a classic picture of it coming out of World War I. A soldier had ventured out into the battle zone to repair a broken telephone cable that was cutting off communication between the allied forces. Although he died in his mission, he had accomplished it—he was holding in either hand the severed wires, and the live current was passing through his body. His hand had literally become a passing link. Beneath the picture was written one big word—and then a smaller one. The smaller one was "Mission accomplished"; the larger one was *through*. Those words can be written over the cross, our eternal mercy seat—*through*. Through the split veil into God's presence—through our weakness to God's power—through our sin to His salvation. *Through*—by the mercy of God.

An extraordinary thing about this mercy seat was its name, because it was not a seat, but a lid—a lid over the ark of the covenant. There was no seat among the furniture of the tabernacle. There was no need for one. C. W. Slemming suggests the rich meaning of this. The priestly work was never finished. Each priest continued to minister until he was relieved by another, and so, in relays, the ministry of the priests went on continuously. Only once do we ever read of a

315

priest finishing his work and sitting down. He was the great High Priest, Jesus Christ Himself. Listen to Hebrews 10:11, 12: "And every priest stands ministering daily and offering repeatedly the same sacrifices, which can never take away sins. But this Man [Jesus], after He had offered one sacrifice for sins forever, sat down at the right hand of God."

Do you see the vivid suggestion here? It is the suggestion of a *finished* work. In the priestly administration of the tabernacle service, there was no end. Christ alone could say: "It is finished."

Note that this was called more than a seat. It was a *mercy seat*. It was that which covered the law that had been deposited in the ark. Man could not keep the law. That was proved when Moses came down from the mountain with the first two tablets of stone and found the people worshiping the golden calf. There was no way for man to keep the law, no way for man to save himself. So what happened? God covered His law with mercy—with the mercy seat. Not through our own accomplishments, but through Jesus Christ we have a resting place, and we can say what the psalmist said, "Surely goodness and mercy shall follow me/ All the days of my life;/ And I will dwell in the house of the Lord/ Forever" (Ps. 23:6).[1]

Let's return now for one more specific look at the ark.

Remember, now, that when the tabernacle was in place, the ark was always in the holy of holies, and no one saw that ark except the high priest—and that only once a year, because no one was allowed in the holy of holies but the high priest on the annual day of atonement. It was there in the holy of holies, with the mercy seat covering the ark, that the high priest would take the blood of sacrificed lambs and pour it on the mercy seat as a sacrifice for the sins of the people.

But the tabernacle was not always in place, because Israel was a wandering people, wandering through that desert land. And wherever they went, of course, they would take the ark. It symbolized God's presence with them.

Let's look at the ark in three different places, as a reminder of God's presence.

The Ark at Jordan: Prevenient Presence

Look first at the ark at Jordan when Joshua was leading the people to the promised land.

So it was, after three days, that the officers went
through the camp; and they commanded the people,
saying, "When you see the ark of the covenant of the
Lord your God, and the priests, the Levites, bearing
it, then you shall set out from your place and go after
it. Yet there shall be a space between you and it,
about two thousand cubits by measure. Do not come
near it, that you may know the way by which you
must go, for you have not passed this way before."
And Joshua said to the people, "Sanctify yourselves,
for tomorrow the Lord will do wonders among you."
Then Joshua spoke to the priests, saying, "Take up
the ark of the covenant and cross over before the
people." So they took up the ark of the covenant and
went before the people.

Josh. 3:2–6

The ark at Jordan teaches us about God's prevenient presence.
When the people set out from their tents to pass over Jordan, following Joshua's leadership, the priests were ahead of them bearing the
ark of the covenant. Then comes one of the most beautiful stories in
the Scripture, almost as dramatic as the crossing of the Red Sea.
When the priests who bore the ark came to the Jordan, the Jordan
was overflowing its bank. But do you know what happened? The
priests didn't stop. What a dramatic sight—the overflowing Jordan,
stretching out before them, the ark of the covenant being borne by
them. The call of God to go burned in the priests' minds, so they
didn't stop. They went straight ahead. And when they stepped into
the waters, the waters flowing down toward the sea stopped. The
waters separated and the people passed through the Jordan. There's
a marvelous picture of it expressed in Joshua 3:17. "Then the priests
who bore the ark of the covenant of the Lord stood firm on dry
ground in the midst of the Jordan; and all Israel crossed over on dry
ground, until all the people had crossed completely over the Jordan."

It's a picture for me of the prevenient presence of God—God going before us in what John Wesley described as prevenient grace on
our behalf. Do you believe that? That God goes before you to prepare the way, that He will be there at every crucial time in your life?

The Scripture says, "You have not passed this way before" (Josh.
3:4). Much psychic and emotional energy is wasted worrying about

317

coming to those places where we've not been before. We tend to worry ourselves to fever pitch as we anticipate things happening that may never happen, or as we come to those places where we've never been before. F. B. Meyer addresses the problem:

> Do you ever ask what you will do at the swellings of Jordan? Do you fear that heart and strength will fail? Do you dread the touch of the cold water? Do you wish that you'd lived in days when bushes burned with fire, when voices spoke from the mount, when the angels seemed visibly to precede the hosts, and a being like the Son of Man walked the glowing embers with his faithful witnesses? There's no need to cherish such backward yearnings. There is a presence with us—a divine companionship, the angel of the covenant, the Christ of God! Like a voice ringing down a mountain ravine, we hear His imperishable words, "Lo, I am with you all the days, even unto the end." Shall we have the faith to answer, "Yea, though I walk through the valley of the shadow of death, I will fear no evil; for Thou art with me"? Even if our emotions have not yet realized the experience, yet our faith affirms the fact with unfaltering emphasis.[2]

God goes before us preveniently, is preparing the way, and is going to meet us at every overflowing Jordan and at every swelling river of our lives.

The Ark at Jericho: Powerful Presence

The ark at Jericho shows God's powerful presence. Sometimes in reading Scripture and in teaching and preaching, we miss some of the most, if not *the* most, significant truth. We all know the story of Joshua and Jericho, don't we? We know the song "Joshua fit the battle of Jericho, and the walls come a-tumblin' down." What do we know about the story?

If asked to recite the events we could probably say:

• Jericho was a stronghold protected by mighty men of valor, and Israel was not equal to the army of Jericho.

• The strategy of Joshua for taking the city was strange indeed. All of Israel's men of war marched around the city once a day for six days, then on the seventh day, marched around the city seven times.

• Seven priests blowing rams horn trumpets followed the army.

• On the seventh time around the city, when the priests made a long blast on the ram's horn, all the people shouted with a great shout, and the wall of the city crumbled.

That's what we know, and of course, we know the walls came tumblin' down. What many may not know or remember about the story involves the ark of the covenant. In the procession around the city, each of the six days and seven times on the seventh day, priests carrying the ark of the covenant followed the seven priests blowing the trumpets. And that's the key to it all. Not the army showing their strength, not the presence of the priests and the blaring trumpets, not the commitment of those wandering people and their shout of oneness. But the ark!—the powerful presence of God.

Don't miss that: *God's presence is power.* For those who abide in the secret place of the Lord, mountains and hills of fear and discouragement and sickness and pain are made low, and walls of estrangement and separation and loneliness and despair come tumbling down. Here is this truth in extreme:

> He was in a leprosarium. He looked old, but who can tell the age of a leper? His fingers were gone from the knuckles. His nose was eaten off. Teeth hung loose in his jaw, but his eyes were very alive.
>
> I looked at him with pity. "Isn't it hard?" I asked him. He smiled and said enthusiastically: "Christ is a wonderful Saviour!"
>
> He was hoeing in his garden at the leprosarium, holding the hoe clumsily in his fingerless hands. Nearby a younger man, new to the leprosarium, I guess, was struggling with a big weed in his own garden patch. The old man leaned over and between his paws jerked out the weed. Then he showed the younger leper how to jerk the reluctant weeds. Under the hot sun I saw him tremble with the exertion. But the younger smiled his thanks, and the older beamed his pleasure.
>
> "Isn't life hard?" I asked him. He smiled and shook his head: "Our Lord God is so wonderful."[3]

That witness reported to us by Leonard T. Wolcott is extreme, dramatic, far removed from daily experience, but I use it precisely for that purpose, to make the point that God's presence is power. If God's presence is power for those at the lowest place to which life can bring them, isn't it so for the rest of us? *Test it.* Stay alive to God's presence. Cultivate that presence. Don't begin any day without acknowledging His presence and making a willful decision to stay in that presence. It will transform your life. Power, not your own, will be yours. That's the witness of the ark of the covenant in Jericho.

The Ark in Captivity: A Passing Presence

Now we come to a third truth, symbolized in the ark in captivity: God as a passing presence.

God's presence in our lives is not necessarily permanent. Repeat: God's presence in our lives is not necessarily permanent. His is a passing presence.

After arriving in the promised land, Israel grievously sinned. Home from their wilderness wandering, secure in the land God had given them, they sinned, forsook their dependence on God, and were defeated by the Philistines. These pagans took the ark of the covenant back to Philistia.

Now to be sure, that was a mistake on the part of the Philistines. They were unaware of the powerful God with whom they were dealing. Wherever the ark went, it carried destruction to the people and idols of Philistia—so much so that the people were smitten with diseases, and they cried out in 1 Samuel 5:11: "Send away the ark of the God of Israel, and let it go back to its own place."

The powerful presence of God always plays havoc with surrounding evil. But the point to be made here is that because of Israel's sin and unfaithfulness, the divine presence departed.

We make the decision about God's presence. We make the sign of the cross over our lives, or we take the ark of the covenant, God's presence, with us.

On one occasion I was preaching at a prayer and Bible conference. The first evening, as we began the conference, all the people who were going to participate in the service that night prayed together. They laid their hands upon me, and each one of them prayed. I hope I'll never forget Danny Morris's prayer. It went something like this. "Lord, we feel that Maxie is anointed tonight, but help him to know that this anointing is not permanent. But in the power of Your present anointing, let him preach tonight with power to Your glory. Amen."

When Danny offered the part of that prayer which said "help him to know that the anointing is not permanent," I could feel a different kind of vibration through the hands of the people. There was a questioning about that, obviously, and I felt it. After the prayer was over, some chuckling comments were made about how intimidating such a prayer might be. But the truth was there. Danny and I talked about it during the week that followed, and I've remembered it almost daily since, and I hope I'll continue to remember it. Our anointing is not permanent. It is dependent upon our response and our obedience to God. So it is with God's presence in our lives. The ark in the wilderness teaches us that; the presence of God as vital reality in our lives is dependent upon our obedience, response, receptivity, and cultivation of the presence.

Let's review before we move on. The ark at Jordan symbolizes the prevenient presence of God, God going before us in His prevenient grace. The ark at Jericho symbolizes the powerful presence of God, leveling all the walls in our lives and enabling us to overcome any obstacle. The ark in captivity reminds us that the presence of God is passing, and for the reality of His presence to remain in our lives, we have to be responsive and obedient.

THE TABLE OF SHOWBREAD

25:23 "You shall also make a table of acacia wood; two cubits *shall be* its length, a cubit its width, and a cubit and a half its height.

24 "And you shall overlay it with pure gold, and make a molding of gold all around.

25 "You shall make for it a frame of a handbreadth all around, and you shall make a gold molding for the frame all around.

26 "And you shall make for it four rings of gold, and put the rings on the four corners that *are* at its four legs.

27 "The rings shall be close to the frame, as holders for the poles to bear the table.

28 "And you shall make the poles of acacia wood, and overlay them with gold, that the table may be carried with them.

29 "You shall make its dishes, its pans, its pitchers,
and its bowls for pouring. You shall make them of
pure gold.
30 "And you shall set the showbread on the table
before Me always."

Exod. 25:23–30

The second piece of furniture described for the tabernacle is the
table for the showbread, or the "bread of the presence." Literally,
the traditional translation, "showbread," means "bread of the face." It
was bread to be placed before the face of God.

The table was made of acacia wood, two cubits long, one cubit
wide, and a cubit and a half high. It was overlaid with pure gold,
with a molding of gold around it. It must have been a beautiful
thing.

Loaves of bread, called the "bread of the presence," were supposed to be on the table always. According to Leviticus 24:5–9,
twelve loaves of bread were to be set out in the presence of God
every Sabbath. (You may recall that this was the bread given to
David and his soldiers to eat in 1 Samuel 21:1–6.) The bread symbolized an offering to God, but it also was an acknowledgment that
God is the provider of our food.

It's not difficult to interpret the meaning of the bread in light of
the New Testament. Jesus is the "Living Bread" come down from
heaven, to feed our souls. (See commentary on the manna, and Jesus'
understanding of Himself as being the manna of God, pp. 189–204.)

THE GOLD LAMPSTAND

25:31 "You shall also make a lampstand of pure gold;
the lampstand shall be of hammered work. Its shaft,
its branches, its bowls, its *ornamental* knobs, and
flowers shall be *of one piece.*
32 "And six branches shall come out of its sides:
three branches of the lampstand out of one side, and
three branches of the lampstand out of the other
side.
33 "Three bowls *shall be* made like almond *blossoms* on one branch, *with* an *ornamental* knob and a

flower, and three bowls made like almond *blossoms* on the other branch, *with* an *ornamental* knob and a flower—and so for the six branches that come out of the lampstand.

34 *On the lampstand itself four bowls *shall be* made like almond *blossoms, each with* its *ornamental* knob and flower.

35 *And *there shall be* a knob under the *first* two branches of the same, a knob under the *second* two branches of the same, and a knob under the *third* two branches of the same, according to the six branches that extend from the lampstand.

36 *Their knobs and their branches *shall be of one piece;* all of it *shall be* one hammered piece of pure gold.

37 *You shall make seven lamps for it, and they shall arrange its lamps so that they give light in front of it.

38 *And its wick-trimmers and their trays *shall be* of pure gold.

39 *It shall be made of a talent of pure gold, with all these utensils.

40 *And see to it that you make *them* according to the pattern which was shown you on the mountain."

Exod. 25:31–40

The next instruction God gives to Moses is for the making of a lampstand. It was to be made of pure gold with six branches coming out its side. This meant that with the central shaft and the six branches there would be seven lamps.

The elaborate appearance is seen in the details that are given. On each branch there were to be three cups in the form of an almond flower, and on the central shaft, four cups with the almond flower. Tongs for adjusting the wick and snuffers were to be made of pure gold also.

Functionally, the purpose of the lampstand was to illuminate the tabernacle. It was the first piece of furniture to grab the attention of a worshiper as he entered through the door of the tabernacle into the holy place. Certainly it would have been an attractive object of splendor. Various symbolic meanings have been given it. First, it has been seen as God's presence in the midst of His people. Second, it is seen as Israel shining with the light of truth (cf. Isa. 42:6). And, third, of course, it's seen as Christ, the Light of the world.

THE ALTAR OF BURNT OFFERING

27:1 "You shall make an altar of acacia wood, five cubits long and five cubits wide—the altar shall be square—and its height *shall be* three cubits.

2 "You shall make its horns on its four corners; its horns shall be of one piece with it. And you shall overlay it with bronze.

3 "Also you shall make its pans to receive its ashes, and its shovels and its basins and its forks and its firepans; you shall make all its utensils of bronze.

4 "You shall make a grate for it, a network of bronze; and on the network you shall make four bronze rings at its four corners.

5 "You shall put it under the rim of the altar beneath, that the network may be midway up the altar.

6 "And you shall make poles for the altar, poles of acacia wood, and overlay them with bronze.

7 "The poles shall be put in the rings, and the poles shall be on the two sides of the altar to bear it.

8 "You shall make it hollow with boards; as it was shown you on the mountain, so shall they make *it.*"

Exod. 27:1–8

Not only was the tabernacle proper important in the worship life of Israel, the area surrounding the tent was also an important place. In that courtyard outside the tabernacle stood the altar of burnt offerings, and also the bronze laver (we'll discuss the bronze laver later). This altar was to be made of acacia wood, five cubits long, five cubits wide, and three cubits tall, and was to be overlaid with bronze. It was without a base or a top. Many scholars believe that it was filled with earth or possibly stones, upon which the offerings were burned. On each of the corners there was an ornamental horn, made of one piece with the altar. These horns were to hold the sacrificial animal firmly in place. Utensils of bronze for the altar were also to be provided, and a bronze grate with bronze rings at its corners to hold acacia wood carrying poles, also overlaid with bronze.

As symbolic as anything else here are the four horns. In Scripture, the horn is always a symbol of strength, salvation, and security. "[The Lord] will give strength to His king, and exalt the horn of His anointed," Hannah rejoiced over the victory of God in her life (1 Sam. 2:10). In Rev. 5:6, Jesus is described as a "Lamb as though it had been slain, having seven horns." So the horns on the altar speak of salvation and saving power, especially the salvation and saving power of the cross.

The brazen altar was at the very center of the Levitical system. There was a fire continually burning on the altar (Lev. 6:13), and the daily sacrifices of the people were renewed every morning. To this altar the sinner came with his sacrifice.

When the Hebrew brought his offering to the altar, he would lay his hands upon it before killing it, thus identifying himself with the animal. He would then offer this animal as a blood sacrifice in his own place.

It was at this altar that the high priest officiated on the annual day of atonement.

The position of the altar was just outside the entrance to the court of the tabernacle. The meaning is clear. The beginning of fellowship between God and man requires dealing with sin. In the case of the Israelites, it was a system of sacrifice as sin offerings. In the sacrificial system, man understood that he had forfeited his life through sin. Life was returned to him by the forfeiture of the life of the animal he brought. Burnt offerings on the altar suggested man's total commitment to God. Peace offerings there indicated a compact of peace, the covenant between the Almighty Friend of Israel and the individual family.

There is a beautiful movement of understanding about sacrifice in Psalm 50. In verse 5, the word is, "Gather My saints together to Me, / Those who have made a covenant with Me by sacrifice." But, as F. B. Meyer suggests, the psalm indicates that after several centuries had elapsed, a loftier conception of the divine requirement began to prevail:

> Hear, O My people, and I will speak,
> O Israel, and I will testify against you;
>
> . . . .
> I will not rebuke you for your sacrifices
> Or your burnt offerings,

Which are continually before Me.
I will not take a bull from your house,
Nor goats out of your folds.
For every beast of the forest is Mine,
And the cattle on a thousand hills.

. . . .

If I were hungry, I would not tell you;

. . . .

Offer to God thanksgiving,
And pay your vows to the Most High.
Ps. 50:7–10, 12, 14

So the meaning of sacrifice expanded and grew, until we came to that supreme act of reconciliation, the peace offering for the whole world present in One who has given Himself "once and for all" for the sins of the world.

THE ALTAR OF INCENSE

30:1 "You shall make an altar to burn incense on; you shall make it of acacia wood.

2 "A cubit *shall be* its length and a cubit its width—it shall be square—and two cubits *shall be* its height. Its horns *shall be* of one piece with it.

3 "And you shall overlay its top, its sides all around, and its horns with pure gold; and you shall make for it a molding of gold all around.

4 "Two gold rings you shall make for it, under the molding on both its sides. You shall place *them* on its two sides, and they will be holders for the poles with which to bear it.

5 "You shall make the poles of acacia wood, and overlay them with gold.

6 "And you shall put it before the veil that *is* before the ark of the Testimony, before the mercy seat that *is* over the Testimony, where I will meet with you.

7 "Aaron shall burn on it sweet incense every morning; when he tends the lamps, he shall burn incense on it.

326

8 "And when Aaron lights the lamps at twilight, he shall burn incense on it, a perpetual incense before the LORD throughout your generations.

9 "You shall not offer strange incense on it, or a burnt offering, or a grain offering; nor shall you pour a drink offering on it.

10 "And Aaron shall make atonement upon its horns once a year with the blood of the sin offering of atonement; once a year he shall make atonement upon it throughout your generations. It *is* most holy to the LORD."

Exod. 30:1–10

We are changing the order of Scripture again so that we might deal with the furniture in the tabernacle and in the court in sequence.

We indicated earlier, in our discussion about the mercy seat, that the furniture in the tabernacle provided a witness. The mercy seat was a witness to redeeming pardon. The altar of incense is a witness to prevailing prayer.

This altar stood just before the holy of holies. It was a small table, one cubit long and one cubit wide and two cubits high.

It was made of acacia wood and covered with pure gold. It also had horns on the corners and a molding of pure gold around it. In order that the altar might be carried from place to place, golden rings were affixed to the two opposite sides into which poles made of acacia wood and overlaid with gold could be fitted. It was right in front of the veil that separated the holy place from the holy of holies (30:6).

As a part of his priestly function, Aaron would refill the lamps each morning, and at the time would burn fragrant incense on the altar. He would do the same thing again in the evening when he lit the lamps. The symbolic meaning here, so powerful in its presentation, is that of prevailing prayer. This little altar of incense stood just before the veil that separated people from the holy of holies. In the holy of holies, remember, was the Ark of the Covenant. This was the dwelling place of God. God had said to the people: "There I will meet with you, and I will speak with you from above the mercy seat from between the two cherubim which are on the ark of the Testimony" (Exod. 25:22).

327

And the entree to that communion is the altar of incense, prevailing prayer.

I like the beautiful suggestion of C. W. Slemming:

> I have sometimes thought of this little piece of furniture standing before the veil as an electric plug such as we use to tap the electric power laid behind our walls. Behind the veil of the tabernacle was the Shekinah Glory of the presence of the Lord, and behind the veil of the sky are all the resources of the great triune God. By putting in the plug of prayer with the hand of faith, we are able to tap those resources and find that "prayer changes things." Great things happen at the hour of prayer when incense is being offered.[4]

For a study of the prevailing power of prayer, look at 1 Kings 18:36–38; Daniel 9:21; Acts 3:1; Acts 10:30–31; Matthew 27:45–51.

Years ago a young preacher named Joseph Parker was called to the pulpit of City Temple in London. Everyone was excited, but he could feel the pressure. On his first Sunday, he was scared, trembling inside and out. He was shown into the vestry and left there to prepare himself for the service. He had worked on his sermon, studied long and hard, but now he was really worried. He paced back and forth in that little room, and suddenly became aware of a vase filled with roses on the table. He leaned down to smell their fragrance and saw a note tucked in among them. It was addressed to him, and when he opened it, he read, "Welcome to your new pulpit at City Temple. We've not come to criticize you, but to pray with and for you. May God bless you." It was signed, "The People of City Temple." Joseph Parker was filled with courage and that was the beginning of a great ministry in that church, a ministry baptized in prayer. Illustration after illustration could be given to confirm the power of prevailing prayer. When we continue in prayer, our prayers come to God as the ascending smoke of the burning incense was interpreted to do by the Hebrew worshipers.

THE BRONZE LAVER

30:17 Then the LORD spoke to Moses, saying:
18 "You shall also make a laver of bronze, with its base also of bronze, for washing. You shall put it

between the tabernacle of meeting and the altar. And you shall put water in it,

19 "for Aaron and his sons shall wash their hands and their feet in water from it.

20 "When they go into the tabernacle of meeting, or when they come near the altar to minister, to burn an offering made by fire to the LORD, they shall wash with water, lest they die.

21 "So they shall wash their hands and their feet, lest they die. And it shall be a statute forever to them—to him and his descendants throughout their generations."

Exod. 30:17-21

The last piece of furniture we consider is the bronze laver. This was a further symbol of the holiness of God and all that made up the sacrificial system. The Lord instructed Moses to put this bronze laver in the courtyard between the tent of meeting and the altar. It was to be filled with water and used by priests to wash their hands and feet before they entered the tent of meeting, or before they performed their priestly duties. This was so crucial in the ritual life of Israel that the priest who overlooked this ritual cleansing would die, for he had violated the holiness of God. The symbol is obvious: Cleansing is essential as we enter the presence of God.

THE RANSOM MONEY

30:11 Then the LORD spoke to Moses, saying:

12 "When you take the census of the children of Israel for their number, then every man shall give a ransom for himself to the LORD, when you number them, that there may be no plague among them when *you* number them.

13 "This is what everyone among those who are numbered shall give: half a shekel according to the shekel of the sanctuary (a shekel *is* twenty gerahs). The half-shekel *shall be* an offering to the LORD.

14 "Everyone included among those who are numbered, from twenty years old and above, shall give an offering to the LORD.

15 "The rich shall not give more and the poor shall not give less than half a shekel, when *you* give an offering to the LORD, to make atonement for yourselves.

16 "And you shall take the atonement money of the children of Israel, and shall appoint it for the service of the tabernacle of meeting, that it may be a memorial for the children of Israel before the LORD, to make atonement for yourselves."

Exod. 30:11–16

The Lord commanded Moses to receive a ransom from every man when he took a census of the children of Israel. Interestingly, each person, rich and poor alike, paid the same amount. This was a reminder that the privilege of worship was available to all.

The word translated "give a ransom" is from the same word as "atonement." This also suggests that the sacrificial system was central to Hebrew worship.

THE HOLY ANOINTING OIL AND THE INCENSE FOR THE ALTAR

30:22 Moreover the LORD spoke to Moses, saying:

23 "Also take for yourself quality spices—five hundred *shekels* of liquid myrrh, half as much sweet-smelling cinnamon (two hundred and fifty *shekels*), two hundred and fifty *shekels* of sweet-smelling cane,

24 "five hundred *shekels* of cassia, according to the shekel of the sanctuary, and a hin of olive oil.

25 "And you shall make from these a holy anointing oil, an ointment compounded according to the art of the perfumer. It shall be a holy anointing oil.

26 "With it you shall anoint the tabernacle of meeting and the ark of the Testimony;

27 "the table and all its utensils, the lampstand and its utensils, and the altar of incense;

28 "the altar of burnt offering with all its utensils, and the laver and its base.

29 "You shall consecrate them, that they may be most holy; whatever touches them must be holy.

30 "And you shall anoint Aaron and his sons, and

consecrate them, that *they* may minister to Me as priests.

31 "And you shall speak to the children of Israel, saying: 'This shall be a holy anointing oil to Me throughout your generations.

32 'It shall not be poured on man's flesh; nor shall you make *any other* like it, according to its composition. It *is* holy, *and* it shall be holy to you.

33 'Whoever compounds *any* like it, or whoever puts *any* of it on an outsider, shall be cut off from his people.'"

34 And the LORD said to Moses: "Take sweet spices, stacte and onycha and galbanum, and pure frankincense with *these* sweet spices; there shall be equal amounts of each.

35 "You shall make of these an incense, a compound according to the art of the perfumer, salted, pure, *and* holy.

36 "And you shall beat *some* of it very fine, and put some of it before the Testimony in the tabernacle of meeting where I will meet with you. It shall be most holy to you.

37 "But *as for* the incense which you shall make, you shall not make any for yourselves, according to its composition. It shall be to you holy for the LORD.

38 "Whoever makes *any* like it, to smell it, he shall be cut off from his people."

Exod. 30:22–38

Blood, water, and oil were all used in the various rituals of the tabernacle. They were symbols of consecration. These verses provide the recipe for making the sacred oil that was used in the anointing service for the consecration of priests. Also, the formula for the incense to be burned on the altar is given.

The warning is clear: The anointing oil and the incense were for the worship of the people, not for personal use.

THE COURT OF THE TABERNACLE

27:9 "You shall also make the court of the tabernacle. For the south side *there shall be* hangings for the court *made of* fine woven linen, one hundred cubits long for one side.

10 "And its twenty pillars and their twenty sockets *shall be* bronze. The hooks of the pillars and their bands *shall be* silver.

11 "Likewise along the length of the north side *there shall be* hangings one hundred *cubits* long, with its twenty pillars and their twenty sockets of bronze, and the hooks of the pillars and their bands of silver.

12 "And along the width of the court on the west side *shall be* hangings of fifty cubits, with their ten pillars and their ten sockets.

13 "The width of the court on the east side *shall be* fifty cubits.

14 "The hangings on *one* side *of the gate shall be* fifteen cubits, *with* their three pillars and their three sockets.

15 "And on the other side *shall be* hangings of fifteen *cubits, with* their three pillars and their three sockets.

16 "For the gate of the court *there shall be* a screen twenty cubits long, *woven of* blue, purple, and scarlet *thread,* and fine woven linen, made by a weaver. It *shall have* four pillars and four sockets.

17 "All the pillars around the court shall have bands of silver; their hooks *shall be* of silver and their sockets of bronze.

18 "The length of the court *shall be* one hundred cubits, the width fifty throughout, and the height five cubits, *woven of* fine linen thread, and its sockets of bronze.

19 "All the utensils of the tabernacle for all its service, all its pegs, and all the pegs of the court, *shall be* of bronze."

Exod. 27:9–19

The tabernacle was surrounded by a rectangular open-air area called the courtyard, or, the court of the tabernacle. It was 100 cubits long from east to west, 50 cubits wide from north to south, and enclosed by curtains of fine-twined linen five cubits high, which were fastened to pillows that had bands of silver set in bronze bases. This courtyard served in two very practical ways. It was a barrier preventing unlawful approach to the sacred building, thus preserving the tabernacle sanctity. It was also a protection; it kept wild animals at a distance.

It also served as a preparation for worship. It formed a distinct line of demarcation between the camp outside and the tabernacle within. Here is again a subtle but very real undergirding of God's call to Israel to be a holy nation, and it's a strong suggestion to us. There is a distinction between God and the world. And though God does not call us to be separated from the world, He calls us to be identified clearly in the world as His people.

The court of the tabernacle gave man the opportunity to think and to prepare himself as he approached God in specific worship. While the holy place remained the place for priests only, and the holy of holies excluded all but the high priests, yet within the court all could come who would, priests and laypersons alike, persons from all stations of life, young and old, rich and poor. This courtyard was the place of sacrifice and was needed by all.

The Care of the Lampstand

> 27:20 "And you shall command the children of Israel
> that they bring you pure oil of pressed olives for the
> light, to cause the lamp to burn continually.
> 21 "In the tabernacle of meeting, outside the veil
> which *is* before the Testimony, Aaron and his sons
> shall tend it from evening until morning before the
> Lord. *It shall be* a statute forever to their generations
> on behalf of the children of Israel."
>
> *Exod. 27:20-21*

These verses describe one of the priest's duties—to care for the lamps. We're not certain whether the lamps were to be kept burning without interruption, but the suggestion is that they were to be lit each night and provided with enough oil to keep them burning until morning. This is the first instance in the Book of Exodus where the tabernacle is called the *"tabernacle of meeting,"* underscoring God's decision to "camp" among His people, mentioned earlier in our discussion.

THE GARMENTS OF THE PRIESTHOOD

28:1 "Now take Aaron your brother, and his sons with him, from among the children of Israel, that he may minister to Me as priest, Aaron *and* Aaron's sons: Nadab, Abihu, Eleazar, and Ithamar.

2 "And you shall make holy garments for Aaron your brother, for glory and for beauty.

3 "So you shall speak to all *who are* gifted artisans, whom I have filled with the spirit of wisdom, that they may make Aaron's garments, to consecrate him, that he may minister to Me as priest.

4 "And these *are* the garments which they shall make: a breastplate, an ephod, a robe, a skillfully woven tunic, a turban, and a sash. So they shall make holy garments for Aaron your brother and his sons, that he may minister to Me as priest.

5 "They shall take the gold, blue, purple, and scarlet *thread*, and the fine linen,

6 "and they shall make the ephod of gold, blue, purple, *and* scarlet *thread*, and fine woven linen, artistically worked.

7 "It shall have two shoulder straps joined at its two edges, and *so* it shall be joined together.

8 "And the intricately woven band of the ephod, which *is* on it, shall be of the same workmanship, *made of* gold, blue, purple, and scarlet *thread*, and fine woven linen.

9 "Then you shall take two onyx stones and engrave on them the names of the sons of Israel:

10 "six of their names on one stone and six names on the other stone, in order of their birth.

11 "With the work of an engraver in stone, *like* the engravings of a signet, you shall engrave the two stones with the names of the sons of Israel. You shall set them in settings of gold.

12 "And you shall put the two stones on the shoulders of the ephod *as* memorial stones for the sons of Israel. So Aaron shall bear their names before the LORD on his two shoulders as a memorial.

13 "You shall also make settings of gold,

14 "and you shall make two chains of pure gold

like braided cords, and fasten the braided chains to the settings.

15 "You shall make the breastplate of judgment. Artistically woven according to the workmanship of the ephod you shall make it: of gold, blue, purple, and scarlet *thread*, and fine woven linen, you shall make it.

16 "It shall be doubled into a square: a span *shall be* its length, and a span *shall be* its width.

17 "And you shall put settings of stones in it, four rows of stones: *The first* row *shall be* a sardius, a topaz, and an emerald; *this shall be* the first row;

18 "the second row *shall be* a turquoise, a sapphire, and a diamond;

19 "the third row, a jacinth, an agate, and an amethyst;

20 "and the fourth row, a beryl, an onyx, and a jasper. They shall be set in gold settings.

21 "And the stones shall have the names of the sons of Israel, twelve according to their names, *like* the engravings of a signet, each one with its own name; they shall be according to the twelve tribes.

22 "You shall make chains for the breastplate at the end, like braided cords of pure gold.

23 "And you shall make two rings of gold for the breastplate, and put the two rings on the two ends of the breastplate.

24 "Then you shall put the two braided *chains* of gold in the two rings which are on the ends of the breastplate;

25 "and the *other* two ends of the two braided *chains* you shall fasten to the two settings, and put them on the shoulder straps of the ephod in the front.

26 "You shall make two rings of gold, and put them on the two ends of the breastplate, on the edge of it, which is on the inner side of the ephod.

27 "And two *other* rings of gold you shall make, and put them on the two shoulder straps, underneath the ephod toward its front, right at the seam above the intricately woven band of the ephod.

28 "They shall bind the breastplate by means of its rings to the rings of the ephod, using a blue cord, so

that it is above the intricately woven band of the ephod, and so that the breastplate does not come loose from the ephod.

29 "So Aaron shall bear the names of the sons of Israel on the breastplate of judgment over his heart, when he goes into the holy *place*, as a memorial before the LORD continually.

30 "And you shall put in the breastplate of judgment the Urim and the Thummim, and they shall be over Aaron's heart when he goes in before the LORD. So Aaron shall bear the judgment of the children of Israel over his heart before the LORD continually.

31 "You shall make the robe of the ephod all of blue.

32 "There shall be an opening for his head in the middle of it; it shall have a woven binding all around its opening, like the opening in a coat of mail, so that it does not tear.

33 "And upon its hem you shall make pomegranates of blue, purple, and scarlet, all around its hem, and bells of gold between them all around:

34 "a golden bell and a pomegranate, a golden bell and a pomegranate, upon the hem of the robe all around.

35 "And it shall be upon Aaron when he ministers, and its sound will be heard when he goes into the holy *place* before the LORD and when he comes out, that he may not die.

36 "You shall also make a plate of pure gold and engrave on it, *like* the engraving of a signet:

37 "And you shall put it on a blue cord, that it may be on the turban; it shall be on the front of the turban.

38 "So it shall be on Aaron's forehead, that Aaron may bear the iniquity of the holy things which the children of Israel hallow in all their holy gifts; and it shall always be on his forehead, that they may be accepted before the LORD.

39 "You shall skillfully weave the tunic of fine linen *thread,* you shall make the turban of fine linen, and you shall make the sash of woven work.

40 "For Aaron's sons you shall make tunics, and you shall make sashes for them. And you shall make hats for them, for glory and beauty.

41 "So you shall put them on Aaron your brother
and on his sons with him. You shall anoint them,
consecrate them, and sanctify them, that they may
minister to Me as priests.

42 "And you shall make for them linen trousers to
cover their nakedness; they shall reach from the
waist to the thighs.

43 "They shall be on Aaron and on his sons when
they come into the tabernacle of meeting, or when
they come near the altar to minister in the holy *place*,
that they do not incur iniquity and die. *It shall be* a
statute forever to him and his descendants after him."

Exod. 28:1–43

"Priest" is originally from the word *kohēn,* the meaning of which is
not certain. Proposed etymologies include "to bend down," which
suggests doing homage; "stand upright," which suggests serving.
Also, "soothsayer," "make prosperous," and "be firm" have been suggested.

We know that priests were not unique to ancient Israel, but the
origin of the priesthood cannot be traced. Ancient Egypt, Babylon,
Assyria and Samaria all had elaborate priesthoods. Earliest priests
ministered only to their own families, the priest usually being the
father. As a system of priesthood evolved, the office became heredi-
tary, passed down from father to son. This was the case in Israel,
and we see it in our text as Aaron's sons became priests with their
father. Eleazar succeeded his father as high priest.

Almost all of Exodus 28 is given to describing the high priest's
(Aaron's) garments, with only four verses (40–43) describing the garments of the ordinary priests, Aaron's sons.

The priests were representatives of God, bridges between the people and God, therefore their vestments were important. That is the
reason that in many churches today there is a tradition of elaborate
vestments, which are highly symbolic. It was natural, given the fact
that these men represented God's presence when they stood before
the people, that their garments sought to communicate some of the
mystery, glory, and beauty of the holy place.

In general terms, the priesthood consisted of Aaron, his sons, and
his tribe. Some have suggested that Aaron alone represents the
priestly ministry of Christ; his sons represent the priestly ministry of

the church, while his tribe symbolizes the ministry of all the children of God, with emphasis on the individual, rather than the corporate body.

The garments were very ornate, of fine linen, intricately embroidered, not to draw attention to the priest, but to the *office*, the function. Seven pieces of apparel are described. Outstanding among them were the ephod and the breastplate. The ephod (28:6–14) included all the colors which have come to symbolize the characteristics of the person of Christ: gold—purity and power; blue—spiritual/divine; purple—sovereign king; scarlet—sacrifice.

Two onyx stones were inscribed, each bearing six names of Israel's sons (tribes). With these names on him at all times when leading worship, the high priest carried with him symbolically, in prayer and total ministry, all of his people. How suggestive is this symbol of the function of those ordained to minister for God. When they are fulfilling their calling, ministers carry in their heart the people whom they are called to shepherd. My friend Rita Snowden, a distinguished writer and a member of the Order of the British Empire, is a deaconess in the Methodist Church. As a young woman, she served in some of the most isolated parts of her home country of New Zealand. She told me of the practice she developed early in her life, out of desperate personal need, and also in response to God's calling. She would spend a long time in prayer early every morning at the altar of the little country chapel. She said, "I vowed not to speak to my people for God until I had spoken to God for my people." This is a beautiful notion that underscores the meaning of the priesthood. On Aaron's ephod were the names of the sons of Israel.

The breastplate was a nine-inch square of fine linen, attached to the ephod. On it were twelve precious stones, each having engraved on it one of the tribes of Israel. The breast (heart) is the place of affection; so again, the priest *loves* his own.

The breastplate was a kind of pouch which served as a container for the "Urim" and "Thummim." These were probably two stones. The words literally mean "light" and "perfection." The stones were probably used as lots by the priest to determine divine will.

Aaron always wore the breastplate with the names of the twelve tribes and these lots (Urim and Thummim) when he went into the holy place.

Our High Priest needs no Urim and Thummim, nor do those who follow Him. Said He, "He who follows Me shall not walk in darkness, but have the light of life" (John 8:12).

THE CONSECRATION OF THE PRIESTS

29:1 "And this is what you shall do to them to hallow them for ministering to Me as priests: Take one young bull and two rams without blemish,

2 "and unleavened bread, unleavened cakes mixed with oil, and unleavened wafers anointed with oil (you shall make them of wheat flour).

3 "You shall put them in one basket and bring them in the basket, with the bull and the two rams.

4 "And Aaron and his sons you shall bring to the door of the tabernacle of meeting, and you shall wash them with water.

5 "Then you shall take the garments, put the tunic on Aaron, and the robe of the ephod, the ephod, and the breastplate, and gird him with the intricately woven band of the ephod.

6 "You shall put the turban on his head, and put the holy crown on the turban.

7 "And you shall take the anointing oil, pour *it* on his head, and anoint him.

8 "Then you shall bring his sons and put tunics on them.

9 "And you shall gird them with sashes, Aaron and his sons, and put the hats on them. The priesthood shall be theirs for a perpetual statute. So you shall consecrate Aaron and his sons.

10 "You shall also have the bull brought before the tabernacle of meeting, and Aaron and his sons shall put their hands on the head of the bull.

11 "Then you shall kill the bull before the LORD, *by* the door of the tabernacle of meeting.

12 "You shall take *some* of the blood of the bull and put *it* on the horns of the altar with your finger, and pour all the blood beside the base of the altar.

13 "And you shall take all the fat that covers the entrails, the fatty lobe *attached* to the liver, and the

two kidneys and the fat that is on them, and burn *them* on the altar.

14 "But the flesh of the bull, with its skin and its offal, you shall burn with fire outside the camp. It *is* a sin offering.

15 "You shall also take one ram, and Aaron and his sons shall put their hands on the head of the ram;

16 "and you shall kill the ram, and you shall take its blood and sprinkle *it* all around on the altar.

17 "Then you shall cut the ram in pieces, wash its entrails and its legs, and put *them* with its pieces and with its head.

18 "And you shall burn the whole ram on the altar. It *is* a burnt offering to the LORD; it *is* a sweet aroma, an offering made by fire to the LORD.

19 "You shall also take the other ram, and Aaron and his sons shall put their hands on the head of the ram.

20 "Then you shall kill the ram, and take some of its blood and put *it* on the tip of the right ear of Aaron and on the tip of the right ear of his sons, on the thumb of their right hand and on the big toe of their right foot, and sprinkle the blood all around on the altar.

21 "And you shall take some of the blood that is on the altar, and some of the anointing oil, and sprinkle *it* on Aaron and on his garments, on his sons and on the garments of his sons with him; and he and his garments shall be hallowed, and his sons and his sons' garments with him.

22 "Also you shall take the fat of the ram, the fat tail, the fat that covers the entrails, the fatty lobe *attached to* the liver, the two kidneys and the fat on them, the right thigh (for it *is* a ram of consecration),

23 "one loaf of bread, one cake *made with* oil, and one wafer from the basket of the unleavened bread that *is* before the LORD;

24 "and you shall put all these in the hands of Aaron and in the hands of his sons, and you shall wave them *as* a wave offering before the LORD.

25 "You shall receive them back from their hands and burn *them* on the altar as a burnt offering, as a

sweet aroma before the LORD. It *is* an offering made by fire to the LORD.

26 "Then you shall take the breast of the ram of Aaron's consecration and wave it *as* a wave offering before the LORD; and it shall be your portion.

27 "And from the ram of the consecration you shall consecrate the breast of the wave offering which is waved, and the thigh of the heave offering which is raised, of *that* which *is* for Aaron and of *that* which is for his sons.

28 "It shall be from the children of Israel *for* Aaron and his sons by a statute forever. For it is a heave offering; it shall be a heave offering from the children of Israel from the sacrifices of their peace offerings, *that is,* their heave offering to the LORD.

29 "And the holy garments of Aaron shall be his sons' after him, to be anointed in them and to be consecrated in them.

30 "That son who becomes priest in his place shall put them on for seven days, when he enters the tabernacle of meeting to minister in the holy *place.*

31 "And you shall take the ram of the consecration and boil its flesh in the holy place.

32 "Then Aaron and his sons shall eat the flesh of the ram, and the bread that *is* in the basket, *by* the door of the tabernacle of meeting.

33 "They shall eat those things with which the atonement was made, to consecrate *and* to sanctify them; but an outsider shall not eat *them,* because they *are* holy.

34 "And if any of the flesh of the consecration offerings, or of the bread, remains until the morning, then you shall burn the remainder with fire. It shall not be eaten, because it *is* holy.

35 "Thus you shall do to Aaron and his sons, according to all that I have commanded you. Seven days you shall consecrate them.

36 "And you shall offer a bull every day *as* a sin offering for atonement. You shall cleanse the altar when you make atonement for it, and you shall anoint it to sanctify it.

37 "Seven days you shall make atonement for the

altar and sanctify it. And the altar shall be most holy. Whatever touches the altar must be holy.

38 *Now this is* what you shall offer on the altar: two lambs of the first year, day by day continually.

39 *One lamb you shall offer in the morning, and the other lamb you shall offer at twilight.

40 *With the one lamb shall be one-tenth *of an ephah* of flour mixed with one-fourth of a hin of pressed oil, and one-fourth of a hin of wine *as* a drink offering.

41 *And the other lamb you shall offer at twilight; and you shall offer with it the grain offering and the drink offering, as in the morning, for a sweet aroma, an offering made by fire to the LORD.

42 *This shall be* a continual burnt offering throughout your generations *at* the door of the tabernacle of meeting before the LORD, where I will meet you to speak with you.

43 *And there I will meet with the children of Israel, and *the tabernacle* shall be sanctified by My glory.

44 *So I will consecrate the tabernacle of meeting and the altar. I will also consecrate both Aaron and his sons to minister to Me as priests.

45 *I will dwell among the children of Israel and will be their God.

46 *And they shall know that I *am* the LORD their God, who brought them up out of the land of Egypt, that I may dwell among them. I *am* the LORD their God.*

Exod. 29:1–46

Exodus 29 gives the plans Moses received from God for the consecration of Aaron and his sons as the priests of Israel. Moses, the deliverer and mediator of the covenant, though not a priest, had the signal honor of ordaining the first priests of Israel.

The entire ceremony marked the solemn act of a few people being set apart for specific ministry. Some of the acts in which all the people participated in sacrificial worship were a part of this consecration: The sin offering indicated that the priest, too, was a sinner; the burnt offering suggested that the priest, too, must offer that *"sweet aroma"* of offering pleasing to God.

The consecration service marked *personal dedication, moral separation* (separation from sin, and unto service), and *revelation*, or spiritual realization. The ceremony was repeated daily for seven days. Seven was the number for completeness, making the "set-asideness" of the priests dramatically clear.

THE APPOINTMENT OF CRAFTSMEN

31:1 Then the LORD spoke to Moses, saying:
2 "See, I have called by name Bezalel the son of Uri, the son of Hur, of the tribe of Judah.
3 "And I have filled him with the Spirit of God, in wisdom, in understanding, in knowledge, and in all *manner of* workmanship,
4 "to design artistic works, to work in gold, in silver, in bronze,
5 "in cutting jewels for setting, in carving wood, and to work in all *manner of* workmanship.
6 "And I, indeed I, have appointed with him Aholiab the son of Ahisamach, of the tribe of Dan; and I have put wisdom in the hearts of all the gifted artisans, that they may make all that I have commanded you:
7 "the tabernacle of meeting, the ark of the Testimony and the mercy seat that *is* on it, and all the furniture of the tabernacle—
8 "the table and its utensils, the pure *gold* lampstand with all its utensils, the alter of incense,
9 "the altar of burnt offering with all its utensils, and the laver and its base—
10 "the garments of ministry, the holy garments for Aaron the priest and the garments of his sons, to minister as priests,
11 "and the anointing oil and sweet incense for the holy *place*. According to all that I have commanded you they shall do."

Exod. 31:1-11

Gifted artisans, filled with the spirit of wisdom, had been selected to make Aaron's garments. Likewise, *"Bezalel the son of Uri, the son of*

Hur, of the tribe of Judah," was filled *"with the Spirit of God, in wisdom, in understanding, in knowledge, and in all manner of workmanship"* along with other artisans so endowed who were chosen as the craftsmen to do the work.

F. B. Meyer has a marvelous word that summarizes the spirit and genius of the building of the tabernacle and the lesson this teaches us about God.

> The tabernacle with its contents was the subject of much divine thought and care. It was not a poor hut run up in an hour. It was not the creation of human fancy. Man was not the creator, but the executor of the divine program and plan. It was thus that God made the heavens and the earth. He was alone when the foundations of the heavens and earth were laid. To Him alone must be attributed, also, the pattern of the human life of our Lord, in which the tabernacle was duplicated in flesh and blood. And He is intimately concerned in the fashioning of all our life. In the minutest details, He is immediately interested; and in the most holy place of our nature, within the veil, there is a shrine, where angels might tread with reverence, because His holy presence is there."[5]

KEEPING THE SABBATH

31:12 And the LORD spoke to Moses, saying,

13 "Speak also to the children of Israel, saying: 'Surely My Sabbaths you shall keep, for it *is* a sign between Me and you throughout your generations, that *you* may know that I *am* the LORD who sanctifies you.

14 'You shall keep the Sabbath, therefore, for *it is* holy to you. Everyone who profanes it shall surely be put to death; for whoever does *any* work on it, that person shall be cut off from among his people.

15 'Work shall be done for six days, but the seventh *is* the Sabbath of rest, holy to the LORD. Whoever does *any* work on the Sabbath day, he shall surely be put to death.

16 'Therefore the children of Israel shall keep the Sabbath, to observe the Sabbath throughout their generations *as* a perpetual covenant.

344

17 'It *is* a sign between Me and the children of Israel forever; for *in* six days the LORD made the heavens and the earth, and on the seventh day He rested
and was refreshed.'"

Exod. 31:12–17

The Sabbath was to be the sign of the perpetual covenant between
Israel and Yahweh. See commentary on the Sabbath (Exod. 20:8–11,
pp. 259–60, and Exod. 23:10–13, p. 286).

The addition to law here, not found earlier, is that whoever profaned the Sabbath by working on that day would be condemned to
death.

WITH THE FINGER OF GOD

31:18 And when He had made an end of speaking
with him on Mount Sinai, He gave Moses two
tablets of the Testimony, tablets of stone, written
with the finger of God.

Exod. 31:18

Let there be no mistake about it: God is the source and authority
of the law given to Moses. *"With the finger of God"* the laws were
written. One thinks of Jesus stooping to write in the sand when the
woman taken in the act of adultery was brought to Him. He was to
pronounce judgment according to the law. But a new law is now in
effect. Jesus Himself is the fulfillment of the law, and that fulfillment is redemption through Him.

NOTES

1. C. W. Slemming, *Made According to the Pattern* (Fort Washington, PA:
Christian Literature Crusade, 1974), pp. 127–28.
2. F. B. Meyer, *Devotional Commentary on Exodus* (Grand Rapids: Kregel
Publications, 1978), p. 303.
3. Story told by Leonard T. Wolcott in *Alive Now,* Sept.–Oct. 1982, p. 57.
4. Slemming, *Made According,* p. 114.
5. Meyer, *Exodus,* p. 302.

CHAPTER SEVENTEEN

Rebellion

Exodus 32:1-33:6

"Atheism is not our greatest danger, but a shadowy sense of God's reality." That's the contention of Harry Emerson Fosdick, and I agree.

Our problem is not atheism—how many atheists do you know? That which is destroying the moral fiber of our nation, weakening the Christian witness, and turning Christian churches into reflections of the club mentality of a secular age is a shadowy sense of God's reality. Just let that image tumble around in your mind for a moment—a shadowy sense of God's reality. Everything is rather vague; nothing is very strong—no clear outline, no driving passion.

Our indifference to the religious foundations of life are reflected in this interesting statement: "Our great grandfathers called it the holy Sabbath; our grandfathers, the Sabbath; our fathers, Sunday. Today we call it the weekend." Isn't this distinctive drift in attitude and commitment to God and His will the problem of every age, especially of our age? It began early in the covenant relationship. Alexander Maclaren provides a moving word picture of the situation.

> It was not yet six weeks since the people had sworn, "All that the Lord hath spoken will we do, and be obedient." The blood of the covenant, sprinkled on them, was scarcely dry when they flung off allegiance to Jehovah. Such short-lived loyalty to him can never have been genuine. That mob of slaves was galvanized by Moses into obedience, and since their acceptance of Jehovah was in reality only yielding to the power of one strong will and its earnest faith, of course it collapsed as soon as Moses disappeared.

We have to note, first, the people's universal revolt. The language of verse 1 may easily hide to a careless reader the gravity and unanimity of the apostasy. "The people gathered themselves together." It was a national rebellion, a flood which swept away even some faithful, timid hearts. No voices ventured to protest. What were the elders, who shortly before saw the God of Israel, doing to be passive at such a crisis? Was there no one to bid the fickle multitude to look up to the summit overhead, where the red flames glowed, or to remind them of a host of Egypt lying stark and dead on the shore? Was Miriam cowed too, and her song forgotten?

We need not cast stones at these people, for we also have short memories for either the terrible or the gracious revelations of God in our lives. But we may learn the lesson that God's lovers have to set themselves dead against the rush of popular feeling, and that there are times when silence or compliance is sin.[1]

That's the setting and the general lesson learned from the section of Scripture at which we look in this chapter.

THE PEOPLE'S FAITHLESSNESS

32:1 Now when the people saw that Moses delayed coming down from the mountain, the people gathered together to Aaron, and said to him, "Come, make us gods that shall go before us; for *as for* this Moses, the man who brought us up out of the land of Egypt, we do not know what has become of him."

2 And Aaron said to them, "Break off the golden earrings which *are* in the ears of your wives, your sons, and your daughters, and bring *them* to me."

3 So all the people broke off the golden earrings which *were* in their ears, and brought *them* to Aaron.

4 And he received *the gold* from their hand, and he fashioned it with an engraving tool, and made a molded calf. Then they said, "This *is* your god, O Israel, that brought you out of the land of Egypt!"

5 So when Aaron saw *it*, he built an altar before it. And Aaron made a proclamation and said, "Tomorrow *is* a feast to the LORD."

> 6 Then they rose early on the next day, offered
> burnt offerings, and brought peace offerings; and the
> people sat down to eat and drink, and rose up to
> play.
>
> *Exod. 32:1–6*

The longer Moses stayed on the mountain, the more restless the people became. Did they believe that something had happened to Moses? Were they getting weary of his leadership? Without him present to keep reminding them of God's presence, did doubt begin to overcome them? Was it a faith struggle? Had the message not yet gripped them? Were they not yet convinced?

When Moses failed to return they went to the next in command and demanded that he make other gods they could serve. Of the ten commandments they were breaking the second one: making a graven image.

Living animals, not idols, were worshiped in Egypt, so this was not a reversion to the gods of their slavery. The bull was often associated with Canaanite Baalism, so it may be that the "golden calf" is a throwback to the bull-image god through common Semitic heritage.

We will focus later in this chapter on this faithlessness of Israel and lessons we may learn, when we look at Moses' confrontation with Aaron and the people on coming down from the mountain.

Note here, however, that Israel's faithlessness, her apostasy, was accompanied by immorality connected with their worship. Look at verse 6. *"And rose up to play"* suggests sexual orgies which accompanied fertility rites, especially in Canaanite Baalism (another indication the golden calf may be a counterpart to the Canaanite bull). The verb translated "to play" (*ṣāḥaq*) supports this. This same verb was used in Genesis 26:8: "Abimelech . . . looked out of a window, and saw . . . Isaac, fondling Rebekah his wife" (RSV). This led the king to know that Rebekah was not Isaac's sister, but his wife.

Though connecting sexual immorality with worship is foreign to us, it still happens. But the lesson for us is that apostasy leads to irresponsible action and gross immorality. Even more applicable to us is the fact that faithlessness leads to a diminishing of moral sensitivity.

IT'S TOUGH TO BE GOD

32:7 And the LORD said to Moses, "Go, get down! For your people whom you brought out of the land of Egypt have corrupted *themselves.*

8 "They have turned aside quickly out of the way which I commanded them. They have made themselves a molded calf, and worshiped it and sacrificed to it, and said, 'This *is* your god, O Israel, that brought you out of the land of Egypt!'"

9 And the LORD said to Moses, "I have seen this people, and indeed it *is* a stiff-necked people!

10 "Now therefore, let Me alone, that My wrath may burn hot against them and I may consume them. And I will make of you a great nation."

11 Then Moses pleaded with the LORD his God, and said: "LORD, why does Your wrath burn hot against Your people whom You have brought out of the land of Egypt with great power and with a mighty hand?

12 "Why should the Egyptians speak, and say, 'He brought them out to harm them, to kill them in the mountains, and to consume them from the face of the earth'? Turn from Your fierce wrath, and relent from this harm to Your people.

13 "Remember Abraham, Isaac, and Israel, Your servants, to whom You swore by Your own self, and said to them, 'I will multiply your descendants as the stars of heaven; and all this land that I have spoken of I give to your descendants, and they shall inherit *it* forever.'"

14 So the LORD relented from the harm which He said He would do to His people.

Exod. 32:7–14

This is one of the sections of Exodus most rich in meaning. The richness of it, I believe, is best revealed as we look at God's response to what was going on.

It's tough to be God. Does that thought shock you? It's tough to be God. How do I know? Well, it's tough to be a parent. How tough? Most of us could tell at least one story that would bring lumps in the throats of the rest of us, and tears to our eyes, as we remember our own sleepless nights, our own painful experiences, seeking to be parents.

And God is our parent, our eternal parent. That was Jesus' favorite title for God, "Abba, Father"—"Daddy." That's really what Jesus called God—Daddy. If you think it's tough rearing three children, just think about God's task, God's responsibility, God's relationship to His children. It's tough to be God. This thought only got my casual attention now and then throughout the book, but it became intense and demanded reflection when I got to this chapter of Exodus. It really jerked at my mind and pierced my heart when I came to verses 9 and 10.

God had laid His life on the line for these people, rescued them from slavery and death in Egypt, delivered them time and time again, guided them, miraculously fed them, saved them from death by thirst. God had identified with them, had made them His people. Now, here they are, still rebellious, seduced by idolatry, unresponsive to the gracious acts of love constantly coming their way. What a description for a stiff-necked people. Is it any wonder that God was ready to allow his wrath to burn hot and consume them? Yes, it's tough to be God.

It's tough to be God *because it's so easy for God's children to be lost.*

See how easy it was for the Israelites. All they had to do was to let Moses get out of their sight. There he was, up on the mountain, in very deep and intense communion with God. And there they were, down in the valley, turning their attention in other directions. It's too easy for God's children to get lost. Look at the prodigal son. All it took was for his mind to start wandering away from the father's house, to start imagining how it would be in the far country—beautiful women, music, festive dancing, money to spend, the good life; none of the restrictions of home, none of the boredom of being an elder brother.

Look at those sheep that Jesus referred to so often, just nibbling away at the grass, paying no attention to the shepherd. They were creatures interested in only that which was close at hand—food for their stomachs—nibbling away until they were far from the flock, away from the care and the protection of the shepherd.

It's easy to get lost. Just take your eyes off the Shepherd. Don't gather with the flock for worship. Don't spend time with God's word. Just nod at it now and then. Don't read it daily; don't let the truth of it penetrate the fiber of your being; don't pay attention to the Bible's witness to God's sovereignty, holiness, and love.

It's easy to get lost. Busy yourself in your profession—your job, your business; it will soon demand all that you are. Center yourself on success and security, and you'll soon come to believe that you've got to have more and more, that your security is not in God, but in your money, your investments. You'll forget about what God said to a man who began to believe the same thing, the one who said, "I will tear down my barns and build more barns and say to my soul, 'Soul, take your ease.'" You remember what God said to that man: "This night your soul will be required of you" (Luke 12:18–20).

It's easy to get lost. Just surround yourself with friends who don't care about God. Just make your cocktail social network your source of fellowship, and seek no "koinonia," no fellowship of the spirit.

It's easy for us to get lost. And that's the reason it's tough to be God.

It's also tough to be God *because it's not easy for God's children to be found.* Look at the shepherd in the New Testament, leaving the ninety-nine safe in the fold and going out to seek that one lost sheep, risking his life, braving the wilds, to find that wandering sheep. Look at that housewife, sweeping every corner of the room, every crevice under the chairs, under the bed as she seeks the lost coin. Look at the picture of God here in this Scripture passage. Moses had to wrestle with God, had to intercede with all the power of his being—what a dramatic plea Moses makes to God (vv. 11–13).

One of the most unique and powerful words in Scripture is found in verse 14. The Revised Standard Version translates it: "And the Lord repented of the evil which he thought to do his people." For God to have a change of heart like that, to stay His anger, to pull back His wrath, shows how difficult it is for God's lost children to be found.

That fact reaches a pinnacle thousands of years later on Calvary. That's how much it took, that's how much love, that's how much sacrifice, that's how much shed blood it took for God's children to be found. It took God's Son, hanging on a cross. It's tough to be God because it's not easy for God's people to be found. God pays a great price to find them.

It's also tough to be God *because God can't rest until all of His children have come home.*

Verse 14, as translated in the Revised Standard Version, rests uneasily on most of our ears. It's a strange idea—God *repented.* But when you reflect on it for a while, you may conclude that it is not only a fitting word for God, but quite descriptive of God's nature. God cannot rest until all His children have come home. He is a seeking God who will have no peace until all of the flock are secure in the fold. It is a vision of the very heart of God.

Paul J. Bauermeister has given us a beautiful word-picture of an occasion in heaven:

> When all the wind-chimes in heaven begin to ring at once, and that only happens when there's a great excited flutter of angel's wings, something has happened that deeply delights the heart of God. And now for the big question. What produces such an agitation of wings and such a rush of wind and such a tinkling, yea crashing, of the celestial wind-chimes? It is simple: a lost one who had rolled under the bed, was misplaced or strayed away or went off on its own, one such lost one, and notice that it seems to require only one, was found! The word whispered from angelic lips to angelic ears throughout all the heavenly palaces is the word, "Found." "Found!" "Found!" Another one! Another one! Another one!
>
> Of course, Yahweh was angry with Israel at Sinai. Who could overlook an insult like a calf of gold? But Moses had some ideas about the heart he addressed. After all, Yahweh had carefully selected an oppressed, slave people to be his people and had led them where they never would have gone by themselves. This Yahweh was not the standard deity who paid off when he was praised and received sacrifices. There was a new element in this desert deity: Mercy! Forgiveness! Grace![2]

It's tough to be God, because God can't rest until all of His children have come home.

We've looked a long time at God. Let's look briefly at Moses. Moses' intercession on behalf of Israel and his bold speech reminding God of who God was and what He had done, reveal a commitment that had moved almost unbelievably from long argument against God's call to standing toe to toe with God for the sake of what God had called him to do in the first place. But even God has reservations! Isn't there a kind of subtle disclaimer in God's word to Moses when He ordered Moses to go down to *your* people. Where was God's commitment to *My* people ("Let My people go")?

Moses' appeal to God was three-fold. First, Israel was God's people whom God had delivered from Egypt (32:11). Second, God must preserve His own honor; otherwise the Egyptians could accuse Him of being evil (32:12). But more important than anything else, the covenant was at stake. The promises God made to Abraham, Isaac, and Jacob must be kept (32:13).

Moses' intercession was effective. We discussed previously God's response: *He repented.* The Hebrew word for "repentance," *nāḥam,* as used of God (see Gen. 6:6) in the Old Testament does not imply the acknowledgment of sin, error, or mistake. Rather, it means that grief and sorrow for what has been done leads to a new course of action. So here in this passage are two big lessons: the compassion of God for a people who need punishment, and the power of one man's intercession, the effectiveness of prayer.

TAUGHT BY A GOLDEN CALF

32:15 And Moses turned and went down from the mountain, and the two tablets of the Testimony *were* in his hand. The tablets *were* written on both sides; on the one *side* and on the other they were written.

16 Now the tablets *were* the work of God, and the writing *was* the writing of God engraved on the tablets.

17 And when Joshua heard the noise of the people as they shouted, he said to Moses, *"There is* a noise of war in the camp."

18 But he said:

"It is not the noise of the shout of victory,
Nor the noise of the cry of defeat,
But the sound of singing I hear."

19 So it was, as soon as he came near the camp, that he saw the calf *and* the dancing. So Moses' anger became hot, and he cast the tablets out of his hands and broke them at the foot of the mountain.

20 Then he took the calf which they had made, burned *it* in the fire, and ground *it* to powder; and he scattered *it* on the water and made the children of Israel drink *it*.

21 And Moses said to Aaron, "What did this people do to you that you have brought *so* great a sin upon them?"

22 So Aaron said, "Do not let the anger of my lord become hot. You know the people, that they *are set* on evil.

23 "For they said to me, 'Make us gods that shall go before us; *as for* this Moses, the man who brought us out of the land of Egypt, we do not know what has become of him.'

24 "And I said to them, 'Whoever has any gold, let them break *it* off.' So they gave *it* to me, and I cast it into the fire, and this calf came out."

25 Now when Moses saw that the people *were* unrestrained (for Aaron had not restrained them, to *their* shame among their enemies),

26 then Moses stood in the entrance of the camp, and said, "Whoever *is* on the LORD's side—*come* to me!" And all the sons of Levi gathered themselves together to him.

27 And he said to them, "Thus says the LORD God of Israel: 'Let every man put his sword on his side, and go in and out from entrance to entrance throughout the camp, and let every man kill his brother, every man his companion, and every man his neighbor.' "

28 So the sons of Levi did according to the word of Moses. And about three thousand men of the people fell that day.

29 Then Moses said, "Consecrate yourselves today to the LORD, that He may bestow on you a blessing this day, for every man has opposed his son and his brother."

Exod. 32:15–29

This is one of the most dramatic stories in Exodus. The impact of Israel's apostasy on Moses is seen in the fact that he became so angry and furious that he smashed on the ground the tablets on which God had written His law. Some contend that this was not just a display of raging anger, but a dramatic sign that the covenant had been annulled by Israel's disobedience. I believe it was both, but the former was the *seed* of the act.

There are many lessons in this event. I name three big ones here which encompass many more.

The Temptation to Idolatry

We think of idolatry as the sin of people who carve wood or stone images, and ignorantly bow down to those images. We think of it as those strange practices we encounter in foreign lands—people bringing food and flowers to a bronze Buddha, or burning paper they've purchased to make incense at the feet of one of a hundred gods in a pagoda temple.

That may be idolatry, but know this: The idolator is not the one who has never known God. Paul writes in Romans 1:21: "Because, although they knew God, they did not glorify Him as God, nor were they thankful, but became futile in their thoughts, and their foolish hearts were darkened."

It is clear from the Exodus story that the people knew God. They had seen His blazing glory and had heard His voice on Sinai; yet they made the calf. So, an idolator is not one who has not known God, but one who, having known God, refuses to glorify Him, or devises some substitute in life for the praise and glory and worship that belong to God.

Idolatry is not the ridiculous mistake of primitive people. It is by no means a dead, irrelevant issue; it is the common sin of most of us.

Put this in the context of the first two commandments. The first was "You shall have no other gods before Me" (Exod. 20:3). The second was the prohibition of the making or the worshiping of an idol: "You shall not make for yourself a carved image" (Exod. 20:4).

Now the Israelites had no desire to break the first commandment and have other gods than Jehovah. If anyone had suggested that Israel would apostatize from the God of Abraham, they would have stoned him to death. Yet, they found the demand of the second commandment too rigid, and they made the golden calf. They had to have a visible image, something they could see and touch.

On the surface, there is nothing wrong with that. To have those things that remind us of God, represent God, may be a tremendous aid to worship for many of us. God is unseen, a Spirit and Power invisible to our eyes. So, we need settings, symbols, places of worship to be vivid reminders of God.

The problem comes when the symbol, the reminder, becomes an idol—when the symbol becomes a substitute, taking the place of God.

The lessons are many and multifaceted, but the core lesson is this: Whenever anyone or anything usurps the place that God should have in our lives, we're guilty of idolatry. (See commentary on Exod. 20:4, pp. 254–56.)

The Trickery of Deceit

The next category of truth taught by the golden calf is the trickery of deception.

I doubt if any incident in the Exodus story reveals more the disposition of our nature as we see it in Aaron. While Moses was up on the mountain holding communion with God, the Israelites began to murmur and complain; they were good at that. They wanted other gods, gods of their own. They were questioning all that Moses had offered them, questioning God Himself working in their lives. Aaron yielded to their pressure, and when they brought him their golden earrings he made out of them a golden calf for them to worship.

You can imagine Moses' anger when he came down the mountain. He first of all destroyed the idol—burned it in the fire, the Scripture says, and ground it into powder, then mixed it with the water and made the people drink it.

Then, Moses confronted Aaron: *"What did this people do to you that you have brought so great a sin upon them?"* (v. 21). I can see Aaron squirming, seeking a way out, unable to face up to his sin and to be honest. He begins to manufacture a story. He pleads with Moses, *"Do not let the anger of my lord become hot. You know the people, that they are set on evil. For they said to me, 'Make us gods that shall go before us,' . . . And I said to them 'Whoever has any gold, let them break it off.' So they gave it to me, and I cast it into the fire, and this calf came out"* (vv. 22–24).

Now Aaron tells a story completely different from the way it actually happened. Aaron himself had fashioned the golden calf, but he has given in to the *trickery of deception.* He's not willing to face up to

356

the truth. He wants to lay the blame somewhere else, and in this instance, he blames it on the furnace. "The fire did it," he said.

How much like Aaron are we? Can you identify with him? How natural it is for most of us—what a common reaction—*diverting blame from self*. It's like that comic line of Flip Wilson's, "The devil made me do it."

When we try to divert blame from ourselves, we're deceiving ourselves. This is the trickery of deception, and it's the root problem in many of our lives.

In his book *There's a Lot More to Health than Not Being Sick*, Bruce Larson tells of visiting a halfway house in Western Ontario. It was a marvelous place to send people who were emotionally disturbed, who needed fresh love, new resources, the gift of hope.

The main meeting room was in an old farm house. Here people would gather and eat and talk in small groups before the roaring fireplace on cold, Canadian winter evenings. But the most memorable thing there was a sign over the fireplace. It said, "Do you want to be right or well?"

That sign summed up the point of view of the director and ministry of that whole place. The director was sure that most people had to make a choice. They could struggle to be right in the eyes of others and in their own sight. That would take a lot of energy. Or, they could decide to be well, and give up the pretensions to perfection. The director was convinced that the need to justify ourselves was one of the major causes of most mental and emotional illnesses.

If you want to make yourself sick, pretend you're right all the time. Try to fix the blame on others. Don't face up to your own responsibility. Keep that "I'm right, I have no problems" mask on all the time, and you'll end up sick unto death.

One of the major things that happens to us when we seek to divert blame from ourselves, thus deceiving ourselves, is that we vacillate between self-pity and self-blame. There's no greater bind in which a person can be. Either of those extremes is destructive to our personhood. Self-pity can turn us into a cringing nothing. Self-blame can drain us of power and make us impotent to live creatively and act responsibly.

But there's another big point here—perhaps the biggest point of all: *deliverance comes only when we own our sin*.

A hundred years ago in a sermon entitled, "The Fire and the Calf," the great preacher Phillips Brooks made one of the most fascinating and telling commentaries on this Scripture that I have found in all of my studies. He contended that there is a need in our lives to recognize and name our sin for our own self-identification. Who is the person who has become a Christian? Who has experienced new birth? Who has come to a newly awakened selfhood? Brooks answers, "A being whom Christ has forgiven, and then in virtue of that forgiveness, made His servant."

Then comes his telling comment.

All his [that servant's] new life dates from and begins with his sin. He cannot afford to find his consciousness of himself only in the noble parts of his life, which it makes him proud and happy to remember. There is not enough of that to make for him a complete and continuous personality. It will have great gaps if he disowns the wicked demonstrations of his selfhood and says, "It was not I," wherever he has done wrong. No! Out of his sin, out of the bad, base, cowardly acts which are truly his, out of the weak and wretched passages of his life which it makes him ashamed to remember, but which he forces himself to recollect and own, out of these he gathers the consciousness of a self all astray with self-will which he then brings to Christ and offers in submission and obedience to His perfect will.

You try to tell some soul rejoicing in the Lord's salvation that the sins over whose forgiveness by its Lord it is gratefully rejoicing, were not truly its; and see what strange thing comes. The soul seems to draw back from your assurance as if, if it were true, it would be robbed of all its surest confidence and brightest hope. You meant to comfort the poor penitent, and he looks into your face as if you were striking him a blow. And you can see what such a strange sight means. It is not that the poor creature loves those sins or is glad that he did them, or dreams for an instant of ever doing them again. It is only that through those sins, which are all the real experience he has had, he has found himself, and finding himself, has found his Saviour and the new life.

So the only hope for any of us is in a perfectly honest manliness to claim our sins. "I did it, I did it," let me say of all my wickedness. Let me refuse to listen for one moment to any voice

which would make my sins less mine. It is the only honest and
the only hopeful way, the only way to know and be ourselves.
When we have done that, then we are ready for the Gospel,
ready for all that Christ wants to show us that we may become,
and for all the powerful grace by which He wants to makes us
be it perfectly.[3]

Deliverance comes when we fight our way free from the trickery
of deception and own our own sin.

The Triumph of Commitment

The final category of truth by a golden calf is the triumph of commitment.

It is pictured clearly in Moses. Look at him. God has called him
down from the mountain because of what Israel has done. God's
anger is at a high pitch. He talks about "a stiff-necked people," and
he says to Moses: "Now therefore, let Me alone, that My wrath may
burn hot against them and I may consume them" (v. 10).

But Moses won't accept that. What commitment! He pleads with
God, lays himself on the line on behalf of his people. He reminds
God of His covenant with Abraham and Isaac and how He had
sworn that He was going to cause Israel to be multiplied as the stars
in the heaven, and give them a land of promise. He prayed, to the
point that the Scripture says: "The Lord relented from the harm
which He said He would do to His people" (v. 14). Moses was triumphant in his commitment.

But that's not all the story. When Moses got down from the
mountain and saw what was happening, the people dancing wildly
around the golden calf, his anger burned hot. He threw the tablets
of Testimony on the ground and smashed them. He then took the
calf which they had made, and he burned it in the fire and ground
it into powder and put it in the water and made the people of Israel
drink it. Then he confronted Aaron, his own brother, and gave the
whole crowd the opportunity to be faithful or not. What a dramatic
picture it is as Moses goes to the gate of the camp and stands there
before all of the people and shouts: *"Whoever is on the Lord's side —
come to me!"* (v. 26).

What followed is an awful story, but a realistic one. The sons of Levi responded to Moses. They became the warriors and about three thousand people—idolators—were slain. Moses' commitment had triumphed.

After this triumph, Moses again prayed to God, confessing his people's sin, but begging God's forgiveness, again laying his life on the line in that dramatic word of verse 32: "Yet now, if You will, forgive their sin—but if not, I pray, blot me out of Your book which You have written."

God didn't respond the way Moses wanted Him to respond—the sins of the people would still be held against them—but the Lord said to Moses: "Go, lead the people to the place of which I have spoken to you. Behold, My Angel shall go before you" (v. 34a).

The call comes to you and me. "Who is on the Lord's side?"

More than a hundred years ago, there was an Episcopal rector in Philadelphia whose name was Dudley Tyng. He had a deep Christian faith and a strong concern about slavery. In March, 1858, he preached to five thousand men, challenging them to stand up for Jesus. One thousand of them responded. A week later he left his study to visit a shed where a horse-powered corn sheller was working. As he reached out to stroke the horse, his study robe caught in the cogs of the machine and his arm was badly mangled. Doctors amputated the arm, but he died from infection and the effects of the wound. He knew he was dying, and he took his father's hand and said, "Stand up for Jesus; and tell my brothers of the ministry wherever you meet them to stand up for Jesus!"

The Reverend George Duffield, a Presbyterian minister, was there and heard that plea. The next Sunday he closed his sermon by quoting the stanzas of a poem he had written for Dudley Tyng's funeral service. Set to music as a hymn, it swept over America, particularly in men's meetings in the YMCAs, and it became a marching song for anti-slavery rallies. Many thousands of persons felt they must fill the gap made by the death of Dudley Tyng. The hymn?

> Stand up, stand up, for Jesus,
> Ye soldiers of the cross!
> Lift high His royal banner!
> It must not suffer loss.
>
> . . . .

> Put on the gospel armor,
> Each piece put on with prayer:
> When duty calls, or danger,
> Be never wanting there!

Who is on the Lord's side? Stand up for Jesus.

POWERFUL INTERCESSION

32:30 Now it came to pass on the next day that Moses said to the people, "You have committed a great sin. So now I will go up to the LORD; perhaps I can make atonement for your sin."
31 Then Moses returned to the LORD and said, "Oh, these people have committed a great sin, and have made for themselves a god of gold!
32 "Yet now, if You will forgive their sin—but if not, I pray, blot me out of Your book which You have written."
33 And the LORD said to Moses, "Whoever has sinned against Me, I will blot him out of My book.
34 "Now therefore, go, lead the people to *the place* of which I have spoken to you. Behold, My Angel shall go before you. Nevertheless, in the day when I visit for punishment, I will visit punishment upon them for their sin."
35 So the LORD plagued the people because of what they did with the calf which Aaron made.

Exod. 32:30–35

Moses had interceded with God earlier on behalf of the people (32:11–14) and had convinced God not to destroy the people. Now he announces to the people that he will mediate for them again. *"Perhaps I can make atonement for your sin"* (v. 30b).

There is a dramatic encounter between Moses and God. Moses is willing to give his own life for his people. "If you won't forgive their sins, then blot me out."

One thinks of the prayer of Jesus in John 17:19b, "for their sakes I sanctify Myself." Though the prayers of Jesus verbally reported in the Gospels are not many, His unselfish intercession is convincing.

361

That unselfishness reached the ultimate height in Jesus' willingness to go to the cross on our behalf, and even there interceding for His enemies, "Father, forgive them; for they know not what they do."

Genuine intercession is unselfish. Our unselfishness is measured by the degree of our willingness to extend ourselves in love, at whatever cost, that our prayers may be answered. In my praying, I sometimes find that, without consciously doing so, I have designed an answer to my prayer. But unselfishness calls for a willingness to let go of our predetermined expectations of the answer, and a willingness to accept the answer which comes.

Harry Emerson Fosdick has given the clearest statement of why we do and don't pray.

> Before a man therefore blames his lack of intercession on intellectual perplexities, he well may ask whether, if all his questions were fully answered, he has the spirit that would pour itself out in vicarious praying. Is his heart really surcharged with pent devotion waiting to find vent in prayer as soon as the logic of intercession is made evident? Rather, it is highly probable that if his last interrogation point were laid low by a strong answer, he would intercede not one whit more than he does now. *Intercession is the result of generous devotion,* not of logical analysis. When such devotion comes into the life of any man who vitally believes in God, like a rising stream in a dry river bed, it lifts the obstacles at whose removal he has tugged in vain, and floats them off. The unselfish prayer of dominant desire clears its own channel. We put our lives into other people and into great causes; and our prayers follow after, voicing our love, with theory or without it. We lay hold on God's alliance for the sake of the folk we care for and the aims we serve. We do it because love makes us, and we continue it because the validity of our praying is proved in our experience. St. Anthony spoke to the point, "We pray as much as we desire, and we desire as much as we love."[4]

The Command to Leave Sinai

33:1 Then the LORD said to Moses, "Depart *and* go up from here, you and the people whom you have brought out of the land of Egypt, to the land of which I swore to Abraham, Isaac, and Jacob, saying, 'To your descendants I will give it.'

2 "And I will send *My* Angel before you, and I will drive out the Canaanite and the Amorite and the Hittite and the Perizzite and the Hivite and the Jebusite.

3 "*Go up* to a land flowing with milk and honey; for I will not go up in your midst, lest I consume you on the way, for you *are* a stiff-necked people."

4 And when the people heard this bad news, they mourned, and no one put on his ornaments.

5 For the LORD had said to Moses, "Say to the children of Israel, 'You *are* a stiff-necked people. I could come up into your midst in one moment and consume you. Now therefore, take off your ornaments, that I may know what to do to you.'"

6 So the children of Israel stripped themselves of their ornaments by Mount Horeb.

Exod. 33:1–6

God's word in verse 3 captures the whole gamut of emotion in this electrically charged encounter of God with His people and His judgment against their apostasy: *"I will not go up in your midst, lest I consume you on the way, for you are a stiff-necked people."* God's anger against Israel's rebellion was so great that He did not even trust Himself to be able to withhold the fire of His judgment.

This passage is a transitional one, and in the next chapter we will talk about Israel's *renewal.* The transition comes with Israel's response to God withdrawing Himself, and sending an angel instead. *"They mourned, and no one put on his ornaments"* (v. 4).

There are two references to the ornaments—this one just noted, and verses 5 and 6 where the word is that God commanded them to take off their ornaments. Roy Honeycutt suggests in his commentary that, rather than being an act of grief, the stripping off of the ornaments was more significant. It was an experience like that at Bethel when Jacob led the people in recommitment to God. The people gave him all the foreign gods they had and all their earrings, and Jacob hid them under an oak near Shechem (Gen. 35:2–4).

This jewelry was probably associated with foreign gods, as was the golden calf. So putting them away was related to rededication to Yahweh. This is confirmed in God's Word, connected with putting away these ornaments: *that I may know what to do to you*" (v. 5).[5]

NOTES

1. Alexander Maclaren, *Expositions of Holy Scripture*, 11 vols. (Grand Rapids: Wm. B. Eerdmans, 1952–59), 1:171–72.

2. Paul J. Bauermeister, "Seventeenth Sunday after Pentecost," *Seminex Preaching Helps*, 10, (January 1983): 53.

3. Phillips Brooks, "The Fire and the Calf," *Twenty Centuries of Great Preaching*, Clyde E. Fant, Jr., and William M. Pinson, Jr., eds., 13 vols. (Waco, TX: Word Books, 1971), 6:170–71.

4. Harry Emerson Fosdick, *The Meaning of Prayer* (New York: Association Press, 1962), p. 173.

5. Roy L. Honeycutt, Jr., *The Broadman Bible Commentary* (Nashville: Broadman Press, 1969), 1:439.

CHAPTER EIGHTEEN

Renewal of the Covenant

Exodus 33:7–40:38

In American history, Abraham Lincoln is known as "the Great Emancipator." But no greater emancipator ever lived than Moses. He was God's chosen deliverer—the one that God had selected to lead His people out of Egyptian captivity. As the great emancipator, Moses was the *mediator* between the people and God. In the last chapter we saw him interceding with God on behalf of Israel, laying his life on the line, as it were, for the people God had called him to serve. So committed was he to their well-being that he was willing to have his name blotted out of the Lord's book if the Lord did not save Israel.

The section of Scripture with which we begin this final chapter of our commentary on Exodus begins with a third intercession of Moses. There will be a fourth, one of the boldest ever in the history of humankind, and there will be that renewing of the covenant, and the building of the tabernacle.

MOSES' THIRD INTERCESSION

33:7 Moses took his tent and pitched it outside the camp, far from the camp, and called it the tabernacle of meeting. And it came to pass *that* everyone who sought the LORD went out to the tabernacle of meeting which *was* outside the camp.

8 So it was, whenever Moses went out to the tabernacle, *that* all the people rose, and each man stood *at* his tent door and watched Moses until he had gone into the tabernacle.

9 And it came to pass, when Moses entered the tabernacle, that the pillar of cloud descended and stood *at* the door of the tabernacle, and *the* LORD talked with Moses.

10 All the people saw the pillar of cloud standing *at* the tabernacle door, and all the people rose and worshiped, each man *in* his tent door.

11 So the LORD spoke to Moses face to face, as a man speaks to his friend. And he would return to the camp, but his servant Joshua the son of Nun, a young man, did not depart from the tabernacle.

12 Then Moses said to the LORD, "See, You say to me, 'Bring up this people.' But You have not let me know whom You will send with me. Yet You have said, 'I know you by name, and you have also found grace in My sight.'

13 "Now therefore, I pray, if I have found grace in Your sight, show me now Your way, that I may know You and that I may find grace in Your sight. And consider that this nation *is* Your people."

14 And He said, "My Presence will go *with you,* and I will give you rest."

15 Then he said to Him, "If Your Presence does not go *with us,* do not bring us up from here.

16 "For how then will it be known that Your people and I have found grace in Your sight, except You go with us? So we shall be separate, Your people and I, from all the people who *are* upon the face of the earth."

17 So the LORD said to Moses, "I will also do this thing that you have spoken; for you have found grace in My sight, and I know you by name."

Exod. 33:7–17

Moses' first intercession was recorded in chapter 32. The Lord had seen how the people had corrupted themselves by the building of the golden calf. He was ready to loose His burning wrath against them and consume them. But Moses pled with Him, reminding God of who He was, and why God must keep faith with the people and not destroy them. (See commentary on Exodus 32:11–14, pp. 349–53.)

In his second intercession (32:31–35), Moses fully acknowledged

Israel's guilt, but begged that Yahweh would forgive. If God would not forgive, then Moses asked that he be blotted out of the Lord's book.

We come now to Moses' third intercession. The people have repented, they have expressed their sorrow and remorse, have divested themselves of the ornaments that were a tie to their former gods. But God has told them that He will not go with them because He might consume them with His wrath.

At this, Moses took his tent and pitched it outside the camp. The Scripture calls that a *"tabernacle of meeting"* because *"everyone who sought the Lord"* would go out to that meeting place *"which was outside the camp."* This tent of meeting is not to be confused with the tabernacle, because the tabernacle has not yet been built. Most commentators believe that this was Moses' private tent where God met with him face to face and spoke *"friend to friend."*

This Scripture passage describes one such meeting when Moses went into the tent. A pillar of cloud descended and stood at the door of the tent, *"and the Lord talked with Moses."* Here, in this tent of meeting, Moses made his third intercession. He sought to change Yahweh's mind about the fact that He would not go up among the people of Israel. Moses appeals on the basis of his own relationship with God (*". . . if I have found grace in Your sight"*). He also appeals on the basis of the covenant: *". . . consider that this nation is Your people"* (v. 13).

Yahweh responded to Moses and gave assent: *"My Presence will go with you, and I will give you rest"* (v. 14).

Two words are important here: *presence* and *rest*. Those two words might be intricately bound. The presence of the Lord does give us rest. But there are occasions when His presence disturbs us instead. One remembers that vivid presence appearing to Isaiah in the temple. Rather than giving rest, it caused Isaiah to tremble and shake and to enter into confession. The presence of the Lord does that; it reveals our sinfulness.

Sometimes the presence disturbs in that it reveals our failure to be who God wants us to be. How often in prayer are we visited by the presence of God and find ourselves keenly aware of our failure in discipleship.

This connecting of the presence of God and rest may very well be like that connection Jesus made: "Take My yoke upon you, . . . for

My yoke is easy and My burden is light" (Matt. 11:29–30). The Lord gives us His presence. With that presence comes responsibility and ministry, but always, there is His presence to make our yoke easy and our burden light.

SHOW ME YOUR GLORY

33:18 And he said, "Please, show me Your glory."

19 Then He said, "I will make all My goodness pass before you, and I will proclaim the name of the LORD before you. I will be gracious to whom I will be gracious, and I will have compassion on whom I will have compassion."

20 But He said, "You cannot see My face; for no man shall see Me, and live."

21 And the LORD said, "Here is a place by Me, and you shall stand on the rock.

22 "So it shall be, while My glory passes by, that I will put you in the cleft of the rock, and will cover you with My hand while I pass by.

23 "Then I will take away My hand, and you shall see My back; but My face shall not be seen."

34:1 And the LORD said to Moses, "Cut two tablets of stone like the first *ones*, and I will write on *these* tablets the words that were on the first tablets which you broke.

2 "So be ready in the morning, and come up in the morning to Mount Sinai, and present yourself to Me there on the top of the mountain.

3 "And no man shall come up with you, and let no man be seen throughout all the mountain; let neither flocks nor herds feed before that mountain."

4 So he cut two tablets of stone like the first *ones*. Then Moses rose early in the morning and went up Mount Sinai, as the LORD had commanded him; and he took in his hand the two tablets of stone.

5 Now the LORD descended in the cloud and stood with him there, and proclaimed the name of the LORD.

6 And the LORD passed before him and proclaimed, "The LORD, the LORD God, merciful and

gracious, longsuffering, and abounding in goodness and truth,

7 "keeping mercy for thousands, forgiving iniquity and transgression and sin, by no means clearing *the guilty*, visiting the iniquity of the fathers upon the children and the children's children to the third and the fourth generation."

8 So Moses made haste and bowed his head toward the earth, and worshiped.

9 Then he said, "If now I have found grace in Your sight, O Lord, let my Lord, I pray, go among us, even though we *are* a stiff-necked people; and pardon our iniquity and our sin, and take us as Your inheritance."

Exod. 33:18–34:9

Here is Moses' fourth intercession, *"Show me Your glory"* (v. 18). This presses God to the limit.

We wrestle in our minds as to how it was that Moses could come to that point of boldness. God had responded to his petitions, had repented of His anger against His people, had renewed His covenant with them to take them into the promised land, and to also go with them. So Moses is at a new place. All along, he has been willing to go on the blanket promise that God had given him at the burning bush. But something had happened. The people's falling into idolatrous sin, God's anger against them, and God's refusal to allow Moses to make atonement, had brought a whole new situation. And obviously Moses felt he needed to know more. He needed to know more of what God was like if he was going to continue to lead a people who had "kept a golden calf up" their sleeve.

There is a sense in which he was asking the same question he had asked years before at this same mountain in the presence of the burning bush. This time he was asking far more. Instead of saying, "Tell me Your name," he said, *"Show me Your glory*—tell me Your way that I may know You." God responds to Moses. He tells Moses that He will show Moses His glory, but He will not show it to him face to face: *"And you shall see My back; but My face shall not be seen."*

This is a warning that there are limitations to revelation. God is not limited, but we are. This idea is expressed throughout the Old Testament (Gen. 16:13; 32:30; Deut. 4:33; Judg. 6:22–23; 13:22;

Isa. 6:5). No one, not even Moses, could know all about God. Even though He has revealed Himself fully in Jesus Christ, there is the sense in which He remains "hidden."

Also, there is the underscoring of God's sovereignty. *"I will be gracious to whom I will be gracious, and I will have compassion on whom I will have compassion."* (See commentary on God's sovereignty, pp. 127–31.)

After God tells Moses that He will share His glory with Moses, God invites him to come up on the mountain and meet with Him the next day. Now what would you feel like if you had an appointment with God at 9:00 A.M. tomorrow? He has given you instructions as to where to meet Him and what to bring with you. Would you be able to eat for the rest of the day? How much sleep do you think you'd get tonight? That was how it was for Moses. Moses was to bring with him two tablets of stone like the ones on which Moses had broken in his wrath against Israel. How gracious God is! He is going to give Moses His testimony on the tablets of stone again.

I'm sure Moses didn't sleep that night—I know I couldn't sleep if I had a date with God the next morning. If God had promised to tell me something that He had never told anybody else, I would be wide-eyed all night long. No wonder the Scripture says that *"Moses rose early in the morning and went up Mount Sinai."* This was to be the day of days; he was going to get a glimpse of God, even if just His back.

What Moses sees on the mountain is important. Here he sees a cloud, and remember, whenever you see a cloud in the Old Testament, open your eyes wide, because God is close by. While Moses is standing in the crevice of the rock, the Lord passes by and Moses senses His presence. But what Moses sees is not nearly as important as what he hears. Because, as the Lord passes by, He says to Moses: *"The Lord, the Lord God, merciful and gracious, longsuffering, and abounding in goodness and truth, keeping mercy for thousands, forgiving iniquity and transgression and sin, by no means clearing the guilty, visiting the iniquity of the fathers upon the children and the children's children to the third and the fourth generation"* (Exod. 34:6–7).

Moses' glimpse of God becomes an answer to the question of the ages: Who is God, and what is God like? This is a Mount Everest affirmation of who God is. It was left for Jesus to become the Incarnation of these words that persons might forever believe that what God said He was, He was.

Look at those words: *"merciful and gracious, longsuffering, and abounding in goodness and truth, . . . forgiving"* (v. 6). There was nothing in the dark, brooding cloud, nothing in the quaking mountain or the flashing lightning to confirm what Moses heard God say. None of the dramatic experiences Moses had had with God pointed in this direction. The terrors of Egypt, the ten plagues, the final banishing of Pharaoh's army in the bowels of the Red Sea certainly did not point to these words. What else had Moses experienced? We don't know, but we do know it had all begun with a God clearly characterized by compassion: "I have seen the oppression of My people, I've heard their cry, I know their sorrow, and I will deliver them."

In a mysterious way, Moses had gotten more than a glimpse. He had heard God's word, and in the depths of his soul, he knew what John knew centuries later after being tutored by Christ: God is love. To be sure, it wasn't crystal clear, and it wouldn't be for centuries until in the fullness of time the "Word became flesh." But even Jesus, that "Word become flesh," spoke no words that made it more clear as to who God was than these words God spoke of Himself to Moses.

These words point clearly to a holy God whose righteousness requires punishment of wrongdoing, and a loving God whose mercy permits and provides forgiveness. So, boil it down; distill it to its most precious essence and what you have is what theologians write volumes about. *God is holy love.*

We will never know all God is, and whenever some fresh insight and meaning comes to us, like Moses on the mountainside, hopefully we will bow our heads in humility and awe and worship. A friend of mine asked his granddaughter when she was going to be four years old. Her priceless response was, "I'm going to be four when I get through being three." Unlike this little girl, we will never get through "being three"—that is, knowing God as holy love. No matter what other revelations come, this is the essence of who God is.

The holiness of God is God's inward character of perfect goodness. One of the primary meanings of the tabernacle is its reflection of a holy God, a God set apart, unique, utterly unstained by the sin of the world. God did not specify rules of cleanliness for those who worshiped there because He had an obsession with personal hygiene, but because in every possible way, people were to be clean, set apart, holy as they entered the place where the holy God actually dwelt. As perfect goodness, God's purpose is to produce that goodness in you

371

and me. So, He takes sides against sin, against all badness, against all evil, against our not being that holy people He called us to be.

John Redhead has provided very helpful commentary on the holiness of God. He states that God cannot help being against sin, because He is for its opposite, righteousness and truth. That fact explains some of the words in the Bible which we have a hard time understanding. The Bible talks about "our Father" and in the same breath speaks of the "wrath of God." That does not mean God loses His temper; it simply describes the reaction of His holiness toward sin. He is bound to be against sin because of who He is. Or, the Bible talks about God's being a consuming fire. That does not mean that God is capricious—one moment a father and the next a consuming fire. It means that because God is a father of perfect goodness, He cannot put up with badness, any more than you could put up with someone's making improper advances to your daughter.

> In the light of that fact, then, we are ready to take in the meaning of one thing God said to Moses. He said, "The Lord, the Lord God . . . will by no means clear the guilty, visiting the iniquity of the fathers upon the children and upon the children's children, upon the third and the fourth generation." What He is saying is that because He is holiness itself, He can never put up with anything that is unholy—that He not only cannot put up with it, He will not put up with it.[1]

But not only is God's holiness His inward character of perfect goodness, the love of God is the inward compassion that is God's nature moving him to be merciful and gracious, longsuffering and abundant in goodness and truth, keeping mercy for thousands, for giving iniquity and transgression and sin.

A woman took a friend with her when she went to a photographer to have her picture taken. The beauty parlor had done its best for her. She took her seat in the studio and fixed her pose. While the photographer was adjusting his lights in preparation for taking the shot, she said to him, "Now be sure to do me justice." The friend who had accompanied her, said, with a twinkle in her eye, "My dear, what you need is not justice but mercy."

It doesn't take us long as we look at our lives to realize that's our need—not justice, but mercy. And our God who is holy love provides that.

It is true that while God is often forced to visit our iniquity upon us because of His holiness, He is still merciful and gracious and forgiving.

I'm sure it has happened with you, as it has happened with me. When you love somebody, you can't stand for anything to come between you and that other person. If something happens to bring about estrangement, or there's something that poisons the relationship or gets you "at odds" with the other, you can't rest in your love. Love will not let you have peace until that estrangement is dissolved. The way the estrangement is dissolved, usually, is that you go and tell that person how much you love him or her. You tell him or her that you love him or her enough to forgive, and that you want to be forgiven. Sometimes it's the tears of knowing that love is there which melt down the barrier standing between us and another. And that's the way it is with God and us. When that happens, when the tears of knowing that love is there begin to flow, then the barriers are melted and you can sleep again. You have peace; joy returns to the relationship.

The best example of it, I think, is the relationship between parents and children. I believe that a parent who has a wayward child can understand the love of God better than anyone else. That parent knows how much he loves his child, even in his waywardness. And that parent will fall down on his face to worship God when he realizes that God loves him in an even greater and deeper way.

That's who God is: holy love.

Hearing the word that God had spoken about Himself, Moses *"made haste and bowed his head toward the earth, and worshiped"* (34:8). That's the only response of any person who begins to know who God is. Moses presses the issue now in a beautiful act of commitment, but also in a boldness of faith: *"If now I have found grace in Your sight, O Lord, let my Lord, I pray, go among us, even though we are a stiff-necked people; and pardon our iniquity and our sin, and take us as Your inheritance"* (v. 9). That was Moses' plea and God responded, as we will see in the following section.

RENEWAL OF THE COVENANT

34:10 And He said: "Behold, I make a covenant. Before all your people I will do marvels such as have not been done in all the earth, nor in any nation; and all the people among whom you *are* shall see the work of the LORD. For it *is* an awesome thing that I will do with you.

11 'Observe what I command you this day. Behold, I am driving out from before you the Amorite and the Canaanite and the Hittite and the Perizzite and the Hivite and the Jebusite.

12 'Take heed to yourself, lest you make a covenant with the inhabitants of the land where you are going, lest it be a snare in your midst.

13 'But you shall destroy their altars, break their *sacred* pillars, and cut down their wooden images

14 '(for you shall worship no other god, for the LORD, whose name *is* Jealous, *is* a jealous God),

15 'lest you make a covenant with the inhabitants of the land, and they play the harlot with their gods and make sacrifice to their gods, and *one of them* invites you and you eat of his sacrifice,

16 'and you take of his daughters for your sons, and his daughters play the harlot with their gods and make your sons play the harlot with their gods.

17 'You shall make no molded gods for yourselves.

18 'The Feast of Unleavened Bread you shall keep. Seven days you shall eat unleavened bread, as I commanded you, in the appointed time of the month of Abib; for in the month of Abib you came out from Egypt.

19 'All that open the womb *are* Mine, and every male firstborn among your livestock, *whether* ox or sheep.

20 'But the firstborn of a donkey you shall redeem with a lamb. And if you will not redeem *him*, then you shall break his neck. All the firstborn of your sons you shall redeem. And none shall appear before Me empty-handed.

21 'Six days you shall work, but on the seventh day you shall rest; in plowing time and in harvest you shall rest.

22 'And you shall observe the Feast of Weeks, of the firstfruits of wheat harvest, and the Feast of Ingathering at the year's end.

23 "Three times in the year all your men shall appear before the Lord, the LORD God of Israel.

24 "For I will cast out the nations before you and enlarge your borders; neither will any man covet your land when you go up to appear before the LORD your God three times in the year.

25 "You shall not offer the blood of My sacrifice with leaven, nor shall the sacrifice of the Feast of the Passover be left until morning.

26 "The first of the firstfruits of your land you shall bring to the house of the LORD your God. You shall not boil a young goat in its mother's milk."

27 Then the LORD said to Moses, "Write these words, for according to the tenor of these words I have made a covenant with you and with Israel."

28 So he was there with the LORD forty days and forty nights; he neither ate bread nor drank water. And He wrote on the tablets the words of the covenant, the Ten Commandments.

29 Now it was so, when Moses came down from Mount Sinai (and the two tablets of the Testimony *were* in Moses' hand when he came down from the mountain), that Moses did not know that the skin of his face shone while he talked with Him.

30 So when Aaron and all the children of Israel saw Moses, behold, the skin of his face shone, and they were afraid to come near him.

31 Then Moses called to them, and Aaron and all the rulers of the congregation returned to him; and Moses talked with them.

32 Afterward all the children of Israel came near, and he gave them as commandments all that the LORD had spoken with him on Mount Sinai.

33 And when Moses had finished speaking with them, he put a veil on his face.

34 But whenever Moses went in before the LORD to speak with Him, he would take the veil off until he came out; and he would come out and speak to the children of Israel whatever he had been commanded.

35 And whenever the children of Israel saw the face of Moses, that the skin of Moses' face shone,

> then Moses would put the veil on his face again, un-
> til he went in to speak with Him.
>
> *Exod. 34:10–35*

God responds to Moses' intercession with as bold a promise as had been the request: *". . . all the people among whom you are shall see the work of the Lord. For it is an awesome thing that I will do with you"* (v. 10). So, the covenant is renewed.

Even with the renewing of the covenant, God expects the people to conform in obedience to His law. He sets that law down very specifically, in verses 12–26.

The undergirding principle of the covenant, and the lesson we learn from it, is that the obedient, loving person with whom God dwells is the one who is the recipient of God's promises. The highlight of this section of Scripture is in the person of Moses. When he came down from the mountain and called his people together to share with them what God had shared with him on the mountain, the skin of his face shone. In fact, it shone so brightly that the people were afraid to come near him.

Moses was reflecting in his very being the glory of God. And so it is with us, when we live in fellowship with God, our lives reflect His life.

There is another observation to be noted, relating to the fact that Moses put a veil over his face when he spoke to the people, in order that the radiant glory of God shining on his face would not be too blinding to the people. In 2 Corinthians 3, Paul gives an allegorical interpretation to this veil. He says that Moses wore the veil so that Israel would not see the glow gradually wearing away. Paul was thinking that the glory of the old covenant, of the old relationship between God and humankind in the covenant made on Sinai, was a fading glory. It was destined to be overshadowed, not as the wrong is overtaken by the right, but as the incomplete is surpassed by the complete. As William Barclay reminds us, the revelation that came by Moses was true and great, but it was only partial. The revelation that came in Jesus Christ is full and final and complete. Then Barclay quotes Augustine, who wisely put it long ago: "We do wrong to the Old Testament if we deny that it comes from the just and good God as does the New. On the other hand we do wrong to the New

Testament, if we put the Old on a level with it. The one is a step to glory; the other is the summit of glory."[2]

Then Paul goes on in pressing the meaning of the veil. He compares the veil to the blindness of Israel, which enabled them to read their Scripture and not see the meaning in it. That veil could be removed only through Jesus Christ.

In the 33rd and 34th chapters of Exodus as we have considered them thus far, the big lessons may be outlined as follows: (1) Sin separates us from God. (2) No matter who we are and where we are in our commitment to God, we must not relax our guard because the temptation to idolatry is always a powerful one. (3) If the presence of God in our lives is forfeited, any other success we achieve is meaningless. (4) If we spend time in God's presence as Moses did, other persons will know that we are in a close relationship with God.

CONSTRUCTION OF THE TABERNACLE

35:1 Then Moses gathered all the congregation of the children of Israel together, and said to them, "These *are* the words which the LORD has commanded *you* to do:

2 "Work shall be done for six days, but the seventh day shall be a holy day for you, a Sabbath of rest to the LORD. Whoever does any work on it shall be put to death.

3 "You shall kindle no fire throughout your dwellings on the Sabbath day."

4 And Moses spoke to all the congregation of the children of Israel, saying, "This *is* the thing which the LORD commanded, saying:

5 'Take from among you an offering to the LORD. Whoever *is* of a willing heart, let him bring it as an offering to the LORD: gold, silver, and bronze;

6 'blue, purple, and scarlet *thread*, fine linen, and goats' *hair*;

7 'ram skins dyed red, badger skins, and acacia wood;

8 'oil for the light, and spices for the anointing oil and for the sweet incense;

9 'onyx stones, and stones to be set in the ephod and in the breastplate.

10 'All *who are* gifted artisans among you shall come and make all that the LORD has commanded:

11 'the tabernacle, its tent, its covering, its clasps, its boards, its bars, its pillars, and its sockets;

12 'the ark and its poles, *with* the mercy seat, and the veil of the covering;

13 'the table and its poles, all its utensils, and the showbread;

14 'also the lampstand for the light, its utensils, its lamps, and the oil for the light;

15 'the incense altar, its poles, the anointing oil, the sweet incense, and the screen for the door at the entrance of the tabernacle;

16 'the altar of burnt offering with its bronze grating, its poles, all its utensils, *and* the laver and its base;

17 'the hangings of the court, its pillars, their sockets, and the screen for the gate of the court;

18 'the pegs of the tabernacle, the pegs of the court, and their cords;

19 'the garments of ministry, for ministering in the holy *place*—the holy garments for Aaron the priest and the garments of his sons, to minister as priests.'"

20 And all the congregation of the children of Israel departed from the presence of Moses.

21 Then everyone came whose heart was stirred, and everyone whose spirit was willing, *and* they brought the LORD's offering for the work of the tabernacle of meeting, for all its service, and for the holy garments.

22 They came, both men and women, as many as had a willing heart, *and* brought earrings and nose rings, rings and necklaces, all jewelry of gold, that is, every man who *made* an offering of gold to the LORD.

23 And every man, with whom was found blue, purple, and scarlet *thread,* fine linen, goats' *hair,* red skins of rams, and badger skins, brought *them.*

24 Everyone who offered an offering of silver or bronze brought the LORD's offering. And everyone with whom was found acacia wood for any work of the service, brought *it.*

25 All the women *who were* gifted artisans spun yarn with their hands, and brought what they had spun, of blue, purple, *and* scarlet, and fine linen.

26 And all the women whose hearts stirred with wisdom spun yarn of goats' *hair.*

27 The rulers brought onyx stones, and the stones to be set in the ephod and in the breastplate,

28 and spices and oil for the light, for the anointing oil, and for the sweet incense.

29 The children of Israel brought a freewill offering to the LORD, all the men and women whose hearts were willing to bring *material* for all kinds of work which the LORD, by the hand of Moses, had commanded to be done.

30 And Moses said to the children of Israel, "See, the LORD has called by name Bezalel the son of Uri, the son of Hur, of the tribe of Judah;

31 "and He has filled him with the Spirit of God, in wisdom and understanding, in knowledge and all manner of workmanship,

32 "to design artistic works, to work in gold and silver and bronze,

33 "in cutting jewels for setting, in carving wood, and to work in all manner of artistic workmanship.

34 "And He has put in his heart the ability to teach, *in* him and Aholiab the son of Ahisamach, of the tribe of Dan.

35 "He has filled them with skill to do all manner of work of the engraver and the designer and the tapestry maker, in blue, purple, and scarlet *thread,* and fine linen, and of the weaver—those who do every work and those who design artistic works.

36:1 "And Bezalel and Aholiab, and every gifted artisan in whom the LORD has put wisdom and understanding, to know how to do all manner of work for the service of the sanctuary, shall do according to all that the LORD has commanded."

2 Then Moses called Bezalel and Aholiab, and every gifted artisan in whose heart the LORD had put wisdom, everyone whose heart was stirred, to come and do the work.

3 And they received from Moses all the offering

which the children of Israel had brought for the
work of the service of making the sanctuary. So
they continued bringing to him freewill offerings
every morning.

4 Then all the craftsmen who were doing all the
work of the sanctuary came, each from the work he
was doing,

5 and they spoke to Moses, saying, "The people
bring much more than enough for the service of the
work which the LORD commanded *us* to do."

6 So Moses gave a commandment, and they caused
it to be proclaimed throughout the camp, saying, "Let
neither man nor woman do any more work for the offering of the sanctuary." And the people were restrained from bringing,

7 for the material they had was sufficient for all
the work to be done—indeed too much.

8 Then all the gifted artisans among them who
worked on the tabernacle made ten curtains woven
of fine linen, and of blue, purple, and scarlet *thread;*
with artistic designs of cherubim they made them.

9 The length of each curtain *was* twenty-eight cubits, and the width of each curtain four cubits; the
curtains *were* all the same size.

10 And he coupled five curtains to one another,
and *the other* five curtains he coupled to one another.

11 He made loops of blue *yarn* on the edge of the
curtain on the selvedge of one set; likewise he did on
the outer edge of *the other* curtain of the second set.

12 Fifty loops he made on one curtain, and fifty
loops he made on the edge of the curtain on the end
of the second set; the loops held one *curtain* to another.

13 And he made fifty clasps of gold, and coupled
the curtains to one another with the clasps, that it
might be one tabernacle.

14 He made curtains of goats' *hair* for the tent over
the tabernacle; he made eleven curtains.

15 The length of each curtain *was* thirty cubits,
and the width of each curtain four cubits; the eleven
curtains *were* the same size.

16 He coupled five curtains by themselves and six curtains by themselves.

17 And he made fifty loops on the edge of the curtain that is outermost in one set, and fifty loops he made on the edge of the curtain of the second set.

18 He also made fifty bronze clasps to couple the tent together, that it might be one.

19 Then he made a covering for the tent of ram skins dyed red, and a covering of badger skins above *that*.

20 For the tabernacle he made boards of acacia wood, standing upright.

21 The length of each board *was* ten cubits, and the width of each board a cubit and a half.

22 Each board had two tenons for binding one to another. Thus he made for all the boards of the tabernacle.

23 And he made boards for the tabernacle, twenty boards for the south side.

24 Forty sockets of silver he made to go under the twenty boards: two sockets under each of the boards for its two tenons.

25 And for the other side of the tabernacle, the north side, he made twenty boards

26 and their forty sockets of silver: two sockets under each of the boards.

27 For the west side of the tabernacle he made six boards.

28 He also made two boards for the two back corners of the tabernacle.

29 And they were coupled at the bottom and coupled together at the top by one ring. Thus he made both of them for the two corners.

30 So there were eight boards and their sockets—sixteen sockets of silver—two sockets under each of the boards.

31 And he made bars of acacia wood: five for the boards on one side of the tabernacle,

32 five bars for the boards on the other side of the tabernacle, and five bars for the boards of the tabernacle on the far side westward.

33 And he made the middle bar to pass through the boards from one end to the other.

34 He overlaid the boards with gold, made their rings of gold *to be* holders for the bars, and overlaid the bars with gold.

35 And he made a veil of blue, purple, and scarlet *thread,* and fine woven linen; it was worked *with* an artistic design of cherubim.

36 He made for it four pillars of acacia *wood,* and overlaid them with gold, with their hooks of gold; and he cast four sockets of silver for them.

37 He also made a screen for the tabernacle door, of blue, purple, and scarlet *thread,* and fine woven linen, made by a weaver,

38 and its five pillars with their hooks. And he overlaid their capitals and their rings with gold, but their five sockets *were* bronze.

37:1 Then Bezalel made the ark of acacia wood; two and a half cubits *was* its length, a cubit and a half its width, and a cubit and a half its height.

2 He overlaid it with pure gold inside and outside, and made a molding of gold all around it.

3 And he cast for it four rings of gold *to be set* in its four corners: two rings on one side, and two rings on the other side of it.

4 He made poles of acacia wood, and overlaid them with gold.

5 And he put the poles into the rings at the sides of the ark, to bear the ark.

6 He also made the mercy seat of pure gold; two and a half cubits *was* its length and a cubit and a half its width.

7 He made two cherubim of beaten gold; he made them of one piece at the two ends of the mercy seat:

8 one cherub at one end on this side, and the other cherub at the *other* end on that side. He made the cherubim at the two ends *of one piece* with the mercy seat.

9 The cherubim spread out *their* wings above, *and* covered the mercy seat with their wings. They faced one another; the faces of the cherubim were toward the mercy seat.

10 He made the table of acacia wood; two cubits *was* its length, a cubit its width, and a cubit and a half its height.

11 And he overlaid it with pure gold, and made a molding of gold all around it.

12 Also he made a frame of a handbreadth all around it, and made a molding of gold for the frame all around it.

13 And he cast for it four rings of gold, and put the rings on the four corners that *were* at its four legs.

14 The rings were close to the frame, as holders for the poles to bear the table.

15 And he made the poles of acacia wood to bear the table, and overlaid them with gold.

16 He made of pure gold the utensils which were on the table: its dishes, its cups, its bowls, and its pitchers for pouring.

17 He also made the lampstand of pure gold; of hammered work he made the lampstand. Its shaft, its branches, its bowls, its *ornamental* knobs, and its flowers were of the same piece.

18 And six branches came out of its sides: three branches of the lampstand out of one side, and three branches of the lampstand out of the other side.

19 There were three bowls made like almond *blossoms* on one branch, with an *ornamental* knob and a flower, and three bowls made like almond *blossoms* on the other branch, with an *ornamental* knob and a flower—and so for the six branches coming out of the lampstand.

20 And on the lampstand itself *were* four bowls made like almond *blossoms, each with* its *ornamental* knob and flower.

21 *There was* a knob under the *first* two branches of the same, a knob under the *second* two branches of the same, and a knob under the *third* two branches of the same, according to the six branches extending from it.

22 Their knobs and their branches were of one piece; all of it *was* one hammered piece of pure gold.

23 And he made its seven lamps, its wick-trimmers, and its trays of pure gold.

24 Of a talent of pure gold he made it, with all its utensils.

25 He made the incense altar of acacia wood. Its length *was* a cubit and its width a cubit—*it was* square—and two cubits *was* its height. Its horns were *of one piece* with it.

26 And he overlaid it with pure gold: its top, its sides all around, and its horns. He also made for it a molding of gold all around it.

27 He made two rings of gold for it under its molding, by its two corners on both sides, as holders for the poles with which to bear it.

28 And he made the poles of acacia wood, and overlaid them with gold.

29 He also made the holy anointing oil and the pure incense of sweet spices, according to the work of the perfumer.

38:1 He made the altar of burnt offering of acacia wood; five cubits *was* its length and five cubits its width—*it was* square—and its height *was* three cubits.

2 He made its horns on its four corners; the horns were *of one piece* with it. And he overlaid it with bronze.

3 He made all the utensils for the altar: the pans, the shovels, the basins, the forks, and the firepans; all its utensils he made of bronze.

4 And he made a grate of bronze network for the altar, under its rim, midway from the bottom.

5 He cast four rings for the four corners of the bronze grating, *as* holders for the poles.

6 And he made the poles of acacia wood, and overlaid them with bronze.

7 Then he put the poles into the rings on the sides of the altar, with which to bear it. He made the altar hollow with boards.

8 He made the laver of bronze and its base of bronze, from the bronze mirrors of the serving women who assembled at the door of the tabernacle of meeting.

9 Then he made the court on the south side; the hangings of the court *were of* fine woven linen, one hundred cubits long.

10 There *were* twenty pillars for them, with twenty bronze sockets. The hooks of the pillars and their bands *were* silver.

11 On the north side *the hangings were* one hundred cubits *long,* with twenty pillars and their twenty bronze sockets. The hooks of the pillars and their bands *were* silver.

12 And on the west side *there were* hangings of fifty cubits, with ten pillars and their ten sockets. The hooks of the pillars and their bands *were* silver.

13 For the east side *the hangings were* fifty cubits.

14 The hangings of one side *of the gate were* fifteen cubits *long, with* their three pillars and their three sockets,

15 and the same for the other side of the court gate; on this side and that *were* hangings of fifteen cubits, *with* their three pillars and their three sockets.

16 All the hangings of the court all around *were of* fine woven linen.

17 The sockets for the pillars *were* bronze, the hooks of the pillars and their bands *were* silver, and the overlay of their capitals *was* silver; and all the pillars of the court had bands of silver.

18 The screen for the gate of the court *was* woven of blue, purple, and scarlet *thread,* and of fine woven linen. The length *was* twenty cubits, and the height along its width *was* five cubits, corresponding to the hangings of the court.

19 And *there were* four pillars *with* their four sockets of bronze; their hooks *were* silver, and the overlay of their capitals and their bands *was* silver.

20 All the pegs of the tabernacle, and of the court all around, *were* bronze.

21 This is the inventory of the tabernacle, the tabernacle of the Testimony, which was counted according to the commandment of Moses, for the service of the Levites, by the hand of Ithamar, son of Aaron the priest.

22 Bezalel the son of Uri, the son of Hur, of the tribe of Judah, made all that the LORD had commanded Moses.

23 And with him *was* Aholiab the son of Ahisamach, of the tribe of Dan, an engraver and designer, a weaver of blue, purple, and scarlet thread, and of fine linen.

24 All the gold that was used in all the work of the holy *place*, that is, the gold of the offering, was twenty-nine talents and seven hundred and thirty shekels, according to the shekel of the sanctuary.

25 And the silver from those who were numbered of the congregation *was* one hundred talents and one thousand seven hundred and seventy-five shekels, according to the shekel of the sanctuary:

26 a bekah for each man (*that is*, half a shekel, according to the shekel of the sanctuary), for everyone included in the numbering from twenty years old and above, for six hundred and three thousand, five hundred and fifty *men*.

27 And from the hundred talents of silver were cast the sockets of the sanctuary and the bases of the veil: one hundred sockets from the hundred talents, one talent for each socket.

28 Then from the one thousand seven hundred and seventy-five *shekels* he made hooks for the pillars, overlaid their capitals, and made bands for them.

29 The offering of bronze *was* seventy talents and two thousand four hundred shekels.

30 And with it he made the sockets for the door of the tabernacle of meeting, the bronze altar, the bronze grating for it, and all the utensils for the altar,

31 the sockets for the court all around, the bases for the court gate, all the pegs for the tabernacle, and all the pegs for the court all around.

39:1 Of the blue, purple, and scarlet *thread* they made garments of ministry, for ministering in the holy *place*, and made the holy garments for Aaron, as the LORD had commanded Moses.

2 He made the ephod of gold, blue, purple, and scarlet *thread*, and of fine woven linen.

3 And they beat the gold into thin sheets and cut *it into* threads, to work *it* in *with* the blue, purple, and scarlet *thread*, and the fine linen, *into* artistic designs.

4 They made shoulder straps for it to couple *it* together; it was coupled together at its two edges.

5 And the intricately woven band of his ephod that *was* on it *was* of the same workmanship, *woven of* gold, blue, purple, and scarlet *thread*, and *of* fine woven linen, as the LORD had commanded Moses.

6 And they set onyx stones, enclosed in settings of gold; they were engraved, as signets are engraved, with the names of the sons of Israel.

7 He put them on the shoulders of the ephod *as* memorial stones for the sons of Israel, as the LORD had commanded Moses.

8 And he made the breastplate, artistically woven like the workmanship of the ephod, of gold, blue, purple, and scarlet *thread*, and of fine woven linen.

9 They made the breastplate square by doubling it; a span *was* its length and a span its width when doubled.

10 And they set in it four rows of stones: a row with a sardius, a topaz, and an emerald was the first row;

11 the second row, a turquoise, a sapphire, and a diamond;

12 the third row, a jacinth, an agate, and an amethyst;

13 the fourth row, a beryl, an onyx, and a jasper. *They were* enclosed in settings of gold in their mountings.

14 *There were* twelve stones according to the names of the sons of Israel: according to their names, *engraved like* a signet, each one with its own name according to the twelve tribes.

15 And they made chains for the breastplate at the ends, like braided cords of pure gold.

16 They also made two settings of gold and two gold rings, and put the two rings on the two ends of the breastplate.

17 And they put the two braided *chains* of gold in the two rings on the ends of the breastplate.

18 The two ends of the two braided *chains* they fastened in the two settings, and put them on the shoulder straps of the ephod in the front.

19 And they made two rings of gold and put *them* on the two ends of the breastplate, on the edge of it, which *was* on the inward side of the ephod.

20 They made two *other* gold rings and put them on the two shoulder straps, underneath the ephod toward its front, right at the seam above the intricately woven band of the ephod.

21 And they bound the breastplate by means of its rings to the rings of the ephod with a blue cord, so that it would be above the intricately woven band of the ephod, and that the breastplate would not come loose from the ephod, as the LORD had commanded Moses.

22 He made the robe of the ephod of woven work, all of blue.

23 And *there was* an opening in the middle of the robe, like the opening in a coat of mail, *with* a woven binding all around the opening, so that it would not tear.

24 They made on the hem of the robe pomegranates of blue, purple, and scarlet, and of fine woven *linen.*

25 And they made bells of pure gold, and put the bells between the pomegranates on the hem of the robe all around between the pomegranates:

26 a bell and a pomegranate, a bell and a pomegranate, all around the hem of the robe to minister in, as the LORD had commanded Moses.

27 They made tunics, artistically woven of fine linen, for Aaron and his sons,

28 a turban of fine linen, exquisite hats of fine linen, short trousers of fine woven linen,

29 and a sash of fine woven linen with blue, purple, and scarlet *thread,* made by a weaver, as the LORD had commanded Moses.

30 Then they made the plate of the holy crown of pure gold, and wrote on it an inscription *like* the engraving of a signet:

HOLINESS TO THE LORD.

31 And they tied to it a blue cord, to fasten *it* above on the turban, as the LORD had commanded Moses.

32 Thus all the work of the tabernacle of the tent of meeting was finished. And the children of Israel did according to all that the LORD had commanded Moses; so they did.

33 And they brought the tabernacle to Moses, the tent and all its furnishings: its clasps, its boards, its bars, its pillars, and its sockets;

34 the covering of ram skins dyed red, the covering of badger skins, and the veil of the covering;

35 the ark of the Testimony with its poles, and the mercy seat;

36 the table, all its utensils, and the showbread;

37 the pure *gold* lampstand with its lamps (the lamps set in order), all its utensils, and the oil for light;

38 the gold altar, the anointing oil, and the sweet incense; the screen for the tabernacle door;

39 the bronze altar, its grate of bronze, its poles, and all its utensils; the laver with its base;

40 the hangings of the court, its pillars and its sockets, the screen for the court gate, its cords, and its pegs; all the utensils for the service of the tabernacle, for the tent of meeting;

41 and the garments of ministry, to minister in the holy *place:* the holy garments for Aaron the priest, and his sons' garments, to minister as priests.

42 According to all that the LORD had commanded Moses, so the children of Israel did all the work.

43 Then Moses looked over all the work, and indeed they had done it; as the LORD had commanded, just so they had done it. And Moses blessed them.

40:1 Then the LORD spoke to Moses, saying:

2 "On the first day of the first month you shall set up the tabernacle of the tent of meeting.

3 "You shall put in it the ark of the Testimony, and partition off the ark with the veil.

4 "You shall bring in the table and arrange the things that are to be set in order on it; and you shall bring in the lampstand and light its lamps.

5 "You shall also set the altar of gold for the incense before the ark of the Testimony, and put up the screen for the door of the tabernacle.

6 "Then you shall set the altar of the burnt offering before the door of the tabernacle of the tent of meeting.

7 "And you shall set the laver between the tabernacle of meeting and the altar, and put water in it.

8 "You shall set up the court all around, and hang up the screen at the court gate.

9 "And you shall take the anointing oil, and anoint the tabernacle and all that *is* in it; and you shall hallow it and all its utensils, and it shall be holy.

10 "You shall anoint the altar of the burnt offering and all its utensils, and consecrate the altar. The altar shall be most holy.

11 "And you shall anoint the laver and its base, and consecrate it.

12 "Then you shall bring Aaron and his sons to the door of the tabernacle of meeting and wash them with water.

13 "You shall put the holy garments on Aaron, and anoint him and consecrate him, that he may minister to Me as priest.

14 "And you shall bring his sons and clothe them with tunics.

15 "You shall anoint them, as you anointed their father, that they may minister to Me as priests; for their anointing shall surely be an everlasting priesthood throughout their generations."

16 Thus Moses did; according to all that the LORD had commanded him, so he did.

17 And it came to pass in the first month of the second year, on the first *day* of the month, *that* the tabernacle was raised up.

18 So Moses raised up the tabernacle, fastened its sockets, set up its boards, put in its bars, and raised up its pillars.

19 And he spread out the tent over the tabernacle and put the covering of the tent on top of it, as the LORD had commanded Moses.

20 He took the Testimony and put *it* into the ark, inserted the poles through the rings of the ark, and put the mercy seat on top of the ark.

21 And he brought the ark into the tabernacle, hung up the veil of the covering, and partitioned off the ark of the Testimony, as the LORD had commanded Moses.

22 He put the table in the tabernacle of meeting, on the north side of the tabernacle, outside the veil;

23 and he set the bread in order upon it before the LORD, as the LORD had commanded Moses.

24 He put the lampstand in the tabernacle of meeting, across from the table, on the south side of the tabernacle;

25 and he lit the lamps before the LORD, as the LORD had commanded Moses.

26 He put the gold altar in the tabernacle of meeting in front of the veil;

27 and he burned sweet incense on it, as the LORD had commanded Moses.

28 He hung up the screen *at* the door of the tabernacle.

29 And he put the altar of burnt offering *before* the door of the tabernacle of the tent of meeting, and offered upon it the burnt offering and the grain offering, as the LORD had commanded Moses.

30 He set the laver between the tabernacle of meeting and the altar, and put water there for washing;

31 and Moses, Aaron, and his sons would wash their hands and their feet *with water* from it.

32 Whenever they went into the tabernacle of meeting, and when they came near the altar, they washed, as the LORD had commanded Moses.

33 And he raised up the court all around the tabernacle and the altar, and hung up the screen of the court gate. So Moses finished the work.

34 Then the cloud covered the tabernacle of meeting, and the glory of the LORD filled the tabernacle.

35 And Moses was not able to enter the tabernacle of meeting, because the cloud rested above it, and the glory of the LORD filled the tabernacle.

36 Whenever the cloud was taken up from above the tabernacle, the children of Israel would go onward in all their journeys.

37 But if the cloud was not taken up, then they did not journey till the day that it was taken up.

391

38 For the cloud of the LORD *was* above the tabernacle by day, and fire was over it by night, in the
sight of all the house of Israel, throughout all their
journeys.

Exod. 35:1–40:38

All these chapters are printed here without comment, because
they tell how the instructions for the tabernacle given to Moses in
chapters 25–31 were carried out. In many cases, with the exception
of a substitution of the past tense for the future tense, the sections
are verbatim.

It is to our edification to note in chapter 36 that the people responded with such overwhelming generosity that Moses had to
give a commandment that people were to do no more work for the
offering of the sanctuary. The people were restrained from bringing material, because they had *"sufficient for all the work to be
done—indeed too much"* (36:7). This is a beautiful picture of how
God's people should respond to God's call. But it is especially an
inspiring picture of what the church could be if people were faithful in their stewardship.

The Book of Exodus closes in a beautiful affirmation of God's
promise fulfilled. When the tabernacle was completed, the glory of
the Lord filled the whole place. Moses was not able to enter the
tabernacle, because the glory of the Lord filled it. When the cloud of
God's glory was taken up from above the tabernacle, the children
of Israel went onward in all their journeys. If the cloud was not
taken up, they remained where they were and continued only when
the cloud was again taken up. The cloud of the Lord by day, and the
fire by night were still God's Presence in the sight of all the house of
Israel, throughout the rest of their journey into the promised land. So
the book closes with the fulfillment of the promise of God's Presence which had been given in 29:45 and renewed again in chapter
33. God's Presence would sanctify, protect, and bring Israel to her
destination.

When I think of Moses, I think about Mark Connally's classic play
Green Pastures, in particular one moving scene. That play does not
come from the Book of Exodus but from the later story of Moses
leading God's people, and the scene to which I refer is one in which
Moses watches the people as they go into the promised land. It

seems to be one of the tragedies of the whole story. Though Moses had given his life to deliver the people out of bondage, he could not go with them into the promised land. The setting is Mount Moab. From the mountain, Moses can look across the horizon and see the destination, the end toward which they had been moving for forty years. He knows that he is not going to be able to go with them. His day is coming to an end, and Joshua has already taken his place.

With powerful imagination, Mark Connally has Moses on the stage, sitting on a rock, in brooding reflection, as the twelve tribes pass by to receive his final blessing. They pass him by and march off toward the land of Caanan. As they go, the mighty emancipator's shoulders sag, and his head bows low. With every sound of the retreating footsteps of his fellow Hebrews, the light on the stage grows dimmer and dimmer, until the stage is almost in total darkness.

Suddenly, you are aware that Moses is not alone. There's somebody else on the stage, behind him. The Presence walks over to where Moses is sitting. Gently, He lays His hand on Moses' shoulder. Without looking up, Moses, who has experienced that Presence so vividly time and time again, knows who it is. Slowly, almost imperceptibly, his shoulders begin to straighten and he raises his head. He says, "You's wid me, Lawd, ain't ya? You's wid me."

And back comes the answer, "Co'se, Ah is, my chile; co'se Ah is."

That's all Moses needed to know, and that's all we need to know, isn't it? That the God who is holy love is with us.

NOTES

1. John A. Redhead, *Getting to Know God* (Nashville: Abingdon, 1954), pp. 25–26.

2. William Barclay, *The Letters to the Corinthians*, The Daily Study Bible (Edinburgh: Saint Andrew Press, 1954), pp. 214–15.

Bibliography

Barclay, William. *The Ten Commandments for Today.* New York: Harper & Row, 1983.

Buber, Martin. *Moses.* New York: Harper & Row, 1958.

Buttrick, George A. *The Interpreter's Bible,* vol. 1, Genesis-Exodus. New York: Abingdon-Cokesbury Press, 1952.

Chadwick, G. A. *The Book of Exodus.* The Expositor's Bible Commentary. Grand Rapids: Zondervan, 1979.

Croatto, Jose Severino. *Exodus: A Hermeneutics of Freedom.* Maryknoll, NY: Orbis Books, 1981.

Durham, John I. *Exodus.* Word Biblical Commentary, vol. 3. Waco, TX: Word Books, 1987.

Eller, Vernard. *In Place of Sacraments.* Grand Rapids: Wm. B. Eerdmans, 1972.

Ellison, H. L. *Exodus.* Daily Study Bible Series. Philadelphia: Westminster Press, 1982.

Fant, Clyde E., Jr., and William M. Pinson, Jr., eds. *Twenty Centuries of Great Preaching.* 13 vols. Waco, TX: Word Books, 1971.

Honeycutt, Roy L., Jr., *The Broadman Bible Commentary.* Nashville: Broadman Press, 1969.

Huey, F. B., Jr. *Exodus: A Study Guide Commentary.* Grand Rapids: Zondervan, 1977.

Hyatt, James Philip. *Commentary on Exodus.* New Century Bible Commentary Series. Grand Rapids: Wm. B. Eerdmans, 1980.

Maclaren, Alexander. *Expositions of Holy Scripture,* vol. 1. Grand Rapids: Wm. B. Eerdmans, 1952–59.

McGee, J. Vernon. *Genesis-Deuteronomy.* Thru the Bible with J. Vernon McGee, vol. 1. Nashville: Thomas Nelson, 1981.

Meyer, F. B. *Devotional Commentary on Exodus.* Grand Rapids: Kregel Publications, 1978.

Meyer, Lester. *The Message of Exodus.* Minneapolis: Augsburg Publishing, 1983.

Myers, T. Cecil. *Thunder on the Mountain.* Nashville: Abingdon Press, 1965.

Napier, B. Davie. *Exodus.* Layman's Bible Commentary, vol. 3. Richmond, VA: John Knox Press, 1963.

BIBLIOGRAPHY

Noth, Martin. *Exodus, a Commentary.* Old Testament Library. Philadelphia: Westminster Press, 1962.

Pink, Arthur W. *Gleanings in Exodus.* Chicago: Moody Press, 1981.

Rawlinson, George. *Exodus.* The Pulpit Commentary, vol. 1. Ed. H. D. Spence and T. S. Exell. Grand Rapids: Wm. B. Eerdmans, 1959 reprint.

Rowley, H. H. *The Faith of Israel.* London: SCM Press, 1956.